Praise for *The Adobe SiteCatalyst Handbook*

"I made Adam Greco a Senior Partner at Web Analytics Demystified because he is the world's singular authority on the Adobe Omniture platform and because he is a fantastic communicator. Readers of this book gain access to both aspects of Adam, and I have little doubt that *The Adobe SiteCatalyst Handbook* will quickly become required reading for SiteCatalyst users around the world."

> —Eric Peterson
> Founder and CEO, Web Analytics Demystified and author of *Web Analytics Demystified*

"*The Adobe SiteCatalyst Handbook* is a must-have for any serious analyst's desk. The tips, tricks, and knowledge contained within this book go deep into the mechanics of Site-Catalyst to deliver information that isn't readily available anywhere else. Adam's real-world examples and clear mastery of the technology deliver a comprehensive how-to guide to fully utilize the extensive capabilities of SiteCatalyst."

> —John Lovett
> President, Digital Analytics Association

"For more than seven years now, Adam Greco has helped leading companies get maximum value out of Adobe SiteCatalyst. He has long been one of the most respected digital analytics consultants in the industry, and his insightful, powerful knowledge has finally been codified in these pages. If you want to make sure you're pushing SiteCatalyst to its limits, keep this book handy and use it often."

> —Ben Gaines
> Product Manager, Adobe Systems, Inc.

"Adam has an extraordinary understanding of Adobe Site Catalyst and an equally impressive ability to effectively teach others how to use the various aspects of the tool. His in-depth knowledge of the platform has allowed him to learn a lot of invaluable tips and tricks for making SiteCatalyst even more productive!"

> —Andreas Dierl
> Founder, Adlytics

"Adam Greco knows Adobe SiteCatalyst inside out, having used it as both a power user and consultant for 10+ years. More important, Adam is skillful at guiding people through its many features and sharing how their organizations can tangibly benefit from them."

> —Brent Dykes
> Evangelist, Customer Analytics, Adobe Systems, Inc.
> Author, *Web Analytics Action Hero*

"Adam's like the Miles Davis of SiteCatalyst—unparalleled in his command of the subject matter and infinitely inventive in its application. Pair that with his business savvy, quick wit, and a trove of great stories from his experience as a SiteCatalyst consultant, trainer, and practitioner, and it makes for a fun and enlightening must-read."

—Melinda Driscoll
    Web Analytics Manager, Best Buy

"Adam is the premier SiteCatalyst doctor in our industry. Whether your analytics implementation needs a quick checkup or a triple bypass, there is no SiteCatalyst surgeon I trust more than Adam to get the job done. His recommendations are the prescriptions you need to take your analytics program to the next level."

—James Niehaus
    Director of Analytics, Symantec

The Adobe®
SiteCatalyst®
Handbook

AN INSIDER'S GUIDE

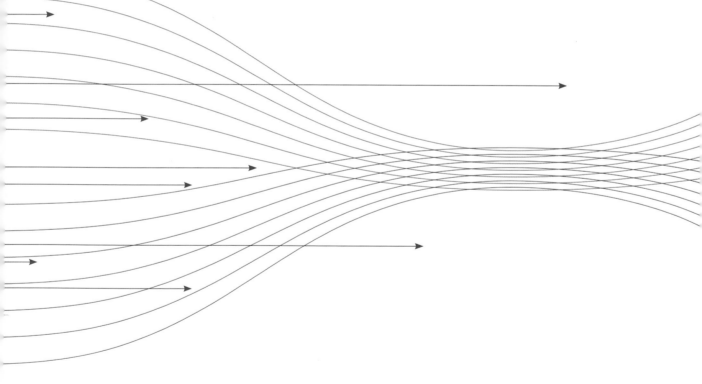

ADAM GRECO

Adobe

Adobe

The Adobe® SiteCatalyst® Handbook: An Insider's Guide
Adam Greco

Adobe Press books are published by Peachpit.
Peachpit is a division of Pearson Education.
For the latest on Adobe Press books, go to www.adobepress.com.
To report errors, please send a note to errata@peachpit.com.

Adobe Press Editor: Victor Gavenda
Project Editor: Nancy Peterson
Development Editor: Anne Marie Walker
Technical Editor: Ben Gaines
Copyeditor: Scout Festa
Proofer: Liz Merfeld
Production Editors: Katerina Malone and David Van Ness
Compositor: Kim Scott/Bumpy Design
Indexer: Jack Lewis
Cover and Interior design: Mimi Heft

Printed and bound in the United States of America

ISBN 13: 978-0-321-85991-4
ISBN 10:   0-321-85991-X

9 8 7 6 5 4 3 2 1

To my father, who always dreamed of being an author.

To my boys, Josh and Zack, may they always strive for knowledge.

Acknowledgments

Creating this book has been a labor of love and has taken much more time and effort than I ever could have imagined. I wrote my first Adobe SiteCatalyst blog post in August of 2008 and since then I've written over 500 pages of SiteCatalyst-related material, which has evolved into this handbook. However, none of this happens in a vacuum; therefore, I would like to thank the folks who helped make this possible.

I want to thank the folks at Omniture (now Adobe) who allowed me to be part of their amazing organization from its early days and participate in the creation of products and services that have helped so many organizations. Thank you to Brian Watkins for encouraging me to write that first blog post and to the many technical folks who have helped me through the years by making sure most of what I wrote in my blog was accurate. Specifically, I'd like to thank Josh West, Jeff Terry, Nick Hecht, Jared Cook, Bret Gundersen, Ryan Ekins, and Shawn Reed. Thanks to Kevin Willeitner for his contributions to Chapter 11 and for his general support over the years. Ben Gaines deserves an extra thank you for his help in technical editing this book and for being a great support system and advocate over the years. Additionally, I'd like to thank the folks at Salesforce.com who let me share with the world some of the cool things we were doing with SiteCatalyst so that others could learn. I am also grateful to my wife for allowing me to spend countless nights writing blog posts. Thank you to my Web Analytics Demystified partners, Eric Peterson, John Lovett, and Brian Hawkins, for their help and guidance throughout the process.

I'd like to thank Brent Dykes for introducing me to the folks at Adobe Press and to the entire Adobe Press team for making this book happen. Thanks to Victor Gavenda, who helped get the ball rolling. Thanks to my editors, Nancy Peterson, Anne Marie Walker, and Scout Festa, who took on the enormous editing challenge of turning a blogger into an author. I would also like to thank Katerina Malone and Kim Scott for working behind the scenes to make this book look better than I ever expected.

Last, but by no means least, I'd like to thank all those who have read my past blogs, commented on them, tweeted them, and taken the time to share how much they helped in learning and understanding SiteCatalyst and web analytics in general. Over the years I have received so many heartwarming e-mails and have even been stopped at conferences by strangers who pulled me aside to thank me for helping them with SiteCatalyst. It is these folks that motivate me to keep doing what I'm doing. Thank you.

About the Contributors

 Kevin Willeitner, author of Chapter 11 "Adobe ReportBuilder," (@willeitner) is a partner at Web Analytics Demystified. Formerly with the Adobe Consulting group, Kevin is a recognized expert in Adobe SiteCatalyst, Discover, and ReportBuilder. While Kevin focuses in all industry vertical markets, he has held leadership roles in the retail space and frequently presents at Adobe conferences. He works with Web Analytics Demystified clients to ensure they're maximizing the value they receive from web analytics implementations, reports, and dashboards.

 Ben Gaines, our technical editor, is the Product Manager for Adobe SiteCatalyst. In this role he manages the planning and design of new features, and works closely with Adobe customers to understand their needs. Previously, he was a manager of digital analytics at ESPN, a Community Manager and Technical Writer at Adobe, and a Technical Support Engineer at Omniture prior to its acquisition by Adobe. Ben has an MBA from the University of Utah and a BA from Brigham Young University. He currently lives near Salt Lake City, Utah, with his wife and three children.

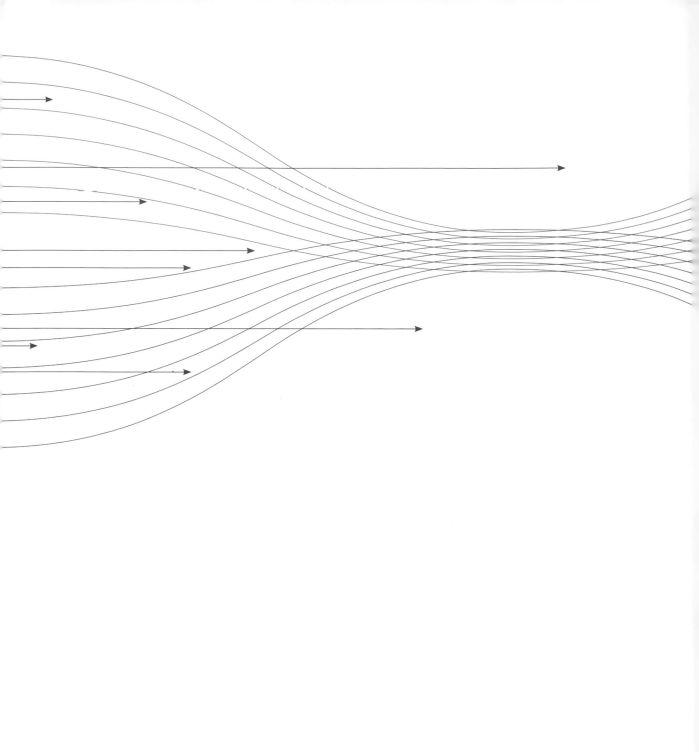

Contents

Preface xvii

| SECTION 1 | Behind the Scenes of Adobe SiteCatalyst | 1 |

| CHAPTER 1 | What Is Adobe SiteCatalyst? . . . . 3 |

A Brief History of SiteCatalyst 4
SiteCatalyst's Role in the Organization 4
How Does SiteCatalyst Work? 6
Why It's Important to Understand SiteCatalyst 7
Learning SiteCatalyst 9
Conclusion 9

| CHAPTER 2 | Company Logins, Report Suites, and Rollups . . . . 11 |

Company Logins 12
Report Suites 13
Report Suite IDs 15
General Report Suite Settings 16
Multi-suite Tagging 17
Rollup Report Suites 22
Conclusion 23

| CHAPTER 3 | SiteCatalyst Traffic Variables . . . . 25 |

SiteCatalyst Variables 26
Traffic Metrics 27
Traffic Variables (sProps) 28
Not Persistent 31
Pathing 32
Enabling Traffic Metrics for Traffic Variables 33
The Instances Metric in Traffic Variable Reports 34
List Props 35
List Prop Limitations 36
Hierarchy Variables 37
Conclusion 38

CHAPTER 4   Success Events 39

Key Performance Indicators 40

Understanding Success Events 41

Shopping Cart Success Events 43

Counter Success Events 44

Currency and Numeric Success Events 45

Setting Currency and Numeric Success Events 48

Enabling Currency and Numeric Success Events 48

Success Event Serialization 49

Types of Serialization 49

Calculated Metrics 52

What Are Calculated Metrics? 52

Creating and Using Calculated Metrics 54

Success Event Participation 57

Important Details to Know About Success Event Participation 59

Conclusion 59

CHAPTER 5   Conversion Variables 61

Conversion Variable (eVars) Fundamentals 62

Conversion Variable Persistence 64

Conversion Variable Settings 64

The "None" Row 74

List Variables 76

List Variable Settings 78

Products Variable 79

Understanding the Products Variable 79

Campaign Variable 83

Setting the Campaign Variable 85

Merchandising Conversion Variables 87

Why Merchandising eVars? 87

Using Merchandising eVars 88

Instances Metrics in Conversion Reports 90

Using Instances for Quality Assurance in Conversion
Variable Reports 90

Using Instances in the Products Report 91

Using Instances in the Campaign Report 92

Using Instances in Search Engine Reports 92

Instances Metrics and Calculated Metrics 93

Conclusion 93

CHAPTER 6   Variable Classifications 95

Understanding Classifications 96
    Creating SAINT Classifications 97
    Using SAINT Classifications 100
    Classifying the None Row 103
    Removing Classification Data 104
Numeric Classifications 104
Classification Hierarchies 106
Conclusion 107

CHAPTER 7   Advanced SiteCatalyst Features 109

SiteCatalyst JavaScript Plug-ins 110
    Get Query Parameter Plug-in 111
    Previous Value Plug-in 112
    Cross-Visit Participation Plug-in 113
    Get & Persist Plug-in 115
    Time Parting Plug-in 115
    Time to Complete Plug-in 119
    Get Val(ue) Once Plug-in 120
    Visit Number Plug-in 120
    Days Since Last Visit Plug-in 120
Data Sources 120
Transaction ID 123
Genesis Integrations 124
    E-mail Marketing Integrations 125
    Voice of Customer 126
    Customer Experience Management 126
    Other Genesis Integrations 126
Data Feeds 127
VISTA Rules 127
    Important Facts About VISTA 129
DB VISTA Rules 129
Conclusion 130

SECTION 2   Using Adobe SiteCatalyst   131

CHAPTER 8   Creating Reports in SiteCatalyst 133

Metric Reports 134
Ranked Reports 136
    Ranked Report Settings 137

Default Metrics 138

Ranked Report Search Filters 139

Trended Reports 143

Breakdown Reports 145

Traffic Correlations 145

Conversion Variable Subrelations 147

Pathing Reports 149

Types of Pathing Reports 149

Other Uses of Pathing Reports 154

Conversion Funnel Reports 156

Conclusion 160

CHAPTER 9   Using the SiteCatalyst Interface 161

General Interface Layout 162

Report Toolbar 163

Download Report 163

Send Report 164

Bookmark Report 166

Add Report to Dashboard 166

Alerts 170

More Actions 176

Targets 180

Publishing Lists 182

Comparison Reporting 184

Date Comparisons 184

Report Suite Comparisons 186

Segment Comparison Reports 187

Pathing Comparison Reports 188

SiteCatalyst Interface Time-savers 188

Update Dashboard Reports 188

Reorganize Menus and Hide Menu Items 188

Double-click to Add/Remove Metrics 188

The Magic Triangle 189

Graph Check Boxes 189

5x5 Subrelation Report 190

Remove Subrelation Breakdowns 191

Conclusion 192

CHAPTER 10 Segmentation 193

Segment Builder 194

Containers and Events 194

Segment Canvas—Nesting Containers 197

Segment Canvas—Exclude 199

DataWarehouse 201

Advanced Segment Insight (ASI) 204

Instant Segmentation (v15+) 205

Instant Segmentation vs. Multi-suite Tagging 209

Conclusion 211

CHAPTER 11 Adobe ReportBuilder 213

What Is Adobe ReportBuilder? 214

SiteCatalyst vs. ReportBuilder 214

Using ReportBuilder 216

Installing ReportBuilder 216

ReportBuilder Toolbar 217

Creating Data Requests 217

Request Manager 221

Refreshing Requests 222

Scheduling Workbooks 222

Other ReportBuilder Items 223

Real-world Examples 225

Using ReportBuilder Templates 225

Using Dependent Data Requests 228

Conclusion 231

SECTION 3 Applying Adobe SiteCatalyst   **233**

CHAPTER 12 Tracking Website Content 235

Naming Pages, Sections, and Sites 236

Naming Pages 236

Naming Site Sections 238

Site Variable 239

Page Types 240

Page Type Pathing 242

Implementing Page Types 243

Bounce Rates 244

Page Influence 246

File Downloads 248
   File Download Limitations 249
   Tracking File Downloads with Custom Variables 249
   File Download Pathing 250
Conclusion 252

CHAPTER 13   Shopping Cart Tracking 253

Product Pages 254
   Product Pathing 254
   Product Page Tab Usage 255
   Product List Views 256
Cart Additions and Checkouts 259
   Product Merchandising 260
   Money Left on the Table 262
Revenue, Orders, and Units 266
   Validating Orders and Revenue 266
   Product Returns 270
   Recurring Revenue 272
   Revenue and Orders to Date 274
Conclusion 278

CHAPTER 14   Campaign Tracking 279

External Campaign Tracking 280
   Unified Sources 280
   Marketing Channels 281
Internal Campaigns 283
   Internal Campaign Click-through Rates 283
   Internal Campaign Influence 286
Conclusion 288

CHAPTER 15   Lead Generation 289

Lead Generation Forms 290
   Form Views and Form Completions 290
   Form Conversion 292
   Form IDs 293
   Form Submit Clicks 295
   Form Errors 295
   Form Field Abandonment 299
Phone Conversion 300
   Click-to-Call 301
   Dynamic Phone Numbers 301
Conclusion 302

CHAPTER 16 Onsite Search Tracking 303

Frequently Asked Tracking Questions 304

Onsite Searches and Phrases 304

Number of Search Results 305

Search Result Click-through Rates 306

Onsite Search Phrase Pathing 307

Conclusion 308

CHAPTER 17 Visitor Engagement 309

KPI Pathing 310

Website Engagement Score 311

Visitor Scoring 313

Other Uses of Visitor Scoring 315

Conclusion 317

APPENDIX SiteCatalyst Cheat Sheet 319

Index 331

Preface

In 2005, when I became employee 165 at Omniture and joined the Omniture Consulting group after being one of the earlier Adobe SiteCatalyst customers, I thought I knew everything there was to know about SiteCatalyst. I had used the product for years, had created hundreds of reports, and had presented data to the highest levels of my organization. Then I began working side by side with the small band of consultants, and with each passing day, I quickly realized that I had much more to learn. My fellow consultants had implemented solutions and answered business questions that I had never dreamed possible, and had a ninja-like mastery of SiteCatalyst that put me to shame. As I learned from them and began working with great, cutting-edge clients, I got to the point where I could honestly call myself knowledgeable in SiteCatalyst. After going through this evolutionary process, I was often quoted as saying, "If every SiteCatalyst client could learn as much about the product as I learned in the process of transitioning from a SiteCatalyst client to a SiteCatalyst consultant, we'd have a lot more clients doing amazing things with our products."

With this thought in mind, I vowed that I would help as many SiteCatalyst customers as possible learn what I had learned over the years. At first this took place via one-on-one interactions with my consulting clients and later with a broader audience through my *Inside SiteCatalyst* blog. Time and time again I meet SiteCatalyst clients who are using 20–30 percent of the product's capabilities due to a lack of education or simply not knowing about the existence of key features. As evidence of this, many years ago I did an experiment at an Omniture Summit. I gave a presentation on SiteCatalyst power strategies, which was very atypical in that it focused on SiteCatalyst features versus general web analytics concepts. Those in attendance were self-described "power users," and many contacted me afterwards to say they weren't familiar with many of the concepts I had discussed. If these power users learned something new, I could only imagine what the rest of the SiteCatalyst user base had the potential to learn.

Based on this experience, I created my blog to help folks interested in transitioning from SiteCatalyst novices to experts, so that they could know enough to maximize their investment in SiteCatalyst. Over the past few years, I've written over 100 blog posts related to SiteCatalyst. The goal of this handbook is to share how the SiteCatalyst product works and how it can be applied to solve day-to-day web analytics questions. Although this handbook does not delve into the technical (tagging) aspects of Site-Catalyst, it does provide a solid foundation that anyone using the product should have.

In my experience, possessing a complete understanding of the tool your organization uses for web analytics can have a significant impact on whether or not you are successful. As I like to say, "Knowing how to effectively use SiteCatalyst will not guarantee success, but *not* knowing how to take advantage of all that SiteCatalyst has to offer will undoubtedly guarantee failure."

With this in mind, I hope that you find this handbook useful, and if you have any further questions, feel free to reach out to me at adam.greco@webanalyticsdemystified.com.

Behind the Scenes of Adobe SiteCatalyst

Before undertaking the detailed process of learning how to use a product like SiteCatalyst, it is worthwhile to consider its purpose and why the product was initially created. At its heart, SiteCatalyst is a web analytics collection and reporting tool. Organizations invest money in SiteCatalyst because they want to gain insight into what the visitors to their sites are doing. Every website has objectives or actions that visitors are meant to complete. Some websites sell products, others are informational, and some generate income through onsite advertising. Regardless of the objective, those investing money in building and improving websites have a desire to understand how well the website is performing against goals set by the organization.

This desire to see website behavior in a click-by-click manner is what spawned the web analytics software industry, and SiteCatalyst has emerged as one of the leading products in this space.

## CHAPTER 1

What Is Adobe SiteCatalyst?

SiteCatalyst is part of Adobe's Digital Marketing Suite of products, which together help online marketers monitor and improve website performance. Organizations use SiteCatalyst to track how website visitors are engaging with videos, applications deployed to mobile devices, and to some extent social media networks, such as Twitter and Facebook. SiteCatalyst customers can leverage a platform they already know to track and analyze new and emerging data sets.

This chapter explains SiteCatalyst's role, how it works, and the importance of understanding and learning the application.

A Brief History of SiteCatalyst

In the early days of the Internet, most organizations captured website data via "log files" stored on their own servers. But over the years, it became more efficient to take advantage of economies of scale by outsourcing this data collection and aggregation to software companies who specialize in web analytics. Products like SiteCatalyst offer SaaS (software as a service) models that allow thousands of organizations to share servers and features in ways that few internal departments can match.

Starting around 2004, most organizations migrated to web analytics tools and abandoned internal efforts to manage website behavior data. As a result of this outsourcing, organizations have had to learn the specific ways that web analytics tools collect and store data. For SiteCatalyst, this means learning how to use its specific JavaScript code and how different variables collecting data act in different situations. This differs from the proprietary methods employed previously but brings with it the benefit of standardization. There are now many established best practices related to SiteCatalyst that your organization can take advantage of, as well as a large talent pool of people with SiteCatalyst expertise and job experience.

SiteCatalyst was originally used to track basic website behaviors, but over the years it has grown in sophistication and is now capable of more advanced data collection than ever before. As the function of web analytics has broadened over the years to include multidevice and multichannel data, so has SiteCatalyst.

SiteCatalyst's Role in the Organization

It is important to understand where web analytics tools like SiteCatalyst fit into the overall organization. Typically, SiteCatalyst is owned and used by marketing departments, although in some cases Information Technology (IT) will be the owner of web analytics tools. The reason SiteCatalyst normally falls under marketing is that it is primarily used to answer marketing questions. Some common questions I've been asked to answer using SiteCatalyst include the following:

► Which pages on the website are leading to success?

► Which products on the website are performing the best?

► Which content or tools on the website are having the biggest impact on converting visitors?

- ▶ Which marketing campaigns are driving the most people to the website and successfully converting visitors into customers?

- ▶ Where are website conversion funnels breaking down and causing the organization to lose visitors?

- ▶ Which lead generation forms on the website are converting? If they're not converting, where are visitors getting stuck?

- ▶ Which website promotions are getting visitors to click and convert, and which are not?

As you can see, most of these questions are marketing related. Although there will be IT questions that SiteCatalyst can answer (such as whether a site has "broken" pages), most questions will be from marketers looking to sell more product or boost website conversion rates.

Once an organization has decided that it wants to improve its digital analytics capabilities and invest in SiteCatalyst, it will go through a standard deployment, which involves the following:

1. Identifying the business questions to be answered

2. Determining the best way to collect the data required to answer those questions

3. Technical implementation (tagging)

4. Report or dashboard creation

5. Analysis

Depending on the size of the organization and the availability of resources, this process can take days to months. Many organizations get off on the wrong foot because at steps 1 and 2 they fail to fully understand the capabilities of SiteCatalyst. Customers new to SiteCatalyst tend to learn how the product works after step 3, by which time they've missed their opportunity to fully explore the requirements and data collection methods at their disposal. This is one of the reasons I've worked diligently to educate SiteCatalyst customers on the inner workings of the product, and reading this handbook can help your organization avoid this mistake. By fully understanding how SiteCatalyst works prior to generating business requirements and selecting the ways that the product will be deployed, you greatly increase your chances of successfully collecting web analytics data and providing impactful web analysis. Even if your organization has already deployed SiteCatalyst, reading this handbook will empower you to rethink your current deployment and consider whether there are better, more efficient ways to capture and analyze website behavior.

How Does SiteCatalyst Work?

Like most web analytics products, SiteCatalyst depends on browser cookies to collect data from website visitors. Using JavaScript and related technologies, data is passed from the visitors' Internet browsers to SiteCatalyst data collection servers, where it is processed. The data is then reported on via the SiteCatalyst interface or exported to other reporting tools. In the SiteCatalyst interface, end users are able to run reports that show how often specific website actions take place—and break down these actions into more granular detail—so that site owners can better understand what is working and what is not working. SiteCatalyst also provides a mechanism for understanding the sequence in which visitors complete website actions, which can be valuable to those who are architecting the site. At most organizations, web analytics data is consolidated into standard reports or dashboards and presented to different parts of the organization. The goal of this reporting is either to show historical progress or to drive action (which normally takes the form of changes to the website or to a website process). In this handbook, you'll explore all of the ways that SiteCatalyst can collect and report on website behavior, and you'll see examples of the reports that can be generated.

If you take a step back and look at the entire marketing technology ecosystem, you see that SiteCatalyst sits squarely in the web analytics quadrant. If you work in the web analytics space, you'll hear terms like click-stream data, voice of customer, customer experience management, session replay, heat maps, personalization, testing, and so on. Each of these technologies answers different questions related to website behavior. Through other products in the Adobe Digital Marketing Suite and the Genesis ecosystem, SiteCatalyst can integrate and share data with many of the preceding technologies, but at its core, it is a website data collection and reporting tool.

But even though SiteCatalyst is a web analytics tool, it is by no means limited to collecting and reporting on only website behavior. There are many ways in which SiteCatalyst can collect and report on data that takes place off the website. In fact, sometimes the most meaningful web analyses are those that combine online and offline (post-website) data. For example, a bank might use SiteCatalyst to track credit card applications on its website but not know for several weeks if those completing applications are approved or denied. Without this data, the bank can go only so far in making recommendations related to applications. But by importing post-website data into SiteCatalyst, the bank can see the full picture of how online marketing campaigns are performing when it comes to generating new customers. This is just one of many examples of how SiteCatalyst can be used beyond the website experience. So be careful not to artificially limit your perception of what SiteCatalyst can and cannot do for your organization. One of the goals of this handbook is to expand your thinking about what is possible in

SiteCatalyst, and my hope is that after reading this book you'll push your organization to do more than it ever thought possible with the tool.

But remember that SiteCatalyst is meant to be a *directional* reporting tool. Unlike other software products, such as Oracle or Salesforce.com, SiteCatalyst is not meant to be a "system of record" or 100 percent reliable database for the marketing department. I often find that clients try to turn SiteCatalyst into something that it was never meant to be—a marketing data warehouse. My theory is that this is done because SiteCatalyst is easier to configure than many other database tools, and it is often quicker to do this than to create large, relational marketing data warehouses. However, I would caution against doing this. SiteCatalyst was created to be a "catalyst" for improving websites (hence the product's name). Although SiteCatalyst will likely collect key website data like revenue, orders, and lead submissions, there are reasons these data points will not match operational back-end systems. The reasons range from cookie deletion, bandwidth constraints, image request tag length, and the list goes on and on. In most cases, SiteCatalyst data should be within five percent of back-end databases, but your objective should be to have data be close, not perfect. The goal of perfect matching data can often lead into a "web analytics abyss" from which you may not recover—and you will waste time that could be spent improving your website. By acknowledging that web analytics is not an exact science and that SiteCatalyst is a directional tool, you will avoid lots of heartache.

Why It's Important to Understand SiteCatalyst

Over the years, I've met many types of web analytics folks. Some were managers of the web analytics program. Others were hard-core analysis geeks who like to dig into data and make pivot tables all night. Some were developers who like to "geek out" on Java-Script code. Many are everyday marketers who want to know how to extract the data they need from tools like SiteCatalyst. Regardless of their role, almost all of these folks claim that there is no real need for them to understand how SiteCatalyst works to do their job effectively. "It's just the tool" I hear them say over and over again, as if knowing how to use the web analytics product their company has invested in would set their careers back in some way.

But in my experience, nothing could be further from the truth. Although I can understand why certain folks wouldn't want to learn the technical tagging aspects of Site-Catalyst (which, by the way, will not be covered in this handbook), I can't understand why anyone wouldn't want to have a deeper understanding of how the product collects, stores, and reports on website data. Repeatedly, I've found that the folks who have a deep understanding of how SiteCatalyst works are much further along than those who do not. Why is this? If you look at the common roles on a web analytics team, you can see the specific benefits of SiteCatalyst product knowledge for each role:

▶ **Web analytics team managers** are often in meetings with executives who want to know if it is possible to report on this thing or measure that thing. Managers without product knowledge are forced to provide bland responses ("I'll check with my team") that don't instill confidence and can often cut off a discussion before it has a chance to evolve into a meaningful idea for data collection.

▶ **Web analysts** dig into data that they don't understand and reach inaccurate conclusions. For example, they might pull data using one variable type that persists across multiple visits when they think they are pulling data that lasts only one page view, or they might build segments without understanding how different segment criteria affect the data output.

▶ **Developers** who don't understand the differences in the variable types might set variables that make no sense or produce data that is unintelligible to its intended audience of marketers. This could manifest itself in reports consisting of nothing but codes that make sense to someone who knows about back-end databases but not to an executive who is trying to do web analysis.

▶ **Marketers** are often the worst culprits of all. They invest in SiteCatalyst yet are too "busy" to attend training, understand how reports work, or learn when one report should be used instead of another. One client had spent hundreds of thousands of dollars on SiteCatalyst and couldn't figure out why she couldn't add a Leads Submitted metric to the Internal Search Term report. When I asked her why she was trying to add a Conversion metric to a traffic report, she looked at me as if I were speaking a foreign language!

In many respects, she hit the nail on the head: I was speaking a foreign language. Understanding a web analytics tool like SiteCatalyst is very much like learning a foreign language. Over the years, when people have asked me how I've been able to write so many blog posts about solving business problems with SiteCatalyst, I reply that I am merely translating online marketing questions into the language of SiteCatalyst. Instead of nouns, verbs, and adjectives, I use success events, eVars, and sProps.

Understanding the inner workings of SiteCatalyst provides a way for all of the preceding web analytics constituencies to come together and communicate in a common language. Ironically, when I first started using SiteCatalyst at CME, I would call my account manager and hear her rattle off sentences such as, "You need to enable full subrelations and then you can see that breakdown with a classification," and I'd think that she was crazy; now I talk in a similar way and people look at me like *I* am crazy. But clients who speak this language are more successful than those who are afraid to learn it. For this reason, everyone on your web analytics team stands to benefit from reading this handbook and learning the language of SiteCatalyst. Bienvenidos, benvenuto, bienvenu to the world of SiteCatalyst.

Learning SiteCatalyst

Now that you know what SiteCatalyst is (and is not), you can begin the process of understanding how SiteCatalyst works. This handbook is divided into the following sections:

▶ **Section 1** explains the core elements that any SiteCatalyst expert should know. This includes data report suites, traffic metrics, traffic variables, conversion variables, success events, and variable classifications. This section also includes a bonus "advanced" chapter that covers topics that many SiteCatalyst clients have never heard of.

▶ **Section 2** teaches you how to use your data after it is collected in SiteCatalyst. Covered topics include using Metric reports, Ranked reports, Trended reports, Breakdown reports, Pathing reports, Fallout reports, and Conversion reports. This section also shows how end users navigate the SiteCatalyst interface, including using menus, running reports, and sharing reports throughout the organization, and also provides some handy interface time-savers. Once you become familiar with the general interface, the important topic of segmentation is explained. Also included is a special chapter on how you can use Adobe ReportBuilder to pull SiteCatalyst data into Microsoft Excel and build robust dashboards.

▶ **Section 3** brings together all that you've learned in the first two sections and demonstrates ways that you can apply your SiteCatalyst knowledge to solve practical web analytics questions. This section shows real-world applications of SiteCatalyst: tracking website content, shopping carts, online marketing campaigns, onsite search, and visitor engagement.

Conclusion

In this chapter, you learned the history of the SiteCatalyst product and where it normally sits in the organization. You also learned why it is important for those in many different web analytics roles to understand how SiteCatalyst works to be successful in their job.

Unlike traditional books, you do not have to read the chapters of this handbook in sequential order, but I've done my best to have most chapters build upon previous ones. Because many people have different roles related to SiteCatalyst, you may find that some chapters are more valuable to your function than others. However, I encourage you to read all of the topics covered in this book; knowing information that is seemingly unrelated to your primary function can, at times, help in unforeseen ways.

## CHAPTER 2

Company Logins, Report Suites, and Rollups

SiteCatalyst is built on a shared infrastructure, so all data collected is routed to central data collection servers. For this reason, each bit of data sent to Adobe must be sent to specific tables on specific servers. To keep this straight, SiteCatalyst uses company logins, report suites, and (to a lesser extent) rollups to collect and share the right data with the right companies. In this chapter, you'll learn how your company can leverage company logins and report suites to mirror the websites, companies, or brands for which your organization wants to perform web analysis.

Company Logins

The easiest way to understand SiteCatalyst is to start from the highest level, so I'll begin by discussing the company login. A company login is a container of all SiteCatalyst elements. When an organization purchases SiteCatalyst, Adobe creates a company login that allows customers to log in and access data. Although you may have 50 SiteCatalyst users at your company, most likely all will use the same company login. On the Site-Catalyst login page, you would enter the login credentials provided by your SiteCatalyst administrator. **Figure 2.1** shows the login page for Greco, Inc., the fictional company I'll use as an example throughout this book.

Company logins can contain various SiteCatalyst elements, including data sets (report suites), users, admin settings, and so on. For example, the company login for Greco, Inc. might contain a data set for a U.S. website, a United Kingdom website, and a global data set that has data for all countries. However, as a SiteCatalyst user you're not required to have and remember a different username and password to access all three of these data sets because they are all part of the same company login. Company logins help minimize how much administration has to take place and are extremely useful when your organization has multiple data sets.

Although it is somewhat rare, there are some cases in which a company would choose to have more than one company login. One reason for having a second company login might be to have separate data sets within the same organization. For example, a large multinational organization might have several different business units that are

Figure 2.1 Sample Site-Catalyst company login screen.

completely unrelated to each other. The organization might own an automotive company and a shampoo company. In this scenario, it is unlikely that the data sets for these distinct businesses would be similar, and aggregating the data for these different business units might not add significant value. In addition, there are most likely very few end users who would log in to both of these SiteCatalyst data sets. In this scenario, even though the two companies are technically part of the same organization, they are so different that there are not many economies of scale to be produced by merging them into the same company login. In fact, there might be cases where having them in the same company login could increase the amount of administration required to maintain different user settings, report suite settings, and so on.

Another common example of using a separate company login is for company intranets. Often, organizations realize that they can leverage their investment in SiteCatalyst by implementing it on their corporate intranet. These intranets often produce minimal traffic, so their cost is insignificant (fees for SiteCatalyst typically depend on how much data is being collected by your organization). However, what is tracked on the intranet varies greatly from what is tracked on the corporate website, as does the intended audience, which normally consists of internal human resources employees. In this scenario, the organization would be advised to create one company login for the public website and a separate one for the intranet.

Keep in mind that it is possible for one data set (report suite) to reside within two company logins. There are some situations where this is helpful, although there are some nuances you need to be aware of. These nuances are primarily related to user security, variable settings, menu customization, and so on, and they can be explained in detail by your Adobe account manager or ClientCare.

For the most part, you should not have to worry too much about company logins, because the odds are that your organization will have only one and it will mainly serve as your gateway into SiteCatalyst.

Report Suites

The next level below company login in SiteCatalyst is report suites. A report suite is a collection of data for a particular website or application. When data is collected by Site-Catalyst (normally via a JavaScript image tag), it is sent to the SiteCatalyst servers in an Adobe data center and then into a specific SiteCatalyst report suite. Every piece of data collected by SiteCatalyst must be assigned to at least one report suite. The report suite to which data for a specific web page is being sent is set using the **s_account** variable

```
/* SiteCatalyst code version: H.24.2.
Copyright 1996-2012 Adobe, Inc. All Rights Reserved
More info available at http://www.omniture.com */
/*********************** ADDITIONAL FEATURES
    Plugins
*/
var s_account="grecous"
var s=s_gi(s_account)
```

Figure 2.2 JavaScript code showing **s_account** setting.

Figure 2.3 Report suite selection drop-down box.

in the first few lines of the JavaScript code (**Figure 2.2**). You can think of report suites as private databases that your organization owns that just happen to reside on servers owned by Adobe. Each report suite is part of one or more company logins, and only those who have access to that company login can see the data contained within that report suite. Contained within each report suite is a full set of all SiteCatalyst reports your organization will use to perform web analysis.

As mentioned, many organizations will have a different report suite for each website. For example, if your organization has websites in ten countries, it might have ten report suites—one for each website. Doing so allows the organization to see web analytics data separately for each country instead of having to parse data within one global report suite. As I'll discuss in later chapters, there are pros and cons of having multiple report suites, but for now it is only important to understand what they do and why they exist.

When you have successfully logged in to SiteCatalyst, at the top of the screen you will see a drop-down box that contains all of the report suites assigned to that company login (**Figure 2.3**). Selecting a specific report suite will instantaneously change all of the reports to reflect the data for the newly chosen report suite. If report suites are set up consistently, switching from one report suite to another while in a SiteCatalyst report will often automatically render the same report for the new report suite. For example, if you were looking at the Pages report for the U.S. report suite and then changed to the Australian report suite, you would immediately see the top Australian pages instead of the top U.S. pages. If, however the new report suite you selected was not identical to the previous one, you may notice that the menus change to reflect the data collected in the newly selected report suite.

Report Suites: Why It Pays to Understand SiteCatalyst

Report suites provide a great illustration of why it is important to understand Site-Catalyst fully prior to implementation. Several organizations I've encountered have had many report suites when they should have had one or have had one when they should have had many. This is often caused by a lack of understanding—at implementation—of how SiteCatalyst works. The unfortunate irony of SiteCatalyst implementations is that the most important architectural decisions usually need to be made in the beginning—when organizations are least knowledgeable about the product. This is why it is important to understand as much as you can about SiteCatalyst before you make key decisions that will be harder to change down the road.

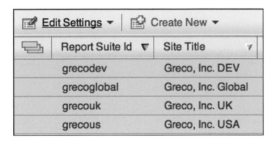

Figure 2.4 Administration console showing report suite IDs.

Report Suite IDs

When you're looking at the drop-down box of report suites, keep in mind that it shows the "friendly" name of each report suite. This friendly name will make sense to your end users, but it is not how SiteCatalyst sees each report suite. Instead, SiteCatalyst uses a report suite ID (RSID) to uniquely identify each report suite within each company login. The report suite ID is somewhat obfuscated from day-to-day end users, but it can be seen by using the SiteCatalyst administration console. In **Figure 2.4** you can see how the report suites for Greco, Inc. would appear in the administration console. The three report suites previously described each have a friendly Site Title and then a more obscure report suite ID. It is this report suite ID that is used in the **s_account** variable in the JavaScript file to send data to the correct company login and report suite within the Adobe data centers.

General Report Suite Settings

When you create a report suite, there are a few key settings to address to make sure data is collected properly. You can access these settings (**Figure 2.5**) from within the administration console (which requires administrator privileges).

▸ **Site Title** is the friendly name for the report suite, which your end users will see in the drop-down box in the SiteCatalyst interface.

▸ **Base URL** doesn't affect data collection (and may often be blank or have a value of "."); it is merely there as your own reminder of which website data is being collected.

▸ **Time Zone** determines the time zone for which data is associated. It is important to note that all data will be shown relative to this time zone, not the time zone where website visitors reside or the time zone of your SiteCatalyst users. For example, because the Greco, Inc. USA report suite shown in Figure 2.5 is set to the Central time zone, even if a visitor accesses the site from Australia, the data will be associated with the current time in the Central time zone.

▸ **Conversion Level** determines whether your organization has the conversion aspects of the SiteCatalyst product (success events and conversion variables) enabled. In most cases, this will be enabled, so you shouldn't have to worry about this setting.

▸ **Default Page** is used only if you are tracking page names using URLs (which I'll later demonstrate should *not* be done) and helps avoid one URL from being subdivided into multiple pages.

Figure 2.5 Administration console showing the general report suite settings.

General Account Settings

Use this page to specify report-suite level settings. Settings on this page will permanently affect the way data is p

Site Title:	✓ Greco, Inc. USA
Base URL:	✓ http://www.grecoinc.com
Time Zone:	✓ US Central Time [GMT-06:00]
Conversion Level:	✓ Enabled
Default Page:	✓
IP Obfuscation:	✓ Disabled
Activated:	Yes
Multi-byte Character Support:	Disabled
Base Currency:	United States Dollars

▶ **IP Obfuscation** allows you to turn IP addresses into unrecognizable text strings. This might be used if your country or organization has strict rules concerning the tracking of IP addresses of website visitors.

Some of the other report suite settings can be set when you're creating a report suite, but they will subsequently need to be configured by an Adobe account manager. These include the following settings:

▶ **Activated** determines whether the current report suite is live and running. There may be cases where you deactivate a report suite so that no new data is collected, but you can still see historical data.

▶ **Multi-byte Character Support** allows a report suite to accept data in languages that use multi-byte characters, such as Japanese.

▶ **Base Currency** sets the currency of the current report suite. The base currency is used to show revenue and other currency metrics in the correct type of currency. For example, a report suite could be set to US Dollars, Australian Dollars, British Pounds, Euros, or Japanese Yen. If you have data from multiple countries being sent to one report suite, SiteCatalyst will use the base currency setting to determine the currency that reports should be viewed in, and it will convert foreign currencies into the base currency using a fixed daily exchange rate.

There's much more to learn about creating reports suites in the administration console, but these are the main settings you should be familiar with to get started creating report suites.

Multi-suite Tagging

As you become more sophisticated at using SiteCatalyst, there may be times when you decide you want some website data collected in more than one report suite. Multi-suite tagging is a fancy name for sending SiteCatalyst data to two or more report suites. Here are some cases in which passing data from one web page to multiple report suites might make sense:

▶ Your organization has a website for each country but also wants to have a global report suite that shows data for all countries combined. For example, Greco, Inc. may have executives who want to see total orders and revenue by product across the globe without having to manually total data from each country site.

▶ Your organization has multiple brands and each has its own report suite, but you also want to see a combined view of website data for the entire company. For example, you might have a shoe brand and a coat brand that each have different websites but track similar data, and you want a data set that combines both for executives to review.

▶ Your organization has a website with various sections and wants a report suite that is a subset of the website for which only a small number of employees can see data. For example, you might want a group of customer service employees to have access to your website's customer service data, but not necessarily to its shopping cart data.

If this or a similar scenario applies to your organization, you need to understand the concept of multi-suite tagging. When you send data from all of your individual websites to one master report suite, it traditionally has been called a *global* report suite. Sending data to multiple report suites will result in additional fees paid to Adobe because you're asking for data to be collected and stored more than once; however, these fees are reduced for the additional data being sent (referred to as secondary server calls).

Multi-suite tagging example

The value of multi-suite tagging can best be understood through an example. Imagine that Greco, Inc. has retail brands under different names. Both retail brands (let's call them Brand A and Brand B) provide similar products. Greco Inc.'s CEO wants to see website data for each business separately but also have a combined view that shows performance across all of Greco, Inc.

To accomplish this, each page on the Brand A website would send data to the "greco_brand_a" and "grecoglobal" report suites, and each page on the Brand B website would send its data to the "greco_brand_b" and "grecoglobal" report suites. Therefore, each page on both sites is sending data to two SiteCatalyst report suites: one for the brand site and one to a global suite that consolidates all data. The most common ways to implement multi-suite tagging are the following:

▶ Modifying the **s_account** value in your JavaScript file to include more than one report suite ID. This is done by adding a comma followed by a second report suite ID (**Figure 2.6**).

▶ Utilizing a VISTA rule to route data to additional report suites. I'll discuss VISTA rules later in the book, but for now, it is a server-side rule that SiteCatalyst can run on your behalf that sends data to one or more report suites.

```
/* SiteCatalyst code version: H.24.2.
Copyright 1996-2012 Adobe, Inc. All Rights Reserved
More info available at http://www.omniture.com */
/************************ ADDITIONAL FEATURES ******
    Plugins
*/

var s_account="greco_brand_a, grecoglobal"
var s=s_gi(s_account)
```

Figure 2.6 JavaScript code showing **s_account** with multiple report suite IDs.

Regardless of the method you use, the result is that all data collected on a page is sent to more than one data set within SiteCatalyst.

It is also worth noting that you are not limited to sending only two server calls to SiteCatalyst. In fact, you can send as many as you want, but each server call will cost you more money. To illustrate this, let's consider an old client of mine that was sending web page data to four SiteCatalyst report suites for every page of its website. In this situation, the client was a hotel and wanted one report suite that captured data for the specific hotel being looked at, one report suite for the brand that the hotel was part of (because it owned multiple brands), one report suite for the region the current hotel site was part of (because it owned multiple hotels in each region), and one global report suite to collect all hotel data. Employees who worked at the local hotel could see data only for that hotel. The brand manager could see data for that hotel combined with all other hotels in the brand across the country. The regional manager could see data for that hotel combined with all other hotels in the region regardless of the brand. Executives could see all hotel activity by looking at the global report suite. This report suite architecture, albeit complex, allowed this organization to partition who could see what data based on their role. In this scenario, there were four report suite IDs in the **s_account** variable on every web page, and they were paying Adobe full price on the primary server call and a reduced price on the additional three server calls.

This solution isn't for everyone, but it is a good illustration of how multi-suite tagging can be used to partition web analytics data within the organization. Keep in mind, however, that there are other ways (segmentation) to partition your data, and later in the book I'll discuss the pros and cons of multi-suite tagging versus the alternatives.

Additional benefits of multi-suite tagging

In addition to the value of combining metrics in reports and limiting who can see what data, there are several other key advantages of using multi-suite tagging. These benefits are derived from the fact that one of the report suites is common to both websites, so as far as SiteCatalyst is concerned, each visitor has the same visitor ID for the combined global report suite. Therefore, someone who had visited the websites of both Brand A and Brand B would be recognized as the same individual in the global report suite. This means that in the global report suite, Greco, Inc. can take advantage of the following:

▶ **Summary metrics.** All success event and traffic metrics in multi-suite tagged (global) report suites are aggregates of corresponding metrics from individual report suites. This allows you to see summary metrics across countries or brands.

▶ **Cross-website pathing.** If a person visits the websites of both Brand A and Brand B, SiteCatalyst recognizes that person as the same individual in the global report suite and allows you to see how the person navigated from one site to the other. In effect, pages for both websites would be seen in the global report suite as one big website encompassing all pages from both sites. This allows you to see how often visitors are floating between the two brand sites at a page level or website level, depending on your specific SiteCatalyst implementation.

▶ **De-duplicated unique visitors.** Because SiteCatalyst, in the global report suite, sees each person visiting both websites as the same visitor, the global report suite will only count that individual as one unique visitor. For example, if the Brand A website had 10,000 unique visitors and the Brand B website had 5000 unique visitors (for a total of 15,000 unique visitors companywide), the individual report suites would reflect those numbers for each website. However, if 1000 of those visitors had visited both the Brand A and Brand B websites, the global report suite would show 14,000 unique visitors instead of 15,000, taking into account the fact that 1000 visitors were common to both websites. This de-duplication makes overall company reporting more accurate and can also show how effective your organization is at getting visitors to view your multiple websites.

▶ **Multi-site segmentation.** In the global report suite, when you are building a segment (segmentation will be covered in a later chapter) of visitors or visits, you have the advantage of using data from both websites. For example, you may want to target visitors who have purchased a product on the Brand A website and who have looked at but never purchased a product on the Brand B website. This type of segment would only be available using the global report suite, which contains data from both Brand A and Brand B.

▶ **Cross-website participation.** Participation will be covered in a later chapter, but it is essentially a way to determine which elements (commonly pages) lead to success. Although this is powerful in a regular report suite, in a global report suite it is possible to see how a page in one website leads to success in another website. For example, it might be the case that a specific page on Brand A's website drove a lot of visitors to Brand B's website, where they purchased at an above average rate. This insight would be impossible to see in Brand B's SiteCatalyst data set, because participation would only work starting with the first page of the visit. However, using multi-suite tagging and a global report suite, it is possible to see how pages on Brand A's website influence sales on Brand B's website.

▶ **Improved campaign attribution.** Most organizations use marketing campaign reports in SiteCatalyst to determine how each visit was sourced. Did visitors come from a paid search keyword (SEM), from a natural search keyword (SEO), or from a social media site like Twitter? The source is normally captured in SiteCatalyst so it can be reported on. However, what happens if someone comes to Brand A's website from a paid search keyword and then clicks over to Brand B's website and purchases a few products? If you are looking at Brand B's report suite, the sale would be attributed to a referral from Brand A's website. This is valuable information to have, but what is interesting is that if you looked at the global report suite, that same purchase would be attributed to the original paid search keyword used to get to Brand A. The reason is that the visit in the global report suite includes the pages in both the Brand A and Brand B sites, which reflects the way the visit actually transpired. According to the global report suite, the paid search keyword drove the overall visit, so it would get credit for any successful purchases on Brand A's site or Brand B's site. This is an example of how multi-suite tagging can show you different views of your data, but it requires that you understand how to interpret it correctly.

With great power comes great responsibility

There are some great reasons to learn about and consider using multi-suite tagging. These include securing data by user type, seeing aggregate data, and so on. However, there is one important detail to consider before embarking on a multi-suite tagging approach: report suite standardization. In general, it is a best practice to have most if not all of your SiteCatalyst report suites set up in the same way. This includes key report suite settings and capturing the same data with the same variables in all report suites. But there is nothing in SiteCatalyst that mandates that you take this approach.

For example, in the Greco, Inc. scenario, there is nothing stopping Brand A from tracking onsite search phrases (phrases website visitors searched on) in one variable (say, eVar1) and Brand B from tracking this same value in a different variable (eVar2). At the same time, Brand B might store city values in its eVar1. Doing so won't be a problem if you are looking at data only in the Brand A report suite or the Brand B report suite. However, the trouble begins when you later decide to embark on multi-suite tagging. In this situation, when you begin passing data to a multi-suite tagged global report suite that combines Brand A and Brand B data, SiteCatalyst will merge the data for eVar1 from all suites in the global report suite. This means that for eVar1 in the global report suite, you will be see a mixture of onsite search phrases from Brand A's website and cities from Brand B's website! This is not ideal at all; the eVar1 variable in the global report suite is now useless because it is impossible to make sense of the disparate data.

As this example demonstrates, as soon as you decide to implement multi-suite tagging, you must determine if all of the data sets you plan to combine are configured in a standard way so when data is combined in the global report suite, it is done so correctly. Unfortunately, I encounter many cases in which clients are merging data and not realizing what they've done. Usually, the reason is that by the time multi-suite tagging was implemented, several of the report suites had been configured differently. This is why it is best to plan out your entire configuration from the beginning and decide if multi-suite tagging is something your organization needs. Alternatively, you can follow one of my best practices and be sure to set up all of your report suites the same way. Even if there are some websites that will never use the variables you have set for other websites, I suggest that you continue to allocate them the same way for every report suite. Then, if you ever decide to implement multi-suite tagging, you won't have to recalibrate all of your report suites.

Another important point is that you cannot create multi-suite tagged data sets retroactively. This means that if you decide six months after your SiteCatalyst rollout that you made a mistake and want to have multi-suite tagging, it is not possible to go back and add historical data to your global report suite. Instead, you'd have to start the global report suite from that day forward and use the individual report suites for the past six months' worth of data or use a report suite rollup. This is yet another reason why planning is so important to SiteCatalyst implementations and why understanding key architectural topics like multi-suite tagging should happen sooner rather than later.

Rollup Report Suites

In addition to global report suites created via multi-suite tagging, SiteCatalyst offers a feature called *rollups*. A rollup is an aggregation of certain aspects of SiteCatalyst data for report suites. Rollups can be created in the administration console by your Adobe account manager or ClientCare and do not have an additional cost. Once configured, rollups add together the metrics found in each of the variables for the report suites included in the rollup. Unfortunately, rollups have several limitations, which restrict their use to specific scenarios:

▶ **Unique visitors are not de-duplicated.** Unlike global report suites, rollups cannot de-duplicate unique visitors.

▶ **Next-day, not real-time, availability.** Rollups are processed once a day, so your data will normally be available the following day (rather than in real time, as global report suites are).

▶ **No inter-site pathing.** Pathing across different report suites is not supported in rollups, as it is in global report suites.

▶ **Limited variables.** Not all variables can be seen in rollups—or if they are seen, they are only at a high level.

There are many other limitations, but these are the main ones I've encountered. I am more inclined to recommend the use of global report suites created through multi-suite tagging instead of rollups, but if you want to learn more about rollups, speak to your Adobe account manager or ClientCare.

Conclusion

In this chapter, you started learning the ways in which SiteCatalyst partitions the data you send to it. This includes company logins and report suites, which are dedicated to your organization's data. You also learned how organizations can use multi-suite tagging to increase web analysis capabilities, and you learned some of the best practices for standardizing report suites. In addition, you reviewed the differences between multi-suite tagging and rollup report suites.

These concepts, although not difficult, have the potential to dramatically change how you approach your SiteCatalyst infrastructure. The more you understand about the capabilities of each, the more likely it is that you'll choose the right architecture for your SiteCatalyst implementation. This will pay dividends down the road if your organization expands into new regions, brands, or product areas.

## CHAPTER 3

SiteCatalyst Traffic Variables

With any software product, you need to understand a few fundamental building blocks to be successful. In SiteCatalyst, these building blocks are the three core variable types in which all web analytics data eventually resides: traffic variables (sProps), conversion variables (eVars), and success events. In this chapter, you'll learn a bit about variables in general and then take an in-depth look at traffic variables.

SiteCatalyst Variables

If you take a step back and look at the web analytics profession at a macro level, the general objective is to perform meaningful analysis on data collected about website behavior in hopes of improving the user experience or making the website more profitable. To do this, you need to have the right data set, collected in the optimal manner. And to collect data, you need a place to store data, which is the purpose of the various SiteCatalyst variables. Even the most complex SiteCatalyst implementation can be broken down into the specific variables that are used to capture data. What some clients fail to see is that SiteCatalyst is not a prescriptive tool that you implement and that automatically answers your questions. Instead, it is a platform upon which you can define and collect the data that is important to your business—albeit a powerful platform with features that make the collection and usage of data easier than if you had to do it yourself. But to take full advantage of this platform, you need to understand how it functions, and the first step is understanding the different SiteCatalyst variable types that will house your web analytics data.

I'll admit that back when I was a new SiteCatalyst client, I thought I had more important things to do with my time than learn about SiteCatalyst variable types and their capabilities. But over time I came to understand that these variables are the foundation of all SiteCatalyst reporting, so if I wanted to use SiteCatalyst reports to measure my website success, I had better suck it up and learn about these three variable types.

To use an analogy, think of the movie *The Karate Kid*. A young karate student (Daniel) receives training from an elder karate master (Mr. Miyagi) in preparation for a tournament. Daniel is afraid that he doesn't know enough karate to survive the tournament, but Mr. Miyagi reassures him by saying, "You trust the quality of what you know, not quantity."

Mr. Miyagi shows Daniel that a strong understanding of the fundamentals—like balance, honor, and discipline—is the key to success in karate.

Similarly, a solid understanding of the SiteCatalyst variables and how to use them will go a long way toward your SiteCatalyst education and proficiency. For this reason, I encourage you to read and reread these variable chapters until everything in them makes sense to you. When I encounter frustrated SiteCatalyst customers, a simple training (or retraining) on these variable concepts is often all that is needed to get them back on track again.

The most basic type of variable in SiteCatalyst is the traffic variable. These variables are often referred to as sProps (or "props") because that is how they were labeled in earlier SiteCatalyst versions. The official name for traffic variables is custom traffic variables, which is how they are labeled in the administration console.

But to fully understand traffic variables, you first need to understand traffic metrics.

Traffic Metrics

Since the dawn of the Internet, organizations have been tracking "hits" to their websites. SiteCatalyst refers to these numbers (hits, page views, or visits) as traffic metrics. Out of the box, SiteCatalyst will show you these numbers for each hour, day, week, and so on. SiteCatalyst will also show you how many visits and unique visitors your website receives. A visit is defined as a session on a website. A visit can contain many page views and lasts until there is 30 minutes of session inactivity or until the session reaches 12 hours in duration (whichever comes first) (**Figure 3.1**).

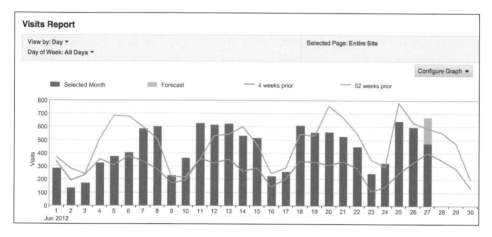

Figure 3.1 A Visits report.

A unique visitor is defined as a unique instance of a cookie ID (or close approximation) during a specified time frame. If the same person with the same SiteCatalyst cookie ID visits your website multiple times in the same day, that activity would count as multiple visits but as only one unique visitor (**Figure 3.2**).

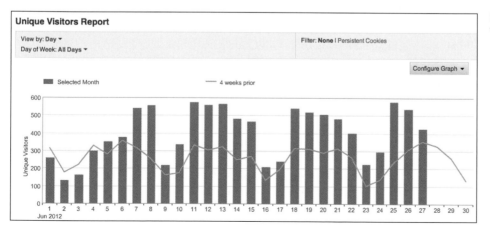

Figure 3.2 A Unique Visitors report.

Keep in mind that unique visitors does not necessarily mean unique people. For example, if someone visited your website during the day from a work computer and then again in the evening from a home computer, SiteCatalyst would treat that one person as two unique visitors because SiteCatalyst has two different cookie IDs for those visits (unless you were doing some advanced visitor "stitching"). In fact, even if someone came to your website twice in the same hour but did so from two different browsers, SiteCatalyst would treat that person as two unique visitors.

Traffic metrics are captured automatically once you begin tracking your website with SiteCatalyst. These metrics are normally viewed as a trend, and as you'll learn in a later chapter, they can be divided by each other to create new metrics. For example, you can create a new metric that divides page views by visits to see an average number of page views per visit (**Figure 3.3**).

Figure 3.3 Traffic metrics can be used to make new calculated metrics.

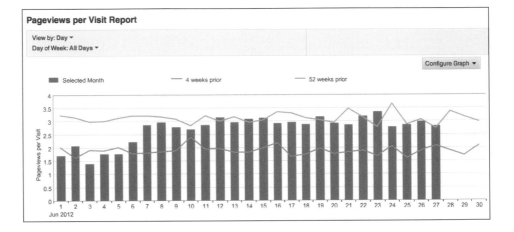

Traffic Variables (sProps)

Now that you have a basic understanding of traffic metrics, you can begin to see why traffic variables are useful. The primary purpose of traffic variables (sProps) is to allow you to break down page views, visits, and unique visitors into meaningful buckets. Although SiteCatalyst provides reports for those metrics, most web analysis needs to take place at a more granular level. For example, you can look at a Page Views report and see that your website had 33,351 page views in the specified time frame (**Figure 3.4**). But how many of those page views were to the website home page? How many were to the onsite search results page? Unfortunately, in this report it is impossible to tell, because all you have is a total by date. To answer your questions, you need a way to divide all of these page views into buckets that show you a breakdown by the

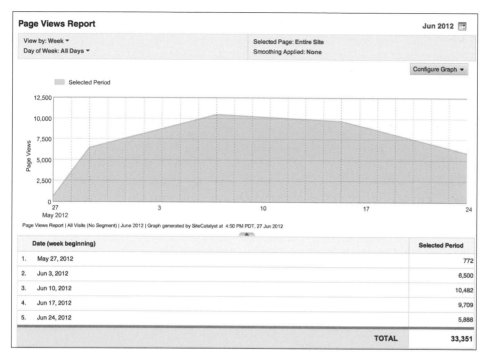

Figure 3.4 A Page Views report.

data point you are interested in, which in this case is page name. This is what traffic variables allow you to do.

If you assign a page name to each page on the website through your SiteCatalyst Java-Script file, SiteCatalyst will use a traffic variable to count how many page views the home page received and how many every other page received. You just need to plan ahead and recognize that page name is one of the variables by which you want to break down your traffic metrics. Doing this would result in a traffic variable report that shows you all page views broken down by page name (**Figure 3.5**).

	Pages	Page Views ▼	
1.	greco:us:home:homepage	7,095	21.3%
2.	greco:us:products:products-landing	6,237	18.7%
3.	greco:uk:home:homepage	5,236	15.7%
4.	greco:us:search:search-results	3,469	10.4%
5.	greco:us:products:sale	2,760	8.3%
6.	greco:uk:search:search-results	2,101	6.3%

Figure 3.5 A Pages report.

To get you started, SiteCatalyst comes with a few predefined traffic variables that it assumes most organizations will want to use:

▶ **Page Name** (`s.pagename`) stores a unique name for every page on your website. If you do not set a "friendly" value for this variable, it will capture the URL by default (although this is not recommended).

▶ **Site Section** (`s.channel`) captures the section of the website in which each page resides. Normally, these will mirror your website navigation architecture.

▶ **Server** (`s.server`) stores the name of the web server your organization is using to render each page of the website.

Although these three traffic variables can be used for other purposes, it is recommended that you use them as planned or simply leave them unused. The Page Name and Site Section variables have some unique capabilities that I'll cover later, but other than that, those predefined traffic variables are similar to the custom traffic variables that you can enable in the administration console. But keep in mind that this is just one example of a traffic variable report. SiteCatalyst provides 75 custom traffic variables for each report suite. This enables you to determine the ways in which breaking down traffic metrics makes sense for your organization.

Each traffic variable that you assign will get its own variable number in the administration console. Your developers must know the exact variable number to use when tagging your site, or you'll end up with the wrong data. Within the administration console, you can assign friendly names to your traffic variables, and these names will appear in the menus and at the top of each traffic variable report (**Figure 3.6**).

Property #	Name	
1	☑	Onsite Search Terms
2	☑	Text Font Style
3	☑	Page Language
4	☐	Custom Insight 4
5	☐	Custom Insight 5

Figure 3.6 Traffic variables in the administration console.

Let's look at an example of how you might use a custom traffic variable. Imagine that you work for Greco, Inc. and have a website with about 3000 pages. On each page is a utility that allows the visitor to switch the font from normal to large. The chief marketing officer, who felt that this would be a popular feature for those with poor eyesight, forced the team to add this feature a few months ago. Unfortunately, this feature is now causing some technical issues on the website, so you must decide whether to abandon the feature or re-implement it, which would take many development hours. As part of the project due diligence, the web analyst sets on each page of the site a traffic variable with a value of Normal Font or Enlarged Font; that way, each page view would have to fall into one of those two buckets. The web analyst wants to see what percentage of the page views are taking advantage of this feature to determine if the development effort is worth the time or could be spent on higher value projects. After a month, the web analyst uses SiteCatalyst to see a full report of font enlargement usage (**Figure 3.7**).

	Text Font Style	Page Views ▼	
1.	Normal Font	32,737	98.2%
2.	Enlarged Font	614	1.8%

Figure 3.7 A traffic variable report showing a custom font enlargement report.

As you can see, only 1.8 percent of all page views used the enlarged font. And given its prominence on the web page, no argument could be made that visitors hadn't seen the feature. So armed with this data, the web analyst convinces the chief marketing officer that the company's target audience isn't having an issue with font size, and development resources are reallocated to more pressing projects.

As this example shows, there is really no limit to what data you can capture using custom traffic variables. The key is to plan ahead and think about the ways your organization needs to see data.

So far, you've learned that traffic variables are used to break down traffic metrics into buckets. Now let's look at some other attributes of traffic variables.

Not Persistent

One of the most important facts to remember about traffic variables is that they are not persistent. They do not retain their value from one page to the next. When a page loads on your website, data is sent to Adobe's servers with the information you have chosen to record about that page view, including all traffic variables. But once that data is sent to Adobe, each traffic variable is reset and is ready to accept new values on the subsequent page view.

The easiest way to understand traffic variables is to think back to the most popular one: Page Name. Let's assume a visitor to your site starts on the home page, and the value Home Page is passed into the Page Name traffic variable. From the home page, the visitor clicks a link and is taken to the Contact Us page. You would not want the value of Home Page to persist and be passed into the Page Name traffic variable on this next page, or it would look like the home page had received two page views rather than each page having one page view. But for some reason, SiteCatalyst customers sometimes assume that they have to set traffic variable values only once—this is not the case. Think back to the font size traffic variable in the earlier example: Some customers think that they can set a value of Normal Font on the first page and that each page thereafter will get that value until a page is encountered where the value is Enlarged Font; unfortunately, that is not the case. I sometimes refer to traffic variables as "dumb" variables, because they remember only one page at a time.

Pathing

Traffic variables are the only variable that can be enabled with pathing. I discuss pathing in great detail in a subsequent chapter, but for now, think of pathing as the order in which values are passed to a traffic variable within a specific visit. For example, let's say that each page on your site has a page name and that the values passed to the Page Name traffic variable are Page A, Page B, and Page C. If pathing is enabled for the Page Name traffic variable, SiteCatalyst will record the order in which the values are passed and allow you to view reports that show the percentage of times that site users went from Page A to Page B, and so on (**Figure 3.8**).

Figure 3.8 A Pathing report.

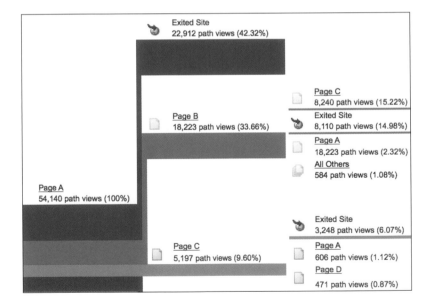

Pathing can be enabled on any traffic variable. Note that there can be additional costs associated with enabling pathing on multiple traffic variables, but that there is no technical limitation on doing so. In fact, one of the advantages that SiteCatalyst has over other clickstream web analytics tools is its ability to enable pathing on more than just pages and site sections. Pathing is enabled on the Page Name traffic variable by default and often on the Site Section variable as well. In future chapters, I demonstrate some cool uses of this type of pathing, but for now just remember that pathing is possible only for traffic variables and that any traffic variable can have pathing enabled.

Enabling Traffic Metrics for Traffic Variables

Visits and Unique Visitors are two other metrics that apply to traffic variables. When a traffic variable is enabled, by default you'll be able to see the Page Views metric associated with values passed to the variable. Unless you are using SiteCatalyst v15 or later, however, you will not be able to see the Visits and Unique Visitors metrics by default; these metrics can be enabled for any traffic variable, but they have to be enabled by your account manager or ClientCare. Depending on your contract with Adobe, there may be a cost or limit to how many traffic variables can have these extra metrics enabled. However, if you are using SiteCatalyst v15 or later, each traffic variable will have the following metrics enabled: Page Views, Instances, Visits, Unique Visitors, Daily Unique Visitors, Weekly Unique Visitors, Monthly Unique Visitors, Quarterly Unique Visitors, and Total Time Spent.

An easy way to determine if a traffic variable has these metrics enabled is to click the Add Metrics button while looking at a specific traffic variable report and see what metrics are available. If no additional metrics have been enabled, the metrics screen might look like **Figure 3.9**.

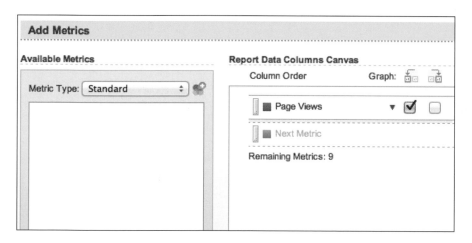

Figure 3.9 A traffic variable with no additional metrics enabled (SiteCatalyst v14).

If the Visits and Unique Visitors metrics have been enabled, you will see them in the Available Metrics column. If pathing has been enabled, you will see even more metrics, including Entries, Exits, and Bounces, all of which I'll cover later in the book (**Figure 3.10**). In the earlier example of normal and enlarged fonts, if Visits or Unique Visitors had been enabled for the traffic variable, you would have been able to see these metrics for each traffic variable value in the traffic report.

Figure 3.10 A traffic variable with additional metrics enabled

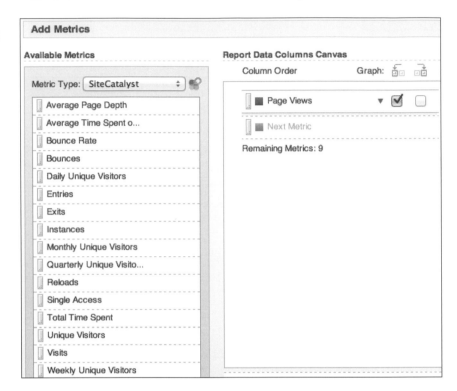

The Instances Metric in Traffic Variable Reports

At some point when you're adding metrics to custom traffic reports, you'll notice that a strange metric named Instances is available to you (**Figure 3.11**). The Instances metric represents how many times a particular value was passed to the traffic variable. For example, if you are passing onsite search terms to a traffic variable, one instance is recorded each time you pass in the search phrase. In many cases, the number of instances will be identical to the number of page views. I generally don't use the Instances metric in traffic variable reports, but now you know why it's there.

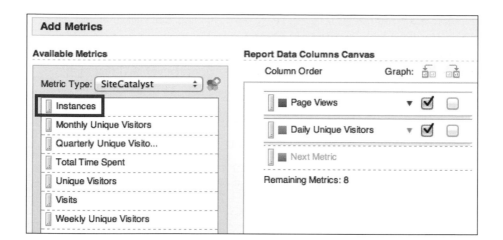

Figure 3.11 The Instances metric in a metric selection list.

List Props

A list prop is a traffic variable that can accept multiple values at once. These values are passed in using a delimited list (the delimiter can be a comma, a colon, and so on). After the data is collected, each of the delimited values is broken out into its own line item. This is useful when you want to break down page views by a traffic variable, but the same page view can be attributed to multiple values.

Let's look at an example of a list prop. Imagine that you manage a website that promotes heavyweight boxers. Your site creates valuable articles that talk about each boxer, and your editor wants to know how many page views are being devoted to each boxer to make sure the reporting is balanced. Your plan is to pass the boxer name into a traffic variable on each page, allowing you to break down page views by boxer name. You talk to a developer and figure it will be done by lunch. But the developer realizes the solution won't work and reminds you that articles can, and often do, mention more than one boxer, especially if two boxers have a big fight coming up. How do you want the developer to account for the fact that multiple boxers can be present on each page? Your first thought is to simply concatenate the names of the multiple boxers in the traffic variable. That way, if two boxers are mentioned in an article, the traffic variable value would be something like **Muhammad Ali:Joe Frazier**, and you could possibly download the SiteCatalyst data to Excel and find a way to add together all of the cases where the name Muhammad Ali was mentioned by itself and then all the cases where it was mentioned with other boxers. But when you think about it, you realize the possible combinations could be endless: **Muhammad Ali**, **Muhammad Ali:Joe Frazier**, **Muhammad Ali:Joe Frazier:Rocky Balboa**, and so on. This won't work. You're stuck and will have to spend your weekend figuring out a solution.

Then it hits you—you recall the concept of the list prop. You realize that all you have to do is pass in the names of boxers mentioned on each page to a list prop, and Site-Catalyst will break this out by boxer name in the report. You show your SiteCatalyst developer a sample page where Muhammad Ali, Joe Frazier, and Rocky Balboa are all mentioned and instruct them to use this sample code:

```
s.prop10="Muhammad Ali,Joe Frazier,Rocky Balboa";
```

When this is done, you run a report that breaks down page views by boxer and answers your business question—and you don't have to work all weekend (**Figure 3.12**).

		Boxer Name	Page Views ▾	
	1.	Muhammad Ali	12,250	24.5%
	2.	Joe Frazier	10,725	21.5%
	3.	Rocky Balboa	9,060	18.1%
	4.	Apollo Creed	7,320	14.6%
	5.	Clubber Lang	5,060	10.1%
	6.	Mike Tyson	2,325	4.7%

Figure 3.12 A list prop report.

Note that the total at the bottom of a list prop report is the total of all of the broken-out page views. This means that the report total does not reflect the total number of page views for the website during the specified time frame, but rather the total number of page views that appear in that list prop report. So it will likely not match the overall Page Views metric.

List Prop Limitations

Although list props can be very useful, they have some limitations that you need to be aware of:

▶ **Page views only.** Page Views is the only metric that can be used with list props unless you are using SiteCatalyst v15. That means no visits or unique visitors if you are using an older version.

▶ **No pathing.** Pathing is not possible for list props.

▶ **No traffic data correlations.** In a later chapter, I'll discuss traffic data correlations, which are breakdowns of one traffic variable by another traffic variable. These types of breakdowns are not available for list props.

Hierarchy Variables

A hierarchy variable is a special traffic variable that allows you to group your content into hierarchies. Using a delimiter, you can assign content into levels and sublevels, and have the ability to see views, visits, and unique visitors for each level. Hierarchy variables are not used often, but there are cases in which they can be helpful, especially if your website has a lot of content.

Let's say your website has a careers section (level 1) that contains content by language (level 2), which in turn contains functions that can be used, such as search (level 3). If a visitor navigates to this third level, the code you would use might look like this:

```
s.hier1="car,us-en,search";
```

This would result in a hierarchy report that looks like the one in **Figure 3.13**. As you can see, it is possible to see totals and percentages at each level.

Level 1 : Level 2 : Level 3	Total Hierarchy Views		Total Visits		Total Unique Visitors	
car	493,055	57.33%	115,280	48.18%	101,066	48.45%
us-en	131,807	26.73%	36,461	31.63%	31,937	31.60%
Level 3	**Hierarchy Views▼**		**Visits**		**Unique Visitors**	
1. search	44,174	33.5%	13,937	38.2%	12,718	39.8%
2. jobs	29,641	22.5%	9,760	26.8%	8,686	27.2%
3. microsites	15,341	11.6%	4,996	13.7%	4,252	13.3%
4. working	14,969	11.4%	6,451	17.7%	6,091	19.1%
5. careers	11,222	8.5%	8,111	22.2%	7,819	24.5%
6. landing-pages	4,224	3.2%	3,859	10.6%	3,717	11.6%

Figure 3.13 Sample hierarchy report.

Here are some details to note about hierarchy traffic variables:

▶ The maximum total length for hierarchy variables is 255 characters.

▶ You can choose which delimiter you use, but it cannot be a character that appears in any of the values being passed to the hierarchy variable (which would create unwanted hierarchy levels).

▶ Each report suite is limited to five hierarchy variables.

▶ You must be careful about using blank spaces in hierarchy variables because they can lead to the creation of unwanted hierarchy levels.

▶ Hierarchy variables must be enabled by your Adobe account manager or ClientCare.

Conclusion

In this chapter, you learned about traffic metrics and how traffic variables can be used to break them down. Understanding the key attributes of traffic variables, including lack of persistence, ability to enable pathing, and so on, will help you understand when they should and should not be used. It will also help you distinguish traffic metrics and traffic variables from conversion variables, which are discussed in the next two chapters.

## CHAPTER 4

Success Events

SiteCatalyst is divided into two broad categories: traffic and conversion. In the previous chapter, you learned about traffic variables; now you'll move into the area of conversion. Conversion consists of two types of elements: success events and conversion variables (also known as eVars), which work together to help you determine how successful your website is at achieving its goals.

In this chapter, you'll learn about success events and how you can use them to monitor the success of your website. But before exploring success events and how they are used, it is worthwhile to discuss key performance indicators (KPIs).

Key Performance Indicators

If you are in the web analytics field, there's a good chance you're already familiar with KPIs. But just in case you're not, *KPIs* are the metrics used to determine the health or success of a website. If the goal of your website is to get visitors to purchase items, your KPIs might be revenue, orders, and units. Alternatively, if the goal of your website is to generate leads, you might monitor a "leads generated" KPI. The reason it's important to understand KPIs is because most website KPIs take the form of success events in SiteCatalyst; in fact, so much so that the two terms are often used interchangeably. Normally, KPIs are raw metrics or ratios that represent a target goal for the organization. As such, they can be quantified to see how the organization is doing against its stated goals. Hence, most KPIs are numbers, and as you'll see, in SiteCatalyst numbers are represented by success events.

So what are success events? Simply put, *success events* are metrics that count the number of times site visitors complete an action on your site. A success event can technically represent anything that happens on your website. You could set a success event when visitors view product pages on your retail site or when a visitor downloads a file from your site. Or, you could set a success event when visitors "Like" you on Facebook or "Tweet" an article on your site. SiteCatalyst provides over 100 success events, and you get to choose which KPI you want to assign to each.

KPI Identification Trick

If your organization is struggling to determine what its KPIs should be, here is a trick I use to get the ideas flowing. Pretend that your organization has no website and that you must pitch your executives to build one and ask for millions of dollars to make it happen. Also assume that your executives are not fans of the Internet and think they can continue to run their business the way they always have. Make a list of all the benefits that the website would bring with it that could not be done without building a website. Then assume that your cranky executives are skeptical that you will achieve any of the benefits on that list. Finish the exercise by writing down how you would quantify (with numbers) each benefit to prove to your cranky, nontechnology-loving executives that the website had in fact realized the benefits you foretold. For example, if on your list you had a benefit that the website could capture leads all day instead of just during business hours, you might write down Leads Generated as the KPI to be used to quantify how successful the website would be at collecting leads. The numbers you associate with each website benefit should be a good starting point for your website KPIs.

An important aspect of succeeding in web analytics is to have well-thought-out KPIs. In fact, when I work with clients, I first look at the success events they are capturing in SiteCatalyst to determine if they have correctly identified their KPIs. If I see that clients have only two success events with data, I know they're in trouble. Conversely, if I see clients with more than 50 success events, I get a bit nervous about how they are tracking their website (unless they are very advanced and doing some sophisticated calculations that require many success events). Overall, my suggestion is that you take the time necessary to accurately identify the key metrics (numbers) that are important to your business before you begin implementing SiteCatalyst. This will make the entire process of setting up and implementing success events much easier.

Understanding Success Events

Recall in the discussion of traffic variables (sProps) in the previous chapter that those variables stored values like page names or the names of professional boxers. This is not possible with success events, because they can only store numbers. In fact, success events are more akin to the traffic metrics discussed in Chapter 3, which included page views, visits, and unique visitors. Eventually, when you start to master SiteCatalyst, you'll realize that these traffic metrics are similar to success events but are predefined by SiteCatalyst. In contrast, success events are metrics that you choose to collect. In fact, starting with SiteCatalyst v15, many traffic metrics, such as page views, visits, and unique visitors, are also available in the conversion part of the product. In some respects, the lines between the traffic and conversion parts of the product are beginning to blur, but I'll discuss that in more detail in later chapters. For now, just remember that success events are metrics that you choose, and they can only collect numbers.

In general, success events collect data when a visitor takes an action on the website. This action can be a button click or simply loading a specific page. Often, success events are set on the page following the action taken by the visitor. For example, when a visitor adds an item to the shopping cart, the success event might be set on the subsequent shopping cart page. When you send data to a success event, SiteCatalyst records the date and time that the event took place, and creates a report for each success event that shows you these numbers by date (hour, day, week, etc.). This metric report will look pretty much the same for every success event you have, only the actual numbers will be different (**Figure 4.1**, on the next page).

Each success event that you want to capture is assigned to its own success event number in the administration console. It's important to use the correct success event number when you're setting success events in your code, or else the numbers in your success event reports will be incorrect. You can also use the administration console to create "friendly" names for each success event. This is better than forcing your end

Figure 4.1 Sample success event report.

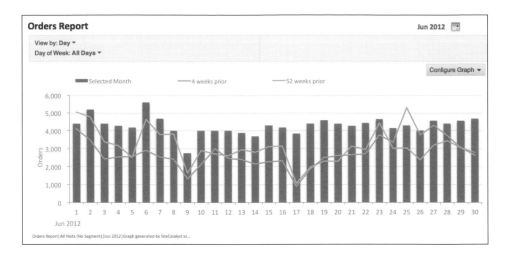

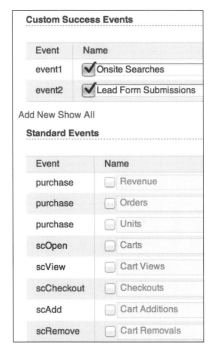

Figure 4.2 Success events in the administration console.

users to remember that "Event 1" is onsite searches or that "Event 2" is lead form submissions. Note that there are some predefined shopping cart success events in the administration console (**Figure 4.2**). These predefined shopping cart success events (Orders, Revenue, Cart Additions, etc.) are similar to the predefined traffic variables you saw for page name and site section. They function the same as custom success events that you choose but are simply predefined because many websites tend to use them.

Shopping Cart Success Events

The following sections explain the predefined shopping cart success events in more detail.

Revenue, Orders, Units (purchase)

The Purchase event in SiteCatalyst is unique in that it populates three distinct success event metrics: Revenue, Orders, and Units. This event is set in combination with the products variable, which is discussed in a later chapter. For now, all you need to know is that when you set the Purchase event (often on the order confirmation page), Site-Catalyst will use values you pass to the products variable to determine how much was spent (Revenue) and how many items were ordered (Units), and will count one successful Order.

Carts (scOpen)

The Carts (**scOpen**) success event is intended to represent how many shopping carts are created or opened during the specified time frame. Some websites open the shopping cart each time a product is added to it. In this scenario, the Carts success event will be set at the same time as the Cart Additions (scAdd) success event, but the Carts success event should be set only once during the visit.

Cart Views (scView)

The Cart Views (**scView**) success event represents the number of times visitors have viewed their cart during the specified time period.

Checkouts (scCheckout)

The Checkouts (**scCheckout**) success event is set when visitors reach the checkout stage of the shopping cart, which is normally the step directly before a purchase takes place.

Cart Additions (scAdd)

The Cart Additions (**scAdd**) success event is set when visitors add products to the shopping cart.

Cart Removals (scRemove)

The Cart Removals (**scRemove**) success event is set when visitors remove items from their shopping cart. In reality, very few clients use this event because its data is questionable due to the fact that many website visitors don't take the time to physically remove cart items, choosing instead to simply leave items in the shopping cart when exiting the website.

Product Views (prodView)

The Product Views (**prodView**) success event doesn't appear in the administration console but is meant to be set when visitors view a product detail page on the website. There are some slight issues with this success event, which are covered in a later chapter, but it should be set and is often mistakenly omitted by SiteCatalyst customers.

As mentioned previously, these success events are simply predefined but can be used for any purpose. If your website doesn't have a shopping cart, but does have a conversion funnel similar to a shopping cart, feel free to adapt these success events to your business model.

Counter Success Events

Although all success events are numbers, there are three different types of success events—Counter, Currency, and Numeric. Each of these success event types has a purpose and unique qualities. Let's examine Counter success events first. In my experience, about 90 percent of all success events are Counter success events, so they are the most important to learn. For the most part, Counter success events increase their count by "1" each time the success event is set (which normally takes place via JavaScript code). For example, if you've set a Counter success event for lead form submissions and a new visitor accesses your website and successfully submits a lead form, you might set the Counter success event on the submission confirmation page. Setting the Counter success event tells SiteCatalyst that the success event took place, and it "counts" it as one more lead submission.

Let's say you had assigned "event 2" in the administration console to "lead form submissions." You would then set success event 2 on the submission confirmation page using code like this:

```
s.events="event2";
```

Once this is set and data is collected, when you open the metric report for that success event 2, SiteCatalyst will add all of the "counts" of lead submissions that took place in the specified time frame and show you totals by day, week, month, and so forth (**Figure 4.3**).

Although it doesn't happen often, as you advance in your use of success events, there will be times when you'll set more than one success event at the same time. To do this, you simply add the second success event directly after the first success event, separated by a comma (no spaces), like this:

```
s.events="event2,event20";
```

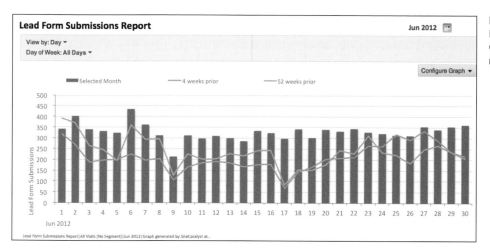

Figure 4.3 Sample Lead Form Submission Counter success event report.

Currency and Numeric Success Events

Although Counter success events will meet most of your success event needs, there will be times when you'll need to do more than just "count" how often actions happen on your website. For example, what if your executives want to analyze how much customers are paying for shipping or taxes? Those figures can vary with every transaction, so to quantify the total shipping costs for each day, you'd have to pass in the exact shipping cost for each order to a success event on the order thank you page. Using a Counter success event, you could "count" how many times a customer had to pay for shipping, or if you are using an updated version of SiteCatalyst code, you could capture a rounded integer that approximates shipping costs, but there would be no way to capture the exact shipping amount (e.g., $4.52).

This shortcoming in Counter success events is what led to the creation of Currency and Numeric success events (previously referred to as Incrementor success events). Currency and Numeric success events allow you to pass any number you want to them, which allows you to add up any figures you need for your business. The only difference between Currency and Numeric success events is that the Currency events will show the base currency of the report suite in reports and translate any foreign monies into the base currency if needed.

So what are some situations in which you might want to use Currency or Numeric success events? The following are some examples I've seen over the years:

▶ Capture tax or shipping metrics.

▶ Capture a sale or discount amount associated with an order.

▸ Capture a page value or assign "points" to a page or action taken by the visitor.

▸ Capture currency values entered into a loan calculator.

▸ Capture actual or estimated advertising impression revenue if your website generates revenue from onsite advertising.

▸ Import metrics from other software tools into SiteCatalyst using the Genesis network. When you import data from other systems into SiteCatalyst, you need to use Currency and Numeric events because you are using batch uploads to increase metrics by more than a count of "1."

To dig a bit deeper into Currency and Numeric success events, let's walk through an example. Imagine that Greco, Inc. has a banking subsidiary. The owners of this website want to understand the values of home loan mortgages that site visitors are requesting so they can compare it to the loan amounts that are ultimately provided. For example, if the bank consistently ends up loaning 79 percent of the amount of home loans that are requested online, it can use this information for future estimates.

During the loan application process, applicants fill out a form and are required to enter a loan amount, as shown in **Figure 4.4**.

Figure 4.4 Greco, Inc. loan application form.

In this scenario, Greco, Inc. could create a Currency success event and possibly name it Requested Loan Amount. It would then instruct its developers to tag the site so that the appropriate Currency success event number is passed a value of 250,000 on the subsequent page. This would result in the Requested Loan Amount success event being increased by 250,000 for the current date. As this same process is repeated with multiple visitors, the bank subsidiary would eventually see a success event report like the one in **Figure 4.5**.

Once the Requested Loan Amount values were captured in the Currency event, the bank subsidiary could download the loan amounts by date and begin to analyze how these Requested Loan Amounts correlate with actual loan amounts in the following months.

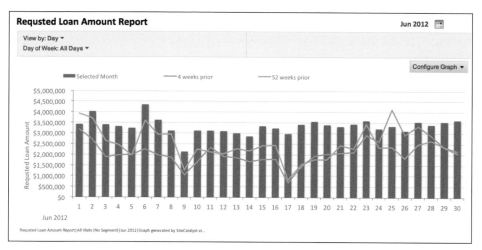

Figure 4.5 Sample Requested Loan Amount report.

After this data is collected, it could be used in a number of interesting ways. For example, if Greco, Inc. was tracking which sources of traffic were driving visitors to the website, it could easily add this new Requested Loan Amount metric to a Marketing Channel report and determine which marketing channels were leading to the highest Requested Loan Amount values. To take it further, Greco, Inc. could divide the Requested Loan Amount by the number of visits from each marketing channel to determine which channel got the most Requested Loan Amounts per visit to the site (**Figure 4.6**). In the figure, you can see that SEO, SEM, and E-mail are doing better than some of the other marketing channels. I'll cover marketing channel tracking in a subsequent chapter, but this type of reporting illustrates some of the valuable uses of Currency and Numeric success events.

		Marketing Channel	Visits ▼ ⑦		Requested Loan Amount		Requested Loan Amount / Visit
	1.	Typed/Bookmarked	2,669,277	21.3%	$18,540,000	18.5%	$6.95
	2.	SEO	2,346,203	18.7%	$22,980,000	23.0%	$9.79
	3.	SEM	1,969,807	15.7%	$18,450,000	18.5%	$9.37
	4.	Social Media	1,304,840	10.4%	$6,500,000	6.5%	$4.98
	5.	E-mail	1,038,226	8.3%	$9,540,000	9.5%	$9.19
	6.	Display Advertising	790,432	6.3%	$5,400,000	5.4%	$6.83
	7.	Affiliates	658,693	5.3%	$2,900,000	2.9%	$4.40

Figure 4.6 Sample use of Currency success event in Marketing Channel report.

Setting Currency and Numeric Success Events

The tagging behind Currency and Numeric success events is, unfortunately, a bit more complex than it is for Counter success events. In addition to using the **s.events** string, Currency and Numeric success events also require the use of the products variable string. I'll cover the products variable in a future chapter, but here is the general syntax for the products string:

```
s.products=[Category1];[Product1];[Quantity];[Total Price];
[Incrementor];[Merchandising],[Category2];[Product2]...
```

In the preceding Requested Loan Amount example, the code used to set the Currency success event might have looked like this:

```
s.events="event20";

s.products=";Home Loan;;;event20=250000";
```

This code would instruct SiteCatalyst to place a value of 250,000 into event20 for that visitor.

Enabling Currency and Numeric Success Events

Like other success events, Currency and Numeric events are enabled through the administration console. Simply open the success events definition page, click the Add New link, enter a success event name, and then choose from the Type drop-down box (**Figure 4.7**).

When you're selecting event types, even though there are several choices, the main types used are Counter, Currency, and Numeric. Note that you'll see versions of each of these success events that include "no subrelations." If you choose that option, you won't be able to use that success event in any out-of-the-box or customer conversion reports. Instead, you'll just have a metric report for that metric. I never choose the "no subrelations" option and recommend that you choose the regular version of each event because it offers more flexibility.

Figure 4.7 Enabling a Currency success event in the administration console.

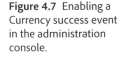

Event	Name	Type
event1	☐ Onsite Searches	Disabled Counter (no subrelations) Counter
event2	☐ Lead Form Submissions	Currency (no subrelations)
event3	☑ Requested Loan Amount	✓ Currency Numeric (no subrelations)
event4	☐ Order Discount Amount	Numeric

Custom Success Events

Add New Show All

Success Event Serialization

As you can imagine, as you start setting SiteCatalyst success events for your website KPIs, it is important that these metrics be as accurate as possible. Your organization will be making potentially significant website decisions based on the metrics reported in SiteCatalyst success events. Therefore, part of your job is to safeguard these metrics like your career depends on them (which it might). Unfortunately, the Internet is a messy, nonlinear place. Website visitors have complete control of the experience and can navigate your website in any order they choose. They can start a process on your website, abandon it, and then restart it a week later. In some respects, measuring success on a website is akin to attempting to herd cats.

For this reason, SiteCatalyst developed the concept of success event serialization. *Success event serialization* is the process of de-duplicating the setting of success events. By using success event serialization, you can limit how often success events are counted by session or by user. For example, if you look back at the Lead Form Submission success event discussed earlier, you can imagine a scenario in which a visitor successfully submits a lead but then decides to click the browser Back button and once again views the Lead Form Submission confirmation page. If you are setting your Counter success event on the loading of that page, you could accidentally set the Lead Form Submission success event twice for the same person. Although this might make your metrics look impressive to your bosses, it is not the desired outcome (because your conversion rates will ultimately decrease). In this scenario, the Lead Form Submission success event should not be set again for the same person for that particular form in the same session (or possibly ever again). This is where success event serialization saves the day. Through success event serialization, you can ensure that only the first instance of this success event will be counted in conversion reports.

Types of Serialization

There are two different methods of using success event serialization: One method is Event ID serialization and the other is Once Per Visit serialization. Although both types of serialization achieve the same goal, they do so in a slightly different manner.

Event ID serialization

Event ID serialization is an approach in which you manually assign an ID with the success event being set. This ID is unique to that instance of the success event being set and can never be repeated. An example of the code required to do this might look like this:

```
s.events="event12:123456789";
```

> ## Be Careful When Setting Success Event ID Serialization IDs
>
> Many times in my career I've seen clients inadvertently make mistakes when it comes to setting Event ID serialization IDs. You must think through these IDs or horrible repercussions can occur. For example, one of my clients decided he only wanted each visitor to get credit for one lead form submission per day, so if the visitor filled out three forms, it would only be counted as one for that day. Therefore, he set the serialization ID to the date, so the code looked like this:
>
> ```
> s.events="event25:05_05_2011";
> ```
>
> Shortly thereafter, the data in the event25 report plummeted. Can you see what this client did wrong? Because he serialized the event to the date, after the first person visiting the website on that date completed a form, no other success events were counted until the next day when, again, the first form submission would be counted and then none other until the next day. In this situation, the client should have made the serialization string more unique to each visitor to possibly look like this:
>
> ```
> s.events="event25:05_05_2011_11223344";
> ```
>
> So be careful when you're setting your Event ID serialization codes, and monitor your metrics immediately thereafter. You should see a modest drop in data due to de-duplication, but a massive drop in data may signify an issue with your serialization IDs.

Once this code is set, if SiteCatalyst ever sees the same success event (event12 in this case) being set with the same serialization string (123456789 in this case), it will ignore the success event completely. If the user refreshes the page, uses the Back button, or even comes back the next day, and SiteCatalyst sees the same event and serialization string combination, the success event will not be re-counted.

The method you use to generate the serialization ID is completely up to you. However, there are some parameters to keep in mind when setting serialization IDs:

- Serialization IDs must be 20 characters or less.
- Serialization IDs must be alphanumeric characters.
- Serialization IDs are separate for each SiteCatalyst success event. Therefore, you can use the same ID for multiple success events if needed, just not for the same success event.
- Serialization IDs are tied to the report suite, so if you are using multi-suite tagging to send data to multiple report suites, keep this in mind.

- ▸ Serialization IDs never expire, so even if the same ID is used years later, the success event will not be counted again.

- ▸ Cookie deletion does not prevent Event ID serialization because serialization IDs are stored in tables on Adobe's servers and are not cookie-based.

- ▸ The one success event with which it is not possible to use Event ID serialization is the Purchase event, which uses a special **s.purchaseID** variable for serialization.

Once Per Visit serialization

Another way to use success event serialization is to use the Once Per Visit approach. This method of success event serialization forces SiteCatalyst to count only one instance of the desired success event in a given session or visit. You can enable this setting for any success event through your Adobe account manager or ClientCare. Because it is set on the back end, this approach is much easier than manually setting an Event ID for a success event as described in the previous section. In fact, this approach requires absolutely no tagging whatsoever.

There are some downsides with this approach that you should be aware of when determining which approach is best for your situation:

- ▸ Once Per Visit serialization will not prevent the same success event from being set multiple times by the same person if that person visits the site in multiple sessions.

- ▸ Because Once Per Visit serialization is cookie-based, if visitors delete their cookies, the same success event can be set more than once in a session. However, visitors would have to delete their cookies mid-session for this to have an impact, so it is not a common occurrence.

In general, I use Once Per Visit serialization to prevent obvious duplication of success events that take place via page refreshes and Back button clicks.

Have Your Cake and Eat It Too

There may be some situations in which you want to see a regular and de-duplicated version of success events. An example might be for onsite searches in which you want to see how many raw onsite searches take place, but also see a de-duplicated count of onsite searches. For example, there may be a business reason to count all onsite searches and a separate reason to just count how many visits contained at least one onsite search. In this situation, there is no reason you couldn't set two onsite search success events and call one Onsite Searches and the other Onsite Searches (De-duplicated). The latter would be a great use case for using Once Per Visit Serialization because it would meet the objective of only counting an onsite search once in the visit and would require no additional tagging.

Calculated Metrics

In the world of web analytics, KPIs (success events) are great, but ratios are better. For example, if you manage a lead generation website and your form completions are increasing by five percent each week, you'd probably be pretty happy. However, what if I then told you that in the same time frame visits to your website increased ten percent each week? Would you still feel great about your five percent lift in form completions? Using ratios, you can normalize data and get a better perspective. In many cases, the only reason you create the success events you just learned about is to create a website conversion metric. In SiteCatalyst, these conversion metrics are created using calculated metrics. In this section, I'll review SiteCatalyst calculated metrics so you understand how they're created and used.

What Are Calculated Metrics?

Calculated metrics are SiteCatalyst metrics that are derived from existing metrics within your report suite. Using common operators, such as addition, subtraction, multiplication, and division, you can create new metrics from existing metrics for use in your web analyses. In fact, most of my calculated metrics are ratios using division as I divide two existing metrics to create a third metric. There are several ways to create calculated metrics, but the most common way is to create them by using the Add Metrics link within a report. When you click this link, you can select the Metric Type drop-down box and choose Calculated to see a list of all existing calculated metrics (**Figure 4.8**).

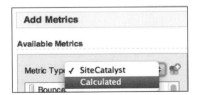

Figure 4.8 Selecting calculated metrics in the Add Metrics window.

If you don't see the metric you desire in the list, you may have to create a new calculated metric. To do this, click the multicolored icon with the plus (+) sign 🔧, which will take you to the Calculated Metrics Manager (**Figure 4.9**). In the Calculated Metrics Manager, click the Define New Metric button to access the calculated metric formula builder (**Figure 4.10**).

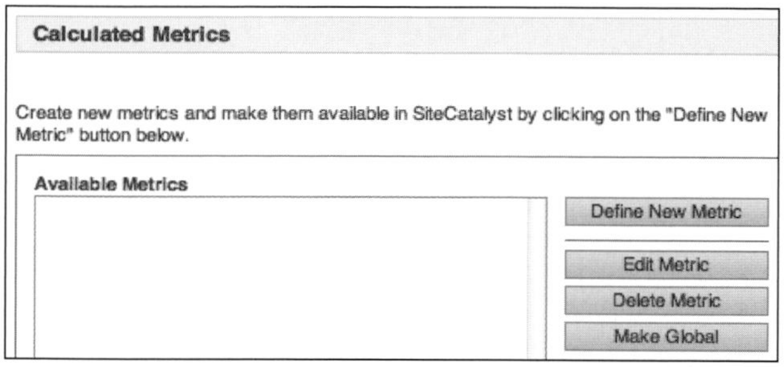

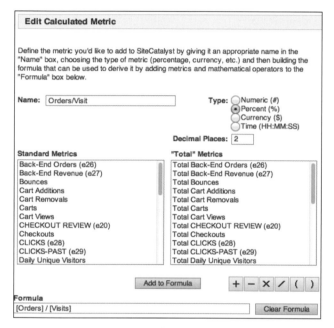

Figure 4.9 Calculated Metrics Manager.

Figure 4.10 Calculated metric formula builder.

On this screen, you can name the calculated metric, choose its type, and specify the formula to be used. In Figure 4.10, I've created a metric to determine how many Orders take place per Visit as a percentage. When you save this metric, you'll be taken back to the previous screen, and the newly created calculated metric will appear in the list of available metrics. Note that from this screen, if you have administrator rights, you can make a calculated metric "global," so it is visible to all SiteCatalyst users. This is an easy way to standardize your organization on common metric definitions.

Creating and Using Calculated Metrics

After you've created a new calculated metric, you can use it in many ways. To begin with, you can add it to a report as a metric as you would any other metric. For example, if you had a Visit Number Conversion Variable report, you could add the newly created Orders/Visit calculated metric (**Figure 4.11**).

Figure 4.11 Sample report using a calculated metric.

	Visit Number	Orders ▼ ⑦		Visits ⑦		Orders/Visit
1.	Visit 1	27,427	21.3%	2,843,883	22.7%	0.96%
2.	Visit 2	24,107	18.7%	2,572,041	20.5%	0.94%
3.	Visit 3	20,240	15.7%	2,028,357	16.2%	1.00%
4.	Visit 4	13,407	10.4%	1,317,387	10.5%	1.02%
5.	Visit 5	10,668	8.3%	920,080	7.3%	1.16%

As you can see in Figure 4.11, because there was data for the two components of the calculated metric, SiteCatalyst can display the ratio for each of the conversion variable values. In this case, it looks like the website is converting slightly better with each incremental visit to the website.

Note that you can use calculated metrics in conversion and traffic reports. However, as you'll recall, there are certain metrics that are available in traffic variable reports (traffic metrics) and others that are available in conversion reports (success events). Therefore, depending on whether you are viewing the list of available calculated metrics in a traffic or conversion variable report, you'll see only those metrics that use underlying metrics that are valid in that report.

In addition to using calculated metrics in traffic and conversion reports to see ratios for each report value, you can also view the overall calculated metric for the entire report suite. This type of metric report is identical to what you would see when you're looking at the raw data of a SiteCatalyst success event. You open this report by choosing Favorites > Calculated Metrics in the SiteCatalyst toolbar and selecting the metric you want to see (**Figure 4.12**).

The resulting report will show you the calculated metric data in a similar format to a success event metric (**Figure 4.13**).

Figure 4.12 Opening calculated metric reports.

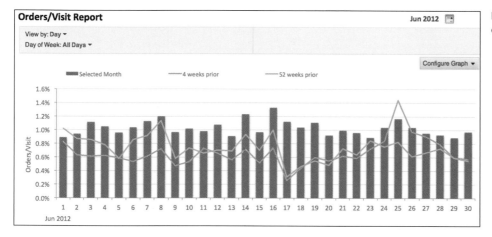

Figure 4.13 Sample calculated metric report.

If you instead have administrator rights for your SiteCatalyst implementation, in addition to creating or editing calculated metrics from within the Add Metrics window, you can also access and modify them from within the administration console, as shown in **Figure 4.14**. The administration console can also be used to replicate the same calculated metric to multiple report suites, provided that each report suite contains the metrics used in the calculated metric.

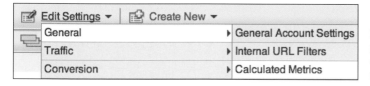

Figure 4.14 Accessing global calculated metrics via the administration console.

Total metrics

While creating the new Orders/Visit calculated metric earlier (Figure 4.10), you may have noticed that each metric available to add to the formula was shown as a standard metric and on the right side as a Total metric. Most of the time you'll choose the standard metric on the left side of the screen. Those standard metrics are your raw traffic or success event metrics. The Total metrics on the right represent the sum total of the selected metric for the specified reporting period. For example, let's say you create a new calculated metric using the formula Orders divided by Total Orders (**Figure 4.15**).

Figure 4.15 Calculated metric formula using a Total metric.

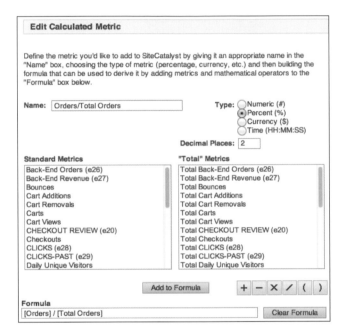

Once this is created, if you add it to a report, you'll see that for each row it divides the numerator (Orders in this case) by the Total metric selected (also Orders in this case) to provide a report like the one in **Figure 4.16**. In this case, the calculated metric demonstrates that the new metric using the Total Orders metric will match the percentage of row items for total Orders, so you've basically re-created these row percentages using a Total metric.

I don't use these Total metrics very often, but at times they can be useful. For example, let's say you have a report of your products and you are curious to see if some products make up a large percentage of orders but not as much of a percentage of revenue, or vice versa. One way to do this is to create two calculated metrics that use Total metrics: One would be Orders divided by Total Orders, and the other would be Revenue divided by Total Revenue. Then you could add these metrics to the Products Conversion report and see a report like the one in **Figure 4.17**.

	Products	Orders ▼ ②		Orders/Total Orders
	1. 101808	274	17.5%	17.45%
	2. 200610	247	15.7%	15.73%
	3. 200632	212	13.5%	13.50%
	4. 101508	119	7.6%	7.58%
	5. 600200	95	6.1%	6.05%
	6. 600067	85	5.4%	5.41%

Figure 4.16 A SiteCatalyst report showing a calculated metric using a Total metric.

	Products	Orders/Total Orders ▼	Revenue/Total Revenue
	1. 200632	28.57%	28.86%
	2. 200560	28.57%	25.96%
	3. 300376	14.29%	2.10%
	4. 600260	14.29%	5.79%
	5. 101808	14.29%	22.85%

Figure 4.17 A SiteCatalyst report showing two calculated metrics using Total metrics.

In this report, you can see that the first two products have a similar percentage of Orders and Revenue, the next two products have a higher percentage of Orders than Revenue, and the last product shown has a higher Revenue percentage than Orders. This type of report allows you to dig deeper into your Orders and Revenue data to see if there are any underlying issues that need to be addressed.

Success Event Participation

One of the more advanced features related to success events is success event participation. *Participation* is an optional setting that you can enable for success events and is used to determine which conversion or traffic variables "participated" in a success event taking place. To fully understand participation, it is helpful to first understand success event allocation. *Success event allocation* is the process of dividing credit among conversion or traffic variable values for a success event. For example, if a visitor viewed four pages on the website and then completed a Form Submission success event, each page would be allocated evenly (also known as *linear allocation*) at 0.25 for the form submission. So if you added the Form Submission success event to the Pages report, you'd see a rounded number of partial page credits for that success event. Conversion variables have a few more possible allocation options. For conversion variables, in addition to evenly allocating a success event to all values, you also have the option of giving credit for the success event to the first value or the last value (which I'll cover in more detail in the next chapter). However, all of these options have one commonality: They divide the credit for success events among one or more variable values.

Now that you understand a bit about allocation, let's return to the topic of participation. Participation assigns *equal* credit to each variable value that "participates" in the flow leading to a success event. So in the preceding example in which a visitor viewed four pages on the website, allocation would divide the Form Submission success event, but participation would assign full credit of "1" to every page (or value) the variable received up to the point the success event took place. If the visitor had viewed four pages prior to the form submission, when viewing the Form Submission Participation metric in the Pages report, SiteCatalyst would show "1" for each of these four pages and also show a total percentage of how often each page "participated" in all Form Submission success events. SiteCatalyst customers use participation metrics for web analyses that should not divide success event metrics by the number of values (pages) viewed by the visitor. There are cases in which you want to use participation to had full credit for a success event to the values leading to that event. For example, if you assume a website with a small amount of traffic for the day, you might see a report that looks like the one in **Figure 4.18**.

Figure 4.18 A sample Page report showing a participation metric.

	Page	Page Views ▼		Form Submissions		Form Submissions Participation	
1.	Page 1	50	50.0%	3	10.0%	33.3%	(10)
2.	Page 2	25	25.0%	2	6.7%	23.3%	(7)
3.	Page 3	15	15.0%	1	3.3%	16.7%	(5)
4.	Page 4	10	10.0%	1	3.3%	6.7%	(2)

In this report, you can see how many Page Views each page received in the first metric column. In the next column to the right, you can see the raw Form Submissions metric; each page has been given a portion of the form submissions that took place after visitors viewed that page. In the last column, you see the Participation metric for Form Submissions. Here you can see that Page 1 was seen prior to 33 percent of all Form Submission success events. The number in parentheses indicates how many success events each page participated in, so you can deduce from these figures that a total of 30 form submissions have taken place in the chosen reporting period. Keep in mind that you're looking at a Pages report in this example, but you can use participation metrics in virtually any traffic or conversion variable report. It often takes SiteCatalyst clients a bit of time to get their heads around how participation metrics work, but once you use them for a while, they begin to make more sense.

Important Details to Know About Success Event Participation

Success event participation metrics are an advanced feature and, as such, come with some caveats. The following are some important details to know about success event participation:

▶ To enable success event participation, you need to contact your Adobe account manager or ClientCare.

▶ You can enable success event participation metrics with or without "subrelations." If enabled without subrelations, you won't be able to use participation metrics in breakdown reports with other variables. Conversely, enabling participation metrics with subrelations allows you to use them in breakdown reports (which is the option I recommend).

▶ Once success event participation is turned on for a success event, you add participation metrics to reports by using the drop-down box in the Add Metrics window.

▶ Success event participation is calculated on a per visit basis, not across multiple visits. This means that it only gives full credit to values it sees in the visit in which the success event for which participation is enabled takes place.

Conclusion

In this chapter, you began the process of learning conversion variables starting with success events. Using success events, you can track your organization's KPIs and see how your website is performing. You learned how to use the three different types of success events: Counter, Currency, and Numeric. The use of event serialization for success event de-duplication was reviewed, along with ways to create calculated metrics using success events. In addition, you learned the difference between success event allocation and participation. In the next chapter, you'll learn about conversion variables and how they are used with success events to report on your website success.

## CHAPTER 5

Conversion Variables

So far you've learned about SiteCatalyst traffic variables and success events. As previously discussed, traffic variables allow you to break down traffic metrics (page views, visits, and unique visitors), whereas success events capture metrics around conversion actions taken by website visitors. Next, you learned about success events and how you can use them to capture metrics that are meaningful to your website. However, you've not yet learned a way to break these success event metrics into buckets. Just as there is a need to break down traffic metrics into buckets, traffic variables break down success event metrics into buckets. As you'll see in this chapter, this is the purpose of Site-Catalyst conversion variables.

Conversion Variable (eVars) Fundamentals

SiteCatalyst *conversion variables* (also known as eVars) allow you to subdivide your KPIs so you can look for differences when you're doing web analysis. Conversion variables break down success events into manageable buckets. For example, in the previous chapter you saw an example of Greco, Inc. using a Currency success event to capture requested loan amounts on the website page in **Figure 5.1**.

Figure 5.1 Greco, Inc. loan application form.

But what if your executives want to see a report of requested loan amounts broken down by state within the United States? To do this, you need a way to partition all of the requested loan amount values so you can see which ones took place in Illinois, California, Pennsylvania, and so on. If you used only success events, you'd need to set a different event for each state (using half of your allotted success events). However, this is easy to do using one conversion variable. In this scenario, you would create a "State" conversion variable (let's say it's eVar1) and update the code you saw in Chapter 4 to capture the state selected in a conversion variable like this:

```
s.products=";Home Loan;;;event20=250000";
s.eVar1="Illinois";
```

By doing so, the $250,000 amount is assigned or bound to the value of "Illinois" in the eVar1 report. Next, you can open the State (eVar1) report in SiteCatalyst and add the Requested Loan Amount metric to the report, and if—for this example only—you pretend that this visitor was the only one who accessed the website to date, you would see a report like the one in **Figure 5.2**.

	State	Requested Loan Amount ▼	
1.	Illinois	$250,000	100.0%

Figure 5.2 A conversion variable report showing one requested loan amount by state.

	State	Requested Loan Amount ▼	
📊	1. New York	$21,275,000	21.3%
📊	2. California	$18,700,000	18.7%
📊	3. Pennsylvania	$12,340,000	12.3%
📊	4. Illinois	$8,540,000	8.5%
📊	5. Ohio	$6,310,000	6.3%
📊	6. Florida	$5,850,000	5.9%
📊	7. New Jersey	$4,480,000	4.5%
📊	8. Wisconsin	$4,100,000	4.1%

Figure 5.3 A conversion variable report showing all requested loan amounts by state.

Of course, there would (hopefully) end up being many more website visitors interested in loans, so the report might eventually end up looking like the one in **Figure 5.3**.

Conversion variables have a direct relationship to success events, and they complement each other. When a SiteCatalyst success event takes place (e.g., a visitor takes an action that results in a success event being set), SiteCatalyst assigns credit for that success event instance to one value *in each conversion variable report* (you may need to re-read this a few times). For example, in the Greco, Inc. loan example, if Greco, Inc. has a second conversion variable (eVar2) that captured the Day of Week and that variable had been set with the value of Monday on the same page or a previous page, the same $250,000 that was passed to the Currency success event would be assigned to the value of "Monday" in the eVar2 report. Again, if only one visitor accessed the website, the Day of Week (eVar2) report would look like the one in **Figure 5.4**.

	Day of Week	Requested Loan Amount ▼	
📊	1. Monday	$250,000	100.0%

Figure 5.4 A conversion variable report showing one requested loan amount by day of week.

Bear in mind that there is still only $250,000 total passed into the Requested Loan Amount success event, but in the State (eVar1) report that $250,000 is credited to Illinois, whereas in the Day of Week (eVar2) report that same $250,000 is credited to Monday. If there were 20 additional conversion variables in the Greco, Inc. implementation, one value in each of those reports would get credit for the same $250,000 in that specific report.

Conversion Variable Persistence

If you read the previous section closely, you may have noticed that I slipped something new into the example scenario. When discussing the Day of Week conversion variable, I mentioned that the day of the week could have been set on that page *or previously* so you could learn about conversion variable persistence. Recall that in Chapter 3 you learned that traffic variables lose their value after each page view (I even went so far as to call them "dumb"). Conversely, conversion variables are able to retain their value from page to page. In fact, your organization has the ability to choose exactly how long each conversion variable should retain values that have been passed to it. In the preceding bank loan example, the Day of Week could have been passed to the eVar2 conversion variable on the first page of the visit and the loan application page might not have been seen until 20 pages thereafter. Conversion variable values can persist for specified durations of time (an hour, a day, a month) or until a specific success event takes place (Order, Form Submission, Onsite Search, etc.). This capability to retain values in conversion variables is called *persistence*, and it is a key factor that differentiates them from traffic variables. Because success events can take place anytime within the website visit, it makes sense that conversion variables would persist their values beyond a page view so that they can do their job of breaking down success events. As you saw in the example of the Day of Week conversion variable, there is no disadvantage to allowing every success event set during the visit to be broken down by the day of the week, so you might as well set its value early on and persist it for the entire session.

But what happens if you pass a second value into a conversion variable? For example, what if you set an Onsite Search Term conversion variable and pass to it the search phrases entered in the search box on your website? It is possible that a visitor will search for the phrase "loans" and then a few pages later search for the phrase "application." How would one conversion variable deal with two different values being passed on two different pages? And if the visitor entering these onsite search phrases completed a key success event, like a loan application form submission, which onsite search term would get the credit—the first term or the last term?

These are great questions and they highlight the inherent complexity that comes with conversion variable persistence. The good news is that SiteCatalyst has anticipated these questions and provides a way for you to decide on a conversion-variable-by-conversion-variable basis how you want to address these questions. Each conversion variable has its own settings, which you can access in the administration console (if you have administrator privileges). The following section explains these settings in detail.

Conversion Variable Settings

In the administration console, you can see every SiteCatalyst variable setting. Conversion variables, due to their complexity, have more settings than the other variable types. However, if you understand how conversion variables work, all of the settings should make sense. In the basic implementation for Greco, Inc., you can see that there are two conversion variables so far—State (eVar1) and Day of Week (eVar2). You can see these on the variable definition screen, where we are also in the process of adding the next conversion variable—Onsite Search Terms (eVar3) (**Figure 5.5**).

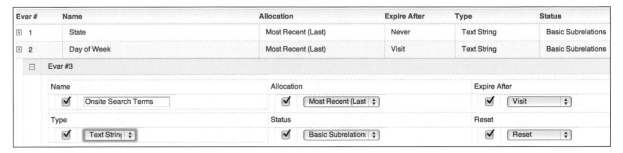

Evar #	Name	Allocation	Expire After	Type	Status
⊞ 1	State	Most Recent (Last)	Never	Text String	Basic Subrelations
⊞ 2	Day of Week	Most Recent (Last)	Visit	Text String	Basic Subrelations

⊟ Evar #3			
Name	Allocation	Expire After
☑ Onsite Search Terms	☑ Most Recent (Last ⇕)	☑ Visit ⇕
Type	Status	Reset
☑ Text String ⇕	☑ Basic Subrelation ⇕	☑ Reset ⇕

Figure 5.5 Conversion variable settings shown in the administration console.

For each conversion variable you can set a Name, Allocation, Expiration, Type, and Status. Let's walk through each of these settings.

Conversion variable names

The Name setting represents what your users will see as the "friendly" name for a conversion variable within SiteCatalyst. Your developers may need to know that eVar #1 is State and eVar #2 is Day of Week, but your SiteCatalyst users do not. You can choose any name that you think your end users will understand, keeping in mind that this name will be displayed in the menus and at the top of the report. In the example shown in Figure 5.5, I've chosen to name the new eVar #3 Onsite Search Terms.

Conversion variable allocation

In the earlier example of onsite search terms, you saw a dilemma about which onsite search term should receive credit for the successful loan application form submission. The visitor had searched on "loans" and then "applications" prior to the KPI taking place. The Allocation setting can be used to address this problem. Allocation is a way to tell SiteCatalyst if you want the first conversion variable value, the last conversion variable value, or all conversion variable values to be associated with subsequent success events (**Figure 5.6**). If you want the first value that gets passed to a conversion variable to get credit for subsequent success events, you would choose Original Value (First). If you want the last value passed to the conversion variable to get credit for subsequent success events, you'd choose Most Recent (Last). And, if you want all values passed to a conversion variable within the visit to get credit for subsequent success events, you'd choose the Linear option. The Linear option divides credit evenly between the values that have been passed to the conversion variable at the time that the success event takes place.

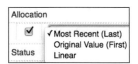

Allocation	
☑	✓ Most Recent (Last)
	Original Value (First)
Status	Linear

Figure 5.6 Conversion variable Allocation settings.

Advanced Variable Naming Techniques

As you become more proficient with SiteCatalyst, you may want to consider a few "best practice" variable naming tricks that have helped SiteCatalyst folks over the years. One trick is to add a variable identifier to the name of each variable. For example, there may be reasons you have an Onsite Search Term conversion variable and an Onsite Search Term traffic variable, because each variable type has its own benefits. If this happens, when you look at the menus or in reports, it is sometimes difficult to figure out if you are looking at the conversion or traffic version of the variable. To mitigate this problem, many customers add the phrase "(Prop3)" or "(eVar3)" to the end of the variable name in the administration console. In Figure 5.5, the new conversion variable created might be named Onsite Search Terms (eVar3) to help distinguish it from the similar traffic variable.

Another popular variable naming trick is to name variables that are not yet implemented in all capital letters. Because you are limited in the ways you can annotate SiteCatalyst variables, you can use uppercase variable names to tell your end users that a variable is planned but not yet implemented. For example, if the onsite search term conversion variable was planned to be in eVar #3 but had not yet started collecting data, its name in the administration console might be set to ONSITE SEARCH TERMS (EVAR3) until such time as it had data. As you'll learn, variables can also be hidden, but this uppercase approach provides a way for everyone to see what is and is not yet implemented, and what exciting new variables are coming soon.

In the previous example, if the Onsite Search Terms conversion variable had been set to Original Value (First) Allocation, the Loan Application Form Submission success event would have been credited to the term "loans" in the eVar #3 report because that was the first value SiteCatalyst saw in the visit. Conversely, if the Onsite Search Terms conversion variable had been set to Most Recent (Last) Allocation, the Loan Application Form Submission success event would have been credited to "applications" in the eVar #3 report because that was the last value SiteCatalyst saw prior to the success event taking place. And if the Onsite Search Terms conversion variable had been set to Linear Allocation, 0.5 credit would have been given to the term "loans" and 0.5 credit would have been given to "applications" because these were the only two search terms prior to the success event taking place. In this specific scenario, it would be up to you to decide which allocation is best for your Onsite Search Terms conversion variable.

What do you suppose would happen if you chose Linear Allocation and the same visitor who searched on the preceding two phrases proceeded to search for a third phrase and then completed a different website success event? SiteCatalyst would see three different Onsite Search Terms conversion variable values at the time the new success event took place, so the new success event would give 0.3333 credit to each of these three terms.

But what if the success event is a Currency success event? How is credit assigned if Linear Allocation is used? Currency success events operate in the same manner, but instead of search phrases receiving 0.5 credit or 0.3333 credit for the success, the currency amount associated with the currency success event is divided by the number of distinct values being linearly allocated. If you think back to the requested loan amount currency event example (which was set for $250,000), if there had been two onsite search terms ("loans" and "application") prior to the Currency success event being set, each search term would be credited with $125,000 (or half credit) when the Requested Loan Amount success event is added to the Onsite Search Terms conversion variable report.

Linear isn't the only type of allocation that can get complex at times. Some clients also struggle with conversion variables set to Original Value (First). When you set a conversion variable to this allocation, you need to understand that no matter how many times you pass a value into the variable, the conversion variable will retain the first value it received (although the conversion variable will capture other values as Instances, as described in Chapter 3), provided that its value has not yet expired (expiration is discussed in the next section).

For example, I've had clients who want to capture the first online marketing campaign code (e.g., specific paid search keyword) a visitor used to find them and keep that as their "original" campaign code. To do this, they correctly capture campaign codes in a conversion variable and set it to Original Value (First). But then I notice that they set the conversion variable to clear its value (expire) at the end of each visit. By doing so, they negate their initial intention of preserving the original campaign code used to reach the website.

Technically, in this configuration, the conversion variable acts the same as if it were set to Last Value Allocation except in the situation where a visitor comes to the website more than once from two different campaign codes all within the same visit time frame (which is what I tell them when they ask me why their Original Value conversion variable data is almost identical to their Most Recent version of the conversion variable). Therefore, when you're using the Original Value (First) Allocation, be mindful of your variable expiration settings.

Warning: Linear Allocation and Multiple Visits

Sometimes SiteCatalyst customers set a conversion variable to Linear Allocation as a way to attribute success to conversion variable values across multiple visits. However, Linear Allocation only takes into account values from the current visit and the last value it receives from the previous visit (if there is one). Therefore, it cannot be used to do true multi-visit attribution, especially if more than two visits take place. Keep this limitation in mind when you're deciding on your approach to your conversion variable Allocation settings.

Fortunately, Most Recent (Last) is the allocation type used most often and the easiest to configure and understand. As values are passed to conversion variables with the Most Recent (Last) Allocation, they simply overwrite the previous value, and whatever value remains at the time success events take place is what gets credit for the success. In my experience, about 90 percent of all conversion variables use this type of allocation.

However, there will be times when you're not quite sure which conversion variable allocation you should set for a particular conversion variable. If this happens, keep in mind that you can set the same values to multiple conversion variables and use a different allocation for each. For example, if you were really unsure about which type of allocation to set for the Onsite Search Terms conversion variable, you could pass the same onsite search phrases to eVar #3, eVar #4, and eVar #5, and set the allocation differently, as shown in **Figure 5.7**.

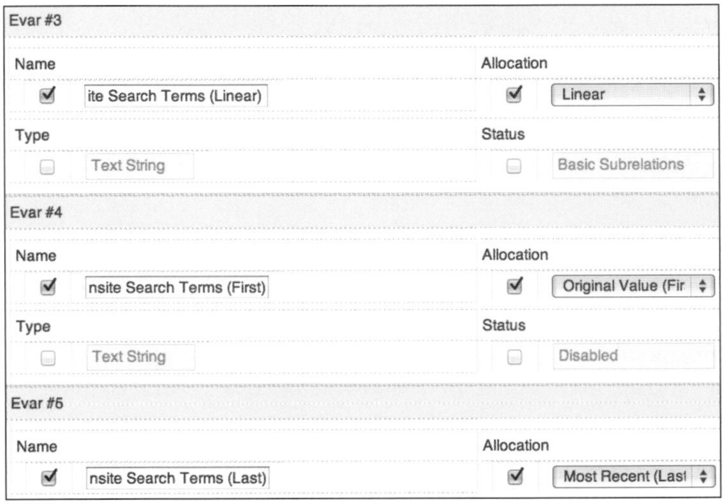

Figure 5.7 Same conversion variable with multiple settings.

Obviously, this is not something you should make a habit of doing, lest you run out of conversion variables. But this just illustrates that you are not confined to only one view of how success events are allocated to conversion variables.

Conversion variable expiration

Conversion variable expiration was mentioned in some of the previous examples. And as you've learned, conversion variable values are persistent, meaning they can be retained beyond a page view or visit. You use conversion variable expiration settings to specify, for each conversion variable, how long you want the conversion variable to retain this value. The process of clearing out a conversion variable value from a user's

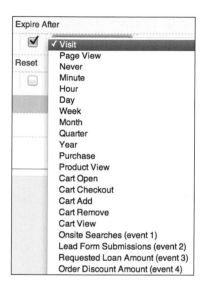

Figure 5.8 Conversion variable expiration options.

SiteCatalyst cookie is known as *expiration*, or expiring the value. Conversion variables can be expired based on a time frame (hour, day, month) or based on the setting of a success event (**Figure 5.8**).

When you choose the expiration setting and save the conversion variable, from that point forward, visitors receiving a value in that conversion variable will retain that value in their SiteCatalyst cookie until they reach the specified expiration (or have their cookies deleted, which wipes out all SiteCatalyst cookie information, including conversion variable values). Over the years, I've learned some snags related to conversion variable expiration that can trip people up, so keep the following items in mind:

▶ If a conversion variable is set to Most Recent (Last) Allocation, even if it has an expiration that has not been reached, it will still accept new values that are passed to it.

▶ When a conversion variable with a time-based expiration (e.g., 60 days) receives a new value, the clock starts over. So if expiration was set for 60 days and 30 days had passed when it received a new value, the new value would then persist for 60 more days.

▶ If you set a conversion variable to expire when a specific success event takes place (e.g., Purchase), keep in mind that the conversion variable value may persist for a long time because it will retain its value until a Purchase success event occurs. In some cases, a Purchase success event might not take place for years, which could result in strange values receiving credit for purchases. Unfortunately, there is currently no way to expire a conversion variable based on a time period *or* a success event taking place (whichever happens first).

► There is currently no way to expire a conversion variable when multiple success events take place. For example, there may be cases in which you want to expire a conversion variable if success event 3 *or* success event 5 takes place (and the order of the success events taking place doesn't matter). Unfortunately, the administration console allows you to select only one success event for expiration, so this is not possible. But I've created a workaround for this, which I call *Über success events* (see the sidebar "*Über* Success Events").

► Notice that there is a Never option to expire. This is an especially powerful option because it means that the value in the conversion variable will remain forever unless visitors delete their cookies. Be especially careful about setting a conversion variable to Never expire if you have Allocation set to Original Value (First), because that could cause a visitor to get one value and retain it forever.

In practice, most conversion variables expire at the visit, a few expire at key success events, and a few are set to expire Never. I suggest that you look at each conversion variable and determine the best expiration for how you plan to use it.

Über Success Events

The inability to expire a conversion variable when one of many possible success events takes place can cause issues at times within SiteCatalyst. For example, imagine that you are a B2B Lead Generation website that sells its products online or allows its visitors to fill out a form and work with a sales rep to complete the purchase. You have a standard conversion flow with three steps (success event 1, success event 2, success event 3). However, when visitors reach the third step of the process, they can proceed to purchase online (scCheckout, purchase) or view and submit a form (success event 4, success event 5) to have a sales rep call them and finish the sale. In this situation, a website visitor can be viewed as successfully completing the conversion funnel two different ways: One way is to purchase online, and the other is to submit a form. It's as if there is a fork in the road, but both paths can lead to a successful conversion. But what if you want to expire several conversion variables when visitors order *or* they submit a lead generation form to a sales rep? You are pretty much out of luck, because you can only pick one event in the administration console to use for expiration purposes.

To solve this dilemma, my *Über* success events method allows you to expire conversion variables when one of any number of success events takes place. In the preceding scenario, what you can do is set a new success event at the same time that you set the Order (purchase event) *and* the Form Submission (event5) success events. In this case, you might set event20 at the same time you set the purchase event and event5. By doing so, not only can you use event20 to sum all of the successes (orders and form submissions), but also now have one success event that represents both types of successes. This *Über* success event (event20) can be used in the administration console to expire any conversion variables that you want to expire when one or the other of these two success events occurs. To do this, you simply set conversion variables to expire when event20 takes place. This handy workaround can be extended in many ways, but the overall theme is that it gives you more control over when you can expire conversion variables when there are multiple versions of success.

Good Uses for the Never Expiration Setting

So when should you use the Never expiration option with conversion variables? As a general rule, I use Never when I've collected a piece of data that will most likely not change for the user over multiple visits. For example, if you have a form on your website and one of the fields is Country of Residence, you could capture that in a conversion variable and retain it perpetually by using the Never expiration option. The rationale is that most people do not move from one country to another frequently, and if you retain it forever, the next time the visitor comes to the website, even if the visitor doesn't fill out a form, you'll still know what country that person is from. This increases the number of success event metrics you can tie to a country. Although you could expire this conversion variable at the end of the visit, why would you when you can extend its value beyond the life of the visit?

Other examples of data points that are worth retaining forever include:

▸ Website visitor IDs

▸ E-mail ID (not e-mail address, but ID of visitor in e-mail tool)

▸ Customer ID

▸ State

▸ Zip code

▸ Gender

Conversion variable type: Text String vs. Counter

The two types of standard conversion variables are Text String and Counter (**Figure 5.9**).

Text String conversion variables accept text (alphanumeric) values. These values can be words like "chicago," "texas," or "google," or can be numbers like "20" or combinations like "20 years old." About 98 percent of conversion variables will be Text String because most conversion variables are used to store alphanumeric values describing values. Text String values can be no longer than 255 characters in length (less if you're using multi-byte characters).

Figure 5.9 Conversion variable Type options.

Counter conversion variables are somewhat tricky to grasp at first. Counter conversion variables are similar to all other conversion variables in that they persist values, have an expiration period, and break down success events. Where they differ is that instead of passing text values to them, you pass numbers, and these numbers are added to the total that the visitor previously had in that Counter conversion variable. Some example uses of Counter eVars might include:

▶ Tracking how many campaign codes are used prior to a purchase taking place.

▶ Tracking how many articles are read prior to registering on the site.

▶ Tracking how many blog posts are read prior to signing up for an RSS feed.

▶ Tracking how many flight searches a user conducts prior to booking travel.

▶ Tracking how many cars a visitor configures prior to requesting a quote from a dealer.

The best way to understand Counter conversion variables is through an example. Imagine that you want to know how many pages on a website each visitor had seen at the time each decided to use onsite search. In this case, you would want to keep a running tally of how many pages the visitor had viewed and increase it by one with every page view. Although you could find a way to store this value in your own corporate cookie, it would be a good use of a Counter conversion variable. On each page of the website, you would set the Counter conversion variable like this:

```
s.eVar15="+1";
```

That's it. Once this is set on each page, SiteCatalyst will add "1" to the existing eVar #15 value in each visitor cookie on every page of the website. For example, if I were new to the website and came to the home page, my value in eVar #15 would be "1.0." After I had viewed three more pages, the eVar #15 value in my SiteCatalyst cookie would be "4.0." Now let's say that I decide to do an onsite search and a success event is set. Once this happens, just like any other conversion variable, in the eVar #15 report, the Onsite Search success event is assigned or credited to the current eVar #15 value in the cookie, (which includes setting the Counter conversion variable on the same page as the success event) after "5.0." Therefore, if you assume I had been the only visitor to the website and were to look at eVar #15 and add the Onsite Search success event to the report, you would see the results shown in **Figure 5.10**.

What can be confusing about Counter conversion variables versus Text String conversion variables is that you can also pass numbers into Text String conversion variables,

🔲	# of Pages Viewed	Onsite Searches ▾	
🔲	1. 5.0	1	100.0%

Figure 5.10 Sample Counter conversion variable report.

but the difference is that Counter conversion variables keep a running tally or count of all numbers that have been passed to them, whereas a number in a Text String conversion variable is simply a string with numbers (no math is involved). However, it's important to understand that even though both conversion variable types can contain numbers, they are not metrics that you can see in charts. Only success events and traffic metrics can be seen in metric reports.

Another cool aspect of Counter conversion variables is that you don't have to increase them by just "1" when they are set; you can increment them using any number, including numbers with decimals. But as mentioned initially, I rarely see SiteCatalyst customers using Counter conversion variables, so you'll most likely not come across them very often. In future chapters, I'll cover some advanced ways Counter conversion variables can be used in real-world situations.

Conversion variable status

Conversion variables can have four status types (**Figure 5.11**):

▸ **Disabled.** Conversion variable is turned off and cannot be seen in the menus. This is normally only used for conversion variables that have not yet been activated.

▸ **No Subrelations.** Conversion variable can be seen with any success event metrics, but cannot be seen in any breakdown reports. This is rarely used.

▸ **Basic Subrelations.** Conversion variable can be seen with any success event metric and in breakdowns with any conversion variable that has Full Subrelations, the campaign variable, the products variable, and Traffic Source reports.

▸ **Full Subrelations.** Conversion variable can be seen with any success event metric and can be broken down by any other conversion variable.

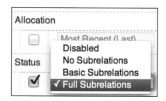

Figure 5.11 Conversion variable Status settings.

Prior to SiteCatalyst v15, the distinction between Basic Subrelations and Full Subrelations was very important. Most SiteCatalyst contracts provided a handful of conversion variables that had Full Subrelations and the rest had Basic Subrelations. Full Subrelations were valuable because it meant that you could perform many more report breakdowns. This meant you had to pick them strategically for the conversion variables you thought you would use in report breakdowns most often or pay Adobe more money.

However, once you migrate to SiteCatalyst v15, this distinction becomes moot because in v15 all conversion variables have Full Subrelations, meaning that any conversion variable can be broken down by any other conversion variable. If you are using Site-Catalyst v15 or later, since all conversion variables have Full Subrelations, the Status setting only provides the ability to enable or disable a conversion variable. Prior versions will continue to have the preceding option settings.

Conversion variable Reset setting

The final setting related to conversion variables is the Reset setting. The two options for this setting are Reset and Do Not Reset. The only time you would use this feature is if you were reusing a conversion variable for a completely different purpose. For example, let's say that eVar #7 has been used for Hour of Day ever since the initial implementation, but you've run out of conversion variables and need to reuse it for a new, more important data value. In this scenario, you would select the Reset option and save the conversion variable. Once you click through the warning messages, the conversion variable will be reset.

However, many SiteCatalyst customers fail to understand what this resetting actually does. Performing these steps will not remove historical data for this conversion variable. It does not wipe the slate clean. Instead, it simply instructs SiteCatalyst to clear out any existing values for that conversion variable in all visitor cookies. It is the equivalent of a one-time conversion variable expiration for all users. Once all values have been expired, from that point forward, you should see only the newly tagged values passed to the conversion variable (although caching may cause old values to appear for a few weeks). Because this reset action does not clear historical data, it is suggested that you use previously unused conversion variables for new data collection if you want to avoid seeing historical data in the same reports as new data.

The "None" Row

As you begin to use SiteCatalyst conversion variable reports, you'll inevitably encounter the dreaded None row in reports. The None row has probably caused more confusion to SiteCatalyst customers than anything else. I often hear, "What is the None row in conversion variable reports, and how can I get rid of it?" However, if you fully understand how conversion variables work, the None row should not scare you. Simply put, if there is no value stored in a conversion variable for a user at the time a success event takes place, SiteCatalyst gives credit to None in that conversion variable report for that success event, so the total at the bottom of the conversion variable report will equal the total success events for that metric. An easy way to remember this is to replace the term None in conversion variable reports in your head with the phrase "cases in which SiteCatalyst didn't know the [*conversion variable name*]." In the report in **Figure 5.12**, you see that the conversion variable is State and the success event shown is Lead Form Submissions.

	State	Lead Form Submissions ▼	
🔲	1. None ⑦	3,460	34.6%
🔲	2. New York	1,870	18.7%
🔲	3. California	1,570	15.7%
🔲	4. Illinois	1,040	10.4%

Figure 5.12 Conversion variable report showing the None row.

	Marketing Channel	Lead Form Submissions ▼	
🔲	1. SEO	3,654	36.5%
🔲	2. SEM	2,945	29.5%
🔲	3. None ⑦	1,245	12.5%
🔲	4. Social Media	1,040	10.4%
🔲	5. E-mail	712	7.1%

Figure 5.13 Marketing Channel report showing the None row.

For this website, visitors are asked to enter the state they live in on forms, but it is not a required field. Therefore, not every form submission will have a value. If the visitor does enter a value, it is passed into the State conversion variable when the Lead Form Submission success event takes place. As you can see in the report, approximately 35 percent of the time that visitors submit the form they did not enter a State value. Therefore, SiteCatalyst doesn't know which state to give credit to for these Lead Form Submissions. If SiteCatalyst were to omit these cases altogether, the report would be inaccurate because it would be missing 3,460 Lead Form Submissions. In reality, these Lead Form Submissions did take place, you just don't know the state associated with them. Omitting them from the report would also boost the percentages associated with New York, California, and so on because they would be divided by a smaller denominator. All of these scenarios have the potential to distort your web analytics data. So the logical answer is for SiteCatalyst to communicate that there were additional Lead Form Submissions beyond those that it had a State value for, but that all it can tell you is that they took place and that SiteCatalyst was not told which state they were associated with. When looked at from this perspective, it is easy to see why the None row is important and is actually a good feature to have as part of the product.

In fact, there are some cases in which seeing the None row in a report is the primary objective of a web analysis. For example, let's say someone wants to know what percentage of time people submitted lead forms without having come from any marketing channel. The answer can be found by simply adding the Lead Form Submissions success event to a Marketing Channel report and looking at the percentage of the None row, as shown in **Figure 5.13**. In this report, the None row represents cases in which visitors reached the site without using any standard marketing channels, like SEO, SEM, or social media. These folks most likely had the website bookmarked or typed in the URL manually. By using the None row in this report, you can see that 12.5 percent of the Lead Form Submissions came from visitors not using any predefined marketing channel.

In general, however, you want to reduce the number of cases in which you see a None row so that more of your success events are tied to specific conversion variable values. If you want to minimize how often you see the None row, here are a few suggestions:

▶ **Set conversion variables as soon as you know them and as early in the visit as possible.** For example, if you know that the current visitor is a customer of yours as soon as the first page of the visit (through a cookie value), don't wait to pass this value into a conversion variable until later in the visit. Set it as early on as possible. Doing so will maximize the number of success events that will be associated with the conversion variable value of "Customer" throughout the visit.

▶ **Revisit your conversion variable expiration settings.** The more frequently you are expiring conversion variables, the more likely these variables will have no value at the time success events occur and have higher percentages of None values.

▶ **Be mindful of which success events you are adding to each conversion variable report.** Some conversion variables will naturally go with success events to which they are related. In the preceding example, the State conversion variable is meant to complement the Lead Form Submission success event. In a perfect world, every Lead Form Submission success event would have a State value. But what if you had added the Onsite Searches success event metric to the State conversion variable report? Because the State conversion variable has no relationship with onsite searches, it is likely that the majority of onsite searches will have no State associated with them and the None row could be as high as 90 percent in that report. All this means is that when the onsite searches success event took place, 90 percent of the time visitors doing searches had no value in the State conversion variable. The fact that 10 percent had State values means that those visitors probably performed the onsite search *after* they had submitted a lead form, and the State conversion variable was set to persist beyond the Lead Form Submission success event (expiration could have been Visit, Week, Month, or Never).

List Variables

Once you master conversion variables, you are ready to tackle list variables (also known as List Vars). List variables are only available in SiteCatalyst v15 and later, so if your organization has not yet migrated, add this to the list of reasons to do so. *List variables* are conversion variables that allow you to store multiple values in them at one time. In many respects, they are the combination of the list prop and the conversion variable. List variables are similar to conversion variables in that they are persistent, are used to break down success events in conversion reports, and have allocation and expiration, but they can collect multiple values like list props. For these reasons, I treat them as conversion variables with just a bit of added functionality.

Figure 5.14 Sample mailing list subscription page.

So why did SiteCatalyst add list variables to the product? There are times when you'll want to capture multiple conversion values on a page, and prior to having a list variable, the only option available was to use a list prop (which has significant limitations), the products variable (covered later in this chapter), or concatenate values together in a standard conversion variable (which is not scalable). The following are just a handful of examples of situations where you could apply list variables:

▶ You have a website form, and you want to capture all of the fields that produce user errors and tie those to a Form Error success event.

▶ You have several website promotions shown on your home page, and you want to give each one an impression each time the page loads.

▶ You have an advanced search tool, and you want to capture the various options visitors have selected at the point when they click the search button.

Anytime you want to associate a success event with multiple possible conversion variable items, list variables can be helpful. Let's explore list variables a bit more through an example. Imagine that you work for NASA and manage the mailing list page shown in **Figure 5.14**. One of your goals is to get visitors to sign up for one or more of its mailing lists. In this scenario, you would set a Mailing List Subscription success event when visitors click the Subscribe button. However, in this case, the visitor is signing up for three different mailing lists at once. If you were using a traditional conversion variable, you'd have to use code like this:

```
s.events="event22";
s.eVar26="science-at-nasa|earth-space-education|sara";
```

Storing concatenated values like this can be cumbersome, especially when you consider that many different permutations could exist in a list with more items. This example has only four possible items, but imagine how many combinations there could be if there were 20 list items. Fortunately, you can use a list variable to solve this tracking quandary. To capture this using a list variable, you would simply alter the preceding code to look like this:

```
s.events="event22";
s.list1="science-at-nasa|earth-space-education|sara";
```

All you need to do is change the variable to use a list variable, and you're done. In this case, a "|" delimiter is used, but you can use a colon or comma just as easily. When you create a list variable, you choose how you will separate the values, and you need to be sure your developers use the correct separator. Once this code is set and data is collected, an example of the report that you'd see is shown in **Figure 5.15**.

		Mailing Lists	Mailing List Subscriptions ▼	
	1.	science-at-nasa	2,100	42.0%
	2.	earth-space-education	1,800	36.0%
	3.	sara	1,300	26.0%
	4.	nasa-spanish	800	16.0%
		TOTAL	**5,000**	

Figure 5.15 Sample list variable report.

In this report, the single Mailing List Subscription success event is counted once for each selected mailing list. As a result, if you add the rows in a list variable report, there will be more than the total found at the bottom of the report, which de-duplicates the values so the total will match that of the overall Mailing List Subscription success event.

List Variable Settings

As mentioned previously, most settings for list variables are similar to those for conversion variables. Unfortunately, at this time, list variables cannot be configured in the administration console, so you cannot see the setting definitions like you can for conversion variables. Here are the various settings that you can configure for list variables:

▶ **Name** is used to set a "friendly" name for each list variable, which is what Site-Catalyst users will see in the menus and in reports.

▶ **Value Delimiter** is the character used to separate values in the code.

▶ **Expiration** determines when the values in the list variable should expire. This is the same option as in standard conversion variables and includes time-based options (Day, Week, Month, Never) or when a specific success event takes place.

▶ **Allocation** determines how each value gets credit for success events, much like standard conversion variables. However, this setting is slightly different. Unlike the choices of Original Value (First), Most Recent (Last), and Linear, the choices are Full and Linear. Full Allocation gives each list variable value full credit for each success event occurring after it has a value. Linear Allocation is similar to traditional conversion variables in that it divides credit among all list variable values collected prior to the success event taking place.

▶ **Max Values** allows you to set a maximum number of values that can be collected on a page. This is an optional setting and is primarily used when you fear your overall SiteCatalyst image request may be longer than the acceptable number of characters allowed by Internet browsers and want to limit request sizes.

■ **NOTE** *Currently it's not possible to apply SAINT Classifications (to be discussed in Chapter 6) to List Variables.*

Products Variable

As you've learned, SiteCatalyst has predefined traffic variables (Pages, Site Sections) and success events (Orders, Cart Additions), but it also has two predefined conversion variables. In this section, you'll learn about the first of these predefined conversion variables: the products variable.

Understanding the Products Variable

As its name implies, the primary purpose of the *products variable* is to store the name of the product for which a website action is taking place. For example, if you manage a retail website and a visitor views a product detail page, you might choose to set a Product View success event so you can see how many product views your website had each day, week, month, and so on. But if you want to see *which* products visitors were looking at, you'd need to capture the product name or product ID in a variable so you can break down the Product Views success event metric by product (**Figure 5.16**).

Figure 5.16 Sample
Products report.

	Products	Product Views ▼ ⑦		Orders ⑦		Look to Book %
1.	isc.1.0.0.24m	822,806	21.3%	29,221	22.7%	3.55%
2.	isc.1.0.0.12m	723,219	18.7%	26,428	20.5%	3.65%
3.	isc.1.1.0.24m	607,194	15.7%	20,841	16.2%	3.43%
4.	avc.1.0.0.12m	402,218	10.4%	13,536	10.5%	3.37%
5.	pct.1.0.0.12m	320,034	8.3%	9,454	7.3%	2.95%

Based on the previous sections, your first instinct should be to use a conversion variable to capture the product name, because conversion variables are used to break down success events. Although you could certainly do that, SiteCatalyst has assumed that most websites will have products, so it has created a special products variable for this purpose. Therefore, it is recommended that you capture the product name or ID in the products variable (**s.products**).

The following sections describe the different aspects of this unique conversion variable.

Multiple values

One of the key aspects of the products variable is that you can pass multiple values to it concurrently. Until list variables were introduced in SiteCatalyst v15, the products variable was the only conversion variable that had multiple value capability.

Special parameters

Because of all of the different requirements SiteCatalyst customers have thrust upon the products variable, it is the most complex to understand from a tagging perspective. The products variable has many special variable parameters that can be set to achieve all of the business requirements mentioned in the sidebar "Products Variable History." Although these parameters can be a bit confusing for newer SiteCatalyst users, it is important to understand them, and I'll do my best to explain them in nontechnical terms. To begin, look at the following full products variable string with all of the potential parameters set:

```
s.products=[Category];[Product];[Quantity];[TotalPrice];
[Incrementor1]|[Incrementor2];[Merchandising1]|[Merchandising2],
[Category2];[Product2]...
```

Products Variable History

SiteCatalyst created a special products variable for several reasons. To fully understand how the products variable emerged, you need to go back in time. If you think back to the problems the creators of SiteCatalyst were attempting to address with the products variable, you'll understand why it ended up the way it is, and this will help you gain a deeper understanding of its facets.

Because website visitors could purchase multiple products at one time, SiteCatalyst had to provide a way to store multiple product values in a conversion variable. Thus, the products variable was born. However, the ability to pass multiple products at the same time was not the only issue clients encountered. Clients also wanted to find a way to assign products into product categories so they could group Revenue, Orders, and Units by products *and* product categories. Further challenges had to do with the fact that visitors could purchase different quantities of each product and that each product had its own price. For example, a visitor might purchase two units of Product A and three units of Product B. Product A might cost $100 per unit, and Product B might cost $200 per unit. For

this reason, the products variable needed to set different success event metrics for each product, which added a level of complexity.

And SiteCatalyst customers had even more demands. Clients requested the ability to pass in additional metrics besides Orders, Units, and Revenue upon purchase and have those metrics tied to each product. For example, Product A might cost $10 for shipping and have taxes of $5, but Product B might cost $20 to ship and have taxes of $8. Clients wanted to create these metrics and tie them to the product for which they were related. In addition, customers wanted to associate additional conversion variable values with each product upon purchase. For example, Product A might be blue and Product B might be red. If they used a standard conversion variable, it would be impossible to assign a different color to each product and have those colors reflected in success events.

This was a pretty tall order to fulfill. So when you wrestle with the complexity of the products variable, keep in mind that it was customers like you that asked SiteCatalyst for it to be that way.

The following list describes each product variable parameter in detail:

- **Category**. Represents the product category. Unfortunately, this is the only parameter that the SiteCatalyst team didn't execute well, so this feature is normally not used. Its original intent was to place products into product categories, but the way it was constructed it bound products forever to the first product category it saw for each product. This proved to be problematic because the same product could be associated with different product categories in different situations. There are now more flexible ways to assign products to product categories, so this parameter is normally not set (left blank) and primarily remains only for backward compatibility purposes.

- **Product.** Represents the name or ID of the product. Most companies pass product IDs because they are shorter and because product names can change over time. As you'll learn in a later chapter, SiteCatalyst provides an easy way to upload "friendly" product names for each product ID, and these product names can even be updated if product names change over time.

▶ **Quantity.** Represents the quantity of the product being purchased (e.g., a visitor buying two memory cards) when used with the Purchase success event. If no purchase is taking place (e.g., Product View success event), leave this parameter blank.

▶ **Total Price.** Represents the total price for the product being purchased (e.g., a total of $200 for two memory cards) when used with the Purchase success event. If no purchase is taking place (e.g., Product View success event), leave this parameter blank.

▶ **Incrementor.** Recall that Incrementor is the original name given to Currency and Numeric success events. As you saw when Currency and Numeric success events were introduced in Chapter 4, they are set in the products variable. For example, if you charge $2.50 shipping for a product and want to show that separate from Revenue, you can set a Currency success event called "Shipping Costs" and pass "2.5" in this part of the products variable string to add $2.50 to each purchase. Note that you can set multiple Incrementor (Currency/Numeric) success events at the same time within this parameter by separating them with a "|" symbol.

▶ **Merchandising.** Assigns different conversion variable values to each product. (I'll cover merchandising shortly.) These values can be product colors, sizes, product categories, or anything else you want to associate with a product. Note that you can set multiple Merchandising conversion variables at the same time within this parameter by separating them with a "|" symbol.

To synthesize all of this information, let's imagine a scenario in which you work for Apple, Inc. and want to capture Orders, Revenue, Units, Shipping Costs, and Taxes, and also assign each purchase to a Product Type conversion variable. This SiteCatalyst customer (Apple, Inc.) has a visitor who purchases the following:

▶ Two Macbook Pros (Product ID 111) at $1,500 each, $15 shipping, $120 in taxes, and the product type is "notebook"

▶ One iPad (Product ID 222) at $400, $5.50 shipping, $32 in taxes, and the product type is "tablet"

In this scenario, the Products string would look like this:

```
s.events="purchase,event18,event19";
s.products=";111;2;3000;event18=15|event19=120;evar12=notebook,
;222;1;400;event18=5.5|event19=32;evar12=tablet";
```

Note that if multiple products are purchased, a comma is used to separate them. Also note that not all parameters are required. For example, if there is no need to set a merchandising variable or an Incrementor event, these settings can be left blank. The following is a valid way to set the products variable if there is no need to capture shipping or taxes, or set any additional conversion variables:

```
s.products=";111;2;3000"
```

Some other important details to note about the products variable string follow:

▶ There is no explicit setting of an Order metric, but SiteCatalyst will treat the entire string as one Order and associate that Order with all products purchased concurrently.

▶ The products variable does not appear in the administration console with the rest of the conversion variables because it has no configurable settings for persistence, allocation, type, and so on.

▶ Products variable values (second parameter setting) can be broken down by any other conversion variable in any version of SiteCatalyst.

▶ Revenue and Unit settings will only be set when the products variable is used in combination with the Purchase event. They will be ignored in all other cases.

Not persistent

One way the products variable is different from other conversion variables is that it is not persistent, meaning that it does not retain its value from one page to the next. In this respect, it is somewhat similar to traffic variables. For this reason, if you need to associate multiple success events with specific products, you must set the products variable every time you set success events. For example, if a visitor adds three products to the shopping cart, you would pass all three product IDs to the products variable when you set the Cart Addition success event. But if later that visitor purchases one of those products, you need to pass that product name or ID to the products variable again when you set the Purchase success event.

Campaign Variable

The other predefined conversion variable is the *campaign variable*, which captures identifiers of marketing campaigns driving traffic to your website. Most organizations spend time and money on marketing campaigns to increase traffic to the website. These campaigns can take place across multiple channels, including e-mail, SEM, social media, and so on. Each marketing campaign should have tracking codes associated with them that map to the campaign for which they are assigned. Then, when visitors come to the website from one of these tracking codes, the code is captured by SiteCatalyst in

Products Variable and Cart Success Events

One of the ways SiteCatalyst customers can falter is by failing to set the products variable with all Shopping Cart success events. Many organizations set the products variable upon purchase and cart addition, but forget to set the products variable during other shopping cart success events, such as Product View, Checkout, or Cart Views. Failing to do this can leave gaps in your reports. For example, let's say you want to see how often products are added to the shopping cart, brought to checkout, and then purchased, but you only set the products variable at Cart Addition and Purchase. **Figure 5.17** shows what your report would look like.

To avoid these types of product gaps, try to set the products variable with all shopping cart success events.

	Products	Cart Additions ▼ ⑦		Checkouts ⑦		Orders ⑦	
1.	111	68,567	21.3%	0	0.0%	27,200	22.7%
2.	222	60,268	18.7%	0	0.0%	24,600	20.5%
3.	333	50,600	15.7%	0	0.0%	19,400	16.2%
4.	444	33,518	10.4%	0	0.0%	12,600	10.5%
5.	555	26,669	8.3%	0	0.0%	8,800	7.3%

Figure 5.17 Products report without products associated with Checkouts.

the campaign variable. These tracking codes allow SiteCatalyst to record the number of visits each tracking code generated, and these codes can later be rolled up into marketing campaigns.

In most respects, the campaign variable is identical to traditional conversion variables. It has the same Name, Allocation, and Expiration settings as other conversion variables, but does not have Type and Status. The reason the campaign variable has no Type setting is that it will always be of the type Text Value (versus a Counter conversion variable). It has no Status setting because the campaign variable always has Full Subrelations, meaning that it can be broken down by any other conversion variable, and any other conversion variable can be broken down by it. These subtle setting differences are found in the administration console (**Figure 5.18**).

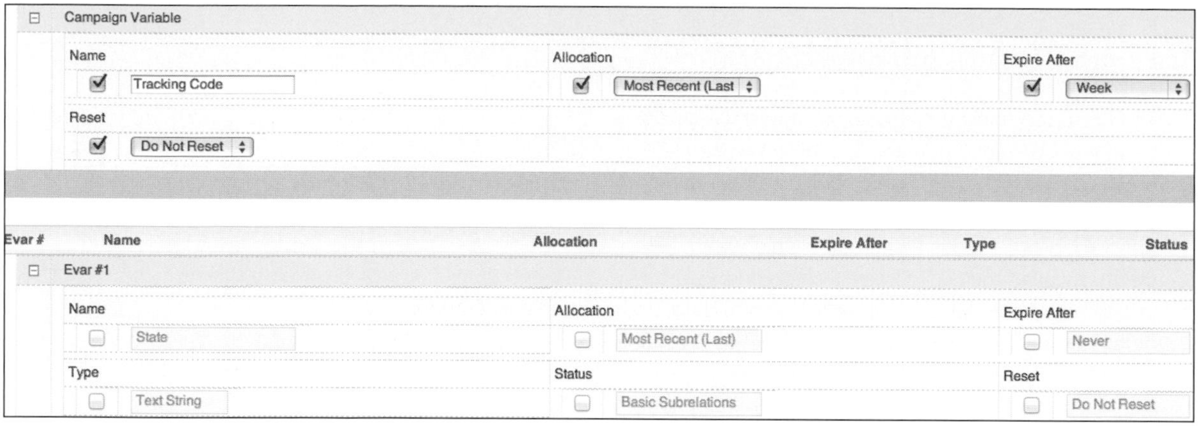

Campaign Variable			
Name		**Allocation**	**Expire After**
☑ Tracking Code		☑ Most Recent (Last) ↕	☑ Week ↕
Reset			
☑ Do Not Reset ↕			

Evar #	Name	Allocation	Expire After	Type	Status
Evar #1					

Name		**Allocation**	**Expire After**
☐ State		☐ Most Recent (Last)	☐ Never
Type		**Status**	**Reset**
☐ Text String		☐ Basic Subrelations	☐ Do Not Reset

Figure 5.18 Campaign variable settings.

You may notice that by default the campaign variable is labeled Tracking Code. As with any other conversion variable, this label can be easily changed, but it is a phrase that has been used for years by SiteCatalyst users. So if you hear others mention campaign variable and tracking code, they are usually synonymous.

Setting the Campaign Variable

Normally, the campaign variable is populated on the first page of the website visit. That is the opportune time to use referrer information to see how the visitor arrived at your website. The syntax for populating the campaign variable looks like this:

```
s.campaign="email_114242";
```

However, most SiteCatalyst clients use a trick to populate the campaign variable by using parameters in the URL query string. Often, when you create a marketing campaign, the publisher or website that you are working with to send traffic to your website allows you to choose the URL on your website that visitors will be directed to when they click the campaign element. For example, if you purchase a keyword from Google, you tell Google what URL to send people to on your site, and you can include a parameter in the URL that identifies the tracking code associated with that specific keyword. When a visitor accesses your website via a tracking code in the URL, you can then use JavaScript code to grab that tracking code and assign it to the campaign variable. In fact, this happens so often that SiteCatalyst has a standard code function (a JavaScript plug-in) that can do this for you so you don't need to manually populate the campaign variable; instead, you would set it using code like this:

```
s.campaign=s.getQueryParam('cid');
```

DigitalPulse Debugger

As you start passing data into SiteCatalyst variables, there will be times when you'll want to see the data being passed. This might be for quality assurance purposes or just to better understand how data flows into variables. To aid in this process, Adobe provides a free tool called the DigitalPulse Debugger that allows you to look behind the scenes and see what data is being passed into SiteCatalyst variables. This tool can be added as a bookmark to your Internet browser toolbar, and once you've loaded a page on your website, clicking the bookmark will bring up a window (**Figure 5.19**).

On the screen you can see all sorts of data being passed, such as the Report Suite ID, page name, success events, traffic variables, and conversion variables. Notice that traffic variables are labeled as "props" with the number that corresponds to the number found in the administration console, and the same holds true for conversion variables, which are labeled as eVars. The campaign variable is labeled as "campaign," and other predefined variables use their special names as well.

I recommend that you learn about this handy tool by reading the Knowledge Base article about it or speaking to ClientCare.

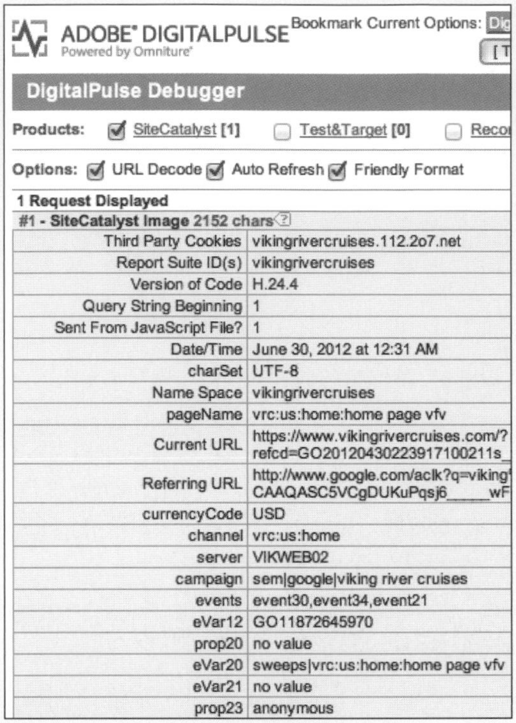

Figure 5.19 Sample DigitalPulse Debugger screen.

You'll learn more about JavaScript plug-ins in a future chapter, but the getQueryParam plug-in is frequently used for the campaign variable.

Regardless of how you collect data in the campaign variable, the end result is a report with a list of campaign tracking codes. Like any other conversion variable, these values are persistent, so if any success events take place on the website during that session, they will be attributed to the campaign tracking code that sourced the visit. This allows you to compare different tracking codes and see which ones are performing well and which are underperforming (**Figure 5.20**).

		Tracking Code	Click-throughs ▼ ⑦		Orders ⑦	
⊤	1.	sem_15252	34,875	4.7%	6,575	5.1%
⊤	2.	sem_15251	30,900	4.1%	5,324	4.1%
⊤	3.	email_114242	29,775	4.0%	5,131	4.0%
⊤	4.	sem_15222	28,800	3.8%	4,834	3.8%
⊤	5.	soc_66252	28,575	3.8%	4,705	3.7%
⊤	6.	email_114247	28,425	3.8%	5,054	3.9%

Figure 5.20 Sample Tracking Code (campaign) report.

Merchandising Conversion Variables

One of the most confusing aspects (in my opinion) of SiteCatalyst is Merchandising conversion variables. *Merchandising eVars* assign a different conversion variable value to each product at the time success events take place. This section explains why they were created and how they are commonly used.

Why Merchandising eVars?

So why did SiteCatalyst make a special type of Merchandising eVar and why are they so complicated? In early versions of SiteCatalyst (version 9.*x*) when Merchandising eVars were nonexistent, there were a few problems. To demonstrate, let's look at an example: You have a retail site that sells ceiling fans, and people can find those fans through the Lighting or Bedroom product categories on your website. However, you want to know how many purchases take place when visitors find ceiling fans through each of these different product categories. It sounds simple enough, right? But it wasn't in the past. If you used the Products string to assign a specific ceiling fan to the Lighting category, it would always be bound to that product category. You'd need a way to dynamically assign the specific product category for each product *in each specific instance* to get the data you were looking for. By doing so, you could see how often the ceiling fan was purchased via the Lighting category and how often it was purchased via the Bedroom category.

Since their introduction, Merchandising eVars have had many different uses, but it's important to understand the underlying problem that they were created to solve so you can comprehend how they work and why they are different from traditional conversion variables.

Using Merchandising eVars

Now that you know a bit about how Merchandising eVars originated, you can learn about how they are used. As you can imagine, connecting a different eVar value to each product is not a simple task. That is a lot of information for SiteCatalyst to keep straight. So how do you implement Merchandising eVars so SiteCatalyst knows when you want each product to be tied to each Merchandising eVar value? Fortunately (or unfortunately), SiteCatalyst has not one but two methods of binding eVar values to products: Product Syntax and Conversion Variable Syntax.

Product Syntax method

The Product Syntax method is the most straightforward and is the method I recommend most often. With this method, you use a special parameter slot within the Products string to declare which Merchandising value you want to assign to each product. To do this, let's revisit the syntax for the Products string:

```
s.products=[Category];[Product];[Quantity];[TotalPrice];
[Incrementor1]|[Incrementor2];[Merchandising1]|[Merchandising2],
[Category2];[Product2]...
```

Toward the end of the Products string a slot is reserved for setting Merchandising eVars. In fact, you can set more than one by using a "|" separator. Using this syntax, if a Cart Addition occurs, you can set your Cart Addition success event and Merchandising eVars as shown in this example:

```
s.events="scAdd";

s.products=";Fan-11980;;;;evar1=Lighting";
```

This code manually assigns the value of Lighting to the product category conversion variable (eVar #1 in this case) for the product Fan-11980 at the time of Cart Addition. However, some back-end settings also need to be made to allow for this to function properly. You first need to work with your Adobe account manager or ClientCare and ask that Merchandising be enabled for the appropriate conversion variable (eVar #1 in this case). Once Merchandising has been enabled, you need to access the administration console and select the Product Syntax option under the new Merchandising setting, which will now be visible. When you're using Product Syntax, the second Merchandising setting (Merchandising Binding Event) is disabled (but for some reason looks like you can use it), so just ignore that setting altogether. **Figure 5.21** shows what the settings should look like when you're done.

As with other conversion variables, you have to choose which Allocation setting you want (First or Last) and how long the variable should persist its value before it expires. Beyond that, the hardest part is making sure your developers are keeping track of which

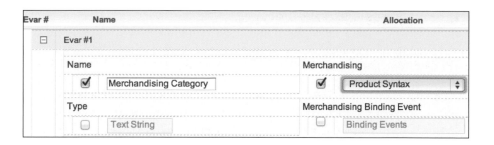

Figure 5.21 Product Syntax Merchandising setting in the administration console.

product categories should be associated with each product. If you know the value that you want to pass to the conversion variable for each product on the page (the product category in the preceding example), I recommend you use the Product Syntax approach.

Conversion Variable Syntax method

The second approach to setting Merchandising eVars is the Conversion Variable Syntax method. This approach is a bit more confusing and is normally used when you want to associate a different conversion variable value to each product, *but the value you want to set in that conversion variable is only known prior to the success event taking place instead of on the same page.* Let's look at an example. Imagine that your boss wants to know which onsite search phrases were used prior to each product being purchased. Now let's pretend that a visitor comes to the website and searches on "ceiling fans," finds Product 123 in the list, and adds it to the cart. Next, the visitor searches for "bathroom vanities," again scans the list, finds Product 789, and adds it to the cart. Then the visitor purchases both items a few pages later. In this example, if you used a traditional conversion variable (with Most Recent allocation), the Cart Addition for both Product 123 and Product 789 would be correctly associated with the correct search phrases, "ceiling fans" for Product 123 and "bathroom vanities" for Product 789—so far so good. But when the visitor purchases both products, guess which onsite search phrase would get credit for both purchases? If you guessed "bathroom vanities" you'd be correct! Because that was the *last* search phrase SiteCatalyst was passed, it would get credit for both products upon purchase. Unfortunately, this result isn't quite accurate and misrepresents the data because it omits the search on the phrase "ceiling fans." This is because a traditional eVar cannot associate a different value for each product.

However, by using the Conversion Variable Syntax and Merchandising in this scenario, each product can be associated with the specific search phrase that was used to find it for both the Cart Addition and Purchase success events. So how do you configure this? First, you would work with ClientCare to declare eVar #2 to be a Merchandising conversion variable. Second, you would decide when you want to have SiteCatalyst bind the onsite search phrase to the eVar value. For most clients, the default is to bind at the Product View (**prodView**) event and the Cart Addition (**scAdd**) event (although you can choose from any success events you'd like). By binding to the Product View and Cart

Addition events, you tell SiteCatalyst that if one of those two events happens, you want SiteCatalyst to bind the last value passed to the Merchandising eVar (the onsite search phrase in this example) with the product being viewed or added to the cart. **Figure 5.22** shows how these settings would look in the administration console.

Figure 5.22 Conversion Variable Syntax Merchandising setting in the administration console.

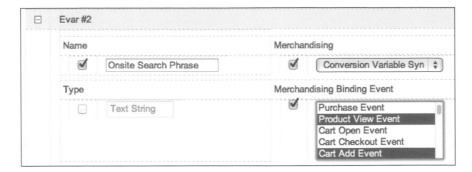

When the Purchase event occurs, each product will have the correct onsite search phrase value associated with it, and you can answer your initial business question of which phrases lead to purchases without incorrectly tying all purchases to the last onsite search phrase.

Instances Metrics in Conversion Reports

In Chapter 3, I touched on the concept of *Instances*, which indicate how often a particular variable received each value in the specified reporting period. As mentioned in Chapter 3, I tend not to use the Instances metric except in rare cases. For better or worse, the Instances metric rears its head again in conversion variable reports but in more significant ways. Therefore, it's best to take the time to see how Instances is used in conversion reports.

Using Instances for Quality Assurance in Conversion Variable Reports

You'll see Instances as a viable metric in every *custom* conversion variable report. In custom conversion reports, the main way I use the Instances metric is to perform variable quality assurance. Because a conversion variable doesn't have to have a value when a success event takes place, it is entirely possible that you'll have conversion variables that show no data for one or more success event metrics that you add to the report. For example, in the report in **Figure 5.23**, you see a conversion variable that concatenates form field errors visitors experience when submitting a form. However, notice that when the Form Views success event is added to the report, no values are shown for this conversion variable.

Form Field Errors (v23)	Form Views (e21)	
None ⍰	744,160	100.0%
TOTAL	**744,160**	

Figure 5.23 Form Field Errors conversion variable shown with Form Views.

Seeing this report you could falsely assume that the conversion variable had no data. However, in this case, the conversion variable doesn't receive its values until *after* the Form View success event takes place, so this report is accurate but the wrong metric was added to see its values. If you added the Instances metric to the same report, you would suddenly see the conversion variable data (**Figure 5.24**). Now you can see that there are, in fact, many values in this conversion variable and that you need to rethink which success event should be added to see those values (in this case, Form Completions).

Form Field Errors (v23)	Instances ▾ ⍰		Form Views (e21)	
txtemailaddress	1,441	37.8%	0	0.0%
ddlcountry	293	7.7%	0	0.0%
txtfirstnametxtlastnametxtemailaddress	280	7.3%	0	0.0%
radreason	247	6.5%	0	0.0%
txtfirstnametxtlastnametxtemailddlcountry	184	4.8%	0	0.0%

Figure 5.24 Form Field Errors conversion variable shown with Form Views and Instances.

Quality assurance of conversion variables is one handy way to use the Instances metric to your advantage. I now make it a practice when I'm learning about a new SiteCatalyst variable or performing quality assurance to always add the Instances metric to conversion variable reports. Because it is impossible to have a None row for the Instances metric, if there is any data in a conversion variable, adding the Instances metric will display it.

Using Instances in the Products Report

As mentioned previously, the Instances metric does not appear in predefined conversion variable reports. One of these reports is the Products report. In this report, Site-Catalyst magically renames the Instances metric to Product Views, which represents how often product names were passed to the products variable. Unfortunately, this can be problematic at times because the passing of a value to the products variable is not always representative of a true product view as defined as a visitor looking at a specific product detail page on the website. In addition, the Instances version of the Product Views metric can only be used in the Products report. This prevents you from adding Product Views to other conversion variable reports or using them on calculated metrics. For these reasons, it is a common best practice to ignore the Instances version of the Product View metric and set your own custom Product Views success event when visitors land on product detail pages. Unfortunately, you cannot remove the Instances version of the Product Views metric, so most SiteCatalyst customers who set a custom Product Views metric name it something like "Product Views (Custom)" or "PDP" (for product detail page). All this can seem extremely confusing, but that's just the way it is.

In addition, you need to be on the lookout for another issue. When it comes to capturing product views on your website, you must set the out-of-the-box Product View success event (**prodView**) *and* your new custom Product View success event. If you fail to set the predefined **prodView** success event, you will not be able to see Conversion Funnel reports filtered by products because that report relies on the predefined product view taking place. Even if you set a custom Product View success event in that report, it won't allow you to filter by product. Therefore, it is a best practice to always set the **prodView** success event and a custom Product View success event on product detail pages like this:

```
s.events="prodView,event30";
s.products=";55525";
```

Using Instances in the Campaign Report

Similar to the Products report, when you're using the Campaign report, Instances are renamed to "Click-throughs" in the metric list. These click-throughs represent instances where the campaign conversion variable was set. To be safe, use the best practice of setting an additional custom success event for campaign click-throughs instead of relying entirely on the Instances metric.

Using Instances in Search Engine Reports

When you're using the out-of-the-box Search Engine reports (Search Engines, Search Keywords), the Instances metric morphs once again and is called Searches. In all Search Engine related reports you'll see the Searches metric, which represents click-throughs from search engines.

Instances Metrics and Calculated Metrics

One major flaw of Instances metrics is that they can wreak havoc on calculated metrics. This is due to the fact that Instances are tied to the specific report you are looking at. At some point, you may have created a calculated metric, seen a metric in the list that appears as Visits (Report-Specific) or Click-throughs (Report-Specific), and wondered what it meant. Let's say, for example, that you are in the Products report and want to create a calculated metric that divides a custom success event, like Registrations by Product Views. In this example, you choose to use the Instances version of the Product Views metric as the denominator and call the metric Registrations per Product View. In the Products report this will be fine and work as designed. However, if you switch over to a Search Engine report, this same calculated metric will now divide Registrations by Searches (the Instances metric of that report). Even though your calculated metric is named Registrations per Product View, you are now looking at Registrations per Search. The denominator in this calculated metric will change based on the report in which you are viewing the calculated metric. If you added the same calculated metric to a custom conversion variable report (e.g., City), your calculated metric would show Registrations divided by the Instances of each conversion variable value (e.g., Chicago, New York, etc.) in that particular conversion variable report.

As you can see, this can get very confusing, so my advice is to avoid using the Instances metric whenever possible (especially in calculated metrics) and always set custom success events for Product Views, Search Engine Clicks, and so on to avoid this mess.

Conclusion

In this chapter, you explored traditional conversion variables, list variables, the products variable, the campaign variable, and Merchandising conversion variables, and learned to watch out for the Instances metric. In all cases, conversion variables are used to break down success events into buckets, so you can conduct deeper web analysis. At different times in your SiteCatalyst implementation, there will be situations in which one of these conversion variables is better to use than the other to answer specific business questions. The more you understand these various types of conversion variables and how they differ from each other, the more likely you'll be able to choose the right variable type to use. Be sure to try using each type in your implementation so you can see how each works.

## CHAPTER 6

Variable Classifications

The previous few chapters discussed how you can use SiteCatalyst variables to store the web analytics data that is important to your business. In this regard, traffic metrics and success events are used to track the metrics or numbers that drive your business, whereas traffic variables and conversion variables are used to break down these metrics into buckets. Once you've mastered traffic variables and conversion variables, the next step is to learn about variable classifications. Classifications provide a way to augment the data that you've collected in your traffic and conversion variables, and can save you time and money if used properly. In this chapter, you'll learn about classifications and how you can use them to enhance your SiteCatalyst implementation.

Understanding Classifications

A *classification* is the addition of attributes (metadata) to an existing traffic or conversion variable to augment the amount of web analyses that can be performed on the variable. Classifications are sometimes referred to as SAINT (SiteCatalyst Attribute Importing and Naming Tool). Technically speaking, when you "classify" a SiteCatalyst variable, you establish a relationship between the variable and the metadata related to that variable.

The best way to explain classifications is to consider a situation in which you would use them and why not having them would make data collection more difficult. Imagine that you are a web analyst and are working with your campaign manager to do some reporting on how online campaigns are performing. Having read about the campaign variable, you instruct your campaign manager to make sure all inbound campaign traffic arrives to the website with a tracking code and that this code is populated into the campaign variable. This allows you to see visits and website success events by campaign tracking code so your campaign manager can judge the success of each campaign.

However, the following week the campaign manager tells you he is using over 1000 unique tracking codes and is getting a bit overwhelmed while doing his analysis. He tells you that what he really needs is a way to see all of these tracking codes rolled up by campaign channel and campaign name, and asks you to provide that somehow. Your first thought is to create two new custom conversion variables—one to capture the campaign channel and another to capture the campaign name. However, you realize that it is almost impossible for you to know the campaign channel and campaign name at the time you collect the tracking code, which is often the first page of the visit. To do this, you would need your campaign manager to change all of his campaign destination URLs so there are more query string parameters present from which you could grab the marketing channel and campaign name. But that would be very time-consuming because there are thousands of tracking codes on multiple websites.

You also realize that the following week the campaign manager might ask you for even more related data points, like the month the campaign ran, the campaign owner, the text used in the campaign, the platform of the creative (e.g., GIF or Flash), and so on. The campaign manager could need as many as 20 different ways to slice and dice information related to these tracking codes. How would all of that data be assigned to the query string of the URL? And imagine if you had to create a different custom conversion variable for each of these. That could result in over 20 conversion variables (out of 75 total) devoted to one item—marketing campaigns.

In this example, you can begin to see the motivation for SiteCatalyst to find a better way to address this situation, which is what led to the creation of classifications. The principle behind classifications was to establish a way to collect one piece of data in a SiteCatalyst variable and then allow additional related data (often referred to as metadata) to be uploaded at a later time. This would allow SiteCatalyst customers to slice and dice metrics by any of the data points (metadata) contained in the upload file instead of having to create additional SiteCatalyst variables. For those of you who use Microsoft Excel, it is similar to the use of a pivot table in which you can group numbers based on metadata added to the root element. In the next section you'll work through this campaign tracking dilemma by learning how to create and use classifications.

Creating SAINT Classifications

In the preceding campaign example, tracking codes are already being collected in the campaign conversion variable, so the next step is to classify this variable in a way that allows you to upload the additional data you're missing. In this case, the data you're missing is campaign channel and campaign name, so you need to let SiteCatalyst know about these additional attributes (metadata) and specify to which variable they are related. Using the administration console, you can select the desired report suite, and then choose the menu option to see conversion classifications (because the campaign variable is a conversion variable) (**Figure 6.1**).

In the administration console, select the conversion variable to which you want to add attributes. In this case, you would select the campaign variable (**Figure 6.2**).

Next, hover your cursor over the icon with the green triangle and click the Add Classification text that appears (**Figure 6.3**).

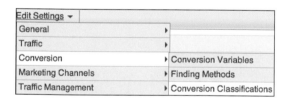

Figure 6.1 Use the Administration Console menu to access the Classification Manager screen.

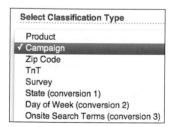

Figure 6.2 Select the variable to be classified.

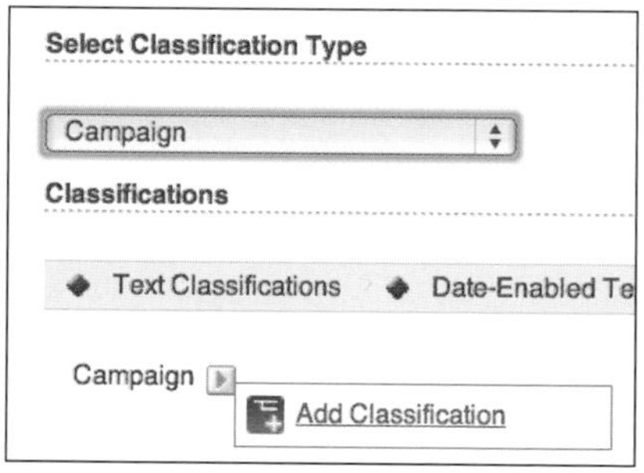

Figure 6.3 Adding a new classification.

Enter a name for the classification (**Figure 6.4**). Because you'll be passing text values into the classification, use the default type of Text (the option to make your classification a Numeric 2 classification is discussed later in the chapter). You'll also notice options to make classifications Date Enabled and to create a Dropdown List, but these features are no longer used and can be ignored. After saving this information and repeating this process for the second classification, you should see a screen like the one in **Figure 6.5**. When this process is complete, SiteCatalyst will display two new reports in the menus—one for Campaign Channel and another for Campaign Name (**Figure 6.6**).

Figure 6.4 Name the classification.

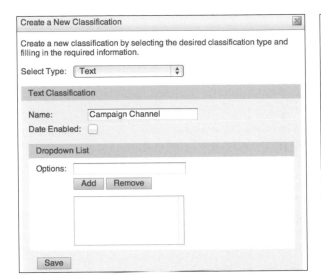

Figure 6.5 Completed classifications.

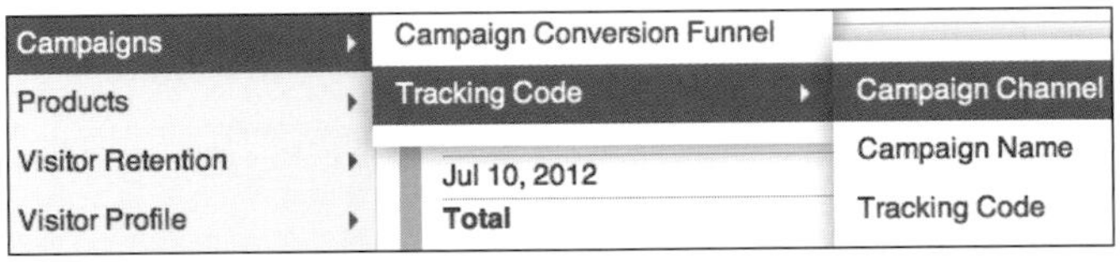

Figure 6.6 New classification reports in the SiteCatalyst menus.

These new reports will always appear directly above the report to which they are related, which in this case is the campaign variable (shown as Tracking Code in the menu). It's as if you added two new conversion variable reports but didn't have to use any of the conversion variables in the administration console. However, at this point, these two classification reports have no data, so when you open them, all data would revert to the None row. The reason is that you haven't yet told SiteCatalyst how to map the values in the tracking code variable to the classification variables (campaign channel and campaign name).

Thus, you need to create this mapping next. When you have created the classifications in the previous steps, SiteCatalyst provides a template you can use to upload the attributes into SiteCatalyst. Anyone with administration rights can access this template from the top menu under the Admin tab by clicking the SAINT Classifications link (**Figure 6.7**).

Figure 6.7 Accessing classification templates.

In the screen that appears, you can download the classification template, open it, and begin entering data. But instead of downloading the template, it's best to use the Browser Export tab to export your current "key" values. These "key" values represent the data that has already been collected for the variable upon which classifications have been enabled. In this case, the "key" values would be tracking codes because this is a tracking code classification. Exporting this file downloads the same template but includes the values that have been captured in the "key" variable (Tracking Code in this case) so you can see which values already have been classified and which have not. Export settings can be configured to allow you to customize how many rows are downloaded or download only those rows missing classification data. Regardless of which method you choose, the result will be a spreadsheet with a Key column and a column for each classification you created using the previous steps (**Figure 6.8**). Therefore, all you need to do is fill in any blank cells and use the SAINT screens to upload your data to SiteCatalyst.

After the classification data is successfully uploaded, SiteCatalyst servers will process it. Depending on how much data you have uploaded, processing can take a few minutes to a few hours.

	A	B	C
1	## SC	SiteCatalyst SAINT Import v:2.0	
2	## SC	'## SC' indicates a SiteCatalyst pre-process header. Please	
3	## SC	D:2012-07-01 13:05:49	A:2828839:53
4	Key	Campaign Channel	Campaign Name
5	tc_1112	Paid Search	Spring Launch Campaign
6	tc_1151	Social Media	Spring Launch Campaign
7	tc_6625	Paid Search	Branded Keyword Campaign
8	tc_5522	E-mail	Product Re-targeting Campaign
9	tc_5413	Display Advertising	Spring Launch Campaign

Figure 6.8 Sample classification upload file.

Using SAINT Classifications

After you have uploaded classification data, it is time to see how it is reflected in Site-Catalyst reports. First, let's look at the Tracking Code report, which served as your "key" for this classification. **Figure 6.9** shows an example of the root Tracking Code report. Directly above this report in the menu, you can click to open the Campaign Channel classification report and see a report like the one shown in **Figure 6.10**.

If you look closely, you'll see that all of the values for tracking codes "tc_1112" and "tc_6625" have been grouped together into a Paid Search row in the Campaign Channel classification report (Figure 6.8). Because you told SiteCatalyst that those two tracking codes are both associated with the Campaign Channel Paid Search, when this classification report opens, it dynamically groups any metrics it sees for those two tracking codes

Figure 6.9 Sample Tracking Code report showing classification "key" values.

		Tracking Code	Orders ▼	
	1.	tc_1112	27,427	28.6%
	2.	tc_1151	24,107	25.2%
	3.	tc_6625	20,240	21.1%
	4.	tc_5522	13,407	14.0%
	5.	tc_5413	10,668	11.1%

		Campaign Channel	Orders ▼	
	1.	Paid Search	47,667	49.7%
	2.	Social Media	24,107	25.2%
	3.	E-mail	13,407	14.0%
	4.	Display Advertising	10,668	11.1%

Figure 6.10 Sample classification report after processing.

Alternatives for Uploading Classifications

There are several ways to upload classification attributes to SiteCatalyst. The easiest way is to use the Browser import, which uses a spreadsheet or text file, and if it is properly formatted, can upload data quickly and easily. Unfortunately, if the file size is greater than one megabyte, you cannot use the Browser import method (or you have to break your file into several files, each less than one megabyte).

The next most common method for uploading classifications is via FTP. SiteCatalyst creates a secure FTP site for any variable you want to classify. Using FTP, you can upload much larger files, and as a bonus, you can upload classification data to multiple report suites concurrently. This can be a real time-saver when you have the same classifications on multiple report suites.

Another mechanism to upload classification data is via the SAINT API. This method is a bit more complex because it requires a developer, but you and your development team should discuss it. Adobe has also created a tool (called SAINT Bernard) that uses the SAINT API to classify data on your behalf but provides a friendly front-end interface. You can learn more about this tool through your Adobe account manager or on the SiteCatalyst developer website (https://developer.omniture.com).

and displays them accordingly. The same takes place for all other tracking codes that have a classification attribute associated with them.

Now that you are more familiar with what classifications are and how they work, let's review why they are so useful:

▶ **No tagging.** As shown in the preceding campaign tracking code example, you were able to create two new conversion variable reports without using any JavaScript tagging. One of the most important benefits of classifications is that as long as you have a "key" that can have attributes (metadata) attached to it, you don't have to spend time tagging additional variables.

▶ **Save variables.** If your organization has a lot of information it wants to track related to the website, you could run low on traffic and conversion variables over time. The use of classifications is a great way to conserve variables because classifications don't utilize precious standard variables.

▶ **Retroactive.** One of the cool aspects of classifications is that they are retroactive. This means that when you upload attributes to SiteCatalyst, they are available to all "key" values, even if those values were collected prior to the classification attributes being uploaded. For example, in the preceding campaign tracking code example, you might have been collecting tracking code values in the campaign variable for months. Therefore, as soon as you upload the classification attribute data, you'll be able to immediately see data for these preceding months grouped by the attributes uploaded. This feature is beneficial because you don't have to wait until you've mapped your attribute data to begin collecting tracking code data. You can start collecting tracking codes anytime and simply upload the attributes when you have them.

▶ **Upload only new/change data.** When you upload classification metadata, there is no need to upload data for "key" values that already have classifications if classification data has not changed. Some clients think they must upload the entire classification attribute file every time they add rows or make a change, but that is not the case and will delay your processing. As a best practice, upload only the rows that have new metadata.

▶ **No success events.** For reasons that should be apparent, you can classify any traffic or conversion variable but cannot classify success events because they are raw numbers.

▶ **No charge.** There is no additional contract cost for applying classifications to variables.

▶ **Breakdowns.** If a breakdown report (covered in a later chapter) is available to the variable that is classified, the same breakdowns are available for any classifications of that variable.

▶ **Column limits.** Although it is technically possible to add as many classification attributes to a variable as you'd like, Adobe only supports the use of 30 attributes per variable. If you need more than this, contact your Adobe account manager or ClientCare.

▶ **No pathing.** If you apply a classification to a traffic variable, you cannot view Pathing reports on the classification values, even if the variable you have classified has pathing enabled. I cannot stress how important this is to remember. Many clients pass in "ugly" values to a traffic variable with the intention of later uploading "friendly" values as a classification, only to then find out that they can view Pathing reports only on the "ugly" values. If you need to see Pathing reports for a traffic variable, you may want to consider taking a bit more time up front to pass in the exact values you want to see in Pathing reports. Note that the ability to see pathing on classifications is a feature available in the more advanced Adobe Discover product.

▶ **No out-of-the-box reports.** It is not possible to create classifications for out-of-the-box traffic and conversion reports in SiteCatalyst. This includes Technology reports, GeoSegmentation, Search Engine reports, and so on. However, you can classify pre-defined variable reports like Products, Campaign, and Page Name. It's also not possible to classify List Variables, although I expect that shortcoming will be addressed in a future release.

Don't Waste Variables

One of the benefits of using classifications is that you can conserve SiteCatalyst variables. Although most SiteCatalyst implementations don't run out of variables, if you are doing some advanced tracking, it is a possibility. Normally, the first variables clients run out of are conversion variables. Therefore, just to be safe, you should make it a practice to conserve as many variables as possible. This means not wasting variables on data elements that could be easily captured using classifications.

Here is a classic example: Later in the book I will discuss a JavaScript plug-in that allows you to store the day of the week in a conversion variable. This is useful if you want to see how different days impact success events or for segmentation purposes. In addition to the day of the week, some clients like to capture whether it is a weekday or the weekend when success events take place. Although this is a reasonable request, it is foolish to dedicate a traffic or conversion variable to this type of data element. The reason this is foolish is that you could easily add a classification to the Day of Week variable in which you classify Monday through Friday as "Weekday" and Saturday and Sunday as "Weekend." This classification takes about five minutes to set up, and unless a new day of the week is invented in the future, you will never have to re-upload data to this classification. Whenever I see clients using a separate variable for weekday/weekend, I know they have not done their homework and don't fully understand the power of classifications.

Keep in mind that this is just one example. Be on the lookout for data elements that you want to capture that are similar or related to a variable that you already capture. Always try to determine if there is way to conserve a variable and avoid more JavaScript tagging, especially cases where you can upload the attribute data once and never have to do it again or only have to do it infrequently.

Beware: The Downside of Retroactive

Although the retroactive nature of classifications is most often a benefit, there is one potential downside to the retroactive nature of classifications: You need to keep in mind that a change made today will impact data in the past.

Let's look at a quick example: Imagine that you have a customer ID and a classification for the city the customer lives in with a row for Joe Smith classified as living in New York City. But then a few weeks later

Joe moves to Chicago. If you reclassify Joe as living in Chicago, any success events (e.g., Orders) tied to Joe over the last few years will suddenly look like they took place in Chicago, whereas the previous month's reports would have shown them having taken place in New York City. Therefore, if you have a data element that you want to ensure is always tied to a value when it happened, consider using a traditional traffic or conversion variable.

Classifying the None Row

There may come a time when you want to classify the None row in conversion variable reports. One common example is when it comes to classifying campaigns or traffic sources. Imagine that you are capturing thousands of unique campaign tracking codes that tell you how visitors are accessing your website and have most of them classified into a campaign channel, such as SEM, SEO, social media, and so on. However, it is inevitable that you will have a None row in your Tracking Code report that represents those who manually entered your URL or came from bookmarks. Because a None row is in your Tracking Code report, you'll have the same (or larger if not all values are classified) None row in the Campaign Channel report. Now let's say that you show this Campaign Channel report to your boss and she gets hung up on the None row in the report. She's afraid that if executives see this report each week, they'll have questions or even think that the data is inaccurate. Although this may sound trivial, executive confidence in web analytics data is always a top concern.

Don't Be a Zero or a #!?*$"

One detail that you have to commit to memory when it comes to classifications is that you cannot classify the number zero. In fact, it's best to avoid passing a "0" or numbers with leading zeros into traffic and conversion variables at all, just in case you decide one day you want to apply classifications.

It's also best to avoid any type of punctuation in values that you want to classify. Punctuation can cause major headaches when it comes to classifying data.

The good news is that the None row of any conversion variable report can be classified. It is not the most intuitive thing to figure out, but once you learn the trick, it's pretty easy. To classify the None row, you download the regular classification template for the variable in question (tracking code in this case), add a "~none~" entry in the Key column, and then add the classification value in the appropriate column (**Figure 6.11**). Once processed, when you open the Campaign Channel report, you should no longer see a None row.

	A	B	
1	## SC	SiteCatalyst SAINT Import	v:2.0
2	## SC	'## SC' indicates a SiteCatalyst pre-proce	
3	## SC	D:2012-07-01 13:05:49	A:2828839:53
4	Key	Campaign Channel	
5	~none~	Typed-Bookmarked	

Figure 6.11 Classifying the None row.

Removing Classification Data

If you ever need to delete classification data, you can use a process similar to what you just learned about classifying the None row. You may want to delete classification data because it is out of date or was uploaded incorrectly. To do this, simply export a version of the classification file that has values you want to delete. Make sure you don't just download the template but rather export a version that has the actual "key" data contained within it. Next, find the classification values you want to delete (you cannot delete "key" values) and change their values to "~empty~" (all lowercase). Then upload the classification file as you normally would.

Numeric Classifications

In addition to text-based classifications, SiteCatalyst offers a set of numeric classifications. Numeric classifications come in two styles: traditional numeric classifications (sometimes referred to as Numeric 1.0) and Numeric 2 classifications (sometimes referred to as Numeric 2.0). Both types of classifications are unique in that they allow you to classify "key" values with numbers. Although numeric classifications aren't used very often, there are some unique situations in which they can be useful.

The most popular use of numeric classifications is to associate a cost value with products so you can calculate a net profit in reports. For example, let's say you are already storing product IDs in the products variable and each product ID has a cost associated with it. Using numeric classifications, you can upload the cost of each product ID so that when the Products report opens, you can see orders, and for each order you can see the cost (either fixed or as a percentage) for each product. The concept is very similar to regular classifications, but instead of uploading text values, you are uploading number values, and SiteCatalyst uses these number values to dynamically calculate the cost as the report renders. These calculations take the form of new metrics in the Products report in **Figure 6.12**.

	Products	Revenue ▾ ⑦	Product Cost	Net Profit
1.	isc.1.0.0.24m	$1,639,768 21.3%	$663,872 22.7%	$975,897
2.	isc.1.0.0.12m	$1,441,300 18.7%	$600,413 20.5%	$840,887
3.	isc.1.1.0.24m	$1,210,076 15.7%	$473,497 16.2%	$736,579
4.	avc.1.0.0.12m	$801,579 10.4%	$307,529 10.5%	$494,050
5.	pct.1.0.0.12m	$637,795 8.3%	$214,782 7.3%	$423,013
6.	isc.1.1.0.12m	$485,572 6.3%	$224,545 7.7%	$261,027

Figure 6.12 Products report using numeric classification.

Other examples of cases in which numeric classifications can be useful include:

▸ Associating costs with tracking codes to calculate ROI on marketing campaigns

▸ Assigning a value to customers based on a customer ID

▸ Assigning "engagement" values to pages on your website

However, over the years, as SiteCatalyst clients implemented numeric classifications as in the preceding example, a tricky problem surfaced. In the example, you were able to associate a product cost with each products variable value, but what happens if product costs change? If you recall from an earlier discussion about classifications, they are retroactive, so if you change the cost of a product today from $25 to $20, it would look as though the product had always cost $20, even though for months or years the cost was $25. As you can see, this can be a major problem because product costs can change frequently.

To address this issue, SiteCatalyst added a new type of numeric classification called *Numeric 2 classifications*. Numeric 2 classifications allow you to associate a date range with numeric classifications. This means you can specify that the product cost was $25 from 1/1/2012 until 5/31/2012 and then the product cost changed to $20 on 6/1/2012. By doing so, SiteCatalyst will calculate the numeric classification metric accordingly, and your reports will be more accurate. Obviously, there is work involved in keeping these Numeric 2 classification files updated, but the functionality is there for you to take advantage of when needed. There are too many detailed aspects of creating Numeric 2 classification files to cover here, so I suggest you read the SiteCatalyst Classification manual found in the SiteCatalyst Knowledge Base before getting started.

One important detail to understand about numeric classifications (Numeric 1.0 and Numeric 2.0) is that they look like any other metric in the Products report, but they are not true metrics like other traffic and success event metrics. The reason they are not "true" metrics is that these metrics are only viewable in the report to which the classification pertains. For example, you cannot see the preceding "Product Cost" metrics in any other report except the Products report, because the metric is really just an attribute of the products variable. As you'll learn in later chapters, there are other methods to import metrics like product cost into SiteCatalyst, which is why numeric classifications aren't used as much as you'd think. However, if your main goal is to use metrics like this in the Products report only, numeric classifications can be useful.

Classification Hierarchies

There are often relationships between the various attributes that you set up as classifications. Classification hierarchies allow you to "nest" classifications so you can take advantage of those relationships. For example, let's say that you sell electronics, have many different types of products, and have already classified products into Product Group, Product SubGroup, and Manufacturer. These classifications allow you to slice and dice all of your product data by any of these elements separately. But what if you wanted to see metrics by Product Group and then a breakdown for each Product Group by SubGroup, and so on? To do this, you would use the classification hierarchies area in the administration console and drag over all of the classifications you want nested, as shown in **Figure 6.13**.

You can choose from any classifications that have been set up for the products variable. In this case, two classification hierarchies were created—one based on Product Group and another based on Manufacturer. These will just provide different breakdowns of

Figure 6.13 Classification hierarchy setup in the administration console.

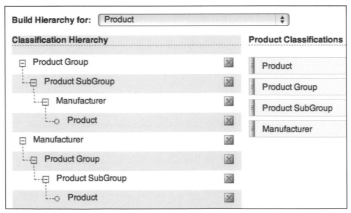

data when viewed in SiteCatalyst. You can then save this hierarchy, and when you look at the Products report area in the menu, you'll see a special icon indicating that a classification hierarchy exists and will have the ability to drill down by all of the items you added to the hierarchy (**Figure 6.14**).

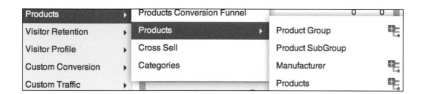

Figure 6.14 Classification hierarchy shown in the SiteCatalyst menu.

If you look at the classification hierarchy by Product Group, you can see a plus (+) sign that allows you to drill down by the other attributes in the classification file (**Figure 6.15**). The figure shows a report in which the plus (+) sign was clicked for Product Group, then Product SubGroup, and then Manufacturer. Success event metrics are available to you for each level of the classification hierarchy. Keep in mind, this is an example using the products variable, but classification hierarchies can be applied to any variable that has classifications.

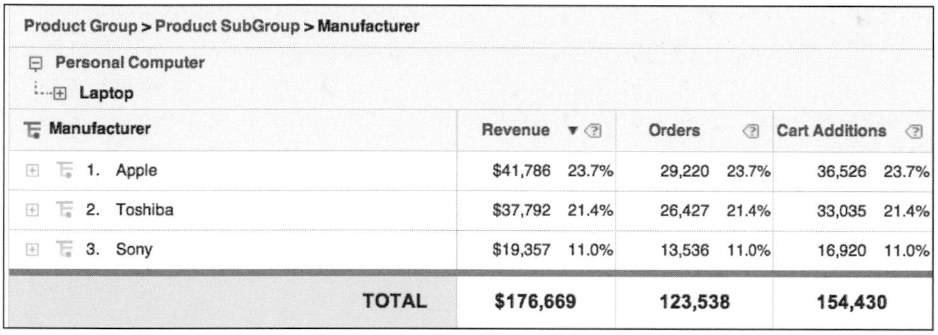

Product Group > Product SubGroup > Manufacturer						
⊟ **Personal Computer**						
⊞ **Laptop**						
Manufacturer	Revenue	▾	Orders		Cart Additions	
⊞ 1. Apple	$41,786	23.7%	29,220	23.7%	36,526	23.7%
⊞ 2. Toshiba	$37,792	21.4%	26,427	21.4%	33,035	21.4%
⊞ 3. Sony	$19,357	11.0%	13,536	11.0%	16,920	11.0%
TOTAL	**$176,669**		**123,538**		**154,430**	

Figure 6.15 Sample classification hierarchy report.

Conclusion

Classifications can be a real boost to a SiteCatalyst implementation if they are used correctly. They can save you time and money, and conserve variables when you understand them and know how to apply them. Be sure to take the time to experiment with classifications in your environment, and remember that unlike normally collected data, you can delete classifications at any time and start over.

## CHAPTER 7

Advanced SiteCatalyst Features

In this first section of the book, I covered the fundamentals that you should know about how SiteCatalyst works behind the scenes. However, there are some aspects of SiteCatalyst that are a bit more complex. These are topics that many SiteCatalyst clients don't even know about. If you want to dig a bit deeper and understand all that SiteCatalyst has to offer, this chapter is for you. You'll learn some advanced ways to collect data, merge online data with offline data, integrate SiteCatalyst with other software products, and more. At this point, if your brain is feeling a bit full and you want to learn how to log in and use SiteCatalyst, you can skip this chapter (for now) and move on to Section 2: "Using Adobe SiteCatalyst." Otherwise, join me for a deep dive into the depths of SiteCatalyst.

SiteCatalyst JavaScript Plug-ins

A *JavaScript plug-in* is a chunk of code that you can add to your SiteCatalyst JavaScript file to address a specific data collection need. As you can imagine, after several years and hundreds of implementations, there have been several common implementation strategies to which SiteCatalyst clients have migrated. As multiple clients ask for similar functionality, Adobe does its best to add it natively to the product. But there will always be features that either don't make sense to add to the product or don't apply to everyone. In these cases, JavaScript plug-ins are sometimes created to fill a gap. JavaScript plug-ins leverage existing code, which makes them easy to add to an implementation. Although not all of these JavaScript plug-ins are officially supported by Adobe, they are prevalent enough to be found in the Knowledge Base of the SiteCatalyst product (**Figure 7.1**).

Most of these JavaScript plug-ins add only a small piece of data or functionality to your implementation, so using them will not magically turn a bad implementation into a great one; rather, they are an easy way to include additional data that can be useful to your organization. You can also modify these plug-ins to suit your needs, which makes them even more useful for your specific business questions. In this section, I'll review some of the most popular JavaScript plug-ins so you can choose whether or not you want to add them to your implementation. For those contained in the SiteCatalyst Knowledge Base, you can even see the code and download documentation directly (**Figure 7.2**).

plug-in		
	Answer ID	**Summary**
1	10092	Why does the Netscape Plug-ins re
2	1422	**PLUG-IN:** getValOnce
3	1420	**PLUG-IN:** getQueryParam
4	10134	**PLUG-IN:** getPercentPageViewed
5	1417	**PLUG-IN:** daysSinceLastVisit
6	1419	**PLUG-IN:** getPreviousValue
7	10093	**PLUG-IN:** detectRIA
8	8424	**PLUG-IN:** APL (appendList)
9	1542	**PLUG-IN:** Time Parting
10	1945	**PLUG-IN:** getNewRepeat
11	1413	**PLUG-IN:** getAndPersistValue
12	10094	**PLUG-IN:** getVisitNum

Figure 7.1 SiteCatalyst plug-ins in the Knowledge Base.

Implementation

To successfully implement this plugin, place the following code within your s_code.js file

```
/*
 * Plugin: getValOnce_v1.1
 */
s.getValOnce=new Function("v","c","e","t",""
+"var s=this,a=new Date,v=v?v:'',c=c?c:'s_gvo',e=e?e:0,i=t=='m'?6000"
+"0:86400000;k=s.c_r(c);if(v){a.setTime(a.getTime()+e*i);s.c_w(c,v,e"
+"==0?0:a);}return v==k?'':v);
```

Once the above code is implemented, define the desired variable using the getValOnce function. The

Preventing the same campaign value from being defined if a duplicate value is detected wit
```
s.campaign=s.getValOnce(s.campaign,'s_cmp',30);
```

Prevents the same eVar1 value from being defined if a duplicate value is detected within 30
```
s.eVar1=s.getValOnce(s.eVar1,'s_ev1',30,'m');
```

Prevents the same eVar2 value from being defined multiple times in the same browser sess
```
s.eVar2=s.getValOnce(s.eVar2,'s_ev2');
```

File Attachments   • getValOnce_v1.0.txt *(1.18 KB)*

Figure 7.2 Sample JavaScript plug-in Knowledge Base documentation.

Get Query Parameter Plug-in

The Get Query Parameter plug-in is by far the most popular plug-in. Most clients use this plug-in by default when it comes to tracking online campaigns. The plug-in looks for query string parameters in the URL and assigns them to the SiteCatalyst variable(s) that you designate. An example of how an organization might use this plug-in is shown in **Figure 7.3** (on the following page). In this case, Disney is tracking paid search keywords with a "CMP" query string, so anything contained after the equal sign will be placed into the **s.campaign** variable, as shown in the DigitalPulse Debugger.

Because it can extract any query string parameter, there are many other uses for this plug-in. Another common use of this plug-in is to move onsite search phrases to a Site-Catalyst variable. For example, on CNN's website, when users conduct an onsite search, the phrase they use is passed in the URL using the query string "query=" on the search results page. This allows the Get Query Parameter plug-in to programmatically assign this value to a traffic variable (**Figure 7.4**).

You can use this plug-in in several ways, including tracking navigation clicks, tracking values populated into a form, and so on. The key is to understand what the Get Query Parameter plug-in does and think about how you can use it to save time and populate more data in your SiteCatalyst implementation.

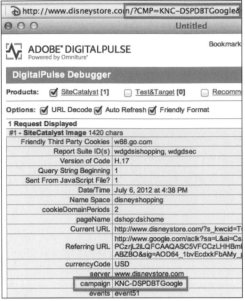

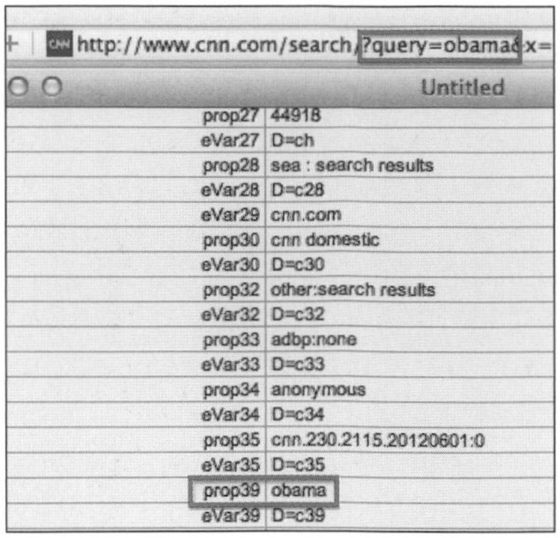

Figure 7.4 Onsite search phrases captured using the Get Query Parameter plug-in.

Figure 7.3 Sample use of the Get Query Parameter plug-in.

Previous Value Plug-in

The Previous Value plug-in allows you to pass a value that was stored on the previous page to a variable on the current page. This plug-in is extremely useful, especially when you use traffic variables, which do not have persistence. A common use of this feature is to pass the page name value of the previous page to a custom traffic variable (sProp) on the current page. Why is this useful? Let's say that you want to see what page users were on when they searched on the term "Obama," as shown in Figure 7.4. Unfortunately, there is not a straightforward way to do this natively in SiteCatalyst. But if the search term is in a traffic variable and the previous page name is in another traffic variable (through this plug-in), and both are in the same image request, you can create a breakdown report between the two. Through this breakdown report, you can see all of the pages that users were on when they searched for "Obama," and you can see the converse, which is the ability to see all of the terms that users searched for while they were on a particular page (e.g., the home page). By combining the Previous Value plug-in and a breakdown report, you can get some pretty valuable data for very little work.

Similarly, I usually recommend that organizations use the Previous Value plug-in to capture the previous page name in a conversion variable on each page. Doing so allows you to see what page visitors were on prior to completing a success event. For example, if one of your success events was the action of a visitor clicking the Add to Cart button, you could use a previous page conversion variable to see the most common pages visitors were on when adding items to the cart.

Cross-Visit Participation Plug-in

Another popular JavaScript plug-in is the Cross-Visit Participation plug-in. This plug-in is a bit more complex and acts as a workaround for some attribution shortcomings in the SiteCatalyst product. To understand this plug-in, recall that SiteCatalyst does not currently have a mechanism for attributing success to conversion variable values across multiple visits. Earlier, you saw that conversion variables are persistent and can retain values for multiple visits but only one value. If desired, you can use two conversion variables—one for First Touch and another for Last Touch. However, beyond these two variables, attribution becomes difficult in SiteCatalyst because the ideal option, Linear Allocation, does not work across multiple website visits. Therefore, if you want to see how more than two values for a conversion variable contributed to a website success event, your options are limited.

To address this problem, some clever folks at Adobe created the Cross-Visit Participation plug-in. This JavaScript plug-in stores a list of values in a cookie and remembers them across multiple visits. These values are concatenated together with a separator of your choosing, and you can configure the plug-in to hold as many values as you like. The most recent list of concatenated values is then passed to a conversion variable, so when a success event takes place, the current value will get credit for success events. This means that if you have three different values from three different website visits concatenated at the time a success event takes place, that three-value string will get credit for the success event. This provides a way to see which multi-session values played a part (participated) in the website success.

Let's look at a real-world example of this plug-in: Your CMO wants to know how often Greco, Inc. is paying to drive people to its site from various marketing channels. The CMO is primarily interested in seeing if there is one marketing channel that is most responsible for website success. Due to budget cuts, advertising spending may need to be cut back, and the CMO needs to identify which channels and channel combinations are important to continue to drive applications.

To answer this question, let's start by looking at how a standard conversion variable storing the marketing channel using Most Recent allocation would present the data (**Figure 7.5**).

		Marketing Channel	Application Completions ▼	
📋	1.	Paid Search	204,045	66.9%
📋	2.	Display Ad	56,273	18.5%
📋	3.	E-mail	44,683	14.7%

Figure 7.5 Marketing Channel conversion variable—Most Recent allocation.

According to this report, only 18.5% of Application Completions are coming from Display Ad, as compared to 66.9% coming from Paid Search (in this case, let's assume e-mails are inexpensive). Based on this information, your first thought might be to cut the Display Ad budget. However, let's imagine that in addition to using a standard Most Recent conversion variable, you use the Cross-Visit Participation plug-in to create a separate conversion variable. You set this conversion variable to capture the last ten marketing channels and expire at the Application Conversion success event. **Figure 7.6** shows what you'll see when you look at this report.

		Marketing Channel	Application Completions ▼	
	1.	Paid Search	93,879	30.8%
	2.	Display Ad	38,095	12.5%
	3.	E-mail	30,317	9.9%
	4.	Display Ad>Paid Search	25,651	8.4%
	5.	E-mail>Paid Search	23,943	7.9%
	6.	Display Ad>Paid Search	22,357	7.3%
	7.	Display Ad>E-mail	21,289	7.0%
	8.	Display Ad>Paid Search>Paid Search	19,978	6.6%
	9.	Display Ad>Display Ad>Paid Search	17,294	5.7%
	10.	Paid Search>Display Ad>Display Ad	12,200	4.0%

Figure 7.6 Marketing Channel conversion variable—Cross-Visit Participation.

Interestingly, Display Ads are often part of the mix that leads to success, but Paid Search is most often the *last* touch prior to conversion. In fact, if you add all of the times that Display Ad is part of the mix (or used individually), the percent impacted is 51.5%. If you looked only at the previous Last Touch report, you'd see a skewed picture because the Most Recent allocation would attribute most of the success to Paid Search. Thus, you have to ask how much of Greco, Inc.'s success would still come through if Display Ad were not in the mix. At 18.5%, you might be willing to eliminate or reduce Display Ad advertising, but at 51.5% you might think twice before doing so or might consider some more in-depth testing prior to making any rash marketing spending decisions. This scenario shows why using the Cross-Visit Participation plug-in can be useful in a Site-Catalyst implementation.

But the value of this plug-in reaches beyond the realm of marketing campaigns. The following are some additional examples of how you can use this plug-in:

▶ Tracking which site tools (e.g., calculators) visitors used prior to success

▶ Tracking which products visitors viewed prior to success

- ▶ Tracking which videos visitors viewed prior to success
- ▶ Tracking which search terms visitors entered on your site prior to success

The list goes on and on. Anytime you want to see a concatenated list of values in the order that they took place across multiple visits, consider using the Cross-Visit Participation plug-in.

The following are some important details to know about Cross-Visit Participation:

- ▶ You must specify the maximum number of values you want to concatenate in the plug-in and the time period for them to be considered germane in impacting conversion.

- ▶ The plug-in can be configured to store or ignore duplicate values based on your needs. For example, in row 9 of Figure 7.6, we're tracking two visits in a row from Display Advertising, but could have configured the plug-in to exclude the duplicate Display Advertising value.

- ▶ There is a 255 byte (character) limit on conversion variables, which will impact how many values you can store. Whenever feasible, make the values used in the Cross-Visit Participation plug-in variable as small as possible to maximize how many values can be concatenated.

Get & Persist Plug-in

The Get & Persist plug-in is very basic but has many effective uses. All it does is pass a value stored in a variable on one page to all subsequent pages. It saves you the time and effort of storing values in your own cookie and lets your SiteCatalyst JavaScript file do the work for you. When would you want to do this? Let's say that you have registered users on your site who log in to use the site. Upon login, you capture their User ID, but it would be great if you could pass that User ID to a traffic variable on every page of the visit. You would then be able to break down reports like Page Name by User ID. The Get & Persist plug-in makes doing this much easier and lets your IT staff focus on more important tagging work.

Time Parting Plug-in

The Time Parting plug-in is very popular and is used to store the Day of Week and Time of Day in SiteCatalyst traffic and conversion variables. Although SiteCatalyst associates all websites with a date and time, there is no easy way to see this information other than using the calendar to select the date range for which you want data. But there are times when you might want to see how a different day or time slot performs; the easiest way to do this is through the Time Parting plug-in.

		Time Parting	Orders ▾ ⑦	
ⲧ	1.	Monday|9:30am	27,427	21.3%
ⲧ	2.	Tuesday|9:00am	24,107	18.7%
ⲧ	3.	Saturday|10:30am	20,240	15.7%
ⲧ	4.	Saturday|11:00am	13,407	10.4%
ⲧ	5.	Saturday|12:00pm	10,668	8.3%
ⲧ	6.	Sunday|4:00pm	8,122	6.3%
ⲧ	7.	Saturday|5:00pm	6,768	5.3%
ⲧ	8.	Friday|5:00pm	5,930	4.6%

Figure 7.7 Sample Time Parting variable.

## SC	SiteCatalyst SAI v:2.0		
## SC	'## SC' indicates a SiteCatalyst pre-process header.		
## SC	D:2012-07-01 1 A:2828839:53		
Key	Hour of Day	Day of Week	Weekday/Weekend
Monday|9:30am	9:30am	Monday	Weekday
Tuesday|9:00am	9:00am	Tuesday	Weekday
Saturday|10:30am	10:30am	Saturday	Weekend
Saturday|11:00am	11:00am	Saturday	Weekend
Saturday|12:00pm	12:00am	Saturday	Weekend
Sunday|4:00pm	4:00pm	Sunday	Weekend
Saturday|5:00pm	5:00pm	Saturday	Weekend
Friday|5:00pm	5:00pm	Friday	Weekday

Figure 7.8 Sample Time Parting SAINT classification file.

In practice, I implement the Time Parting plug-in slightly differently than is suggested in the Knowledge Base. The Knowledge Base recommends that you populate one variable for Day of Week, another for the different times of the day (usually in 15-minute or 30-minute increments), and one variable for weekday or weekend. Because this is a waste of two variables, I suggest that you combine the values into one variable and use classifications. For example, the report in **Figure 7.7** shows what the combined Time Parting variable might look like.

By concatenating these values, you can easily make a Day of Week classification, an Hour of Day classification, and a Weekday/Weekend classification through a SAINT classification file like the one shown in **Figure 7.8**. This way, you conserve two variables and get the same result as setting three standard variables. Also, because the values will never change, you only have to set this classification once. You can then use these variables to see website success events by any of these data points (**Figure 7.9**).

While we are on the topic of Time Parting and classifications, I have had some clients that like to see website behavior by their own customized time window. For example, you might want to see how website performance in the afternoon compares to performance in the morning. This is easy to do by adding one more classification to the Time Parting variable. **Figure 7.10** shows an example of the previous classification file with a column added to account for the Time Window within the day. Obviously, you can use whatever descriptive values you want for these time windows. For example, some clients in the financial services industry like to use Trading Hours versus Nontrading Hours.

In addition to being able to see these various Time Parting values in SiteCatalyst reports, another benefit is the ability to use them in segments. As you'll learn later when I cover segmentation, this one variable and its classifications allow you to isolate visits to a specific time of day or day of the week in which specific success event actions took place (**Figure 7.11**).

		Day of Week	Orders ▼ ⑦	
⊤	1.	Saturday	38,804	30.1%
⊤	2.	Sunday	31,636	24.5%
⊤	3.	Monday	24,107	18.7%
⊤	4.	Friday	14,310	11.1%
⊤	5.	Thursday	9,540	7.4%
⊤	6.	Wednesday	6,575	5.1%
⊤	7.	Tuesday	3,945	3.1%

Figure 7.9 Sample Time Parting report.

## SC	SiteCatalyst SAIv:2.0			
## SC	'## SC' indicates a SiteCatalyst pre-process header. Please do not re			
## SC	D:2012-07-01 1A:2828839:53			
Key	Hour of Day	Day of Week	Weekday/Weekend	Time Window
Monday|9:30am	9:30am	Monday	Weekday	Early morning
Tuesday|9:00am	9:00am	Tuesday	Weekday	Early morning
Saturday|10:30am	10:30am	Saturday	Weekend	Morning
Saturday|11:00am	11:00am	Saturday	Weekend	Morning
Saturday|12:00pm	12:00am	Saturday	Weekend	Mid Day
Sunday|4:00pm	4:00pm	Sunday	Weekend	Afternoon
Saturday|5:00pm	5:00pm	Saturday	Weekend	Afternoon
Friday|5:00pm	5:00pm	Friday	Weekday	Afternoon

Figure 7.10 Sample Time Window report.

Segment Definition Builder

Title: Monday or Friday Orders

Segment Definition Components

Components Library

Containers

⊘ Page Views

⊙ Visits

⬤ Visitors

Segment Canvas

☑ Include ☐ Exclude

⊟ ⊙ **Visit**

⊟ ⊙ **Order**

Rules for: Order
- **Day of Week (v41) (eVar41)** equals **monday**
- or **Day of Week (v41) (eVar41)** equals **friday**

Figure 7.11 Sample segment using the Time Parting plug-in.

Date Stamp variable

You can also use the Time Parting plug-in to set a Date Stamp variable. This variable simply contains the current date and is set at the beginning of each website visit. I'll use a real-life client story to explain why you might want to do this: While working with a client, a unique situation developed. This client was well versed in the usage of the Adobe Discover product and frequently took advantage of its ability to segment by date.

For those unfamiliar with this feature, you might use it to address the following scenario: I want to build a segment of people who filled out a form in the third week of January 2011, but I want to see their behavior for the months of February, March, and April. **Figure 7.12** shows how this segment could be built using Adobe Discover. This functionality is cool because you can use it to limit your population to folks who took some action in a specific time period in the past, but then observe their subsequent behavior in a future time period.

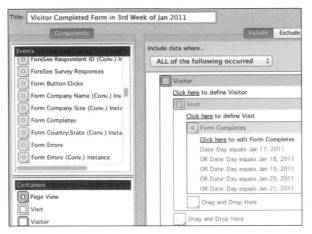

Figure 7.12 Sample Adobe Discover date-based segment.

However, the challenge facing my client was that very few people in the organization had access to Adobe Discover, so the client wanted the ability to apply this date-based segmentation to his SiteCatalyst reports. To mimic what could be done in Adobe Discover in SiteCatalyst, I had the client use the Time Parting plug-in to pass the current date to a traffic variable. He then created a segment that took advantage of this variable to isolate visits that happened in the past (**Figure 7.13**). This segment will make more sense after I cover segmentation in Chapter 10. But for now, you can see that this is a similar segment to the one in Adobe Discover, and you can use it to filter data by past dates directly in SiteCatalyst. If desired, this Date Stamp variable could also be classified into higher-level buckets like Week Of or Month Of (**Figure 7.14**).

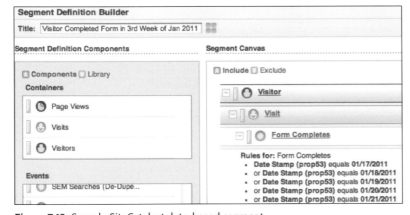

Figure 7.13 Sample SiteCatalyst date-based segment.

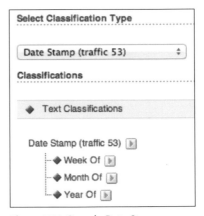

Figure 7.14 Sample Date Stamp classification.

Time to Complete Plug-in

The Time to Complete plug-in allows you to set a timer between any two success events in your implementation. This is handy if you want to see how long it takes visitors to make it through a process on your website. Here are some common examples of how you can use this plug-in:

▸ Track how long it takes visitors to go from Add to Cart to Order

▸ Track how long it takes visitors to finish an application process

▸ Track how long it takes visitors to complete a self-service function (e.g., pay a phone bill)

This plug-in is configured to start a timer when the first success event takes place and then to stop the timer when the second success event takes place. This time frame can be seconds, minutes, or days, and the Time to Complete plug-in has prebuilt time frame buckets it uses for reporting purposes. Normally, this plug-in populates a conversion variable, and this variable is best used when paired with the second success event. For example, let's say that you are using the Time to Complete plug-in to track how long it takes visitors to go from Cart Addition to Order. Once you have collected the data, the ideal report would consist of the Time to Complete conversion variable and the Orders metric (**Figure 7.15**).

Keep in mind that anytime a variable spans multiple visits, it will be subject to cookie deletion issues. Therefore, I recommend that you use this report for directional guidance only and treat its data as a bit more suspect than other SiteCatalyst data you might collect within a session.

		Time Between Cart Add & Order	Orders ▾ ⑦	
	1.	3 minutes	20,627	16.0%
	2.	4 minutes	15,599	12.1%
	3.	5 minutes	12,724	9.9%
	4.	30-60 minutes	11,267	8.7%
	5.	over 3 days	10,668	8.3%
	6.	1-2 days	8,122	6.3%
	7.	11-20 minutes	6,768	5.3%
	8.	6-10 minutes	5,930	4.6%

Figure 7.15 Sample Time to Complete report.

Get Val(ue) Once Plug-in

The Get Val Once plug-in (which I call Get Value Once) is used to prevent SiteCatalyst from accepting the same value multiple times. This plug-in is normally used with conversion variables and especially with those that use the Instances metric. For example, as discussed in Chapter 5, if a visitor comes to the website from a paid search keyword, the Searches metric (Instances) is incremented. However, if the same visitor clicks the Refresh button or clicks the Back button, another Searches instance will be counted. By using the Get Value Once plug-in, you can prevent this and try to make the Searches metric as accurate as possible. In many respects, this plug-in mimics the functionality of Once Per Visit serialization.

Visit Number Plug-in

The Visit Number plug-in simply passes the current Visit Number to a custom variable. This is only needed if you want to apply SAINT classifications to the Visit Number variable, which is not possible for out-of-the-box reports like Visit Number.

Days Since Last Visit Plug-in

The Days Since Last Visit plug-in is similar to the Visit Number plug-in except it passes one of a few predefined values (e.g., "Less Than 7 Days") based on when the active visitor last visited the site.

Data Sources

Although more and more business is taking place on the web each day, online marketers cannot forget about successes and conversions that take place beyond the website. SiteCatalyst can capture all of your online success, but there are times when you'll need to couple this with business metrics that take place offline or in other channels. To do this, SiteCatalyst provides a feature called *Data Sources*, which is a mechanism to manually import supplemental (non-website) metrics and metric dimensions into Site-Catalyst. The primary reason customers import this data is to compare online metrics to non-website metrics. The following are some examples of situations in which you might use Data Sources:

▸ Import historical traffic data from log files or a previous web analytics vendor

▸ Import offline success metrics unrelated to the website or taking place after a visit to the website

▸ Import metrics from a separate channel, such as e-mail or call center, so you can compare them to online metrics and create calculated metrics

▶ Import metrics from other products through Genesis (Adobe's partner network), such as Advertising Network or CRM metrics (most Genesis integrations use Data Sources behind the scenes)

Let's walk through a real-world example of Data Sources. This example discusses a scenario for one of Greco, Inc.'s electronics subsidiaries. Greco, Inc. wants to add the Cost of Goods Sold and Shipping Costs to SiteCatalyst so it can create more realistic calculated metrics for judging campaign success and other analyses. To accomplish this, Greco, Inc. sets up a new Currency success event for each and then determines how it will break down these new offline metrics. For its online sales, Greco, Inc. does most of its analysis using Tracking Code, Order Number, Brand, Product Type, and Coupon (if used). It already created conversion variables for these attributes and regularly looks at online metrics, such as Orders, Units, and Revenue using these variables. Via the Data Sources wizard, Greco, Inc. has set up an FTP account and a Data Sources import template (shown in **Figure 7.16** with one sample line of offline data).

Once all testing is done, Greco, Inc. can begin importing the offline data via Data Sources. This file will add the two currency values to the Currency success events created (COGS and Shipping Costs). It will also allow these offline metrics to appear in any conversion variable report that was uploaded with the metrics, which in this case were Order Number, Product, Brand, Type, Part Number, Coupon, and Tracking Code. This means that if there is online data for any of these conversion variables, the company can see online metrics and offline metrics for cases in which the conversion variable values match (**Figure 7.17**). In the report in Figure 7.17, online Revenue is associated with Tracking Codes and now, through Data Sources, offline COGS data appears for the same Tracking Codes. This allows the company to create a calculated metric that subtracts these two metrics. Obviously, online and offline metrics must have the same Tracking Code values for this to work. Keep in mind that this is only one of the reports for which you can combine online and offline metrics. The same is possible for any of

# Generic Data Source template file (user: 8971 ds_id: 1)									
#	Order #	Product	Brand	Type	Part No.	Coupon	Tracking Code	COGS	Shipping Costs
Date	Evar 16	Product	Evar 2	Evar 3	Evar 6	Evar 15	Tracking Code	Event 5	Event 4
07/07/2012	66524	ink345	HP	Laser	112	sale_001	goog_123	121.75	12.75

Figure 7.16 Sample Data Sources import file.

	Tracking Code	Revenue ▼ ⑦		COGS		Revenue - COGS
1.	goog_123	$1,639,768	21.3%	$611,461	22.7%	$1,028,307
2.	msn_111	$1,441,300	18.7%	$553,012	20.5%	$888,288
3.	yahoo_889	$1,210,076	15.7%	$436,115	16.2%	$773,960

Figure 7.17 Sample conversion variable report showing online and offline metrics.

the data points imported with the offline metrics, including Order Number, Product, and so on. However, if you look at a conversion variable report that was not uploaded with the offline metrics, all offline metrics will be lumped into a None row because Site-Catalyst doesn't know with which conversion variable values they should be associated.

While we are on the subject of Cost of Goods Sold in this example, recall that in Chapter 6 I explained how to import COGS using numeric classifications. In that example, I discussed how difficult it could be to track COGS using numeric classifications because costs change frequently. Data Sources provides an alternate way to add Cost of Goods Sold data to your SiteCatalyst implementation by uploading actual COGS associated with each order. However, this brings up a key point related to Data Sources that cannot be overemphasized: Once you upload Data Sources data into SiteCatalyst, it cannot be removed (ever). There are some tricks to upload additional (negative) data to reverse incorrect data values, but in my experience this can be very cumbersome. Therefore, you must be careful what you upload because you may get only one chance to get it right. In the preceding Cost of Goods Sold example, in some respects Data Sources is easier to implement, but SAINT classifications, albeit more cumbersome, are retroactive and thus more forgiving of mistakes. These are the types of decisions that require ample forethought, and knowing the pros and cons of each approach can help you make the best decision for your organization.

The following are some important details to know about Data Sources:

▸ As stated earlier, once you import Data Sources data into SiteCatalyst, it is difficult to undo. For this reason, you need to be very careful and make sure you've done thorough testing and have a good process in place for automated data uploads. *Always test within a development report suite.*

▸ All data imported via Data Sources is tied to a date, so it does not matter when it is physically imported.

▸ Normally, each row of data imported via Data Sources is charged as a server call at your contracted rate.

▸ You cannot have more than 50 MB of data in your Data Sources FTP account at once (not 50 MB per file but in total across all files), or it will become "locked." It is recommended that you feed data to SiteCatalyst accordingly.

▸ It is not possible to upload more than 30 unique dates at a time.

▸ In some cases, Data Sources values cannot be segmented using the new v15 segmentation capabilities.

▸ Some types of Data Sources imports allow you to see the imported data in Site-Catalyst only, whereas others allow you to see imported data in SiteCatalyst, Data-Warehouse, and Discover. For this reason, it is important to ensure that you select the correct Data Sources type (for more information, read the Data Sources User Manual found in the Knowledge Base).

Transaction ID

Transaction ID is an advanced feature that allows you to connect online and offline data by establishing a "key" that can tie an online visit to offline success. The feature of Transaction ID with the greatest impact is the ability to let you associate offline metrics with previously captured online conversion variable values. To see this, let's walk through an example. In this scenario, Greco, Inc. has a banking subsidiary that generates many loan applications. Currently, the marketing department is measuring itself based on completed loan applications, but it wants to create a more realistic KPI because the business only makes money for *approved* loans. About 30 days after a loan application takes place, the company generates a file that shows whether a loan application was approved or denied. Greco, Inc. wants to upload these results into SiteCatalyst to have a Loans Approved metric it can compare to its online Completed Loan Applications metric. Having both metrics would allow Greco, Inc. to look at various conversion variables (e.g., campaigns) and determine which values lead to completed applications but few approved loans.

The company could use Data Sources, but recall that it would have to manually identify and upload all online variables for which it wanted to see this non-website metric. That means moving data from SiteCatalyst to the back end to merge it with the approved loan data, only to re-upload it to SiteCatalyst through Data Sources. This would be a nuisance, especially because SiteCatalyst already has all of this information up to the point that visitors completed loan applications. Wouldn't it be great if SiteCatalyst could store all of that data somewhere and later if a specific loan application turned into an approved loan, associate that success event with all of the preexisting conversion variable values collected at the time of the completed loan application? That is exactly what Transaction ID does.

So how does Transaction ID work this kind of magic? It's not as complex as you might think. Using the loan application example, when a visitor completes a loan application online, the developers would pass a unique Transaction ID to a special **s.transactionID** SiteCatalyst variable. When that happens, SiteCatalyst would then store all current conversion variable values for that visitor in a separate table and use the Transaction ID as the "key." Later, when non-website data related to that same Transaction ID is uploaded (the approved loan in this example), all of the conversion variable data (e.g., Campaign Tracking Code, Visit Number, etc.) would be associated with the newly uploaded metric(s). This would save the developers the work of having to upload all of this supplemental data with the offline metrics.

Here are a few other potential Transaction ID use cases:

▶ A visitor fills out a lead form on your website and later purchases a product by phone. If you can connect the user's online session and phone call together using an ID, you can see what online campaigns or referral sources led to the phone call, which led to the sale. This helps you justify your investment in online advertising.

▶ A rental car company wants to see which campaigns lead to online car reservations versus which lead to actual car rentals (offline).

▶ A Human Resources department would like to upload performance scores for hired employees and connect those to the original website application. This would allow them to see which marketing campaigns lead to the best employees.

Here are a few important details you need to keep in mind when you're using Transaction ID:

▶ Because SiteCatalyst must store an extra table of data to make Transaction ID work, there are some additional fees involved. Your Adobe account manager can discuss this with you in more detail.

▶ By default, the conversion variable data stored in the Transaction ID table on Adobe's servers is available for 90 days. This means that you have 90 days from the time you set the Transaction ID online to upload the related offline data. This time frame should be adequate for most clients but can be extended if needed for a surcharge. Importing Transaction ID data after 90 days will still allow metrics to be imported but will be treated as traditional Data Sources data, and metrics will not be associated with their corresponding conversion variable values.

▶ The **s.transactionID** string is limited to 100 characters.

Genesis Integrations

Genesis is a network of predefined integrations between SiteCatalyst and other online marketing tools. Instead of starting from scratch each time you want to integrate SiteCatalyst with another vendor, you can take advantage of best-practice, prebuilt integrations that exist as part of the Genesis network. As you become more advanced using SiteCatalyst, it will become apparent that there is no limit to the amount of data you can inject into SiteCatalyst. Having the marketing data from the various tools your team uses in one place allows you to leverage SiteCatalyst's great reports, dashboards, and other tools. For this reason, many SiteCatalyst clients decide to use Genesis to make SiteCatalyst their hub for online marketing data.

However, if SiteCatalyst is to be the central repository for this data, there has to be an easy way to insert data from other online marketing tools into SiteCatalyst. Online marketers use tools to manage e-mail, paid search, display advertising, CRM, and so on.

Imagine if you had five tools with data to be inserted into SiteCatalyst. Setting up Data Sources for each would be very cumbersome. For this reason, the folks at Adobe created the Genesis partner ecosystem. Many of these integrations leverage Data Sources or API integrations but have an easy-to-use front end that masks the complexity and lets you use the data immediately. To be a part of the Genesis network, each vendor must "certify" its integration by architecting a scalable solution and proving to Adobe that the integration is sound. Over 500 integrations are part of the Genesis network, so the odds are that many of the tools you work with are ready to be integrated.

In addition to injecting data into SiteCatalyst, many of these Genesis integrations allow you to export data from SiteCatalyst. Important data captured on the website can be sent to other online marketing tools where its impact can be multiplied. Because there are too many Genesis integrations to review, I'll just review the most popular types of Genesis integrations used by SiteCatalyst clients.

E-mail Marketing Integrations

E-mail Marketing integrations allow you to easily import e-mail metrics into SiteCatalyst and export segments of users back to your e-mail provider. When you use an e-mail tool, typical success metrics include Sends, Delivers, Opens, and Clicks. These metrics are housed in the e-mail tool, but because they are numbers, they can be easily transferred to SiteCatalyst as Numeric success events. Having these metrics in SiteCatalyst allows you to compare how many e-mail clicks arrived at the website and completed website success events. It is even possible to create calculated metrics that combine E-mail metrics and SiteCatalyst metrics (**Figure 7.18**).

	Tracking Code	E-Mail Clicks ▾		Orders ⑦		Orders/ Email Click
1.	email_1112	4,255	21.3%	680	22.7%	16.0%
2.	email_1115	3,740	18.7%	615	20.5%	16.4%
3.	email_1265	3,140	15.7%	485	16.2%	15.4%

Figure 7.18 Tracking Code report with e-mail, online, and calculated metrics.

In addition, most e-mail tools are configured so that a recipient clicking a link in an e-mail will arrive at the website with an E-mail ID in the URL. As you learned earlier, you can use the Get Query Parameter plug-in to place this E-mail ID into a SiteCatalyst conversion variable. Then you can build segments of visitors who meet specific criteria (e.g., added a product to the cart but did not purchase) and export those E-mail IDs back to the e-mail tool where they can be remarketed to accordingly.

Hence, E-mail Marketing integrations demonstrate the bidirectional nature of Genesis, with E-mail metrics being imported into SiteCatalyst and E-mail IDs being exported from SiteCatalyst.

Voice of Customer

Voice of Customer tools, like OpinionLab or ForeSee, are used to gather feedback about your website from real users. Most Voice of Customer Genesis integrations involve setting a survey ID in SiteCatalyst when visitors engage with a page or session survey. Once this ID resides in a SiteCatalyst variable, metadata about the survey can be uploaded as SAINT classifications after the fact. This allows you to add important values like score, visit intent, and so forth to your SiteCatalyst data set where it can be analyzed and used as segmentation criteria. Even though the amount of data is normally small, it can be extrapolated to understand how the larger population feels about specific pages or your website in general.

Customer Experience Management

Customer Experience Management (CEM) vendors, like TeaLeaf and ClickTale, focus on *why* website visitors do what they do. However, instead of asking them, their tools allow you to record website sessions and "watch" them at a later time. Tools like Tea-Leaf allow you to see how visitors navigate from page to page; tools like ClickTale can actually show you when visitors move their mouse within pages. Although these tools are great at letting you visually see the struggles your visitors are encountering on your website, finding the specific sessions that you want to watch is sometimes like looking for a needle in a haystack. To solve this problem, CEM Genesis integrations place recording IDs from these vendors into SiteCatalyst variables. Then you can build segments to isolate the sessions that have a specific problem (e.g., a visitor received an error during checkout) and see if any of these sessions have a recording ID associated with them. You can then focus your time on watching just those problem sessions and hopefully identify a common trend.

Other Genesis Integrations

Other types of Genesis integrations deserve a brief overview:

▶ **Facebook.** This integration allows you to exchange information between Site-Catalyst and Facebook, including tracking usage of your Facebook site, accessing demographic information available from Facebook, informing Facebook marketing campaigns, and more.

▶ **Search Engine Optimization (SEO).** SEO integrations allow you to import natural (and sometimes paid) search data, such as search volume, keyword rank, search positions, positions of competitors, and so on.

▶ **Ad Serving.** These Genesis integrations are used to populate Display Advertising metrics (including View-Throughs) in SiteCatalyst in a similar manner to E-mail Marketing integrations.

► **DemandBase.** The DemandBase Genesis integration allows companies (primarily business to business) to use DemandBase's Real-Time ID database to identify the company that is visiting your website. Often, business-to-business websites don't know which companies have visited their website until after they have completed a form. By using DemandBase's proprietary technology, the company name and other key information can be passed into SiteCatalyst so business-to-business companies can better service and target website visitors with relevant messaging and improve conversion rates.

► **Salesforce.com.** This Genesis integration allows you to pass data back and forth between SiteCatalyst and Salesforce.com. The overall goal is to provide "closed loop marketing" so SiteCatalyst has visibility into what happens after the website visit, which is populated from Salesforce.com.

Data Feeds

A *data feed* is a recurring (normally daily) export of granular, raw data from SiteCatalyst. You learned the ways to import data into SiteCatalyst, but there are many times when you'll want to export raw data from SiteCatalyst. To do this, SiteCatalyst offers a feature called *Data Feeds*. Many organizations have enterprise data warehouses that they use to aggregate data from multiple sources in an effort to unify customer or prospect records across all channels. For these organizations, SiteCatalyst clickstream data is a rich source of information that they can add to an existing data warehouse. Because SiteCatalyst collects an enormous amount of data, most clients customize the data columns they want to export and map those to their own enterprise data warehouse. You can learn more about Data Feeds through your Adobe account manager or ClientCare.

VISTA Rules

VISTA (Visitor Identification, Segmentation & Transformation Architecture) is a way to apply a rule or logic to your SiteCatalyst data *after* it is collected but *before* it is stored in SiteCatalyst's data tables. This technology gives you the ability to tweak or massage the data you are collecting and transform it into different or additional variables, depending on your business needs.

Let's look at an example. Imagine that Greco, Inc. is structured in a way that each U.S. state is assigned to a specific sales representative. As visitors complete website forms, they are assigned to sales representatives based on the state entered on the form. However, if a deal is over $200,000, the lead is assigned to enterprise representatives in each sales region. Greco, Inc. wants to use the data captured from forms to associate a sales representative with each lead in SiteCatalyst so it can measure leads by representative. Initially, the company intended to use SAINT classifications to populate a sales representative conversion variable by state, but this proved difficult because the sales team was different based on the potential deal size. It needed a way to tell SiteCatalyst that if a lead was submitted and it was under $200,000, it was to be assigned to Bob if it was an East Coast state, Jane if it was a Midwest state, and Joe if it was a West Coast state. But if the deal was over $200,000, it was to be assigned to Bill if it was an East Coast state, Ted if it was a Midwest state, and Jill if it was a West Coast state.

Although you can use some tricks to capture this data in a conversion variable and apply SAINT classifications (e.g., Illinois|150000 could be classified as Jane), I'll use this example just as a way to illustrate how VISTA rules work. To create a VISTA rule, you have to work with Adobe's Engineering Services team and pay a setup fee. In this case, you would work with the engineering team to map out the decision tree. You'd first decide whether the deal was over $200,000 and then you'd identify the state. With these two pieces of information, you would hard-code the names of the sales representatives for each state and deal size. When the VISTA rule logic was complete, you'd tell the engineering team which report suite to run on and which conversion variable(s) it should populate with the sales representative name.

The VISTA rule will populate the variable after the submission of the lead form without the use of JavaScript. Instead, the rule runs on SiteCatalyst servers after it collects the lead form data from the JavaScript on the page but before the image request is sent to SiteCatalyst servers for processing. The end result will be the population of a Sales Representative conversion variable, and from an end-user perspective, there is no way to differentiate between variables set by VISTA rules and those set by JavaScript.

Here are some other common examples of how you can use VISTA rules:

▶ Send employee traffic to an internal report suite based on a range of IP addresses.

▶ Add visitors to a segment on the fly based on data found in variables or query string parameters. For example, if your website has a form in which visitors are required to enter Birth Year, State, and Gender, you can write a detailed VISTA rule that will evaluate the responses and assign the visitor into a segment by passing a segment name (e.g., "Middle-aged Midwestern Women") to a conversion or traffic variable.

▶ Pass a value stored in one SiteCatalyst variable to other SiteCatalyst variables. For example, if you capture the Campaign Tracking Code in `s.campaign`, but also want to pass it to a few other conversion variables that have different allocations or expirations, you can use a VISTA rule to pass the same value to all variables instead of having to do additional tagging or JavaScript modification.

▶ Pass data found in GeoSegmentation or Technology reports to custom variables so it can be classified using SAINT classifications.

▶ Set success events based on a URL or a query string parameter.

▶ Look for potentially fraudulent orders (e.g., Revenue > $XX,000) and move them to a separate report suite so SiteCatalyst data is not tainted.

Important Facts About VISTA

The following list contains some important details to know about VISTA:

▶ VISTA rules have access to and can act upon any data point that is available on the page, including IP address, referring URL, query string parameters, traffic variables, conversion variables, success events, and so on. However, VISTA rules do not have access to data that was passed on previous pages.

▶ Making any changes to a VISTA rule normally requires additional fees to be paid to Engineering Services.

▶ VISTA rules can be used to automate certain types of SiteCatalyst tagging, but this is not recommended as a long-term solution because changes in your site could have adverse effects on predefined VISTA rules.

VISTA rules can become quite complex. The good news is that all you have to do is identify the rules you might want to apply to your data, and Engineering Services can help with the rest.

DB VISTA Rules

DB VISTA (Database VISTA) is a VISTA rule that performs a lookup to a database as part of its logic. For the most part, there is very little difference between DB VISTA and VISTA. Both are used to alter or augment data that you have collected in SiteCatalyst prior to it being placed into SiteCatalyst's back-end data tables. However, the database component of DB VISTA makes it much more flexible than traditional VISTA rules.

To illustrate this, let's revisit the preceding sales representative example. Using the VISTA rule in that example, a Sales Representative conversion variable was successfully populated based on deal size and state. However, what if the names of sales representatives change frequently? As mentioned earlier, any changes to VISTA rules cost additional money, so it may not be cost-effective to continually pay Adobe to keep making changes to the VISTA rule each time a sales representative is replaced. To avoid this issue, the company can use a DB VISTA rule to set the Sales Representative conversion variable instead of a VISTA rule. Doing so will provide the ability to upload a table that maps each scenario to a sales representative. This table would have rows that indicate the over $200,000 East Coast rep's name, the under $200,000 East Coast rep's name, and so on, and this table can be updated at anytime via FTP. When the DB VISTA rule is ready to process, it will check the database table for the latest name of the sales representative that matches the current lead criteria. This means that if the over $200,000 East Coast sales representative changes from Bill to Steve midday on July 10, the company could upload the new name, and from that point on, any new leads would be assigned to Steve. The best part is that no additional money is needed to make these database table updates. Initially, DB VISTA rules cost a bit more than VISTA rules but offer more flexibility over the long term, which is why I prefer them to standard VISTA rules.

The following list contains some other ways you can take advantage of DB VISTA functionality:

▶ If you have hundreds or thousands of IP addresses that you want to exclude (and they change frequently), you could upload a table of IP addresses to be excluded by a DB VISTA rule.

▶ If you want to get the latest Cost of Goods Sold from a database table by product ID, you could use a DB VISTA rule and pass it to a Currency success event.

▶ If you have a customer ID captured in a SiteCatalyst variable, you could add customer demographic data (e.g., age, city, state) to the DB VISTA table and use it to populate custom conversion variables.

Conclusion

In this chapter, you learned some advanced SiteCatalyst features that over time you can use to augment your implementation. Most of these topics require additional education, which you can access in the SiteCatalyst Knowledge Base. Some of these topics will also be discussed in more detail in Section 3, "Applying Adobe SiteCatalyst," when I discuss ways to apply SiteCatalyst to your organization.

In Section 1, "Behind the Scenes of Adobe SiteCatalyst," I reviewed the fundamentals that you should know about how SiteCatalyst works as well as some advanced topics. A deep understanding of this information will help you immensely as you plan or reengineer your existing SiteCatalyst implementation. In the next section I'll discuss reporting and explain how you can access the data you've collected so you can begin conducting web analysis.

Using Adobe SiteCatalyst

In Section 1, you learned how SiteCatalyst is used to collect data through the use of report suites, success events, variables, and classifications. These features allow you to configure SiteCatalyst so that it provides the data your business needs to conduct web analysis.

In this section, I'll assume that you've started collecting website data and are ready to view and use this data in SiteCatalyst. Chapter 8 reviews all the different reports that you can use in SiteCatalyst. Chapter 9 shows you how to use the SiteCatalyst interface to easily bookmark and share SiteCatalyst reports with co-workers. Chapter 10 discusses the important subject of report segmentation. And Chapter 11 explains the Adobe ReportBuilder tool, which allows you to move SiteCatalyst data to Microsoft Excel for advanced analysis.

## CHAPTER 8

Creating Reports in SiteCatalyst

When it comes to web analytics, you can never get away from reports. Like it or not, web analysts spend a lot of time looking at reports of data collected to answer specific business questions. SiteCatalyst offers many different types of reports to help you analyze what is taking place on your website. In this chapter I'll dissect the various report types available in SiteCatalyst so you'll be familiar with them and know which ones to use for the different business questions you are asked.

Metric Reports

The most basic report in SiteCatalyst is what I call the Metric report (sometimes referred to as an "over time" report). Metric reports show raw numbers for traffic metrics, success events, or calculated metrics (**Figure 8.1**).

Figure 8.1 Sample Metric report.

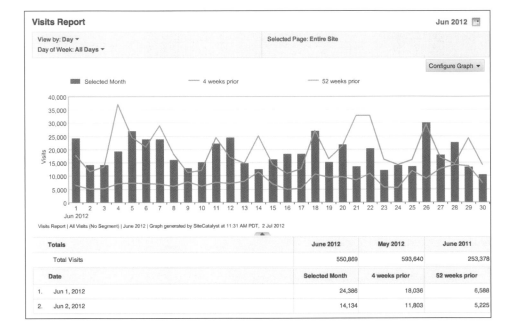

These reports show all raw data for the selected time period and can be viewed by Day, Week, Month, and so on. Looking at this report you can see website visits by day and can also see the previous four-week period. And, if you have enough data, you can see a comparison to the same time frame 52 weeks earlier. There are a few settings you can tweak on Metric reports:

▶ **View by.** This setting allows you to change the report to see data by Day, Week, Month, Quarter, or Year. SiteCatalyst only allows you to choose a View By option that is a shorter date range than the one you selected in the report. For example, if you try to view the report in Figure 8.1 by Month, Quarter, or Year, you'll receive an error message. But you can view it by week because a week is shorter than the chosen date range of a month.

▶ **Day of Week.** This option allows you to filter the report to see data only for a specific day. For example, you might want to see how Mondays are performing week after week. To do this, you would select the Day of Week as Monday and view the resulting report (**Figure 8.2**).

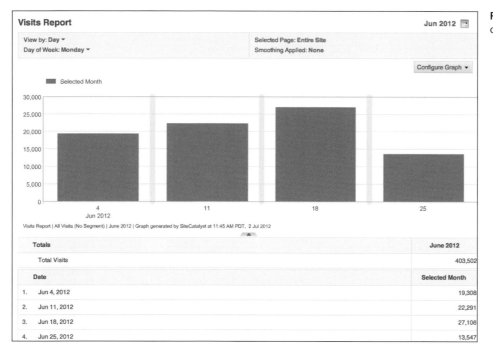

Figure 8.2 Sample Day of Week Metric report.

▶ **Smoothing Applied.** In most Metric reports you can adjust the smoothing aspects of the trend graph. Although this option is not heavily used, it allows you to modify the graph to show a daily moving average or linear view of the data. Most clients do this type of smoothing in a tool like Excel, but it is available to you if needed.

▶ **Selected Page.** For a subset of Traffic Metric reports (Page Views, Visits, Daily Unique Visitors, etc.), you'll see Selected Page as an additional option. The Selected Page option allows you to filter the report for a specific page.

▶ **Persistent Cookies.** In Unique Visitor reports you have the option to filter the report by Persistent Cookies versus Non-persistent Cookies. This simply splits Unique Visitor data by whether or not the visitor accepts persistent cookies and shows what portion of data used the cookie fallback method (**Figure 8.3**).

▶ **Configure Graph.** You can click the Configure Graph button to change the graph type.

▶ **Date Range.** Clicking the calendar will provide the ability to select dates or date ranges from the calendar. Press the Shift key and then click and drag date ranges or use the preset drop-down menu to select commonly used date ranges (**Figure 8.4**).

Because you can't do much with Metric reports, the preceding options are the only ones you really need to know. Again, these are the simplest of the SiteCatalyst reports. Next, I'll move on to Ranked reports, which are the most commonly used reports in SiteCatalyst.

▶**TIP** *The Smoothing option is not available in monthly Metric reports. If you use the preset for Month (the default shown or accessed by clicking on the month name in the calendar), you'll see the trending lines for the past four and 52 weeks but not the Smoothing option. Conversely, if you manually select a date range (even the same month using the calendar), you'll no longer see the historical trend lines but will see the Smoothing option.*

Figure 8.3 Persistent
Cookies filter.

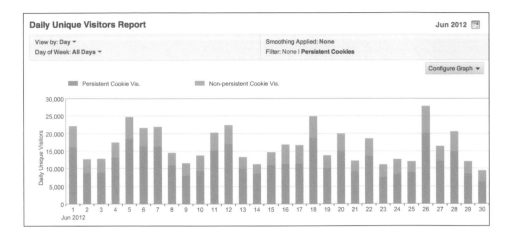

Figure 8.4 Date Range
selection screen.

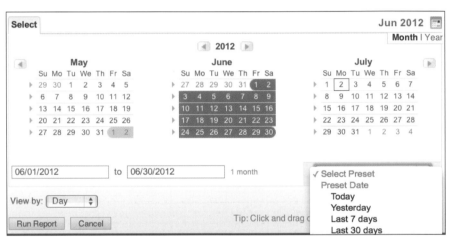

*▶TIP When you're
using the calendar, you
can double-click on the
month or year to select
it and begin loading the
report. You can also click
on the small gray tri-
angles next to a week in
the calendar to select the
entire week.*

Ranked Reports

The goal of a Ranked report is to show you traffic metric, success event metric, or calculated metric data associated with a traffic or conversion variable. Selecting a traffic
or conversion variable from the SiteCatalyst menu opens Ranked reports. **Figure 8.5**
shows an example of a Ranked report.

Ranked reports always have the values of the selected traffic or conversion variable
as the rows and the metrics as the columns. You can add any metric available in the
Metrics Selector to a Ranked report, and you can include up to nine metrics per report.
Clicking on the metric name will sort the report by that metric, and you can always see
which metric is being sorted on by the small green triangle next to the metric name. If
a selected metric is a predefined metric, a "?" help bubble appears, which you can click
to learn more about the metric. Ranked reports can display from 10 to 200 rows of data

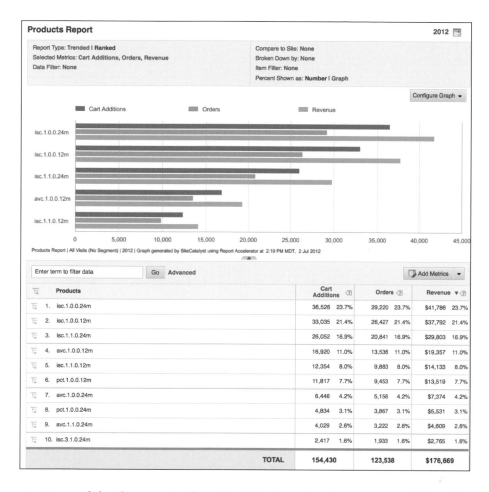

Figure 8.5 Sample Ranked report.

at a time, and they have next and previous links to go to subsequent pages. Normally, Ranked reports appear with a graph at the top, but you can use the toggle directly below the graph to hide this feature. Directly above the raw report data is a filter box where you can enter text values and filter the report on those values.

Ranked Report Settings

At the top of the report are configuration options similar to those for Metric reports. They include the following:

▶ **Report Type.** Allows you to toggle between Ranked and Trended views of the report. Ranked is the report shown in Figure 8.5, and Trended allows you to see *one* metric for a few values for the current variable over the selected date range (more on this in the next section). Note that if you have multiple metrics in a Ranked report, when you click Trended, SiteCatalyst defaults to showing you the leftmost column metric trended, but you can change this if needed.

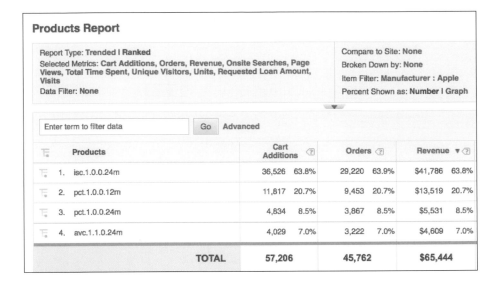

> ▶ **Selected Metrics.** Shows you which metrics are being used in the active Ranked report. Clicking this option is the same as clicking the Add Metrics button and will open the Metric Selector screen.

> ▶ **Data Filter.** Applies a text filter to Ranked reports. This setting shows whether or not you have applied any filters to the selected report.

> ▶ **Compare to Site.** Allows you to compare the current report for the current report suite to the same report for another report suite. Once it is active, this setting also shows you what suites are being compared.

> ▶ **Broken Down By.** Breaks down values in the report by another variable. This setting also shows whether or not any breakdowns are currently applied.

> ▶ **Item Filter.** Appears only if a classification is available for the selected variable. If there is, it allows you to filter the report by one of these classifications. For example, **Figure 8.6** shows the same report as in Figure 8.5 but is filtered to just show Apple products using the Manufacturer classification.

> ▶ **Percent Shown As.** Allows you to choose whether you show report percentages as numbers or graphs within reach row.

Default Metrics

Starting in SiteCatalyst v15, Ranked reports offer the ability to set default metrics for each report. Default metrics allow you to choose which metrics you want to display in a specific report the first time you open it within a SiteCatalyst session. This can be a real time-saver when you have lots of variables and metrics. To set your default metrics, simply open a Ranked report, select the metrics you want as your default, and click the arrow next to the Add Metrics button (**Figure 8.7**).

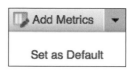

Figure 8.7 Setting Ranked report default metrics.

Note that if you add or remove metrics during a session, SiteCatalyst will retain those metrics (where applicable) when you navigate from report to report. But the first time you view a Ranked report within a SiteCatalyst session, you'll begin with your default metrics. If you want to clear the default metrics, use the same process but choose Clear Defaults to start over. If you are using an earlier version of SiteCatalyst, you can only set default metrics for the entire report suite, and this is done in the administration console.

Ranked Report Search Filters

As mentioned previously, Ranked reports enable you to apply a text search filter on variable values. This search filter can be very useful, especially if you have a lot of values for a particular variable. However, some advanced filter features take a bit of time to learn.

The basics

Let's start with the basics—a Page report (**Figure 8.8**). Now let's say that you want to filter this report to find all "cruises" pages. Because this implementation has logical page names, in this report you can enter ":cruises:" in the search box to see the filtered report (**Figure 8.9**). But what if you want to see all "cruises" pages, but also want to see all "videos" pages? This is easy with the text filter; all you have to do is enter these two phrases with an OR between them (**Figure 8.10**). Note that the word OR must be uppercase or it won't work.

	Page
1.	vrc:us:home:home page vfv
2.	vrc:us:subscribe:signup popup form vpv
3.	vrc:us:aboutyourtrip:pif form vfv
4.	vrc:us:home:find a cruise
5.	vrc:us:regions:europe_packagelist
6.	vrc:us:specialoffers:rivercruising vfv
7.	vrc:us:cruises:grand european tour_itinerary

Figure 8.8 Page report.

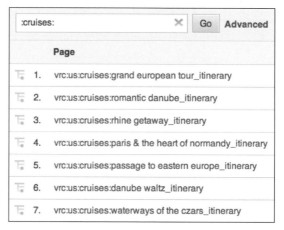

Figure 8.9 Basic Ranked report search filter.

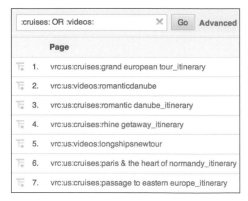

Figure 8.10 Search filter with the OR clause.

Another way to get the same results is to use the Advanced Search tool. Click the Advanced link to the right of the search box to access this tool. Then enter the appropriate phrase in the first box, click the plus (+) sign to add another search criterion, and then enter the second phrase. If you want to use an OR clause, be sure to choose the "If any criteria are met" option from the drop-down menu (**Figure 8.11**). Selecting the "If all criteria are met" option causes the text filter to be an AND clause and only returns rows that meet both criteria. Another way to build an AND clause is to use the basic search and enter AND between phrases (**Figure 8.12**). Again, note that the word AND must be uppercase or it won't work.

Figure 8.11 Advanced Search filter with OR clause.

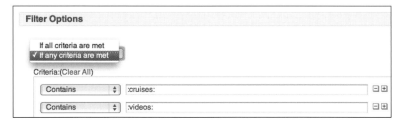

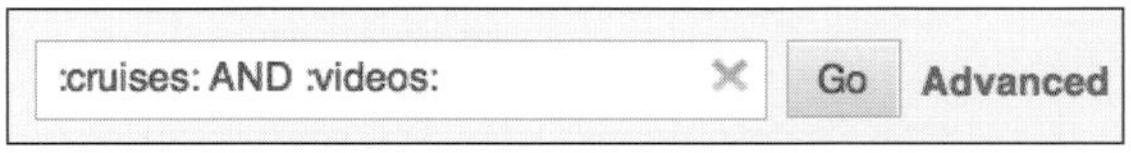

Figure 8.12 Basic search filter with AND clause.

Complex searches

Now that you have the basics, let's get more advanced. Let's build on the preceding example and assume that you want to find pages containing the phrase "cruises" OR "videos" but only if they have the word "France" as well. This gets tricky because OR and AND statements are now being mixed. Using the Advanced Search query builder, **Figure 8.13** shows how to enter this query. The lesson to be learned here is that you must combine any OR and AND statements into each row of the advanced search screen because each search criterion is also treated as an AND or OR clause.

Filter Options

Match:
If all criteria are met

Criteria:(Clear All)

Contains   :cruises: OR :videos:

Contains   france

Figure 8.13 Complex search filter with OR and AND clauses.

Filter Options

Match:
If all criteria are met

Criteria:(Clear All)

Contains   :cruises:

Does not contain   video

Figure 8.14 Complex search filter using the Does Not Contain filter.

In the advanced search area, you can also change the Criteria option, which includes a Contains and a Does Not Contain option. So if, for example, you wanted to see all "cruises" pages but exclude "videos" pages, you would enter the criteria the way you see it in **Figure 8.14**. For this instance, you need to be sure the "If all criteria are met" option is selected.

There is also a "secret" search feature that many SiteCatalyst users don't know about. It has to do with breakdown reports, which haven't been covered yet but should still make sense. Imagine you are looking at a conversion variable report that you have broken down by another conversion variable. **Figure 8.15** shows an example of a Video Name conversion variable broken down by a Day of Week conversion variable. Now, let's say that you wanted to use a search filter to see only items that mention "stateroom" and only when the day is a "Monday." Your first instinct might be to enter into the search box the search criteria in **Figure 8.16**.

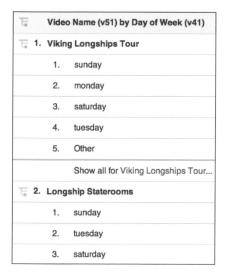

	Video Name (v51) by Day of Week (v41)
	1. **Viking Longships Tour**
1.	sunday
2.	monday
3.	saturday
4.	tuesday
5.	Other
	Show all for Viking Longships Tour...
	2. **Longship Staterooms**
1.	sunday
2.	tuesday
3.	saturday

Figure 8.15 Sample conversion variable breakdown report.

stateroom AND monday   ✕   Go   Advanced

	Video Name (v51) by Day of Week (v41)
	1. **Viking Longships Tour**
	There is no data for the selected criteria.
	2. **Longship Staterooms**
	There is no data for the selected criteria.

Figure 8.16 Incorrect attempt to filter a breakdown report.

However, as you can see, you end up with no results. The problem is that you are searching for two different criteria for two different conversion variables. When you create a breakdown report, SiteCatalyst doesn't know for which of the two conversion variables it should conduct the search filter. To solve this problem, you need to tell SiteCatalyst which search phrase goes with which variable; you do this through the Advanced Search box (**Figure 8.17**). Notice that for each row a different conversion variable is selected using the drop-down menu that appears when SiteCatalyst recognizes that you are using a breakdown report. When you run this search filter, you can see the correct results (**Figure 8.18**).

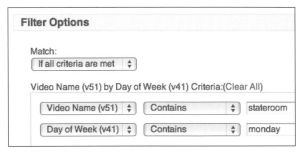

Figure 8.17 Filtering search results for a breakdown report.

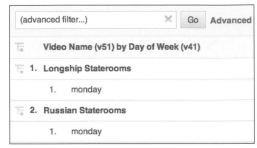

Figure 8.18 Search results for a breakdown filter.

Additional search filter tips

The preceding tips should get you through most of your Ranked report search filter needs, but here are a few additional tips to keep in mind:

▸ You can use the asterisk (*) symbol as a wildcard search.

▸ A <SPACE> is considered a valid separator in SiteCatalyst searches, so items with spaces can be a bit quirky. If you have phrases with spaces, enclose them in quotes and use OR statements. And whenever possible, avoid putting spaces in values that you think you will search on. I try to remove all spaces from page names because that is the variable on which I search the most.

▸ You can use the minus (-) sign to exclude items from search results. This has the same effect as using the Does Not Contain criterion in the advanced search area.

▸ After you've crafted your search criteria, keep in mind that you can bookmark the report or save it to a dashboard and it will retain its search filter criteria. Bookmarking prevents you from having to spend the time reentering the search criteria each time you run a report. It is also useful in cases where you finally have a complex search filter working and don't ever want to figure it out again.

Trended Reports

After mastering Ranked reports, the next step is to use Trended reports. The goal of a Trended report is to track metric trends over time for specific traffic or conversion variable values. Although Ranked reports are great for summary information, they can't tell you if metrics have been steady, increasing, or decreasing each day or week. You can see these trends when you're viewing the Metric reports discussed earlier, but those reports are for the entire population, and there are many times when you'll need to see how specific variable values trend over time. Let's look at an example. Imagine you are looking at a standard Metric report for Visits like the one shown in **Figure 8.19**.

This report shows you some general fluctuations of website Visits, but what if you needed to know how Visits were impacted by Visit Number? This is impossible to know based on this report, so you need to find a way to break it down by Visit Number. To do this, you would use a traffic or conversion variable to capture the Visit Number and then add the Visits metric to the report (**Figure 8.20**).

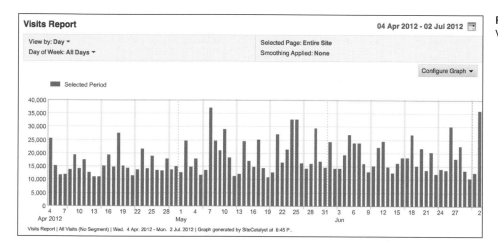

Figure 8.19 Standard Visits report.

	Visit # Grouping	Visits ▼ ⓘ	
	1. First Visit	1,058,684	64.9%
	2. Second Visit	249,086	15.3%
	3. Third Visit	109,624	6.7%
	4. Fourth Visit	58,969	3.6%
	5. Fifth Visit	35,417	2.2%

Figure 8.20 Visit Number report showing Visits.

Once you have the right variable and the right metric, all you have to do is click the Trended link in the report settings area. The report will then dynamically change to the trended view using the metric found in the leftmost column, the selected date range, and the top five variable values (**Figure 8.21**).

Now you can graphically see the breakdown of Visits by Visit Number and do some analysis to see which types of visits might be having issues. By default, the report shows the top five variable values, but you can click the Selected Items link to manually choose any five items you want to see in this report (**Figure 8.22**). If you need to trend more than five values, you can export data to Excel (see Chapter 11).

Figure 8.21 Trended Visit Number report.

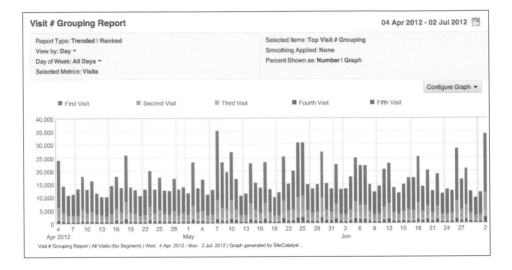

Figure 8.22 Selected Items option.

You can still take advantage of most of the report settings you learned about previously, including smoothing, viewing by day or week, viewing only a specific day, and so on, and can change the graph options as desired. And speaking of graph options, you can choose whether you want to view the raw numbers trended or see the percentages trended (which I prefer). Choose Show Numbers or Show Percentages at the bottom of the Configure Graph options to change the results displayed in the preceding report (**Figure 8.23**).

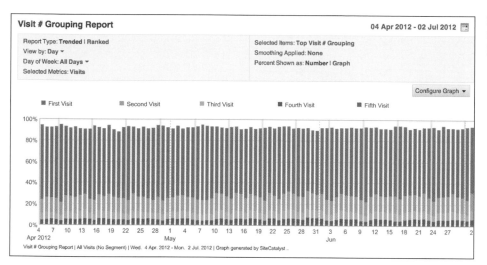

Figure 8.23 Trended report showing percentages.

Breakdown Reports

Web analysts often need to look at relationships between data points to get a full picture of what is taking place. In SiteCatalyst, you can often break down one report by another report to get a deeper understanding of the data. SiteCatalyst is not a relational system that will let you infinitely break down data, but it does allow you two levels of breakdowns. If you require more breakdowns, Adobe offers a more advanced product (Adobe Discover) that provides unlimited breakdown capabilities. This section explores what you can do with SiteCatalyst using breakdown reports called Correlations and Subrelations.

Traffic Correlations

A Traffic Correlation report in SiteCatalyst breaks down one traffic variable by another traffic variable. If you have populated a value in two different traffic variables on the same page, it is possible to see one broken down by the other. For example, let's say that you've passed a Page Name value on each page to the Page Name traffic variable. By default, SiteCatalyst captures the visitor's Browser Height in a traffic variable. Therefore, you can easily see the Browser Height for each Page Name by enabling a traffic correlation between these two traffic variables. To enable traffic data correlations, you use the administration console and select the traffic variables you want to correlate (**Figure 8.24**).

When you "enable" a traffic correlation, SiteCatalyst establishes a data table dedicated to the traffic variables you've specified. After the traffic correlation has been created, you can access it by viewing either of the Traffic Variable reports associated with that correlation and clicking the breakdown icon (▥) (**Figure 8.25**).

▶ **TIP** *In addition to clicking the breakdown icon, it is also possible to correlate traffic variables by clicking on the value (in blue) or by clicking the Correlation Filter link in the report settings area.*

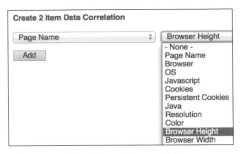

Figure 8.24 Creating traffic correlations.

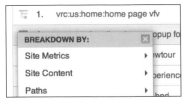

Figure 8.25 A correlation icon appears next to each row.

Figure 8.26 Sample Correlation report; Page Name correlated to Browser Height.

Correlation Summary	Page Views	
Total	276,932	
Page Name = vrc:us:home:home page vfv	18,519	6.69%

Enter term to filter data   [Go] Advanced

	Browser Height	Page Views	
1.	400 to 499	3,602	19.5%
2.	600 to 699	3,454	18.7%
3.	300 to 399	2,245	12.1%
4.	500 to 599	1,828	9.9%

▶**TIP** *Notice that the intersection of any two values are (or should be) identical in either report (Figure 8.27). At the intersection of the Page Name "vrc:us:home:home page vfv" and the Browser Height of "400 to 499" in both reports, the value is the same, "3,602." The reason is that these reports are simply reverse breakdowns of each other.*

In this example, if you clicked the breakdown icon next to a specific Page Name, you'd see a report that shows the various Browser Heights for the selected Page Name and their associated percentages (**Figure 8.26**).

However, when you create a traffic correlation, you're able to see two new reports, not just one, which sometimes confuses SiteCatalyst users. In Figure 8.26, you see a report showing Browser Heights for a specific Page, but using the same traffic correlation, you can also see the converse, which in this case is a report that shows all Page Names for a specific Browser Height (**Figure 8.27**).

There are a few detailed items that you need to remember when it comes to traffic correlations:

▶ It is recommended that you correlate traffic variables that are both present in the same SiteCatalyst image request (normally a Page View). Because traffic variables don't retain their values beyond one page, SiteCatalyst can only correlate traffic variables that are present at the same time. If only one traffic variable has a value, you'll see an "Unspecified" value in the Traffic Correlation report.

- ▶ Traffic Correlation reports can show only the Page Views metric.

- ▶ Traffic correlations can be enabled with many standard traffic variables out of the box, such as Browser, OS, Resolution, and more.

- ▶ Any traffic correlations for a traffic variable will also apply to any SAINT classification for that traffic variable.

- ▶ Traffic data correlations come in several flavors, such as 2-item correlations and 5-item correlations. You can enable up to 15 2-item traffic correlations in the administration console. Although a bit more advanced, 5-item traffic and 20-item correlations can be used to provide many more traffic variable breakdowns but have an additional cost.

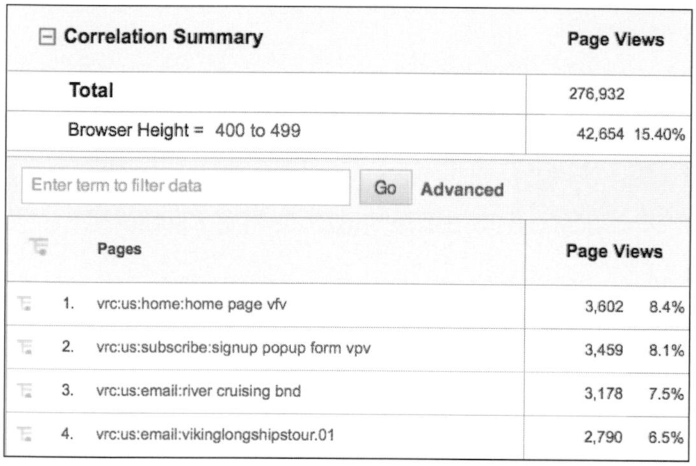

⊟ **Correlation Summary**	**Page Views**	
Total	276,932	
Browser Height = 400 to 499	42,654	15.40%

	Pages	**Page Views**	
1.	vrc:us:home:home page vfv	3,602	8.4%
2.	vrc:us:subscribe:signup popup form vpv	3,459	8.1%
3.	vrc:us:email:river cruising bnd	3,178	7.5%
4.	vrc:us:email:vikinglongshipstour.01	2,790	6.5%

Figure 8.27 Sample Correlation report; Browser Height correlated to Page Name.

Conversion Variable Subrelations

In the previous section, you learned how traffic correlations can be used to break down one traffic variable by another traffic variable. But what if you want to break down a SiteCatalyst conversion variable by another conversion variable? This works in a similar manner to traffic correlations, but SiteCatalyst calls these breakdowns *conversion subrelations*.

Let's look at an example of conversion variable subrelations. Imagine that Greco, Inc. has a website that is trying to get visitors to sign up for a subscription. During the sign-up process, the site captures the city they live in and their age in two different conversion variables. In the analysis, the company wants to see the city of all visitors subscribing broken down by their age. To do this, all you'd need to do is open the City Conversion Variable report, click the breakdown icon for the desired city, and choose the Age report (**Figure 8.28**). You'll then see a subrelation report (**Figure 8.29**).

Figure 8.28 Conversion subrelation icon.

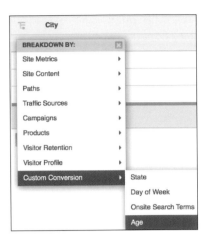

	City by Age	Subscriptions ▾	
	1. Chicago	2,453	
	1. 18 Years Old	356	14.5%
	2. 21 Years Old	308	12.5%
	3. 22 Years Old	270	11.0%
	4. 24 Years Old	209	8.5%
	5. 23 Years Old	158	6.5%

Figure 8.29 Sample subrelation report.

One of the ways that conversion variable subrelations are different from traffic correlations is that you cannot enable a subrelation between just two conversion variables. A conversion variable can have one of the following types of subrelations:

▸ **Full Subrelations.** A conversion variable can be broken down by all other conversion variables.

▸ **Basic Subrelations.** A conversion variable can be broken down by any other conversion variable that has Full Subrelations.

▸ **No Subrelations.** A conversion variable cannot be broken down by any other conversion variable (rarely used).

Therefore, conversion variable subrelations is an "all or nothing" proposition. The good news is that if you are using SiteCatalyst v15 or later, all conversion variables come with Full Subrelations. If you are using an earlier version of SiteCatalyst, the number of conversion variables for which you can enable Full Subrelations is specified in your SiteCatalyst contract. However, the predefined conversion variables for products and campaigns will always have Full Subrelations enabled regardless of which SiteCatalyst version you are using.

Another way that conversion subrelations are different from traffic correlations has to do with the persistent nature of conversion variables. Recall that because traffic variables do not persist values from one page to the next, traffic variables added to traffic correlations must be set on the same image request (page) to ensure that data will exist. However, because conversion variables persist their values, subrelations will work even if values passed to the two conversion variables being subrelated occur on different pages. In the preceding example, the website could have captured the city on the first page of the visit and not captured age until the tenth page of the visit. As long as both conversion variables being subrelated have values prior to the point that a success event takes place, Subrelation reports will have data for each variable. But if one or both of the subrelated conversion variables had no value at the time of the chosen success event, you would simply see the None row in the Subrelation report.

As was the case with traffic correlations, if you have a classification enabled on a conversion variable that has Full Subrelations, all classifications of that variable will also have Full Subrelations. If you are using an earlier version of SiteCatalyst, this may be another reason to use classifications, because it allows you to create more breakdown reports without having to pay additional money to enable Full Subrelations on more conversion variables.

Pathing Reports

Pathing reports show a sequence in which values are collected in a SiteCatalyst traffic variable. The preceding Metric, Ranked, and breakdown reports show aggregated data, but there is no notion of the order in which values were collected. Therefore, Pathing reports were created for situations in which knowing the sequence is important. Pathing reports have basic and advanced uses; both are discussed in this section.

The most basic use of pathing is to see how often website visitors go from Page A to Page B or Page C on your site. By having even the most basic SiteCatalyst code on your site pages, you'll be able to see several different Pathing reports right out of the box. Pathing is commonly used to analyze key website process flows in hopes of identifying opportunities for improvement. For example, you may notice that an unusually high number of site visits show pathing exits after visitors view the shopping cart page. After you have several months' worth of data, you should be able to baseline your standard exit rates and then test changes to key pages and see if these changes have a positive or negative effect.

Types of Pathing Reports

Many Pathing reports are available in SiteCatalyst, but those discussed in the following sections are the ones I use the most.

Next [*Variable*] Flow report

The Next Flow report allows you to see two levels of pathing from the selected variable value so you can visually see the next two values collected after the selected value. **Figure 8.30** shows a Next Flow report for Pages. The thickness of the bars is representative of the path percentages. It is also possible to see a Previous Flow report that starts with one value and works its way backward two levels.

Figure 8.30 Sample Next Page Flow report.

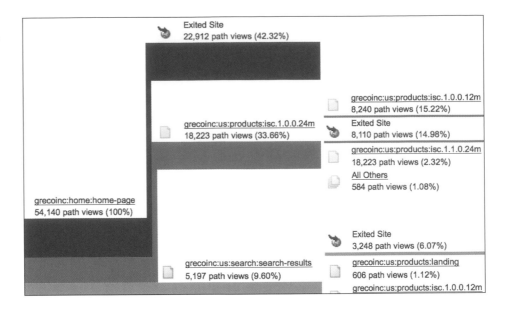

Fallout report

The Fallout report allows you to see how often a visitor's path included one value and then eventually another value. I say eventually because Fallout reports do not have to see values immediately after the previous value as in a Next Flow report. The variable values you add to Fallout reports are called *checkpoints*, and the report identifies cases where visitors hit those checkpoints in the order you specify. For example, a visitor could receive value A, then values X, Y, Z, and then value B. In this case, the visitor would still qualify for a checkpoint of value A to value B because both values were collected in the correct sequence in the same visit. This concept has confused Site-Catalyst users over the years because the report looks like it is a linear process. Another important aspect to remember about Fallout reports (and Pathing reports in general) is that they are all visit-based, so you will not see any Pathing reports across multiple website visits.

Figure 8.31 shows an example of a Page Fallout report for Greco, Inc. In this report, you can see that of all the visitors viewing the Greco, Inc. home page, 33.7% eventually reached the products landing page. These visits could have been directly from the home page or many clicks after the home page was viewed. Of those who viewed the home page *and* the products landing page, 15.2% went on to also view the "isc.1.0.0.12m" product page. Note the use of *and* because when you analyze the third level of this Fallout report, those visitors who viewed the third checkpoint had to have seen both of the previous two checkpoint items (in the correct order). For example, if visitors went from the home page directly to the "isc.1.0.0.12m" product page, they would not qualify to be included in this Fallout report because they did not see the products landing page in

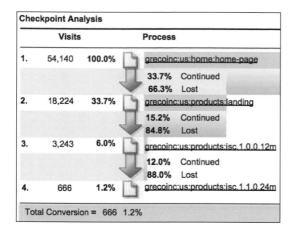

Figure 8.31 Sample Fallout report.

between those two steps. If you removed the products landing page from this Fallout report, you would be guaranteed to see either the same number of "isc.1.0.0.12m" product page views or more because you would include those visitors who saw the home page and eventually reached this page.

Note another detail in the Fallout reports: the percentages listed next to each checkpoint. These percentages show you the percent of visits from the first checkpoint that made it to each subsequent checkpoint. In this case, you can see that approximately 6% of visits that saw the home page made it to the "isc.1.0.0.12m" page, which is simply a division of the checkpoint number and the initial checkpoint value.

To add items to the Checkpoint Canvas of the Fallout report, select the variable for which you want to see fallout, and then choose the Fallout report from the menu. You can then launch the checkpoint screen and begin to add items to the canvas (**Figure 8.32**). The number of items you can add to the Checkpoint Canvas is limited in SiteCatalyst, but you can add as many as you'd like to the canvas if you use the Adobe Discover product.

Define Checkpoints

Order the checkpoints you would like to use in this analysis by dragging pages from the panel on the left to the 'Checkpoint Canvas" on the right. You can also drag and drop within the Canvas to reorder the checkpoints.

Available Items

Search All Available

[Search] [Clear]

Select from Available

- vrc:us:home:home page vfv
- vrc:us:subscribe:signup popup form vpv
- vrc:us:videos:thevikingexperience
- vrc:us:email:river cruising bnd
- vrc:us:videos:longshipsnewtour

Checkpoint Canvas

Begin with All Site Visits

vrc:us:home:home page vfv

vrc:us:specialoffers:rivercrui...

Figure 8.32 Adding checkpoints to Fallout reports.

Pathfinder report

The Pathfinder report is somewhat similar to the Fallout report but allows you to specify more granular criteria for very detailed analysis. For example, in the Pathfinder report, you can see path flows with or without exits, add wildcards, include only visits where visitors entered on a specific page, and so on. **Figure 8.33** shows the types of options available.

Figure 8.33 Pathfinder canvas options.

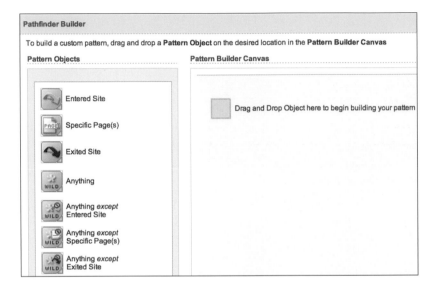

Unlike the Fallout report, the results of a Pathfinder report show a series of path views that match your criteria and the percentage that each represents of all path views. Normally, these percentages are very low, but they can help you see how often a specific scenario is taking place. For example, let's say that your boss wants to see where visitors are going from the home page, but also requires the following criteria:

▶ She only wants to see cases where visitors entered on the home page because she doesn't want to include data when visitors went back to the home page at some point in the visit.

▶ She only wants to see where visitors went on the website and doesn't care about how often they exited the website from the home page.

In this scenario, neither the Next Flow nor Fallout reports will help because both will contain exits and instances when visitors went back to the home page within a visit. It is for these specific types of pathing situations that a Pathfinder report was built. To produce the required results, you would build the Pathfinder canvas shown in **Figure 8.34**. These settings meet the requirements because the report will include only entries to the home page and will exclude exits. **Figure 8.35** shows the results of running this report.

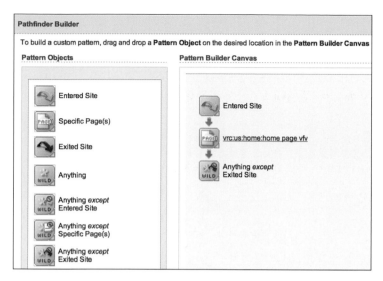

Figure 8.34 Sample Pathfinder canvas.

PathFinder Report

Filter Options: Edit Filter		Percent Shown as: **Number I Graph**	

	Site Path	Path Views	%
1.	Entered Site vrc:us:home:home page vfv vrc:us:home:find a cruise	1,794	27.2%
2.	Entered Site vrc:us:home:home page vfv vrc:us:videos:holiday cruises	534	8.1%
3.	Entered Site vrc:us:home:home page vfv vrc:us:brochures:standalone form vfv	346	5.3%
4.	Entered Site vrc:us:home:home page vfv vrc:us:video:longship-christening	345	5.2%

Figure 8.35 Sample Pathfinder report.

Due to its many options, the Pathfinder report requires that you experiment and try different configurations. But over time you'll learn which use cases are best suited for Pathfinder reports.

Summary report

Another popular Pathing report is the Summary report. This report shows you a summary overview of any value within a report that has pathing enabled. On this summary page, you can see all key metrics for the selected value. The most common use of this report is within page pathing where you are looking at all statistics for a specific page. If you have stakeholders who "own" pages, they will love this report. **Figure 8.36** shows an example of a Page Summary report.

Figure 8.36 Sample
Page Summary report.

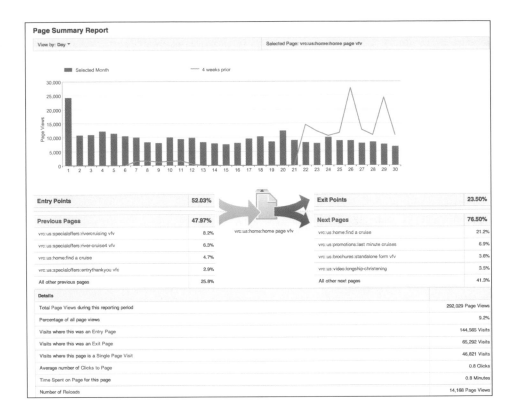

Other Uses of Pathing Reports

One of the most disappointing aspects of SiteCatalyst implementations I encounter is
when I see clients using the preceding Pathing reports only for pages or sections. One
of the advantages of SiteCatalyst compared to other web analytics tools is that you
can enable pathing capabilities on any traffic variable. Although the examples you just
reviewed were page-centric, your use of pathing should not be limited to just pages.
Take a step back for a moment and think about what you just learned about pathing:
Pathing is nothing more than SiteCatalyst's way of storing the sequence in which values
are passed to a traffic variable. In the preceding examples, that traffic variable just happened to be the Page Name traffic variable, but it didn't have to be.

For example, let's say that one of Greco, Inc.'s subsidiaries is a finance-related media
site and its goal is to increase page views so it can increase paid advertising revenue.
It turns out that people are willing to pay top dollar for paid display ads served on
the Apple (AAPL) ticker symbol page. Unfortunately, many of the other ticker symbol
pages don't command such a premium. Therefore, Greco, Inc. wants to find a way to
identify which ticker symbols are similar to AAPL on its site so it can increase overall

advertising revenues. The first thought might be to use page pathing because the ticker symbol is contained in each page name. But it has thousands of pages on its site, and its Page Pathing report is difficult to navigate. Instead, the company would rather see Pathing reports that just include quote pages (which have one ticker symbol per page). This would help create an uncluttered view of how visitors navigate between different ticker symbols. To do this, Greco, Inc. can capture the ticker symbol associated with each quote page on its website in a custom Ticker Symbol traffic variable. Once this data is being collected, pathing can be enabled (this is done by an account manager or Client-Care) to see a report (**Figure 8.37**).

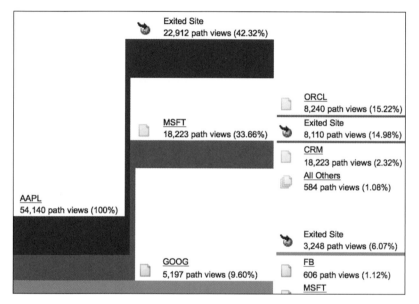

Figure 8.37 Ticker Symbol Pathing report.

Armed with this information, Greco, Inc. can show its advertising clients that the next best thing to AAPL would be ADBE, GOOG, MSFT, ORCL, CRM, and FB. This information might allow Greco, Inc. to charge almost as much for these ticker symbols as it does for AAPL. As a web analyst, this report is an easy way to answer a business question and avoid the clutter associated with all of the pages in the website that had nothing to do with the analysis at hand. Also, keep in mind that this is only one of the many Pathing reports available for ticker symbols because every traffic variable that has pathing enabled gets every Pathing report. The company could have just as easily used a Fallout or Pathfinder report using the preceding ticker symbols. This is just one example of how you can use pathing to answer business questions that are unrelated to pages. In subsequent chapters, you'll see a few more of these examples.

Here are some important details related to pathing that I've learned over the years:

▶ Pathing reports do not span multiple visits. They report on only one website session.

▶ Pathing reports consider that a path has changed only when a new value is passed to the traffic variable. This is important because if you accidentally use the same page name for two different pages, you will not be able to see instances where visitors went from one page to the other.

▶ Pathing reports are not available in DataWarehouse or ReportBuilder.

▶ As mentioned in Chapter 6, you cannot view pathing on a classification of a traffic variable in SiteCatalyst (although you can in Adobe Discover). Therefore, you should take this into account when you're determining whether to capture data values directly into a traffic variable or a classification.

▶ Pathing reports cannot span across multiple SiteCatalyst report suites, so if you want to see pathing for different sites, you need to have a common tag on pages of both sites (multi-suite tagging).

Conversion Funnel Reports

Conversion Funnel reports calculate conversion metrics between success events, provide a high-level view of how your website is performing, and provide the ability to filter performance by conversion variable values.

There are three ways to create Conversion Funnel reports. You'll find three links to Conversion Funnel reports in the Site Metrics menu—Purchases, Shopping Cart, and Custom Metrics. The only difference among the three links is which success events default in the conversion funnel, but these can be changed so it doesn't really matter which one you choose. On the Conversion Funnel screen, click the Selected Events link to access a screen where you can choose the success events you want to see in your Conversion Funnel report (**Figure 8.38**). After selecting your metrics, you'll see the Conversion Funnel report (**Figure 8.39**). In this report, you can see each of the selected success events and the conversion percentage between each. Here you can see that 21.3% of Cart Additions lead to a Checkout, and 55.5% of Checkouts turn into an Order. If desired, you can also show total Orders, Revenue, and Units. Below the funnel, the various conversion metrics for the elements in the conversion funnel are displayed.

However, one key point is important to consider when you're looking at conversion funnels. Many SiteCatalyst clients think that their Fallout reports for the shopping cart pages should mirror what they see in a Conversion Funnel report. Unfortunately, this will never happen due to the many ways these reports differ. Unlike Pathing Fallout reports, Conversion Funnel reports are simply aggregations of success events and are

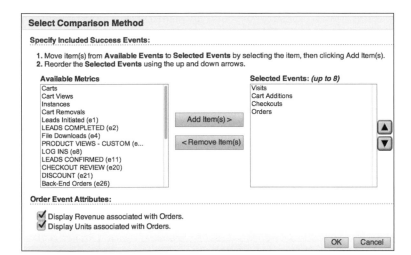

Figure 8.38 Select Conversion Funnel metrics.

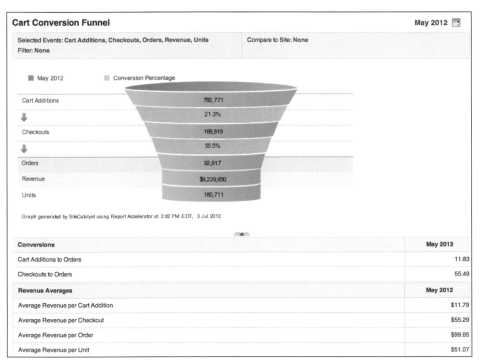

Figure 8.39 Sample Conversion Funnel report.

not tied to individuals or cookie IDs. Even though the Conversion Funnel report looks like a Fallout report, it is different in that each of the items in the funnel do not have to take place sequentially or within the same visit. For example, a visitor could have come to your website on June 6, added something to the shopping cart (Cart Addition), and then left. The same visitor could have then come back a week later and checked out with the item previously added to the shopping cart (Checkout). If the Conversion Funnel report you were looking at encompassed this two-week range (or longer), this visitor would be counted as one Cart Addition and one Checkout in the conversion funnel.

Now, let's contrast this with a Pathing Fallout report. You could build a Fallout report that has the pages associated with these same shopping cart pages, but the results would be very different because Fallout reports are visit-based. This means that the preceding visitor would have a view of the Cart Addition page but not the Checkout page because that happened in a subsequent visit.

One of the advantages of the Conversion Funnel report is the ease in which you can filter it by conversion variables. Once you've learned what you want from your general conversion funnel, you can click the Filter link and choose a specific value from a predefined or custom conversion variable. In this case, let's select Search Engine and filter this conversion funnel by cases where the Search Engine equals "Google" (**Figure 8.40**). Doing so refreshes the conversion funnel to show only cases where selected success events took place when the predefined Search Engine conversion variable was equal to "Google" (**Figure 8.41**).

You can then compare this filtered version of the conversion funnel to the unfiltered version. For example, you can see that the general Revenue per Order rate is $99.65, whereas the same rate for Google visits is $95.95. Both versions of this report can be added to a SiteCatalyst dashboard for comparison purposes. You can filter conversion funnels by any conversion variable, but keep in mind that it will show you success event values only where that conversion value was set with or prior to the success event taking place.

Figure 8.40 Filtering conversion funnels.

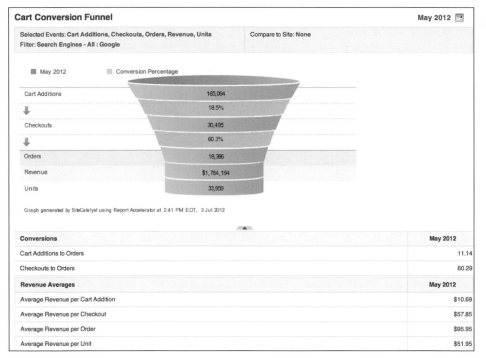

Figure 8.41 A conversion funnel filtered by Search Engine.

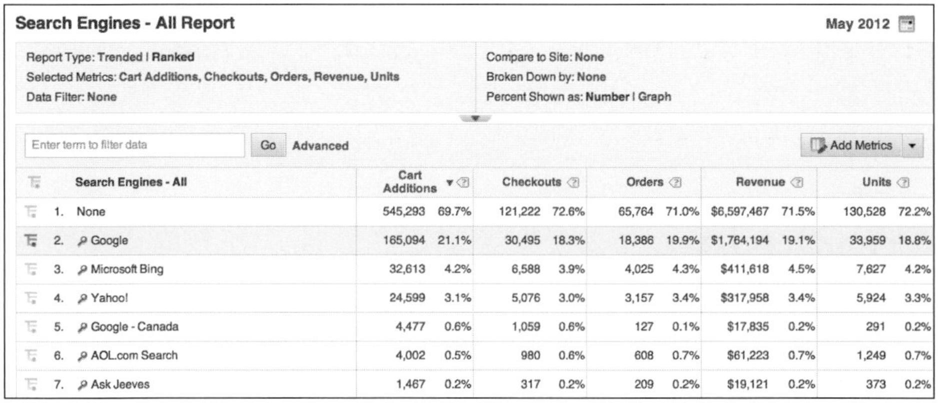

Figure 8.42 Sample Ranked report.

The one downside of Conversion Funnel reports is that when you filter, you can filter on only one value per conversion variable. This can be extremely limiting from a web analysis perspective. For this reason, I don't use conversion funnels very often. Instead, you can use a Conversion Variable Ranked report and add the same success events you would add to the conversion funnel (**Figure 8.42**). Doing so allows you to see those same success event metrics for all conversion variable values instead of just one. Notice in the highlighted row the same numbers for each success event that you saw in the conversion funnel, only this time they are shown horizontally instead of vertically. You can also see similar metrics for other search engines in the same view. The only content you lose with this approach is the individual conversion metrics shown at the bottom of the Conversion Funnel report. But you can create these as global calculated metrics and add them to the Ranked report as well (**Figure 8.43**). This report duplicates the Average Revenue per Order ratio you saw at the bottom of the Conversion Funnel report. As expected, you can see the same $95.95 value you saw earlier when you were looking at the Google row, but now you can see the same metric for other search engines as well, providing you with greater context. Alternatively, you can export this Ranked report to Excel and use formulas in Excel to calculate the same conversion metrics found at the bottom of the Conversion Funnel report.

However, if all you need are topline metrics or metrics filtered by one conversion variable value, Conversion Funnel reports look very cool and go over well with executives.

Figure 8.43 Sample Ranked report with conversion calculated metrics.

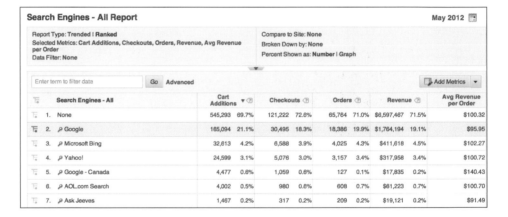

Search Engines - All	Cart Additions ▼ ②		Checkouts ②		Orders ②		Revenue ②		Avg Revenue per Order
1. 🔎 None	545,293	69.7%	121,222	72.6%	65,784	71.0%	$6,597,467	71.5%	$100.32
2. 🔎 Google	165,094	21.1%	30,495	18.3%	18,386	19.9%	$1,764,194	19.1%	$95.95
3. 🔎 Microsoft Bing	32,613	4.2%	6,588	3.9%	4,025	4.3%	$411,618	4.5%	$102.27
4. 🔎 Yahoo!	24,599	3.1%	5,076	3.0%	3,157	3.4%	$317,958	3.4%	$100.72
5. 🔎 Google - Canada	4,477	0.6%	1,059	0.6%	127	0.1%	$17,835	0.2%	$140.43
6. 🔎 AOL.com Search	4,002	0.5%	980	0.6%	608	0.7%	$61,223	0.7%	$100.70
7. 🔎 Ask Jeeves	1,467	0.2%	317	0.2%	209	0.2%	$19,121	0.2%	$91.49

Conclusion

In this chapter, you learned all you need to know about creating and running reports in SiteCatalyst. Whether your analysis requires the use of Ranked, Trended, Pathing, or Conversion Funnel reports, you have more than enough options from which to choose. In the next chapter, you'll learn how to manipulate, download, and share these reports so you can start proliferating web analytics data throughout your organization.

## CHAPTER 9

Using the SiteCatalyst Interface

Over the years, the SiteCatalyst end-user interface has been through several iterations. In the more recent versions, many of the common tasks needed by web analysts have been streamlined and improved upon. Web analysts spend a lot of time within the SiteCatalyst interface, so it is beneficial to understand how it works and optimize its usage. I won't cover all aspects of the SiteCatalyst interface (which are quite extensive) in this chapter, but I'll discuss the most important details you should know about the interface and mention some time-saving tips along the way.

General Interface Layout

▶TIP *If for one reason or another you don't like the way your Site-Catalyst administrator has customized your menus, a setting under Favorites - Report Settings allows you to use the SiteCatalyst default menu structure.*

SiteCatalyst's layout, for the most part, does not change throughout a session. This layout has key quadrants that perform specific functions (**Figure 9.1**):

▶ **Top menu (purple).** The topmost menu is used to access other Adobe Digital Marketing Suite products, Favorites, the Admin area, Community links, and Help.

▶ **Report suite and segment selector (orange).** Below the top menu is the area where you choose which report suite and segment you want to use. Report suites normally mirror different websites or portions of websites. Segments allow you to filter data and are covered in the next chapter.

▶ **Menu toolbar (turquoise).** Below the report suite selector is the report toolbar, which provides easy access to actions often taken related to reports.

▶ **Report area (blue).** The report area is where the real action happens. This area will dynamically switch between Metric, Ranked, Trended, Fallout, and Conversion Funnel reports.

▶ **Left navigation menu (green).** The left navigation menu is the main way to access all of your SiteCatalyst reports. Choosing a menu item shows a fly-out submenu where you can access reports. Administrators can customize this menu, so yours may look slightly different.

Figure 9.1 SiteCatalyst interface layout.

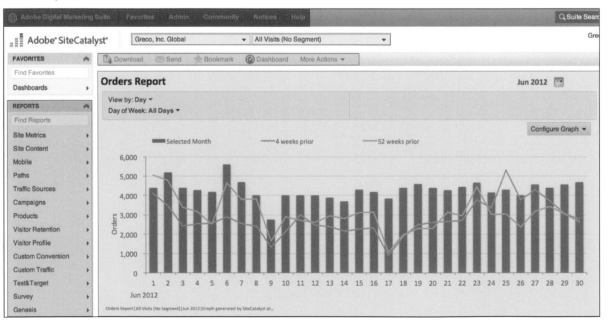

Report Toolbar

In Chapter 8, I discussed most of the settings related to configuring SiteCatalyst reports. In this section, I'll review what you can do with reports after you've created them. For example, let's assume that you're curious to see how often visitors reaching your website from various search engines end up using the onsite search feature. To see this data, you run the Search Engines report, add Visits, the Onsite Searches success event, and a calculated metric that divides these two metrics (**Figure 9.2**).

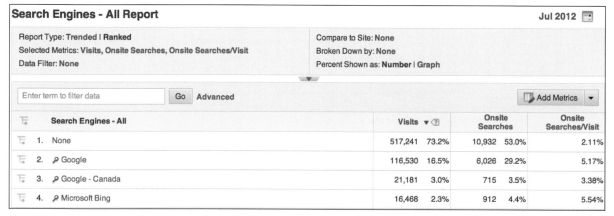

Figure 9.2 Sample SiteCatalyst report.

Now let's look at all you can do with this report.

Download Report

Clicking the Download button allows you to save the current report to your computer in one of a few different formats (**Figure 9.3**).

Figure 9.3 Download report.

Using the downloadable report format buttons shown in Figure 9.3 will download a report with the number of rows currently visible on the screen. If you want to download more data, click the Advanced Download Options link where you can specify the number of rows you want to download. Note that each file format has its own size limits:

- ▶ PDF files can contain a maximum of 500 rows.

- ▶ CSV files can contain a maximum of 50,000 rows.

- ▶ Excel files can contain a maximum of 500 rows.

- ▶ Word files can contain a maximum of 500 rows.

For the most part, I use CSV files because they allow the most data to be downloaded and can be opened in Microsoft Excel.

Send Report

Clicking the Send button allows you to e-mail the current report to yourself or co-workers (**Figure 9.4**). The Send screen consists of options that are similar to those of Download but includes a few additional options:

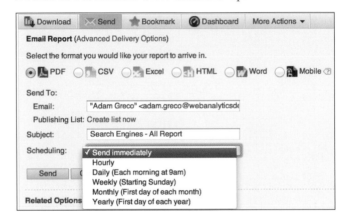

Figure 9.4 Send report via e-mail.

- ▶ **HTML format.** Provides a version of the report in HTML for use on intranets or websites.

- ▶ **Mobile format.** Provides a text-only version of the report that can be more easily viewed on mobile devices.

- ▶ **Publishing Lists.** Are a cool way to send different data for the same report to different groups of people and is explained later in this chapter.

- ▶ **Scheduling.** Provides a drop-down box as a quick way to schedule a report for recurring delivery each hour, day, week, month, or year. Note that under the Advanced Delivery Options area, your scheduling options are extremely granular (**Figure 9.5**).

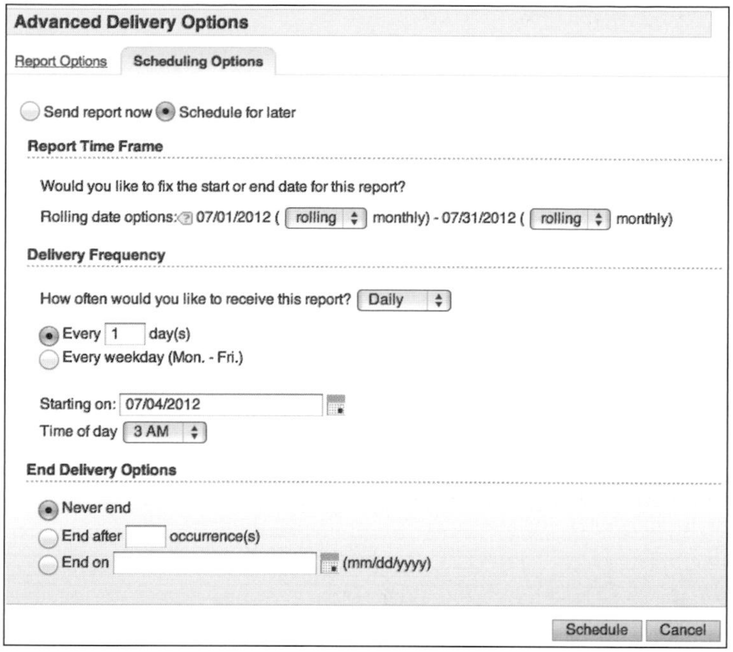

Advanced Delivery Options

Report Options   **Scheduling Options**

◯ Send report now ⦿ Schedule for later

Report Time Frame

Would you like to fix the start or end date for this report?

Rolling date options:⑦ 07/01/2012 ([rolling ⬍] monthly) - 07/31/2012 ([rolling ⬍] monthly)

Delivery Frequency

How often would you like to receive this report? [Daily ⬍]

⦿ Every [1] day(s)
◯ Every weekday (Mon. - Fri.)

Starting on: [07/04/2012] ▦
Time of day [3 AM ⬍]

End Delivery Options

⦿ Never end
◯ End after [   ] occurrence(s)
◯ End on [   ] ▦ (mm/dd/yyyy)

[Schedule] [Cancel]

Figure 9.5 Advanced Scheduling Options.

Avoid Being a Report Spammer

Once you start scheduling daily or weekly reports to be sent to co-workers, you might begin to worry about being labeled as a report spammer. Here are a few tips to help you avoid this reputation. Only send recurring reports to those who really need it. You can always send a one-off report as needed or forward a report you have received. Another best practice is to update the Subject line of the report to use a common term (e.g., ANALYTICS) that can easily be filtered by an e-mail program. This will allow your end users to place recurring reports into a folder to be reviewed later. Most important, be sure to teach your end users how to easily remove themselves from any recurring report. A link is embedded in each recurring report that your users can click to stop receiving that particular recurring report (**Figure 9.6**).

> **Delivery Frequency:** Occurs every hour effective 2012-07-03 at 8 PM. To cancel automatic delivery of this report click here
> (Note: This will not delete your bookmark)

Figure 9.6 Recurring report unsubscribe link.

Bookmark Report

Clicking the Bookmark button allows you to save the current report, similar to the way you would bookmark a website in an internet browser (**Figure 9.7**). The Bookmark screen provides a way to name your bookmark and specify a folder location. Bookmarks can be shared with other users by making them public. You can also have a bookmark open as the first report you'll see when you log into SiteCatalyst. If you are a Microsoft Windows user, you can add SiteCatalyst bookmarks to a Direct Access menu in the Windows Start bar.

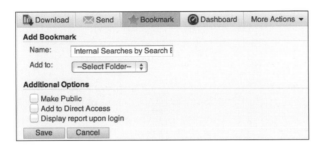

Figure 9.7 Bookmark report.

Add Report to Dashboard

The Dashboard button allows you to add the current report to a SiteCatalyst dashboard. Dashboards are collections of reports that provide a snapshot of activity taking place on your website. You can create dashboards in SiteCatalyst and Microsoft Excel, or export and report on SiteCatalyst data using other third-party tools like Tableau or Cognos. The Dashboard button in the report toolbar adds the current report only to a native SiteCatalyst dashboard. When you click the button, a screen appears that allows you to name the report and select the dashboard to which it should be added (**Figure 9.8**). In this example a brand new Search Engine Dashboard was created, so this will be its first report. Notice that date range options are available to you prior to adding the report to the dashboard. Date ranges can be "fixed" or "rolling." A *fixed* start date forces the report to always use the same start date; a *rolling* start date causes the report start date to change based on the reporting period. For example, a rolling monthly start date would be July 1, 2012 for the month of July and then change to August 1, 2012 on the first day of August, whereas a fixed start date would also retain July 1, 2012 in August.

Another tricky item to keep in mind is that the rolling setting is directly tied to the selected date range used in the calendar shown on the screen. For example, if today is July 3, 2012 and you change the date range in the report to use the Last 7 Days preset, an updated version of the report in Figure 9.8 would look like the report in **Figure 9.9**.

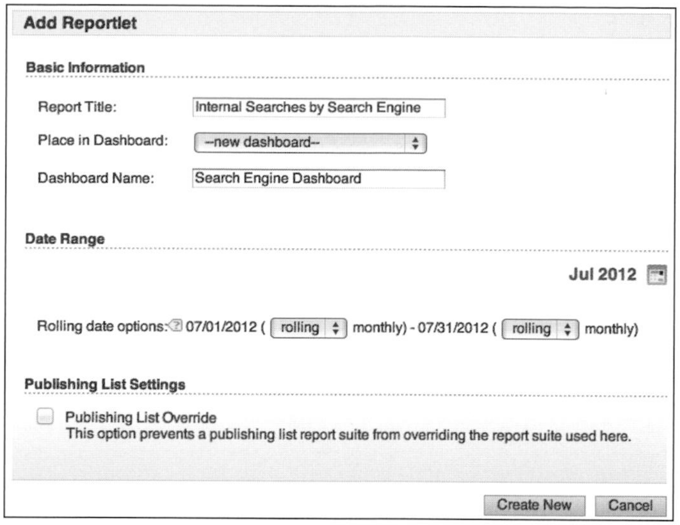

Add Reportlet

Basic Information

Report Title: Internal Searches by Search Engine

Place in Dashboard: --new dashboard--

Dashboard Name: Search Engine Dashboard

Date Range

Jul 2012

Rolling date options: 07/01/2012 (rolling ‡ monthly) - 07/31/2012 (rolling ‡ monthly)

Publishing List Settings

☐ Publishing List Override
This option prevents a publishing list report suite from overriding the report suite used here.

Create New   Cancel

Figure 9.8 Add a report to a dashboard.

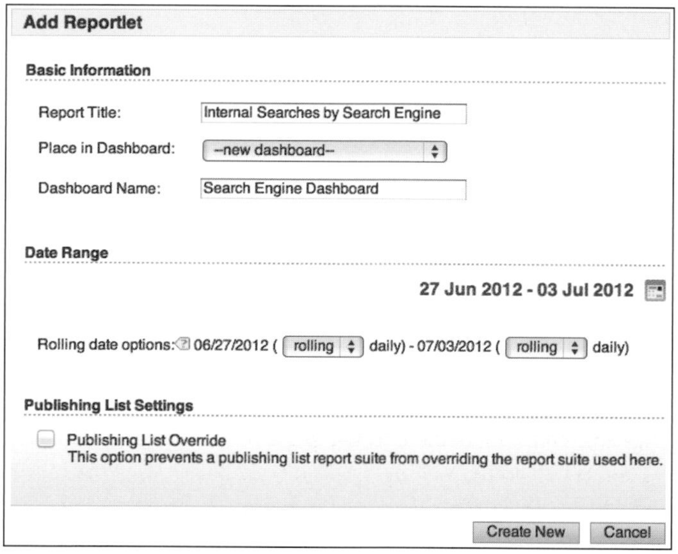

Add Reportlet

Basic Information

Report Title: Internal Searches by Search Engine

Place in Dashboard: --new dashboard--

Dashboard Name: Search Engine Dashboard

Date Range

27 Jun 2012 - 03 Jul 2012

Rolling date options: 06/27/2012 (rolling ‡ daily) - 07/03/2012 (rolling ‡ daily)

Publishing List Settings

☐ Publishing List Override
This option prevents a publishing list report suite from overriding the report suite used here.

Create New   Cancel

Figure 9.9 Updated Add report to dashboard screen using the Last 7 Days preset.

The date range has changed to the last seven days, and instead of rolling monthly, it is now set to roll daily. Making this change results in the report start date and end date rolling forward one day with each passing day. So if this report was added to the dashboard on July 3, it would show data from 6/27/12 to 7/3/12, but on July 4, the data would shift and show data from 6/28/12 to 7/4/12. This takes a bit of practice to get used to, so be mindful of these date range settings.

Working with dashboards

After you've added the preceding report to your new dashboard, you need to configure it. You can access the dashboard from the top navigation Favorites area or from the Favorites area in the left navigation menu. When you access this dashboard for the first time, it will expect you to configure and save it. You first need to choose a layout, which will determine how many reports can be placed on the dashboard (**Figure 9.10**). Then you can drag your new report onto the dashboard canvas (**Figure 9.11**).

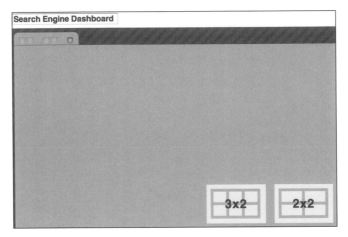

Figure 9.10 Choose a dashboard layout.

Figure 9.11 Drag the dashboard contents onto the dashboard canvas.

From here you can choose to see the table, the graph, or both and how many lines of data you want to see. You can then save the dashboard, and when you open it again, you'll see your completed dashboard (**Figure 9.12**). If you ever want to relaunch the original report, you can do so directly from the dashboard by simply clicking on its title. Also, now that your dashboard exists, anytime you create new reports you'll see the Search Engine Dashboard as a potential location onto which to place them.

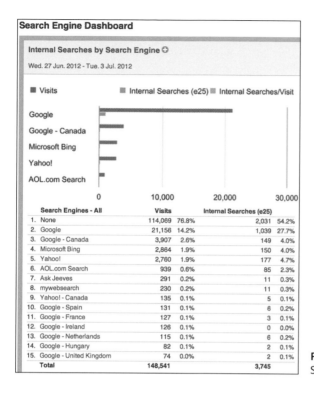

Figure 9.12 A completed SiteCatalyst dashboard.

Another cool aspect of dashboards is that you can easily change the date of all reports on the dashboard by just clicking on the calendar at the top right of the dashboard. However, the next time you log in, the dashboard will revert back to the originally chosen time frame (taking into account fixed or rolling settings). To permanently change the date settings, you must enter Layout mode for the dashboard and resave it.

Other key settings for reports added to dashboards are Report Suite and Segment. Reports added to a dashboard default to the report suite and segment that were associated with them when they were added to the dashboard. However, if while looking at a dashboard you change the report suite and/or segment via the dropdowns at the top of the interface, the dashboard will automatically change to show data from the new report suite and segment. This is a cool way to see the same reports for a different data set, especially if you have a standardized implementation using multi-suite tagging. If for some reason you really want the report suite for a particular report to retain its original report suite when the overall report suite is changed, while in dashboard edit mode, you can "lock" it by selecting the Lock Report Suite check box.

When you're happy with your dashboard, share it with other userss by clicking the Manage Dashboards link within the Favorites area on the top navigation bar (**Figure 9.13**).

Then select the check boxes next to the dashboards that you want to share (**Figure 9.14**). On this screen you can see all of your dashboards and those that have been shared corporate-wide. From here you can also edit your dashboards, share them publicly, push them to specific users, delete them, and so on.

Figure 9.13 Access the Manage Dashboards screen.

Dashboards for User Adam Greco							
Add Dashboard							
My Dashboards		DirectAccess	Shared	Scheduled	View Archive	Push To Users	Manage
My Dashboards ▾							
↑ ↓ Website Overview		🖥	☑	🗎		➡	✎ 🗐 ✕
↑ ↓ Find A Cruise Analysis		🖥	☑	🗎		➡	✎ 🗐 ✕
↑ ↓ Vivian Test		🖥	☑	🗎		➡	✎ 🗐 ✕
↑ ↓ Internal Search Analysis		🖥	☑	🗎		➡	✎ 🗐 ✕
↑ ↓ Video Impact Analysis		🖥	☑	🗎		➡	✎ 🗐 ✕
↑ ↓ SiteCatalyst Usage Dashboard		🖥	☑	🗎		➡	✎ 🗐 ✕
↑ ↓ New Dashboard		🖥	☐	🗎			✎ 🗐 ✕
↑ ↓ Search Engine Dashboard		🖥	☐	🗎			✎ 🗐 ✕

Figure 9.14 Manage dashboards.

There is a lot more to learn about dashboards, but now you have what you need to get started. Here are a few additional details about dashboards:

▸ You can create an unlimited number of SiteCatalyst dashboards.

▸ You can schedule dashboards for e-mail delivery on a recurring basis like other SiteCatalyst reports.

▸ You can use publishing lists to have one dashboard deliver data from different SiteCatalyst report suites to different people (covered later in this chapter).

▸ You can add notes to dashboard reports.

Alerts

Although alerts are not overly complicated, I'm amazed at the number of SiteCatalyst customers I meet who aren't using them. After all, once you set a large number of metrics by which to evaluate your online business, who wants to spend all day checking to see if they go up or down when SiteCatalyst can automatically inform you of major changes?

Figure 9.15 Add Alert.

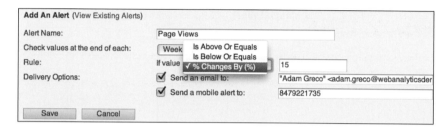

Figure 9.16 Metric report alert.

SiteCatalyst alerts are a mechanism for you or your business users to be alerted when something positive or negative happens related to SiteCatalyst metrics that are important to you. You can set alerts in many different types of SiteCatalyst reports using the icon in the report toolbar (**Figure 9.15**). Alerts are available in all reports except Pathing and some Visitor Retention reports. However, their usage differs slightly based on the type of report you are using. The following sections explain how to use alerts in each of the different report types.

Site Metric alerts

Alerts for Site Metric reports are the easiest to understand because they involve raw numbers only. As a refresher, Metric reports include Page Views, Visits, Unique Visitors, Purchase, Orders, and all of your custom success events. When you set an alert on these reports, you'll see a screen like the one shown in **Figure 9.16**. On this screen, your only options are the following:

▸ **Alert Name.** The name of the alert.

▸ **Time frame (Check values at the end of each).** Specifies when the alert should be checked (Hour, Day, Week, Month).

▸ **Rule.** Allows you to choose from three alert rule types. If you choose Is Above/Below or Equals, you are hard-coding a threshold number that when above or below (depending on your selection) will notify you. The most commonly used option is % Changes By, which alerts you if there is a percent change of more than the percent number you enter in the box (in this example I've entered "15" for 15%). Note that this will alert you of either a positive or negative change. Also, keep in mind that if you use daily alerts, you might receive alerts on Sundays and Mondays if your website traffic is lower during the weekends.

▸ **Delivery Options.** Allows you to choose how you will be notified. The choices are e-mail, mobile phone, or both.

Traffic and Conversion Variable alerts

Alerts for the other reports (Traffic and Conversion Variable) in SiteCatalyst are a bit more involved because:

▸ Unlike a Metric report, instead of having just one possible metric, there are multiple metrics that can be associated with a variable.

▸ Traffic and Conversion Variable reports have many different values, and you need to specify the values about which you want to be alerted.

For example, if you click to set an alert in the Pages report, you'll see the screen in **Figure 9.17**.

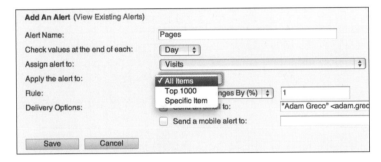

Figure 9.17 Pages report alert.

On this screen, you have a few additional options to select:

▸ **Assign alert to.** Allows you to choose the metric.

▸ **Apply the alert to.** Provides three choices. *All Items* alerts you if the total at the bottom of the report meets the alert criteria set. In many respects this is similar to a metric alert for the chosen metric. The *Top 1000* choice notifies you if any of the top 1000 variable values meet the alert criteria. The alert will list any of the top 1000 values that trigger the alert along with the reason they met the criteria (e.g., percentage difference). The most useful option in this alert type is *Specific Item* because it lets you choose which variable values you want to be alerted about.

To demonstrate the differences among these three choices, I have created three separate alerts: one with All Items, one with Top 1000 items, and one with Specific Items and three specific pages selected. For demonstration purposes, the alert was set to look for a daily Visit percent change of 1% so there would be a greater likelihood of triggering the alerts. **Figures 9.18** through **9.20** show snapshots of the e-mails I received for each when each alert triggered.

As you can see, the All Items alert just presents a total change, the Top 1000 alert shows a list of items and the percentage for which they changed. The Specific Item alert is similar to the Top 1000 but is limited to the three pages that were selected.

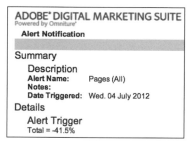

ADOBE® DIGITAL MARKETING SUITE
Powered by Omniture®

Alert Notification

Summary
  Description
    Alert Name: Pages (All)
    Notes:
    Date Triggered: Wed. 04 July 2012
Details
  Alert Trigger
    Total = -41.5%

Figure 9.18 All Item alert.

ADOBE® DIGITAL MARKETING SUITE
Powered by Omniture®

Alert Notification

Summary
  Description
    Alert Name: Pages (1000)
    Notes:
    Date Triggered: Wed. 04 July 2012
Details
  Alert Trigger
    vrc:us:home:home page vfv = -21.2%
    vrc:us:subscribe:signup popup form vpv = -43.0%
    vrc:us:videos:thevikingexperience = -24.4%
    vrc:us:email:river cruising bnd = -19.5%
    vrc:us:videos:longshipsnewtour = -59.1%
    vrc:us:specialoffers:rivercruising vfv = -16.4%
    vrc:us:aboutyourtrip:reading = -24.0%
    vrc:us:emailitinerary:070212.01_euro_pricing = -69.5%
    vrc:us:home:find a cruise = -22.9%
    vrc:us:emailitinerary:070212.01_rhge_pricing = -68.4%
    vrc:us:email:vikinglongshipstour.01 = -67.0%
    vrc:us:emailitinerary:070212.01_roda_pricing = -67.8%
    vrc:us:videos:grandeuropeantouritin = -13.8%

Figure 9.19 Top 1000 alert.

ADOBE® DIGITAL MARKETING SUITE
Powered by Omniture®

Alert Notification

Summary
  Description
    Alert Name: Pages (3 Specific)
    Notes:
    Date Triggered: Wed. 04 July 2012
Details
  Alert Trigger
    vrc:us:home:home page vfv = -21.2%
    vrc:us:subscribe:signup popup form vpv = -43.0%
    vrc:us:videos:thevikingexperience = -24.4%

Figure 9.20 Specific Item alert.

Page	2 Jul. 2012 Visits▼		3 Jul. 2012 Visits		Change	
vrc:us:subscribe:signup popup form vpv	9,841	21.6%	5,606	21.0%	-4,235	-43.0%
vrc:us:home:home page vfv	8,439	18.5%	6,647	24.9%	-1,792	-21.2%
vrc:us:videos:thevikingexperience	6,929	15.2%	5,238	19.6%	-1,691	-24.4%
vrc:us:email:river cruising bnd	6,414	14.1%	5,161	19.3%	-1,253	-19.5%
vrc:us:videos:longshipsnewtour	6,390	14.0%	2,616	9.8%	-3,774	-59.1%
vrc:us:emailitinerary:070212.01_euro_pricing	5,562	12.2%	1,699	6.4%	-3,863	-69.5%
vrc:us:emailitinerary:070212.01_rhge_pricing	4,841	10.6%	1,532	5.7%	-3,309	-68.4%
vrc:us:emailitinerary:070212.01_roda_pricing	4,722	10.4%	1,520	5.7%	-3,202	-67.8%
vrc:us:email:vikinglongshipstour.01	4,613	10.1%	1,521	5.7%	-3,092	-67.0%
vrc:us:aboutyourtrip:reading	2,843	6.2%	2,160	8.1%	-683	-24.0%
TOTAL	**45,602**		**26,673**			

Figure 9.21 Pages report showing the same alert values as in the previous figures.

You can actually see the same data in a regular SiteCatalyst report as well (**Figure 9.21**). In the Pages report, you can see that the percent change in this daily comparison report shows the same percentages as the alerts received. For example, notice that the first three pages changed by –43.0%, –21.2%, and –24.4% respectively, match the alerts in Figure 9.19 and Figure 9.20. You can also compute the total difference in Visits using the report total numbers (which matches the alert total shown in Figure 9.18):

$(26{,}673 - 45{,}602)/45{,}602 = -41.5\%$

Classification alerts

As of SiteCatalyst version 14.7, in addition to setting alerts on traffic and conversion variables, it became possible to set alerts on classifications. Although this addition may not sound that impressive at first, it can be quite valuable. Classification alerts work the same way as the preceding traffic and conversion variable alerts except the criteria are classification values instead of standard traffic and conversion variable values.

Let's walk through an example that shows why classification alerts can be so useful. Imagine that you have a conversion or campaign variable that captures individual website traffic sources. These sources of traffic might be SEO keywords, paid search keywords, e-mail links, or clicks from social networking sites. However, you don't want to be notified every time there is an increase or decrease for a *specific* traffic source; rather, you want to know if there has been a significant change to one of the higher-level marketing channels (SEO, SEM, social media). Before classification alerts were possible, doing so would be virtually impossible (unless you had an additional variable that captured the marketing channel), but this is now easy to accomplish if you use a classification to group your individual traffic sources by marketing channel.

Let's say that your boss wants to be alerted if there is more than a 10 percent change in "Social" referrals to the website from one week to the next. To be alerted about this change, simply open the classification of the traffic source conversion variable (which you've named Marketing Channel) and click the alert icon. From there, you can click on the Specific Item entry and then click the link to see the pop-up screen shown in **Figure 9.22**, which lets you choose the Marketing Channel you want. You can then save "Social" as your selection and configure the rest of the alert until you have a screen that looks like the one in **Figure 9.23**.

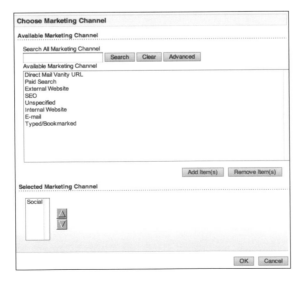

Figure 9.22 Classification alert to choose the desired Marketing Channel.

Add An Alert (View Existing Alerts)

Alert Name:	Social Media Weekly Alert
Check values at the end of each:	Week ↕
Assign alert to:	Bounces ↕
Apply the alert to:	Specific Item ↕ Selected Item: Social
Rule:	If value [% Changes By (%) ↕] 10
Delivery Options:	☑ Send an email to: "Adam Greco" <adam.greco@webanalyticsder
	☐ Send a mobile alert to:

Save   Cancel

Figure 9.23 Sample classification alert showing weekly changes in Social.

This is a great way to take advantage of the time you've already spent applying classifications to your key traffic and conversion variables. It also saves you a lot of time attempting to set alerts for hundreds of individual items.

Some other cool uses of classification alerts include:

▸ Classifying Pages into "Important Pages" and setting an alert when this group of pages changes.

▸ Classifying onsite search terms into buckets and being alerted when specific types of keywords hit a threshold or change significantly.

▸ Classifying countries or cities into regions and being alerted when a metric related to a specific one changes.

▸ Classifying search engine keywords into branded versus nonbranded and having alerts sent when each type changes significantly.

▸ Classifying videos viewed on your website into types and being notified when a video type changes significantly.

These are just a few examples, so I encourage you to think about which of your classifications would make sense to have alerts associated with them.

In addition, a few general alert items are worth noting:

▸ You can send alerts to multiple people by adding e-mail addresses separated by a comma.

▸ You can view all of your alerts and make changes to them in the Alerts area below the Favorites area in the top navigation bar. On this screen you can also disable alerts if there are some that you want to receive only at specific times but don't want to re-create them each time.

▸ As with scheduled reports, every alert e-mail has a link at the bottom that allows you or your co-workers to disable the alert.

▸ You can set alerts on calculated metrics by clicking the alert icon from within the specific Calculated Metric report. However, you cannot use calculated metrics in traffic and conversion variable or classification alerts.

More Actions

The More Actions menu offers several useful report functions (**Figure 9.24**).

Some of these actions are trivial, and others are a bit more involved. Here is a list of the more basic actions:

▶ **Print** allows you to print the current report.

▶ **Extract Data** allows you to create the shell of a report to be delivered via e-mail (see more information in the next section).

▶ **Create Custom Report** allows you to add the current report to a special Custom Reports area in the left navigation menu (**Figure 9.25**). These custom reports are viewable to others within the organization and can only be deleted by administrators.

▶ **Copy Graph** allows you to view and download the current report graph.

▶ **Link to This Report** creates a shortcut link to the current report (**Figure 9.26**) and is one of my favorite features. This shortcut link retains all of the current report settings and is great for e-mailing to co-workers. When they click the link, they will be taken to SiteCatalyst where they can log in and see the exact report you built (assuming they have the appropriate permissions). This is especially handy when you need to quickly review a report with a co-worker because you can e-mail the link and be guaranteed that both of you are looking at the same report. Note that this link will be locked to the current date range (will not roll like dashboard reports). Also, the link is not permanent and expires after 12 months.

▶**TIP** *As a web analyst, you will often embed SiteCatalyst reports and graphs into presentations you create for your organization. A great use of shortcut links is to include them in your presentation by inserting them into these reports or as part of an appendix. This provides an easy way for those viewing your presentation to go back later and see the reports you used in your analysis.*

Figure 9.24 More Actions.

Figure 9.25 Custom Reports in the left navigation menu.

Figure 9.26 Link to This Report option.

▶ **Open New Window** is a handy way to duplicate the report you are looking at in a new window or browser tab. I use this quite often when I want to adjust the current report, but I am worried I won't be able to get back to where I started. This link is like a temporary Save As option; you can preserve the current report and modify the new copy, which you can simply close if your report tinkering fails.

▶ **Launch Discover** only appears if your SiteCatalyst login has access to the Discover product. If you see this option, you can click this link to open the current report in Discover where you can log in and begin to dig deeper.

Data extracts

Also found under More Actions (Figure 9.24) is the Extract Data option. Data extracts are a more advanced method of creating SiteCatalyst reports. These data extracts offer a bit more flexibility because they are not subject to the constraints of the Internet Browser interface. Instead, these reports are sent as a CSV file or downloaded directly into Excel. Not all aspects of data extracts can be covered here, but the following should give you a sense of what they are and how you can use them.

To create a data extract, click the Extract Data ▤ icon in the toolbar. Note that there are some reports for which you cannot use data extracts (e.g., Pathing), so if you don't see the Extract Data option, that report is not supported. If you see the icon, click it and a pop-up window will appear (**Figure 9.27**). This screen defaults to the settings of the current report but can be changed as needed. From this interface, you can configure the

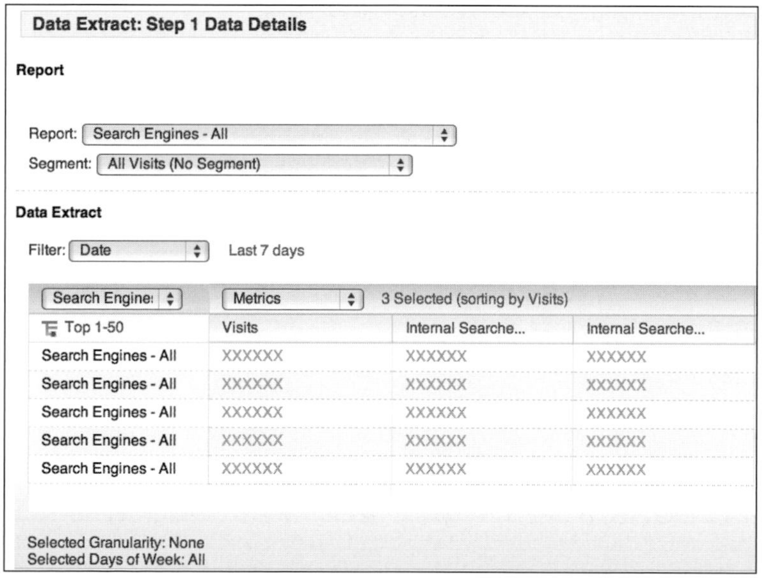

Figure 9.27 Data Extract settings - Step 1.

report, including the date range, which metrics appear, and which variable and segment is being used. You also have access to traffic correlations or conversion variable subrelations, depending on which type of report you have selected, and you can also apply search filter criteria.

To illustrate the flexibility of data extracts, let's have some fun and customize every aspect of this data extract using the following wacky set of criteria:

▸ Apply a segment of First Time Visits (segments are discussed in more detail in Chapter 10).

▸ Change the date range to the month of May and show data only for weekdays.

▸ Narrow down the number of entries to the top 25 and apply a search criterion so only search engines with the word Google are included.

▸ Apply a conversion variable subrelation to break down Search Engines by Day of Week.

▸ Change the layout of the report so the columns are dates and all three success events are shown for each row.

When you've made all of these customizations, the screen should look like the one in **Figure 9.28**.

Figure 9.28
Reconfigured Data
Extract settings - Step 1.

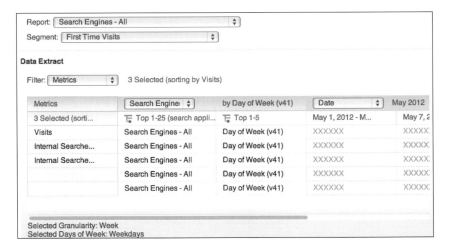

Next, move to the Step 2 screen, which allows you to send the report either once or on a recurring basis. You can also bookmark the data extract to return to it easily at a later date and share it publicly with others (**Figure 9.29**). When you're finished configuring the data extract, you can send it via e-mail and receive the report in a few minutes. You can then open the CSV file, which produces the data shown in **Figure 9.30**.

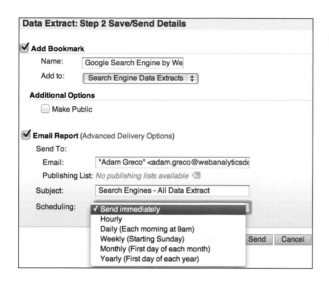

Figure 9.29 Data Extract settings - Step 2.

	A	B	C	D	E
1	**Metrics**	**Search Engines - All**	**Day of Week (v41)**	**May 1, 2012 - May 4, 2012**	**May 7, 2012 - May 11, 2012**
2	Visits	Google	wednesday	2249	2530
3	Visits	Google	friday	2123	2024
4	Visits	Google	thursday	2117	1889
5	Visits	Google	tuesday	1978	2026

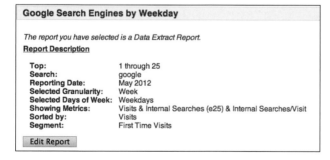

Figure 9.30 Final Data Extract report.

The report is a bit nonsensical, but it shows just how many configurations you can tweak using data extracts. Another important detail to note about data extracts relates to the bookmark you created. Because data extracts are not actual SiteCatalyst interface reports, when you access the bookmark, you may be surprised at what you see. You've actually bookmarked just a placeholder with all of your Data Extract settings, so when you access it, you'll see the description shown in **Figure 9.31,** not the actual report.

Figure 9.31 Data extract bookmark.

Targets

In addition to the report saving and sharing options available in the SiteCatalyst report toolbar, there are some other general report features that can be set globally, one of which is called *targets*. Targets provide a way to establish benchmarks for metrics and variables so that those using SiteCatalyst can see how you are doing against your goals. If a metric is important enough to your organization that it tracks it with a success event, there is a good chance that it has an associated yearly, quarterly, or monthly goal, or target. It's nice to look at your SiteCatalyst reports and see that certain trends are going up or down (depending on which way you want them to go), but sometimes that is not enough. In the real world, some bosses want to hold you accountable for your metrics. If this sounds familiar, you should become familiar with targets. Targets allow you to define the specific values you are expected to achieve. They then show you how you are performing toward the targets that you set.

For example, let's say your company's Revenue graph looked like the one in **Figure 9.32**.

Figure 9.32 Sample Revenue report.

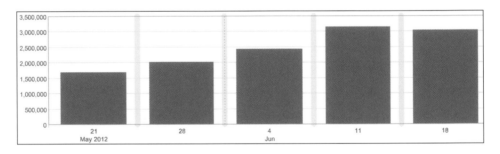

In general, looking at this Revenue graph you'd feel pretty good because revenue is going up and to the right, and it's usually a good sign when revenue increases. In fact, it may be time to head out early, take a well-deserved vacation, or ask for that raise you've been longing for.

But then you see the same graph with a target added that shows where your boss expects revenue to be (**Figure 9.33**). Suddenly, your view of the world changes, and this change is not for the better. In web analytics, context is important, and this target allows you to put your revenue performance in perspective. No one like surprises; therefore, I recommend that you set targets for all of your key metrics, and when you add reports to dashboards, you add them with their targets included so everyone can see where you stand with respect to your KPIs (**Figure 9.34**).

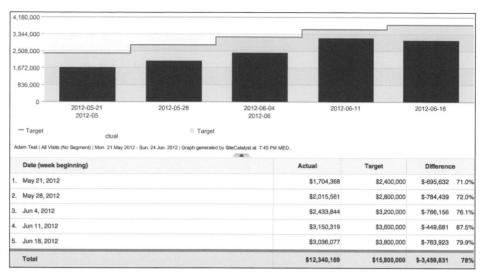

Figure 9.33 Sample Revenue report with target.

Date (week beginning)	Actual	Target	Difference	
1. May 21, 2012	$1,704,368	$2,400,000	$-695,632	71.0%
2. May 28, 2012	$2,015,561	$2,800,000	$-784,439	72.0%
3. Jun 4, 2012	$2,433,844	$3,200,000	$-766,156	76.1%
4. Jun 11, 2012	$3,150,319	$3,600,000	$-449,681	87.5%
5. Jun 18, 2012	$3,036,077	$3,800,000	$-763,923	79.9%
Total	$12,340,169	$15,800,000	$-3,459,831	78%

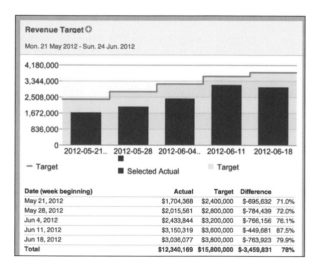

Figure 9.34 Sample dashboard with report target included.

The following are some other details to know about targets:

▶ When you create a target, you can apply it to the entire metric or include only a specific value for a traffic or conversion variable.

▶ An advanced version of targets is called an *accountability matrix*, but it is super-complicated and not used very often. It allows you to set targets at the conversion variable subrelation level. If you are interested in an accountability matrix, contact ClientCare.

Publishing Lists

Publishing lists are another general reporting feature that you can apply to various aspects of report sharing. A publishing list is deceptively simple, yet very effective. It is nothing more than a grouping of end-user e-mail addresses associated with different report suites used to distribute different data sets to different people. This feature is not commonly used, mainly, I fear, because it takes a while to fully understand it. However, if you have multiple report suites and many employees at your organization with which you want to share reports, publishing lists are worth learning. Publishing lists, as well as how they came about and when they should be used, are explained in this section.

Have you ever created a SiteCatalyst report or dashboard only to find out that you need to make several different versions of it for different audiences? Perhaps you have multiple country websites for your organization that all need the same report, but the data needs to come from a different SiteCatalyst report suite. For example, you may have five people in the UK that need to see the report with UK data and three people in France that need to see the same report but with data from the France report suite. Duplicating the same report or dashboard over and over again, only to connect the different people to their correct report suite is tedious and a waste of time. To solve this problem, the Publishing List function was created, which can save you hours of work and make you look like a reporting machine.

A publishing list is normally created from within a report or dashboard, but once it is created, it can be applied to any report or dashboard. You first saw publishing lists mentioned on the Send Report by Email screen (**Figure 9.35**). On this screen, because no publishing lists were created, a "Create list now" link appeared. Note that only administrators can create publishing lists, but once they are created, users can choose them on the screen shown in Figure 9.35. To create a publishing list, click the "Create list now" link or access the Publishing List Manager in the Administration - User Management area (**Figure 9.36**).

Figure 9.35 Report send options with Publishing List option.

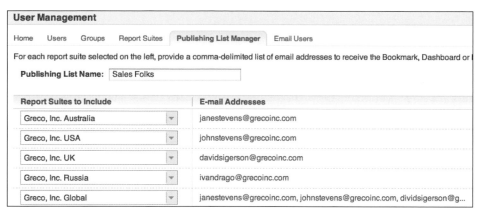

Figure 9.36 Publishing list setup screen.

Then follow these steps:

1. Name the publishing list.

2. Select a report suite.

3. Assign one or more e-mail addresses that should receive data for the selected report suite.

4. Repeat steps 2 and 3 for each report suite that could have data you want to send.

In this example, a publishing list called Sales Folks has been created and has sales-people from four different countries in the list. Because you might want all of these sales folks to see the total data for the global report suite, all of them have been added to that report suite. Each of these sales people will receive two copies of the report or dashboard—one for their local country and the other for the global company as a whole. You could have also added multiple people to each country report suite, but for now let's keep it simple.

With the publishing list complete, if an end user runs a report, that user will see a new Click to Add option, which when clicked, shows the new publishing list (**Figure 9.37**). By selecting this publishing list, when the report or dashboard is run, each person in each country will receive a copy of that report with data from the local report suite, plus a version of all data from the global report suite.

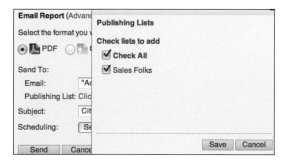

Figure 9.37 Selecting a publishing list.

Comparison Reporting

A big part of web analysis is comparing one set of data to another. These comparisons can be date comparisons, website comparisons, or comparisons of segments of website visitors. In this section, various comparison options available in SiteCatalyst are reviewed.

Date Comparisons

Date Comparison reports are probably the most popular. A Date Comparison report allows you to see how a particular metric or variable differs from one time frame to the next. Common uses of date comparisons are week over week, month over month, and year over year. Previously, you saw that in a Metric report it is possible to see the current month, the past month, and the past year all in one report. However, this is just the beginning of how you can compare data in SiteCatalyst.

To create a Date Comparison report, you simply choose the traffic or conversion variable that you want to compare and open the report. In this example, you'll use the Search Engines report (**Figure 9.38**). In this report, you see Searches and Form Completions by Search Engine for the month of June 2012. You can then click the calendar icon and the Compare Dates link to see a screen with two calendars. On this screen, you'll select the months of May and June and run the report (**Figure 9.39**). The resulting report shows you each metric for May and June and a new comparison column for each (**Figure 9.40**). This type of report is helpful to see which traffic or conversion report values are improving and which ones are declining. In this case, it looks like the number of searches is holding steady and Form Completions are doing better than last month except for the Google - Canada Search Engine.

Figure 9.38 Sample Search Engines report.

	Search Engines - All	Searches ▾		Form Completions (e22)	
1.	Google	165,988	61.5%	13,545	28.0%
2.	Google - Canada	30,284	11.2%	2,244	4.6%
3.	Yahoo!	22,728	8.4%	3,076	6.4%
4.	Microsoft Bing	22,694	8.4%	2,671	5.5%
5.	AOL.com Search	7,611	2.8%	1,031	2.1%
6.	Ask Jeeves	1,919	0.7%	294	0.6%

Figure 9.39 Compare Dates selection screen.

	Search Engines - All	May 2012 Searches▾		June 2012 Searches		Change		May 2012 Form Completions (e22)		June 2012 Form Completions (e22)		Change	
	1. 🔎 Google	161,990	61.3%	165,988	61.5%	3,998	2.5%	12,577	27.0%	13,545	28.0%	968	7.7%
	2. 🔎 Google - Canada	29,263	11.1%	30,284	11.2%	1,021	3.5%	2,351	5.1%	2,244	4.6%	-107	-4.6%
	3. 🔎 Microsoft Bing	22,190	8.4%	22,694	8.4%	504	2.3%	2,665	5.7%	2,671	5.5%	6	0.2%
	4. 🔎 Yahoo!	21,883	8.3%	22,728	8.4%	845	3.9%	2,690	5.8%	3,076	6.4%	386	14.3%
	5. 🔎 AOL.com Search	7,711	2.9%	7,611	2.8%	-100	-1.3%	982	2.1%	1,031	2.1%	49	5.0%
	6. 🔎 Ask Jeeves	1,923	0.7%	1,919	0.7%	-4	-0.2%	236	0.5%	294	0.6%	58	24.6%

Figure 9.40 Sample date comparison report.

However, when you compare ranges that have different numbers of days, your results can be skewed. In this example, it shouldn't be an issue because there is only a one-day difference. But if you have to compare a month to one-half month, it could be problematic. If this scenario arises, be aware of a feature called Comparison Reports – Normalization. In the report settings is a link that allows you to normalize the data. When you do, SiteCatalyst will try to adjust data to make the columns as close to "apples to apples" as possible. In this example, June outpaced May, even though it had a one-day disadvantage. Therefore, if you normalize this report, SiteCatalyst will adjust

	Search Engines - All	May 2012 Searches ▼		June 2012 Searches (Normalized)		Change	May 2012 Form Completions (e22)		June 2012 Form Completions (e22) (Normalized)		Change
1.	Google	161,990	61.3%	182,942	61.5%	12.9%	12,577	27.0%	14,928	28.0%	18.7%
2.	Google - Canada	29,263	11.1%	33,37	165,988 1.2%	14.1%	2,351	5.1%	2,473	4.6%	5.2%
3.	Microsoft Bing	22,190	8.4%	25,012	8.4%	12.7%	2,665	5.7%	2,944	5.5%	10.5%
4.	Yahoo!	21,883	8.3%	25,049	8.4%	14.5%	2,690	5.8%	3,390	6.4%	26.0%
5.	AOL.com Search	7,711	2.9%	8,388	2.8%	8.8%	982	2.1%	1,136	2.1%	15.7%
6.	Ask Jeeves	1,923	0.7%	2,115	0.7%	10.0%	236	0.5%	324	0.6%	37.3%

Figure 9.41 Normalized Date Comparison report.

June's numbers even higher as it attempts to model what would have happened if both months had 31 days (**Figure 9.41**).

The June numbers are way up due to the extra day, but keep in mind that these are mathematically generated figures, not actual figures.

Report Suite Comparisons

▶**TIP** *If you use normalization, here is a handy trick: When you're looking at the column that is being normalized, such as the Searches metric for the June 2012 column in Figure 9.41, hover your mouse over a row value to see a pop-up window showing what the actual value was before it was modified by normalization. By hovering the mouse over the number 182,942 in the report, you can see that the "un-normalized" number is 165,988, which matches what you saw in the original report in Figure 9.40.*

Report Suite Comparison reports are not used as frequently as Date Comparison reports because they are contingent on having multiple report suites and having those report suites configured consistently. The goal of this comparison report is to show the same report for two different report suites. To use Report Suite Comparison reports, you should have the following:

▶ Multiple report suites

▶ Each report suite set up as similar to each other as possible (ideally, the same)

▶ Permission to view both report suites you want to compare

To initiate a Report Suite Comparison report, simply open a Traffic or Conversion Variable report. In this example, you'll start by opening the Greco, Inc. USA Report Suite and using a new or repeat conversion variable with Visits as the metric. After you open the report, you click the Compare to Site link in the report settings area and choose the Greco, Inc. UK Report Suite as the comparison. This results in a report that looks like the one in **Figure 9.42**. A rather large disparity exists between the two report suites due to the fact that the USA site received significantly more volume than the UK site. This is another reason Report Suite Comparison reports are more difficult and less commonly used than Date Comparison reports. However, you can use normalization to get a better comparison and to see a report like the one in **Figure 9.43**.

	New/Repeat	Greco, Inc. USA Visits ▾		Greco, Inc. UK Visits		Change	
1.	New	45,755	81.3%	1,585	69.9%	-44,170	-96.5%
2.	Repeat	10,527	18.7%	684	30.1%	-9,843	-93.5%

Figure 9.42 Sample Report Suite Comparison report.

	New/Repeat	Greco, Inc. USA Visits ▾		Greco, Inc. UK Visits (Normalized)		Change	
1.	New	45,755	81.3%	39,403	70.0%	-6,352	-13.9%
2.	Repeat	10,527	18.7%	16,880	30.0%	6,353	60.3%

Figure 9.43 Normalized Report Suite Comparison report.

Segment Comparison Reports

Segment Comparison reports are also meaningful to web analysts. Although segments are covered in the next chapter, for now you just need to know that they are subsets of data created for analysis purposes. For example, one segment might be First Time Visitors and you may want to compare a variable or metric for that segment to a Loyal Visitor segment (visitors who have been to your website three times or more). Unfortunately, there is not (yet) a great way to compare segments in SiteCatalyst, because much of this type of comparison is done in Adobe Discover, which specializes in segments and segment comparisons.

However, there are some rudimentary ways to compare segments. The first method is to use dashboards. You can create a report for one segment, add it to a dashboard, and then create the same report for another segment and place it directly next to the first. This allows you to see a side-by-side report comparison in the dashboard. You will not be able to see the difference columns like you can in Date and Report Suite Comparison reports, but you will see both data points together.

The second and most common way to compare segments is to pull down data for both to Microsoft Excel using ReportBuilder (covered in Chapter 11). Then you can compare the data side by side and calculate differences as needed.

The third way to do segment comparisons is to take advantage of Advanced Segment Insight (ASI) data slots. As you'll learn in the next chapter, ASI is a way to reprocess your SiteCatalyst data for a particular segment, and doing so creates a data set that is very similar to a report suite. These ASI data slots can be added to Report Suite Comparison reports just like any other report suite. However, ASI has been phased out of the SiteCatalyst product beginning with SiteCatalyst v15, so this method will only work in older versions.

▶**TIP** *One advanced technique I've used when comparing very disparate sets of data is to create a Total metric that divides the metric of interest by the total of that metric. This, in effect, makes the percentage normally shown to the right of the raw figure the main focus of the column. Then when you do a comparison report, you are comparing the percentages instead of the raw numbers. These figures often make the report easier to compare when the raw numbers are dramatically different.*

Pathing Comparison Reports

A few Pathing reports can be compared, but they are rarely used. The following Pathing reports are available for comparison if you want to check them out:

► Next/Previous Page report

► Full Paths report

SiteCatalyst Interface Time-savers

Over the years I've found some cool SiteCatalyst interface features and tricks that I'll share here. Many of these are obscure but could end up saving you time in the long run.

Update Dashboard Reports

If you click on the title of a report from a dashboard, it will take you to that report and provide an update message (**Figure 9.44**). From this screen, you can make updates to the original report, and if you click the Update button, those updates will be applied back to the dashboard. This eliminates the arduous process of having to open the report, make changes, save it to the dashboard, and then remove the old report.

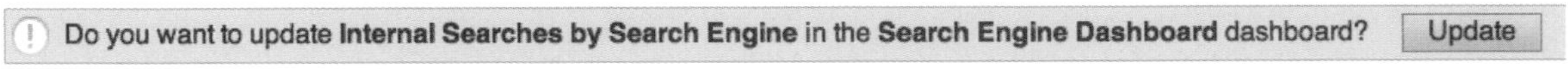

Do you want to update **Internal Searches by Search Engine** in the **Search Engine Dashboard** dashboard? Update

Figure 9.44 Dashboard report update message.

Reorganize Menus and Hide Menu Items

If you have administrator rights, you can make changes to the report menus and customize them for your organization. Using menu customization, you can hide the traditional Traffic Variable and Conversion Variable menu items. You can also hide reports that your organization doesn't use. All of this can be done in the administration console by creating your own menus and adding or removing items. Simply select the desired report suite(s) and open the Menu Customization tool.

Double-click to Add/Remove Metrics

In SiteCatalyst v14 or later, you can double-click to add or remove metrics in the Add Metrics screen.

The Magic Triangle

If you're like me, it may seem like you spend most of your day adding or removing metrics from reports. This can be a very time-consuming process. One time-saving trick I use is to change the column that is used for sorting by clicking the small triangle next to a metric from within the Add Metrics window (**Figure 9.45**). It amazes me how many people add metrics, wait for the report to load, and then click on a column to sort and wait for the report to load again. Multiply that by 20 reports, and it becomes a real time suck. Instead, simply click the triangle until it turns green while you are initially adding metrics, and you're done.

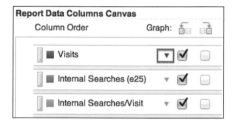

Figure 9.45 Triangle indicating sort metric.

Graph Check Boxes

On the same screen as the sorting triangle are check boxes that you can use to choose which metrics you want to graph with your report. Having too many metrics in graphs can confuse your end users, so be selective. Also, take advantage of the fact that you can display two graphs per report. To do this, select one of the check boxes on the left and right side. This is helpful if some of your metrics are numbers and others are percentages. **Figure 9.46** shows an example. This graph is somewhat useless because it has

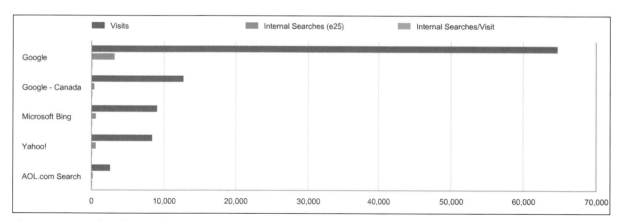

Figure 9.46 Graph with three disparate metrics.

three different metrics; two are raw numbers and the third is a ratio. To fix this, you can click the Add Metrics button and customize what is graphed using the check boxes next to each metric (**Figure 9.47**).

Now when you look at the graph for your report, you see two separate metrics side by side (**Figure 9.48**). This view of the data is a bit more functional, because the graph on the left contains raw numbers and the graph on the right contains percentages.

Figure 9.47 Customize Graph metrics.

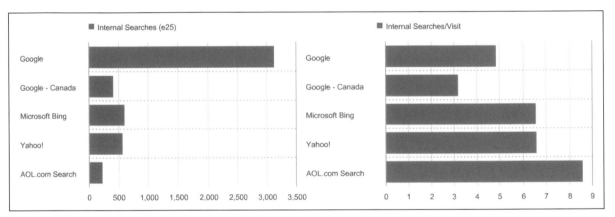

Figure 9.48 Report with side-by-side graphs.

5x5 Subrelation Report

In Chapter 8 you learned that it is possible to break down one conversion variable value by another conversion variable using conversion variable subrelations. However, there may be times when instead of breaking down just one value, you want to break down the top values from the report you are looking at by another conversion variable. There is a secret way to do this that will create what is known as the *5x5 report*, which shows the top five values from the report you are looking at and the top five items to which it is being subrelated. Simply click the breakdown icon at the top left of the conversion report and choose the conversion variable by which you want to break it down (**Figure 9.49**). The result is a 5x5 subrelation report that provides a general overview of the top values (**Figure 9.50**).

	Search Engines - All
	1. None
	2. ⌕ Google
	3. ⌕ Google - Canada
	4. ⌕ Microsoft Bing
	5. ⌕ Yahoo!

Figure 9.49 5x5 subrelation link.

	Search Engines - All by Day of Week (v41)
	1. None
1.	wednesday
2.	thursday
3.	friday
4.	monday
5.	Other
	Show all for None...
	2. Google
1.	sunday
2.	saturday
3.	monday
4.	thursday
5.	Other
	Show all for Google...
	3. Google - Canada
1.	saturday
2.	sunday
3.	tuesday

Figure 9.50 Sample 5x5 subrelation report.

BREAKDOWN BY:
Site Metrics
Site Content
Paths
Traffic Sources
Campaigns
Cruises & Ships
Visitor Retention
Visitor Profile
Custom Conversion
Marketing Channels
Video
None

Figure 9.51 Use the None item in the breakdown area to remove a subrelated variable.

Remove Subrelation Breakdowns

What if, after looking at a conversion subrelation report, you want to view the report without the breakdown? Many SiteCatalyst users click the Internet browser Back button to go back. But what if you made several metric or report setting changes while looking at the subrelation report? Using the Back button would require redoing those settings. A handy trick to remove breakdowns is to click the breakdown icon again and select the bottommost entry, labeled None (**Figure 9.51**). This will retain all of your new report settings and simply remove the item that was subrelated to your original report.

Conclusion

In this chapter, you learned most of what you'll need on a daily basis to navigate Site-Catalyst and share reports you have created with co-workers. As mentioned previously, there are many more interface features to learn, but knowing how to bookmark reports, share reports, and add reports to dashboards should be some of the first tasks you will tackle as a web analyst. When you get more comfortable with the basics, I suggest you begin using alerts and targets, and eventually try out data extracts and publishing lists. These skills along with those related to ReportBuilder (see Chapter 11) will help you find and extract the data you need to be a successful web analyst.

## CHAPTER 10

Segmentation

Ever since the earliest versions of SiteCatalyst, segmentation has been a cornerstone of the product, because business users often have an endless array of questions about data being collected. As a web analyst, there is only so much you can do by analyzing raw traffic metrics and success events. These numbers can give you a high-level view of how your website is performing but cannot provide detailed answers about why your site is doing well or poorly.

You can use various tools in SiteCatalyst to segment data, but all of them have a common goal of helping you isolate the exact website behavior that can answer business questions and, ultimately, improve the website. In this chapter, I'll review the segmentation tools at your disposal in SiteCatalyst.

Segment Builder

To understand segmentation in SiteCatalyst, you must learn how to use the Segment Builder tool. All SiteCatalyst segmentation tools use the same model for creating and using segments, and they are all based on the Segment Builder tool. This tool is extremely robust, and it can be complicated at times. It may take you a while to fully understand it, so don't get frustrated if you don't understand it completely at first. Through experimentation, you'll eventually learn its nuances and begin to feel comfortable building segments.

Containers and Events

To understand the Segment Builder, you first need to understand the various components it uses to build a segment. As shown in **Figure 10.1**, when you enter the Segment Builder, you'll see containers, events, and a Segment Canvas.

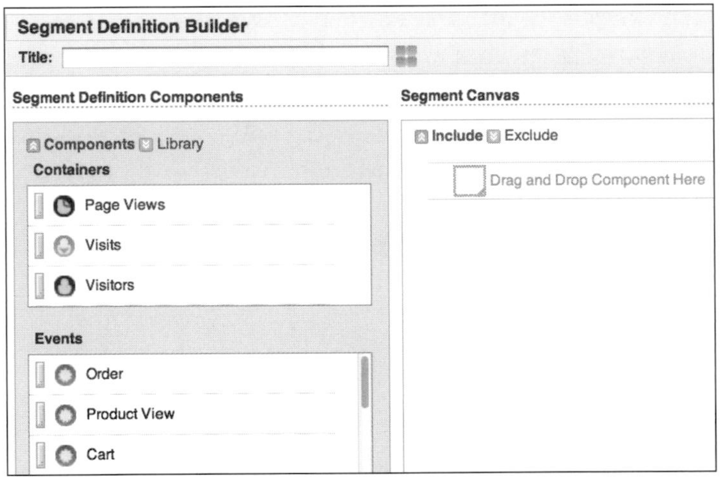

Figure 10.1 Segment Definition Builder.

Let's start by learning about the Segment Builder's various containers:

▶ **Page Views.** Adding a Page View container to the Segment Canvas allows you to define which page views you want to include or exclude from the segment. When evaluating the Page View container, SiteCatalyst scans through each page view it finds within the specified time frame and decides whether it should be included or excluded. Therefore, two different page views from the same visit may or may not be included in the segment. For example, let's say you built a segment in which you wanted only Spanish-language pages and a visitor viewed ten pages during his visit, but only two of those ten pages were viewed in Spanish. Using a Page View container, only those two page views would be included in the segment.

- **Visits.** Adding the Visit container to the Segment Canvas allows you to define which visits you want to include or exclude from the segment. When evaluating the Visit container, SiteCatalyst scans through each visit it finds within the specified time frame and decides whether the entire visit should be included or excluded. Therefore, if any of the criteria are met within the visit, all data from that visit will be included (or excluded if you're using the Exclude tab) in the segment. Using the preceding example, if the segment looking for pages viewed in Spanish was built using a Visit container, the entire visit would be included because at least one of the pages was viewed in Spanish (even though the majority were in English).

- **Visitors.** Adding the Visitor container to the Segment Canvas allows you to define which visitors (cookie IDs) you want to include or exclude from the segment. When evaluating the Visitor container, SiteCatalyst scans through all data it has for each visitor within the specified time frame and decides whether at any time the visitor met the criteria. If it finds that the visitor has met the criteria, all visits and page views for that visitor will be included in the segment. Continuing with the preceding example, if a Visitor container was used and a visitor had six website visits within the specified time frame and during at least one of those visits viewed at least one page in Spanish, data from all six visits would be included in the segment.

▶ **TIP** *Some SiteCatalyst customers incorrectly think that they need to use the Page View container if they want to see page views or the Visit container if they want to see visits. This is not the case. Try to remember that these containers are meant for selecting data to be included in the segment and that you will be able to see all of the page views, visits, and unique visitors in reports for those items that are successfully included in the segment.*

The container you select can have an enormous impact on the data set that is returned to the segment. SiteCatalyst clients sometimes breeze over these container definitions, not realizing how important they are to their web analysis. There are specific situations in which you should use the Visitor container and an equal number of scenarios in which you'd want to avoid using the Visitor container. The same is true for the other containers as well.

Events can also be added to the segment. The Event containers represent the various success events you've identified for your website. If, for example, you are using a Visit container and you add the Order event to it, you are indicating that only visits in which an order took place should be included in the segment.

You can "define" containers and events by clicking on them and adding criteria. Almost any data collected in SiteCatalyst can be used in these segment definitions, as shown in **Figure 10.2**.

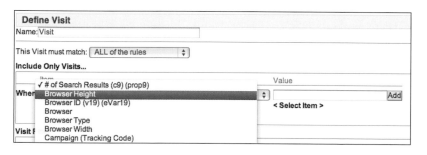

Figure 10.2 Defining containers and events.

▶**TIP** *One of the most common mistakes made in the Segment Builder is adding a criterion but forgetting to click the Add button to add it to the segment. Make a habit of checking that you have not forgotten this critical step.*

Once you choose a criteria element, you then have multiple operator choices you can use to determine which values related to that criteria element will be included, such as an exact match, a contains clause, and others (**Figure 10.3**). In some cases, the definition window will change based on the criteria element you have chosen to include. For example, if you choose Browser Height, SiteCatalyst will remind you that it is looking for a number of pixels in the definition field. As you are adding criteria within each Container, you'll see an AND clause and OR clause in the This Visit Must Match drop-down box above the criteria area. It is important to decide if the criteria you are entering have to all be met or if any item in the criteria is sufficient to include the container element (Visit in this example). As you add criteria, SiteCatalyst will remind you whether you are using an AND or OR clause in the container, as shown in **Figure 10.4**.

Figure 10.3 Definition selection clauses.

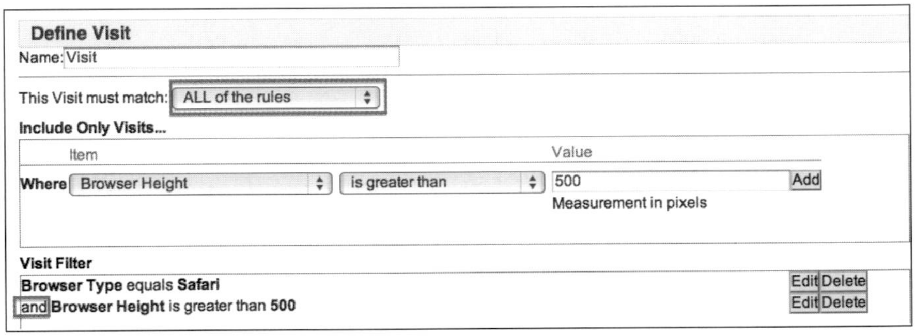

Figure 10.4 Containers include AND and OR clauses.

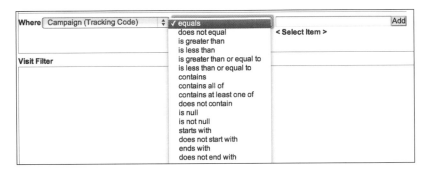

The following are two other items to note about containers and events:

▶ Segment Builder allows you to segment on how many times a success event takes place, which is useful because it adds a numeric count to event containers. For example, if you set a success event each time a visitor conducts an onsite search, you can build a segment that looks for cases where "Total Onsite Searches is greater than 2" to find repeat searchers.

▶ If you are scheduling reports using DataWarehouse (covered later in this chapter), keep in mind that segments built using the Page View container will return data the quickest, followed by the Visit container and the Visitor container. Whenever possible, try to use the lowest-level container needed to get the data you need to improve processing and delivery time.

Segment Canvas—Nesting Containers

Once you understand how each container type functions, the next step is to learn how the different containers can be nested within the Segment Canvas. The nesting of containers can get a bit tricky, but the following explanation of how they work will help you with this task.

Each container has items that can and cannot be nested within it. Think of it as a hierarchy:

▶ Visitor containers sit at the top of the hierarchy and can have nested Visit, Page View, or Event containers.

▶ Visit containers can have nested Page View or Event containers.

▶ Page View containers can only have Event containers nested within them.

The most difficult part of understanding container nesting is the use of OR clauses and AND clauses. If two items are part of the same nesting, they are treated as an AND clause. For this reason, it is not possible to nest the same container twice. For example, SiteCatalyst will not allow you to nest two Visit containers within a Visitor container. Likewise, you cannot nest two Page View containers in a Visit container. If you look closely, when you add the first container to the canvas, SiteCatalyst creates a thin colored line underneath it that separates that container from any other containers added to the canvas. If you initially add a Visitor container, that line will be red like the Visitor container, indicating that only items that are lower than Visitor in the hierarchy discussed earlier can be placed within it. If you want to add two or more items and have all of the conditions met (AND), you want to be sure to nest them above the line of the container. If you want the containers that you add to be OR clauses, make sure they are below the line of the initial container. The good news is that the Segment Builder usually tells you when you are attempting to add an invalid combination, but it is best to learn what you can and can't nest within the Segment Builder.

To reinforce what you've learned, let's walk through an example. Imagine that you want to create a segment that has any visit from the United States where an order occurred. To do this, perform the following steps:

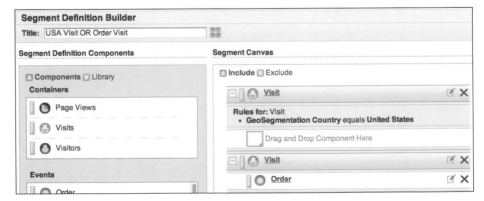

1. Add the Visit container to the Segment Canvas.

2. Click on the Visit container to define it as a Visit where the country is the United States (you can use the out-of-the-box GeoSegmentation Country variable).

3. Add the Order event to the Visit container.

When you're done, **Figure 10.5** shows you what it should look like.

To illustrate the nesting of containers on the canvas, let's now pretend that you need a segment in which a Visit was from the United States *or* an Order took place. One way to create this segment is to add two separate Visit containers to the Segment Canvas and have one Visit be those from the United States and the other Visit be those who placed an Order (**Figure 10.6**). This illustrates a few points. You cannot have two Visit containers together at the same level and have them be an OR clause. Also, any containers that are at the same level in the Segment Canvas are treated as OR clauses. In this example, this would be Visits from the United States OR Visits with an Order, which matches the criteria.

As you get good at using the Segment Builder, you'll learn some tricks along the way. For example, another way to build the preceding OR clause would be to add the single Visit container shown in **Figure 10.7** to the canvas.

Figure 10.5 Sample segment.

Figure 10.6 Sample OR clause segment.

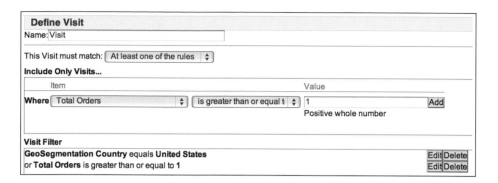

Figure 10.7 An advanced criteria clause within a container.

The Nesting Challenge

When you think you really understand segment nesting, you can take my nesting challenge. Look at the segment nesting shown in **Figure 10.8** and see if you understand the following description.

This segment includes a Visitor container with two Visit containers nested within it. Those two Visit containers would form an OR clause, so if the criteria of either were met, everything for that visitor would be included in the segment. The first Visit container has two Page View containers within it, so if the criteria of either of these Page View containers were met (meaning a page view with an order or a page view with a product view), the entire visit would be included in the segment, meaning that the Visitor container in which the visit was nested would also be included. Below the fold could be more criteria, and you could even have another Visitor container at the same level of the top Visitor container and start the process over

again, keeping in mind that this second Visitor container would be an OR clause at the top of the Visitor container. If this all makes sense, you are on your way to being a segment master.

Figure 10.8 Nesting and more nesting.

Segment Canvas—Exclude

Now that you're feeling confident about adding containers, defining them, and nesting them, you need to know about the Exclude tab. Fortunately, the Exclude area of the Segment Canvas isn't too difficult to grasp. Everything discussed so far was on the Include tab of the Segment Canvas, and you were telling SiteCatalyst what you wanted to include in your segment. Using the Exclude tab, you can tell SiteCatalyst what you don't want in your segment. At times you'll need to use both tabs to narrow down the people or sessions to those in which you are interested.

Let's look at an example: Your boss wants to do some analysis on people who have come close to buying on the website but have not completed the purchase so you can re-market to them. Specifically, she wants to target those who have visited the site at some point and added something to the cart but have not purchased. This is a great use case for the Exclude tab. Unfortunately, you cannot see both tabs on one screen; **Figure 10.9** shows what would be placed on both screens to build this segment.

Once you learn how to create segments, the ultimate goal is to apply them to your SiteCatalyst reports and dashboards. In this regard, SiteCatalyst v15 made a huge leap forward by allowing Instant Segmentation throughout the product. If you are using an older version, you can still segment data, but it is a more involved process. Prior to SiteCatalyst v15, segmentation was limited to DataWarehouse and Advanced Segment Insight (ASI). In SiteCatalyst v15, Instant Segmentation was introduced, which replaced ASI, but DataWarehouse segmentation is still available. The rest of this chapter describes the legacy approaches to segmentation (for those still using older versions) and the latest capabilities of Instant Segmentation.

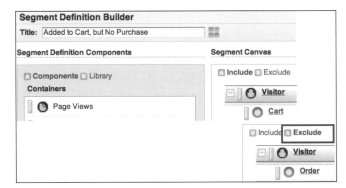

Figure 10.9 Sample segment with Include and Exclude tabs.

Converse Segments

One of the best uses of the Exclude tab in the Segment Builder is to create what I call *Converse segments*, which are two segments that are the complete opposite of each other. For example, I once had a client that wanted to see how sessions in which a video was watched performed as compared to others. To do this, the client created a segment of Visits with Video Views and compared it to the general population. This is OK, but the issue with this approach is that these video sessions were also included in the general population. A better approach might be to create a segment of Visits in which no Video Views occurred and compare that to the segment in which Video Views did occur. Doing this splits your traffic into two parts and no Visit can be in both, allowing for a clearer comparison. To do this, you simply create your initial Video View Visit segment and then use the same criteria in a second segment but move it to the Exclude tab. This creates a Converse segment.

DataWarehouse

DataWarehouse is a back-end repository that stores granular SiteCatalyst data. Technically, DataWarehouse is an add-on product to SiteCatalyst, but it is very rare that a SiteCatalyst client doesn't have DataWarehouse (I tell people that if they can't afford DataWarehouse, they can't afford SiteCatalyst). Unfortunately, some SiteCatalyst customers think DataWarehouse is only a backup of their data, but it is actually much more than that.

To understand DataWarehouse, you need to first understand how it differs from Site-Catalyst. When you use SiteCatalyst, the reports you produce are predefined so they can return quickly in Internet browsers. For this reason, you can only perform one or two levels of report breakdowns in the SiteCatalyst interface. The reason is that more complex queries could take too long to return, resulting in a browser timeout. SiteCatalyst is fine-tuned to provide you with speedy access to 80 percent of the reports you should need on a daily basis. On the other hand, DataWarehouse stores the raw data, which enables it to be used for more complex queries. However, the results are not provided in real time (normally within 24 hours). Instead, results are provided through a flat file of rows and columns, which can be opened in a tool like Microsoft Excel.

DataWarehouse contains all historical data and has the same Segment Builder reviewed earlier to allow you to segment and ultimately download the data you need. In fact, segments you create in SiteCatalyst can be used in DataWarehouse and vice versa. Data requests from DataWarehouse can be done one time or delivered on a recurring basis. If you are using an earlier version of SiteCatalyst, DataWarehouse may be your primary method of segmenting and generating a report that can be analyzed. In SiteCatalyst v15 and later, segmenting and generating a report can be done directly within SiteCatalyst, so the use of DataWarehouse tends to be more focused on cases in which you need a specific file of data for a given segment.

Let's look at how you'd request a DataWarehouse report. You can access DataWarehouse by clicking the Adobe Digital Marketing Suite link at the top left of the SiteCatalyst interface, clicking the SiteCatalyst product menu, and then choosing DataWarehouse. Note that not everyone has access to DataWarehouse, so if you cannot access it, talk to your SiteCatalyst administrator. Once you've launched DataWarehouse, you'll see the DataWarehouse canvas (**Figure 10.10**).

The following list describes each of the elements on the DataWarehouse canvas:

▶ **Name.** An area to name your DataWarehouse request.

▶ **Reporting Date.** In this section, you choose the date for which you want Site-Catalyst to scan data. You can manually choose dates or use the predefined date ranges provided. A Granularity option allows you to see data by hour, day, week, month, quarter, or year.

Figure 10.10
DataWarehouse canvas.

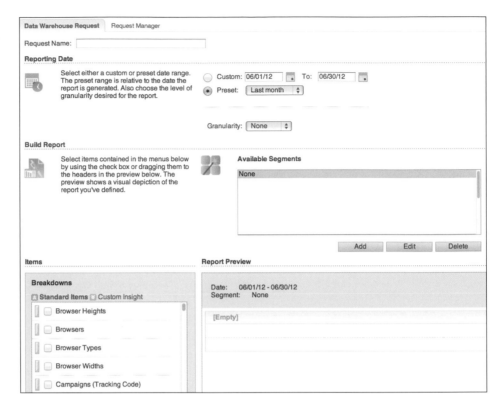

▶ **Build Report.** In this section, you can choose a segment to apply to the request or create a new segment. After selecting your segment, you can begin adding elements to the Report Preview, which shows you an example of what your report will look like when it is returned. Items are divided into Breakdowns and Metrics. Breakdowns show all of your traffic and conversion variables, whereas Metrics show all of your traffic metrics and success events. Note that within each is a tab to differentiate between Standard and Custom elements.

▶ **Schedule Delivery.** This area is where you specify who should receive the report and how often. DataWarehouse reports can be one-time or recurring. Reports can be e-mailed or, if they are large, can be delivered to an FTP site.

Let's walk through an example of how DataWarehouse works. Building on the previous scenario, imagine that your boss not only wants to segment those who have added items to the cart and not purchased, but also wants to see which products they looked at, if a campaign drove them to the site, and what visit number it was when they looked at each product. That is a heavy-duty request but one that is easily tackled in DataWarehouse. We'll start by naming the report "Abandoners Report" and looking at the last four weeks of data. Next you'll add the Looked, But Did Not Buy segment created earlier to the report and then begin to choose the data elements. In this case, your boss wants to

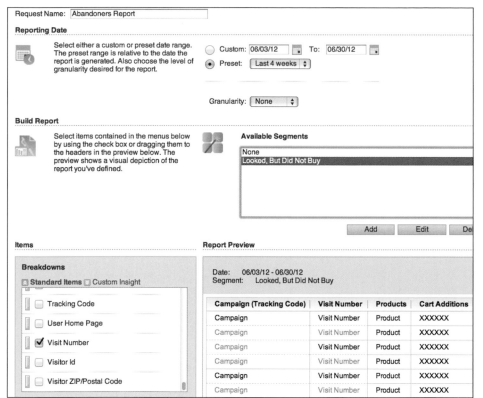

Figure 10.11 Sample DataWarehouse request.

see the products that were looked at, so you'll add Products and the Cart Additions success event. She also wants to know what campaign drove visitors to the website, so add the Campaign variable to the report area. It is up to you to decide if you want Campaign before or after Products, but it will end up resulting in the same data, just configured differently. If you make a mistake, you can drag the column heading left or right, but Metrics must always be on the right. In addition, you'll add Visit Number because your boss wants to know that as well. **Figure 10.11** shows what your screen might look like when you're done. Now all you have to do is decide who you'll send the report to and submit the request. **Figure 10.12** shows what the file would look like.

	A	B	C	D
1	Campaign	Visit Number	Products	Cart Additions
2	11166622	1		0
3	11166622	1	Product1	1
4	11166622	1	Product2	0
5	11166622	1	Product3	0
6	11166622	1	Product4	0
7	11166622	1	Product5	0
8	11166622	1		0
9	11166622	1	Product6	0
10	11161525	1	Product7	0
11	11161525	1	Product8	2

Figure 10.12 Sample DataWarehouse report.

Here are some other tips and facts related to DataWarehouse that I've learned over the years:

▶ **Unlimited breakdowns.** Use DataWarehouse if you need more than the two levels of report breakdowns offered in SiteCatalyst and don't have access to Adobe Discover. DataWarehouse allows you to create an unlimited number of breakdowns.

▶ **Mix traffic and conversion.** In SiteCatalyst, it is not possible to break down traffic variables by conversion variables (or vice versa). However, this can be done in DataWarehouse.

▶ **No unique value limits.** Use DataWarehouse if you have a piece of data that has more than 500,000 unique values per month. Although this doesn't happen too often, there are cases where SiteCatalyst customers need to pass a user ID or some other unique values to a variable that exceeds the 500,000 recommended SiteCatalyst limit. In these cases, the variable in SiteCatalyst is not useful because it shows a "(Low Traffic)" value. But all of the data is stored correctly in DataWarehouse, where you can build the appropriate segments and extract a list of the relevant unique values as needed.

▶ **Test segments.** Building too granular of a segment can at times return no data. Therefore, run a test report for one day of data to be sure the segment is correct before attempting to run it for a month's worth of data (learned the hard way from someone who waited a few days only to receive no data due to user error).

Advanced Segment Insight (ASI)

■ **NOTE** *Remember that ASI does not work if you are using SiteCatalyst v15 or later.*

ASI is a component of DataWarehouse that allows you to create a new data set for a specific segment of users. ASI and DataWarehouse are very similar concepts. Whereas DataWarehouse allows you to build a segment and run *one report* for that segment, ASI takes this a step further by allowing you to see *all reports* for a segment. Although this may not seem like a big distinction, it is. ASI allows you to basically do a Save As of a report suite for a segment of your choosing. Once created, ASI slots (as they are called) look very much like report suites.

When you create an ASI slot, you name it, select or create a segment, and then specify whether the ASI should be for a fixed time frame or should recur daily. If the ASI slot is created for a fixed time frame, SiteCatalyst will cycle through all data in that time frame looking for data that matches the specified segment and include data accordingly, just like it does for a DataWarehouse report. If you choose a daily recurring ASI slot, SiteCatalyst will begin with the specified start date and perform the same process just described but will continue to add one day of data every 24 hours. You can think of ASI as a time machine that goes back in time and re-creates all of the web behavior after the fact for a specific group of people of your choosing. When ASI has examined all the data in the entire date range, you'll be notified via e-mail, although you can use the ASI slot while it is in progress if the time frame is lengthy.

Here is a list of other details you should know about ASI:

▸ You can reuse ASI slots when you are done with them. Let's say you need to see a month's worth of data for a specific segment, but after you've done your analysis, you have no use for it. Simply purge the ASI slot, and after an hour or so it will be ready for reuse.

▸ Any segments that you build in DataWarehouse are available for use in ASI (and Adobe Discover for that matter).

▸ You can manage ASI slot settings using the administration console just as you would any other report suite. Select All in the Report Suites Manager area of the administration console. ASI slots will have report suite IDs beginning with "cyg."

Instant Segmentation (v15+)

With the arrival of SiteCatalyst v15, segmentation took center stage because it became possible to instantly segment any report or dashboard. This change made end users less reliant on DataWarehouse and ASI because those tools required you to wait to get your segmented data. It also increased the importance of understanding how segmentation works in the product because now all SiteCatalyst end users can be expected to build and use segments.

In the SiteCatalyst interface, Instant Segmentation is hard to miss; it is located in the top center of virtually every screen (**Figure 10.13**).

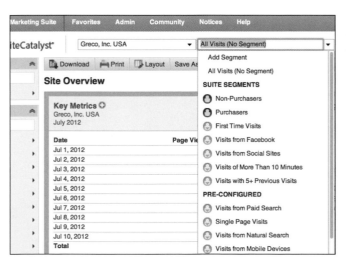

Figure 10.13 Instant Segmentation in the SiteCatalyst interface.

By default, no segment is selected, but the drop-down box allows you to choose from various types of segments:

▶ **Add Segment.** This link allows you to create a new segment.

▶ **Suite Segments.** These are segments that your SiteCatalyst administrator has shared with everyone at the organization. They are set in the administration console. By hovering over a Suite Segment, you'll see a blue information icon (i) that you can click to see the segment definition.

▶ **DataWarehouse.** If you have your own DataWarehouse segments, they will appear in this list as well. By hovering over a DataWarehouse segment, you'll see a series of icons that let you view, edit, or delete the segment, respectively (i ✎ ✖).

▶ **Pre-configured.** These are segments that Adobe has created and are commonly asked for by clients. As with Suite Segments, by hovering over a Pre-configured Segment, you'll see a blue information icon (i) that you can click to see the segment definition.

The power of Instant Segmentation is that you can select a segment from the drop-down box and everything in the report or dashboard you are looking at will dynamically change based on the segment criteria. For example, imagine you are looking at the Browser report shown in **Figure 10.14**. While looking at this report, you can choose to segment it by First Time Visits by clicking on the Instant Segmentation drop-down box, and you'll immediately see the same report, only this time for First Time Visits (**Figure 10.15**).

Figure 10.14 Sample Internet Browser report.

	Browsers	Visits ▼ ⑦		Page Views ⑦	
1.	Microsoft Internet Explorer 9	28,066	25.8%	171,728	27.3%
2.	None	23,052	21.2%	113,267	18.0%
3.	Microsoft Internet Explorer 8	17,527	16.1%	103,717	16.5%
4.	Mozilla Firefox 13.0	9,255	8.5%	57,056	9.1%
5.	Safari 5.1.7	6,946	6.4%	42,891	6.8%

Figure 10.15 Internet Browser report - First Time Visits.

	Browsers	Visits ▼ ⑦		Page Views ⑦	
1.	Microsoft Internet Explorer 9	16,094	26.8%	92,645	27.2%
2.	None	13,534	22.5%	68,609	20.2%
3.	Microsoft Internet Explorer 8	9,839	16.4%	55,407	16.3%
4.	Mozilla Firefox 13.0	5,203	8.6%	31,519	9.3%
5.	Google Chrome 20.0	3,581	6.0%	21,183	6.2%

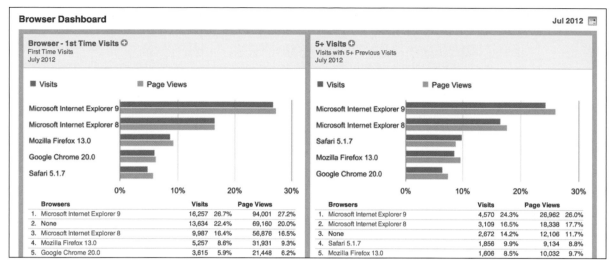

Figure 10.16 Comparing segments using SiteCatalyst dashboards.

As mentioned in Chapter 9, there is currently no way to directly compare segments, but you can add a report to a SiteCatalyst dashboard and place it side by side with a similar report that has a different segment applied. **Figure 10.16** shows an example that compares First Time Visits with 5+ Visits while looking at the same Browser report. Although this doesn't provide the comparison columns you saw with other Comparison reports, it forms a basis for comparison.

One other important detail to note about Instant Segmentation is that it can help circumvent some of the breakdown issues that have plagued SiteCatalyst clients for years. I mention this because many SiteCatalyst clients I work with don't realize how helpful Instant Segmentation can really be. I'll demonstrate using an example. Imagine that you want to see the top Search Engines used to reach your site by Day of Week. You might create a Conversion Subrelation report and use the 5x5 breakdown report trick to see this report (**Figure 10.17**).

Figure 10.17 Sample Subrelation report.

Search Engines - All by Day of Week (v41)	Searches	
1. Google	**26,618**	
1. monday	6,631	24.9%
2. tuesday	5,591	21.0%
3. sunday	5,463	20.5%
4. wednesday	5,135	19.3%
5. Other	3,798	14.3%
Show all for Google...		
2. Google - Canada	**5,444**	
1. monday	1,562	28.7%

Then your boss demands, for some crazy reason, to see this report but only for people who have come to the website between 9:00 a.m. and 10:00 a.m. Now you're stuck. Unless you have Adobe Discover, you'd have to use a DataWarehouse report to get this information because it requires more than the allotted two levels of breakdown permitted in SiteCatalyst. But your boss wants the data ASAP. What do you do? Fortunately, you can use Instant Segmentation to save the day. All you have to do is create a new segment that looks for Visits that take place within that hour (**Figure 10.18**). After you create this segment and apply it to this report, you'll instantly see the original two variables broken down. But behind the scenes, your segment is enabling an extra level of report breakdown by filtering all traffic to use the specified one-hour window (**Figure 10.19**).

If you compare the two reports in Figures 10.17 and 10.19, you can see that this hour window did make a difference on which days were popular for each search engine. But this is just a silly example to illustrate how you can use Instant Segmentation to extend the types of breakdowns you can do in SiteCatalyst.

Figure 10.18 Instant Segmentation creates another breakdown level.

Search Engines - All by Day of Week (v41)	Searches ▼	
1. Google	1,228	
1. wednesday	270	22.0%
2. thursday	253	20.6%
3. tuesday	235	19.1%
4. sunday	222	18.1%
5. monday	216	17.6%
6. friday	1	0.1%
2. Google - Canada	232	
1. sunday	55	23.7%
2. thursday	53	22.8%
3. tuesday	45	19.4%

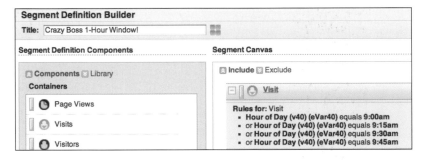

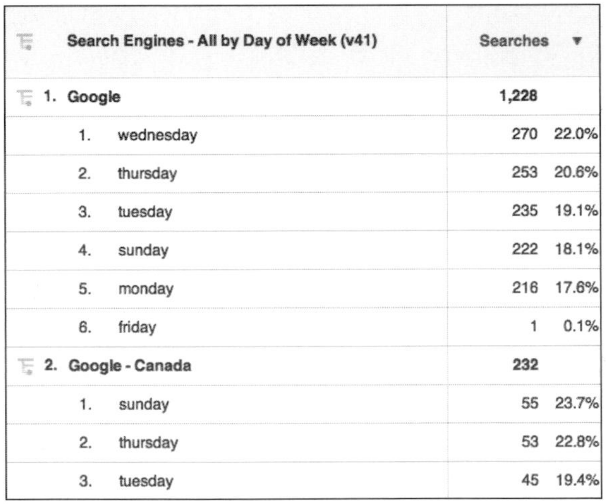

Figure 10.19 Report with three breakdown levels.

Instant Segmentation vs. Multi-suite Tagging

Now that you've learned about the power of Instant Segmentation, one of the most intriguing questions is whether or not clients should take advantage of Instant Segmentation to replace the historic usage of multi-suite tagging. Because this question may arise at your organization, let's review the options at your disposal.

As a quick refresher from Chapter 2, if you have multiple websites, it has traditionally been common to send data to more than one SiteCatalyst report suite (multi-suite tagging). The benefits of multi-suite tagging are as follows:

▶ You can have different suites for each data set (e.g., to see Spain data separately from Italy data).

▶ If you send data to many sub-report suites and one global (master) report suite, you could see de-duplicated unique visitors from all suites in the global report suite.

▶ You can see pathing data across multiple sites in the global report suite to see how people navigate from one website to another.

▶ You can create one dashboard and use the same dashboard for different report suites in SiteCatalyst or in Excel.

▶ You can see metrics at a sub-report suite level, but also aggregate them to see company totals in the global report suite.

Multi-suite tagging offers many benefits, and most large websites to use it as a best practice. Of course, there is a cost. Because you're storing twice as much data in SiteCatalyst, Adobe charges extra for multi-suite tagging, but these "secondary server calls" are charged at a reduced rate. However, Instant Segmentation brought with it the ability to segment your data on the fly. Hence, smart SiteCatalyst clients asked the following question:

"If I track the website name on every page of my websites, why can't I just send all data to one global report suite and build a segment for each website instead of paying extra money to collect my data twice through multi-suite tagging?"

You can reap most of the multi-suite tagging benefits on the preceding list by simply creating website segments. For example, if you currently pass data to a global report suite and an Italy report suite, you could simply pass the phrase "Italy" (or use the abbreviation "it") on every page and build the Italy segment shown in **Figure 10.20**.

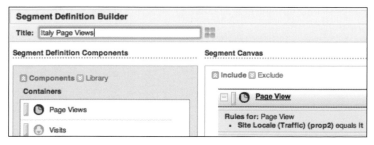

Figure 10.20 Sample Italy segment.

Doing so would narrow the data to just Italy traffic, and you wouldn't have to pay any extra money to Adobe. Most clients are very interested in this concept because it allows them to move some budget money to other needs (like more web analysts or A/B testing). Many companies are taking a "wait and see" attitude while they get comfortable with Instant Segmentation. However, over time, organizations might decide to go this route to save a little money and simplify their implementations (one can only dream about not having to keep 50–100 report suites consistent in the administration console).

So what are the downsides of making this architectural change? Currently, there are some potential downsides that are worth considering, although in the next year I suspect many of these will probably be addressed by product enhancements. The following sections contain some disadvantages to consider before switching from multi-suite tagging to one report suite and Instant Segmentation.

Data security

Currently, there is no way to limit access to SiteCatalyst data based on a segment. With multi-suite tagging, you can assign security at the report suite level. In the preceding Italy example, with multi-suite tagging, it is possible to have some folks in Italy see only Italy data, whereas others can see data for Italy, Spain, United States, and more. If you move to a model of one report suite and rely on segments, you lose this security option. So if locking down your data is important, this is a factor to consider.

More complex segments

Another potential downside is that moving to one report suite will make the creation and usage of segments inherently more difficult. For example, let's say that you create an Italy segment as described earlier. It works well if you are in Italy and want to see all Italy traffic. But what if you are in Italy and want to see all first time visitors from a specific list of keywords who have abandoned the shopping cart? That is a complex segment, and you'd have to be careful to include the Italy part of the segment at the same time or you might incorrectly include or exclude data in your segment. Creating segments is tricky enough, but if you use segments to split out countries (or brands), you have to build even more complex segments to take these countries or brands into account. You and your end users would need to decide when to use an AND clause, an OR clause, combine Visit containers, use a Visitor container, and so on. These are tricky questions for everyday end users, whereas having a separate report suite for each country (or brand) allows you to just focus segments on the task at hand and not worry about the additional country container. For advanced SiteCatalyst users, this nuance shouldn't be a showstopper, but it can definitely hinder novice users and is an issue that should be considered.

Comparing sites

The loss of the ability to compare websites is another downside. As discussed previously, it is easy to compare report suites using the Compare to Site feature. This is a very handy feature when you have multiple geographies or multiple brand websites. Unfortunately, if you choose to abandon your multiple report suites and rely on one report suite and Instant Segmentation, you will lose this capability. The reason is that Instant Segmentation does not allow you to compare two segments in a Comparison report (though you can do this using ReportBuilder, as described in the next chapter). I am hopeful that this feature is coming soon, but it isn't there as of this writing. Therefore, if you want to look at reports side by side for different segments, the multi-suite tagging approach is still the better option at this point.

Conclusion

This chapter covered what you need to know about building segments, using segments in DataWarehouse and ASI, and using segments with Instant Segmentation in Site-Catalyst v15 and later. I've found that those good at identifying and creating useful segments are able to find more insights buried in their SiteCatalyst data. Therefore, even though segmentation takes a while to learn, it is essential to your success as a web analyst.

## CHAPTER 11

Adobe ReportBuilder

As a web analyst, you'll often need to bring together data and manipulate it many different ways. For years, the tool of choice has been Microsoft Excel because it allows you to create great tables, graphs, pivot tables, and so on. Although SiteCatalyst provides some significant reporting and graphing capabilities, it is not meant to replace Microsoft Excel as a daily reporting tool. Therefore, it is incumbent upon web analysts to move SiteCatalyst data to Microsoft Excel, and in this chapter you'll learn the best way to do that using Adobe ReportBuilder. It is not feasible to cover everything you can do with ReportBuilder in this chapter, but I'll cover most of what you need to get started.

What Is Adobe ReportBuilder?

Adobe ReportBuilder is a Microsoft Excel add-on that allows you to easily bring Site-Catalyst data directly into Microsoft Excel. By establishing a data connection between SiteCatalyst and Excel, it is possible to programmatically insert SiteCatalyst data into Excel worksheets. Using ReportBuilder, you can create predefined tables of SiteCatalyst data known as *data requests*. These data requests are configured so that Excel knows which SiteCatalyst report suite, report, metrics, variables, rows of data, breakdowns, text filters, and so on should be inserted.

Using ReportBuilder is far more efficient than the manual process of configuring a report in SiteCatalyst, downloading it to Excel, copying the data to your master spread-sheet, and so on. By taking the time to determine what data you'll need, you can insert SiteCatalyst data easily and even know the exact cells it will be in so you can prepare charts and graphs for when the data arrives. With your data in Excel, you can then apply the many formulas and tools that Excel provides to manipulate or present your data as you please. Once the data requests have been defined, you can easily refresh the data to reflect the most up-to-date information without having to rebuild your requests each time. You can perform this refresh process while you have your Excel workbook open on your desktop, or you can schedule the Excel workbook to be delivered from the Adobe servers via e-mail or FTP.

SiteCatalyst vs. ReportBuilder

One of the first questions SiteCatalyst customers ask is when they should use SiteCata-lyst reports and dashboards, and when they should turn to ReportBuilder. Each one has a better fit for different types of applications. Let's first look at some of the most com-mon advantages that ReportBuilder has over traditional reporting within SiteCatalyst:

▶ **Advanced calculations.** SiteCatalyst allows for calculations to be done using com-mon math operators (addition, division, and so on) and allows you to build line-item or report suite totals into your fomulas. With ReportBuilder you can use all of Excel's formulas (average, mean, median, standard deviation, and so on), and you can per-form calculations between numbers that are in separate reports or report suites. It is also possible to take advantage of advanced Excel functions to show forecast data to give users an idea of what data is expected in the next few days or weeks.

▶ **Advanced graphs.** SiteCatalyst provides many graph options, such as line, bar, area, pie, scatter, and bubble charts, but trending is limited to five items in a report, and you don't have much control over the axes or appearance of the graph. With Report-Builder you can use Excel to trend as many items as you want, use more graph types, and configure the graph to look the way you want it.

▶ **Dynamic templates.** It is common for an analyst to have to take one report or dashboard and then make many copies for different geographies or brands. For example, you may have a product dashboard for a specific product line that uses ten separate SiteCatalyst reports. Now imagine that 30 other product lines want the same dashboard. With SiteCatalyst this can be very time-consuming, but using ReportBuilder you can create your dashboard data requests so they reference common filter criteria (e.g., product line values) contained in a cell of the worksheet. This allows you to produce each separate product line dashboard by simply updating one cell in Excel and refreshing the workbook.

▶ **Many-by-many breakdowns.** In SiteCatalyst, you can create a one-by-many or a 5x5 breakdown. In ReportBuilder, you can go way beyond this to create many-by-many breakdowns.

▶ **Formatting and appearance.** Using ReportBuilder, you can format your reports and dashboards any way you'd like using company logos and colors.

▶ **Data request duplication.** ReportBuilder allows you to easily duplicate data requests, which allows you to create multiple reports using one as a template.

ReportBuilder might be the better approach when you need more advanced capabilities or find that a report or dashboard you are working on needs to be replicated. You can then use SiteCatalyst dashboards and reports for everything else, and they are especially beneficial for the casual users. Here are some of the advantages SiteCatalyst reports and dashboards have over ReportBuilder:

▶ **Standardized.** Most SiteCatalyst reports look the same, so your end users will be familiar with their layout and design. Customized reports and dashboards generated by ReportBuilder can add a level of complexity that is beyond many casual users.

▶ **Unlimited.** There is no practical limit on how many SiteCatalyst reports or dashboards you can create and schedule for delivery to your stakeholders. Conversely, ReportBuilder licenses have a limit to the number of workbooks that are automated (historically ten per license). There are also limits on how many users at your organization will have access to ReportBuilder. This is determined by your Adobe contract.

▶ **Ease of access.** ReportBuilder workbooks are viewed in Excel and are often passed around via e-mail. SiteCatalyst provides a central repository for reports and dashboards, and allows them to be easily shared among users.

▶ **Ad hoc analysis.** ReportBuilder is a great tool when you know the exact report you want to create or automate. However, SiteCatalyst is much better at ad hoc analysis because you can play with the dates, filters, segments, breakdowns, metrics, and so on until you find what you need. This includes the building of segments, which you can do in SiteCatalyst, but not from within ReportBuilder.

Using ReportBuilder

ReportBuilder can help you create amazing reports and dashboards, but it does take time to learn how it works. This section explains how to install ReportBuilder and reviews the basics of its use.

Installing ReportBuilder

■ **NOTE** *Report-Builder does not work on the Mac versions of Microsoft Excel. If you use a Mac, you can use ReportBuilder by running Microsoft Windows on your Mac.*

Two prerequisites allow you to install ReportBuilder. First, your company has to have acquired ReportBuilder licenses, and they need to be activated. If you do not have licenses, contact your Adobe account manager. Second, you'll need to add users to the ReportBuilder user group, which has to be done by your SiteCatalyst administrator. When you have been given access, you can find instructions for downloading Report-Builder from within the SiteCatalyst interface, as shown in **Figure 11.1**. From the download page, select the 32- or 64-bit Excel version (ask your IT team which version of Excel you have) and then click the Download button. When the ReportBuilder executable file has downloaded, open it to install the toolbar. After installation is complete, you'll see the ReportBuilder toolbar under the Add-Ins tab in Excel (**Figure 11.2**).

Figure 11.1 ReportBuilder download link.

ExcelClient

You may have heard of ExcelClient, which is another Adobe Excel add-on that allows you to bring data into Excel. ReportBuilder has many more features and is much more stable than ExcelClient. Adobe has made it clear that ReportBuilder is the tool of choice, and as such, ExcelClient is maintained but no longer receives enhancements. This means that newer SiteCatalyst features like segmentation will be built into ReportBuilder but not ExcelClient. ExcelClient also has many limitations not present in ReportBuilder, so it is advised that if your organization is using ExcelClient that you transition to ReportBuilder. If you have existing reports in ExcelClient, ReportBuilder has a converter that allows you to easily convert workbooks to the ReportBuilder format.

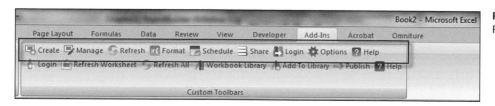

Figure 11.2
ReportBuilder toolbar.

ReportBuilder Toolbar

Let's review the various actions you can take from the ReportBuilder toolbar:

▸ **Create.** Opens the wizard that you'll use to create new data requests.

▸ **Manage.** Is a bulk editor for all data requests in your workbook.

▸ **Refresh.** Updates all the data requests in your workbook.

▸ **Format.** Provides an easy way to open Excel's conditional formatting tool.

▸ **Schedule.** Allows you to schedule and distribute workbooks automatically.

▸ **Share.** Uploads your workbook to a repository from which other users with Report-Builder can access it (rarely used).

▸ **Login.** Allows you to log in and log out of ReportBuilder.

▸ **Options.** Contains general settings, which for the most part never need to be changed.

▸ **Help.** Opens a help reference where you can get additional information related to ReportBuilder features.

The following sections explain these functions in greater detail.

Creating Data Requests

The most important part of using ReportBuilder is creating data requests. A data request is a query created by ReportBuilder that is inserted into an Excel workbook. To create a data request, click the Create button in the toolbar to open the Request Wizard. In this wizard, you'll see the following configuration options (**Figure 11.3**):

▸ **Report Suite.** This is similar to the report suite selector in SiteCatalyst. When you select a report suite from the drop-down list, the request will be bound to that report suite. However, notice that next to the report suite drop-down list is a small icon with a red arrow (Figure 11.3). Clicking this arrow allows you to to pick a cell that contains the report suite ID you want to use. Note this is not the friendly name you see in the drop-down list but the SiteCatalyst Report Suite ID, which you might have to get from your SiteCatalyst administrator. This makes your data request dynamic, and ReportBuilder will use that cell value to determine which report suite

Figure 11.3
ReportBuilder Wizard –
Step 1.

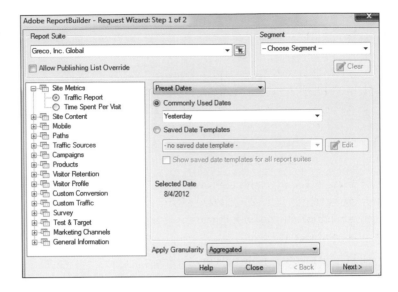

Dynamic cell references make it easy to refresh data for different report suites without having to reconfigure data requests. Also in the same window is an Allow Publishing List Override check box, which allows you to use publishing lists with your requests (which you learned about in Chapter 9).

▸ **Segment.** Use this drop-down list to apply a segment from SiteCatalyst. Notice that you can't create a new segment in ReportBuilder. If you need a new segment, create it in SiteCatalyst first. Click the Clear button to remove a segment.

▸ **Menu.** In the menu portion of the screen, choose the report you want to use in the data request. The options provided are roughly the equivalent of those available for the selected report suite in SiteCatalyst (not all SiteCatalyst reports can be used in ReportBuilder).

▸ **Dates.** Use this area to select dates for the data request. You can use preset date ranges, fixed dates, or rolling dates. Preset date ranges are rolling dates based on commonly used date ranges. Your organization can also create custom date templates if there are specific date ranges it wants to use that are not listed as a preset range. The fixed date option is not often used. Rolling dates allows you to customize the date ranges in any way you desire. For example, you might choose a date range that is "one week, starting 13 weeks ago" to compare to last week for a quarterly comparison. If you're not sure what results your date range configuration will give you, remember to look at the date preview provided and compare it to a calendar to see if it is what you expect relative to today.

▸ **Apply Granularity.** The dates that you've worked with so far are configured to select the total date range for your report. This drop-down list applies a granularity. If you set your date range to be the "last 13 weeks," you could apply a granularity of "week" to see trended metrics by week for the last 13 weeks. If you do not want any granularity applied, simply select Aggregated.

After you have completed the configurations in Step 1 of the data Request Wizard, you'll configure the layout of the data request in Step 2. This portion of the wizard can be separated into three main sections (**Figure 11.4**). On the left (outlined in red) are all of the available elements that you can add to your request. In the top half (outlined in orange) is the report layout. In the bottom half of the right side (outlined in purple) is the report preview. Let's review the elements in this step of the wizard:

▸ **Metrics.** The options on this tab are roughly equivalent to what you would see if you were running a SiteCatalyst report and selected Add Metrics. At the top of the tab is a drop-down list that contains the different types of metrics, including standard, participation, calculated, and lifetime.

▸ **Dimensions.** The tab behind Metrics is Dimensions. Clicking this tab shows you all reports that you can use in a breakdown using the report you selected in Step 1. In the case of conversion variables, it will contain all other conversion variables (if you are using SiteCatalyst v15 or later). In the case of traffic variables, it will contain other traffic variables that have traffic correlations with the report selected in Step 1.

▸ **Pivot Layout.** This allows you to define your report as one consistent block with the report dimensions and metrics along the top or side and the metrics in the middle.

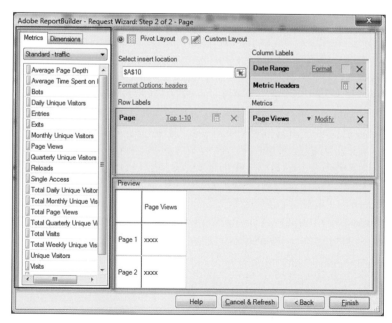

Figure 11.4 ReportBuilder Wizard – Step 2.

▶ **Custom Layout.** This allows you to separate the labels and metrics of your request so they can be inserted into different locations or even hidden from sight. This is a good option if you already have the necessary description of the data in your Excel file. If this is the case, you can hide the labels that would be repetitive and just insert the data that you need. Pivot Layout also provides hiding options but does not allow the flexibility to insert different parts of the request in different locations.

▶ **Insert Location.** Click the cell selector icon to designate the top-left corner of the request that you will insert into your workbook. Be aware of the size of the request in terms of columns and rows. If you try to insert a request that overlaps with another request, ReportBuilder will warn you. However, it will not warn you if your request overlaps with other Excel data that you have created outside of ReportBuilder.

▶ **Format Options: headers.** This link will provide you with some general options for the headers that come with the request. You can opt to display report filters and parameters; otherwise, the filters applied to your data will be hidden from view.

▶ **Hiding/Deleting.** Each item under the row and column label boxes has a red X and a square button just to the left of the X. Click the red X to delete the item from your report. Note that you are required to have at least one dimension (with the exception of event totals pulled from Site metrics) in which case you may see the red X grayed out. There are also small rectangles that you can use to hide row or column labels. Labels provide good context for your data, of course, so hide them only if the appropriate data descriptions are somewhere else in your workbook.

▶ **Filtering/Selecting.** The green link located between the name of your dimension and the Hide button will show filtering options. By default this will display "Top 1–10" which means it will limit the results to the top ten items. However, clicking this link will show the three distinct filter options available. Most Popular allows you to choose a starting rank (begin with the 1st item or the 100th) and specify how many items should be returned in the report (keep in mind that there is a hard limit of 50,000 rows, including breakdowns). Specific Filters allows you to select the exact values you want to appear in the report. You can select these values manually or by using a range of cells in the Excel worksheet. Saved Filters allows you to reuse filters that you or others at your organization have created.

▶ **Prepend/Postpend Text.** This allows you to apply a common prefix or postfix to all elements in your report but is rarely used.

As you can see, there are many ReportBuilder configuration options. As you become more advanced using ReportBuilder, you can experiment with some of the more advanced features to see what data is returned. A great online help system shows you tricks (e.g., using date formulas), so I encourage you to take the time to learn this tool. It will save you time in the long run.

Request Manager

The Request Manager helps you find and edit requests within your workbook. You can access it by clicking the Manage button on the toolbar. When you open the Request Manager (**Figure 11.5**), you'll see a list of the requests in the workbook (if the All Sheets check box is selected) or for the worksheet (if the All Sheets check box is deselected).

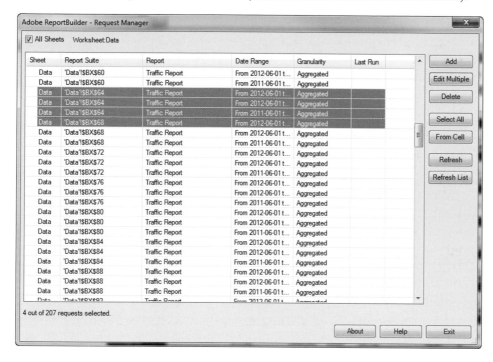

Figure 11.5 Request Manager.

You'll find the following options in the Request Manager:

▶ **Add.** Launches the data Request Wizard to create a new data request.

▶ **Edit/Edit Multiple.** Allows you to do mass edits across data requests to change the report suite, segment, granularity, or date range of the requests. The Edit Multiple feature applies when you have multiple data requests selected and can be a time-saver when you have to make a global change to multiple data requests (e.g., change the segment used).

▶ **Delete.** Provides a mechanism to delete one or more data requests.

▶ **Select All.** Highlights all of the rows in the manager.

▶ **From Cell.** Highlights a data request in the Request Manager by selecting a request in the worksheet with the Request Manager open.

▶ **Refresh.** Refreshes all highlighted requests.

▶ **Refresh List.** Refreshes all requests in the list.

Refreshing Requests

After you've created a workbook, you can refresh data requests whenever you need to see the most up-to-date data. There are two general ways to refresh your data.

The first is to manually refresh by simply opening your workbook in Excel and clicking the Refresh button in the toolbar. You'll then be prompted for the "now" date (also known as the "as of" date). The majority of the time you'll simply use today as the relative date for your data request. However, if you want to back-date the report to past weeks, you can roll back the date by entering a date in the past. After you've selected your date, click OK and wait until the workbook has been completely refreshed. The progress bar that appears during this time will advance, not based on time to completion, but based on the number of requests that have been completed.

The second way to refresh your dashboard is to schedule it for distribution (this is covered in the next section). In general, you would use this method when you don't want to wait for the report to refresh or want it delivered at a designated time in the future. This method uploads the Excel workbook to the Adobe servers, and when the scheduled delivery time is reached, it refreshes the workbook (on the server) and delivers the completed report via e-mail or FTP.

Scheduling Workbooks

The Schedule feature automatically delivers ReportBuilder workbooks to you or your stakeholders. To schedule a workbook, click the Schedule button in the toolbar and then click New to access the Scheduling Wizard (**Figure 11.6**). By default your currently open workbook will appear as the selected report to schedule, but you can click the Select button to choose a different file. Next, you'll select the e-mail addresses to which you want to send the report (manually or by clicking the To button). You can adjust the subject line as desired and choose any advanced scheduling options needed before clicking OK and scheduling your workbook.

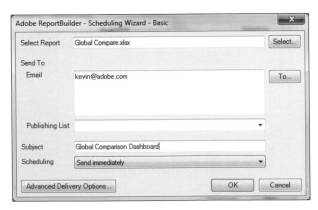

Figure 11.6 Scheduling Wizard.

Other ReportBuilder Items

Before moving on to the next section and examining some real-world ReportBuilder examples, there are two final items worth mentioning: dependent requests and how installing ReportBuilder modifies your right-click context menu in Excel.

Dependent requests

A dependent request occurs when one data request points to a different request, which creates a dependency. As you become more advanced using ReportBuilder, you'll find that at times you'll want one data request to use the values returned in another data request. For example, you may have one data request that inserts the ten most popular pages of the website and then a second data request that uses these ten values as part of its criteria. ReportBuilder knows which requests are dependent and ensures that nondependent requests are refreshed prior to dependent requests in the order of dependency.

Right-clicking in Excel

Once you've installed ReportBuilder and are logged in, it will modify your right-click context menu in Excel by adding two ReportBuilder options. If you right-click on a cell that does not have a request, the following additional options will appear at the bottom of the menu (**Figure 11.7**):

▶ **Add Request.** Launches the data Request Wizard.

▶ **Copy Worksheet w/Requests.** Copies the worksheet you are currently viewing with all the ReportBuilder requests and creates a new duplicated worksheet. Note that this is different than just using Excel to copy the worksheet because traditional Excel functionality will not automatically carry over ReportBuilder data requests to the new worksheet.

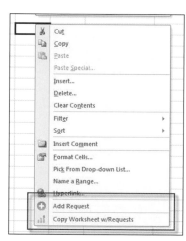

Figure 11.7 Excel right-click context menu without a data request.

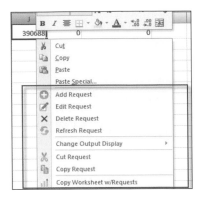

Figure 11.8 Excel right-click context menu with data request.

If you right-click on cells that do contain a ReportBuilder request, the following additional options will appear in the menu (**Figure 11.8**):

▶ **Edit Request.** Opens the ReportBuilder Wizard for this request so you can modify the report.

▶ **Delete Request.** Removes the currently selected request in the worksheet.

▶ **Refresh Request.** Refreshes the currently selected request. This is different than the Refresh button in the toolbar, which refreshes all requests.

▶ **Cut Request.** Cuts the request. This is particularly useful if you inserted the request in the wrong location. After you've cut the request, you can right-click in a new area to insert your request. Be sure to use the Paste Request option, not Excel's native Paste option.

▶ **Copy Request.** Allows you to easily duplicate requests that you have already created through copy and paste.

▶ **Paste Request.** In connection with the Cut or Copy Request commands, this option allows you to make your requests relative as you move or duplicate them. This option appears only if you have cut or copied a request. If a cell reference is in your request, you'll be given the option to paste statically or relatively. Use the Relative option to use cells that contain different report suites, search criteria, number of entries, or any other value that has a cell selector in the data request. You can then build one request that references these cells and then just copy the request across your list of varying inputs. This can quickly create many unique requests. If there are no cell references in your request, you'll just see Paste Request.

Real-world Examples

Let's walk through two examples of using ReportBuilder in real-world situations. These examples demonstrate how the functions described in the preceding section can be applied and show you two popular uses of ReportBuilder: templates and dependent data requests.

Using ReportBuilder Templates

In this example, you'll learn how to create a ReportBuilder template that you can leverage across multiple report suites. Imagine that Greco, Inc. has a retail business that sells products in 15 countries. In SiteCatalyst, Greco, Inc. has one global report suite that is a combination of all countries and 15 country-specific report suites. Each country site is managed by a different team, and you are responsible for creating country-specific reporting for each of these groups. For this example, assume that all of your country report suites are implemented identically and you need to show a trend of visits, orders, and revenue for each country. Because you'll ultimately be distributing this report to different stakeholders in different countries, you'll create a publishing list, as described in Chapter 9, so that each country report suite is assigned to the e-mail addresses to which data should be delivered.

Now let's switch over to ReportBuilder and add a data request to trend visits, orders, and revenue. Click Create in the toolbar and configure the first page as shown in **Figure 11.9**.

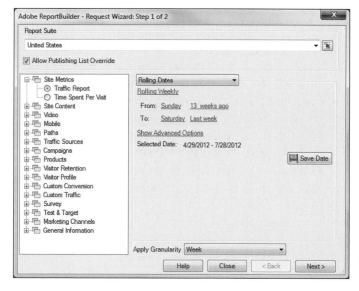

Figure 11.9 Settings for Step 1 in the data Request Wizard.

Note that the Allow Publishing List Override check box is selected. This option will later allow you to dynamically change the data for each report suite. The report suite selected is United States. Also selected is the Site Metrics - Traffic Report because this is where the trended events are located. For the date range you'll use a weekly rolling date that covers the last 13 weeks with weekly granularity.

Next, you'll add your metrics—visits, revenue, and orders—which are under the Standard – Commerce metrics. From here, you can drag your three desired metrics to the Metrics area. You can also click the Format link next to the Week label to modify the start date so that it is in the format of MM/DD/YYYY. Then choose an insert location cell of B2. When you're done with these configurations, your screen should look like the one shown in **Figure 11.10**.

Figure 11.10 Settings for Step 2 in the data Request Wizard.

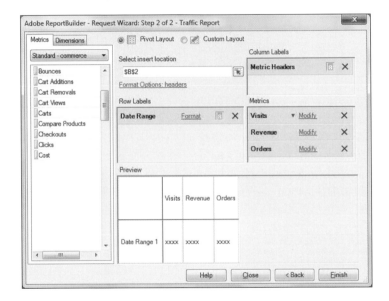

When you click the Finish button, your data should refresh and look something like **Figure 11.11**.

If desired, you can use standard Excel formulas to add calculated metrics, such as Conversion (orders/visits) and Yield (revenue/visits) in the columns to the right of your data request. To make sure that you and your stakeholders know what country the data shown is associated with, you can optionally add a second data request that contains the report suite information. You can do this by inserting a report suite data request using the General Information area of the data Request Wizard. If you want your report to look a bit more polished, you can add some formatting as well. When you've added your conversion rate formulas and report suite information, your report might look like the one shown in **Figure 11.12**.

	A	B	C	D	E
1					
2		Week	Visits	Revenue	Orders
3		04/29/2012	771546	522194	1999
4		05/06/2012	789076	531224	2004
5		05/13/2012	672930	485772	1827
6		05/20/2012	780400	552091	2032
7		05/27/2012	723582	557103	2002
8		06/03/2012	807179	625438	2177
9		06/10/2012	718859	553083	1837
10		06/17/2012	773833	651450	1982
11		06/24/2012	694283	610146	1877
12		07/01/2012	847641	541284	1908
13		07/08/2012	1155539	845687	2752
14		07/15/2012	984737	769833	2394
15		07/22/2012	1192374	1035128	3083
16					

Figure 11.11 Completed data request.

	A	B	C	D	E	F	G
1		United States Country Performance					
2		Week	Visits	Revenue	Orders	Conversion	Yield
3		04/29/2012	77,155	$543,323	2,080	2.70%	$7.04
4		05/06/2012	78,908	$552,719	2,085	2.64%	$7.00
5		05/13/2012	67,293	$505,427	1,901	2.82%	$7.51
6		05/20/2012	78,040	$574,430	2,114	2.71%	$7.36
7		05/27/2012	72,358	$579,645	2,083	2.88%	$8.01
8		06/03/2012	80,718	$650,745	2,265	2.81%	$8.06
9		06/10/2012	71,886	$575,462	1,911	2.66%	$8.01
10		06/17/2012	77,383	$677,810	2,062	2.66%	$8.76
11		06/24/2012	69,428	$634,834	1,953	2.81%	$9.14
12		07/01/2012	84,764	$563,186	1,986	2.34%	$6.64
13		07/08/2012	115,554	$879,906	2,863	2.48%	$7.61
14		07/15/2012	98,474	$800,983	2,491	2.53%	$8.13
15		07/22/2012	119,237	$1,077,012	3,208	2.69%	$9.03
16							
17		Source:					
18		Report Suite	Report Suite Name				
19		usproduction	United States				

Figure 11.12 Completed data request with conversion rates and report suite information.

Your last step is to schedule this template for delivery to different stakeholders in each of the different countries. To do this, select Schedule in the ReportBuilder toolbar and click New. Choose the workbook you've been working on, and then be sure to select the publishing list set up earlier, as shown in **Figure 11.13**. When you click OK, the report will be sent to each publishing list recipient. Keep in mind that each recipient will receive data for the country that person is associated with in the publishing list. You can also click the Advanced Delivery Options button to make this delivery occur on a regular basis (e.g., weekly).

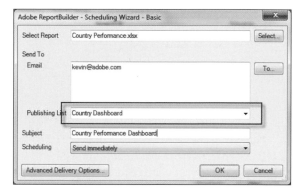

Figure 11.13 Scheduling report using a publishing list.

Using Dependent Data Requests

As mentioned previously, ReportBuilder allows you to create data requests that are dependent on one another. In this example, you'll see how this can be done using a real-world business question.

In this scenario, Greco, Inc. has a sporting goods retail website. It has a number of high-volume pages that it wants visitors to take action on. However, it has noticed a spike in onsite searches and wants to determine which of these top pages are causing visitors to use onsite search, because that might be indicative of page content deficiencies. To accomplish this in ReportBuilder, you'll use two separate SiteCatalyst reports. The first is the Pages report sorted by Page Views. The second is a custom Previous Page to Search traffic variable report. The latter is set using the Previous Value plug-in described in Chapter 7 and is set with Page Name values, but only on the search results page of the site. This Previous Page to Search traffic variable, therefore, has the names of Pages and a Page View count of how many times it was the page being viewed when an onsite search took place. Your goal is to report how many page views each page name received (in general) and how many times those same pages led to searches. By having both of these page view counts for the same page name, you can divide the two and see how many searches take place for each time a page name is viewed. Dependent data requests in ReportBuilder can help you do this.

You'll start by creating a Pages report showing the top 100 pages sorted by Page Views and creating a data request that looks like the one in **Figure 11.14**.

Figure 11.14 Top 100 pages data request.

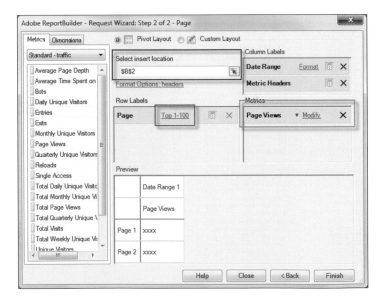

Next, you'll pull in the number of Page Views that led to onsite searches using the custom traffic variable. However, you don't want to see this data for the top 100 pages that led to onsite searches. Instead, you want to see the Page Views associated with the same top 100 pages that are returned from your first data request (Figure 11.14). In effect, you want to tell ReportBuilder to first look at the top 100 page names that are returned in the primary data request and then retrieve the corresponding values from the custom Previous Page to Search traffic variables *for each of those top 100 page names*. This makes it a dependent request because the second data request you're building doesn't know which values to pull data for until the first data request has finished running.

To start, you'll configure the second data request to use the Previous Page to Search traffic variable and insert the top 100 items (**Figure 11.15**).

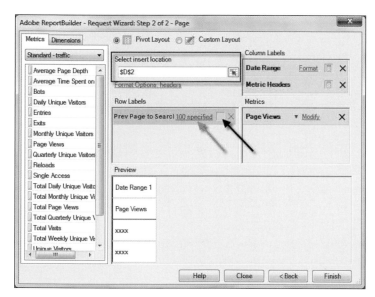

Figure 11.15
Dependent data request settings.

Notice that the dimension (blue arrow) has been hidden and the green link to apply a specific filter (yellow arrow) has been clicked. On the specific filter screen, you can choose a range of cells that will tell ReportBuilder the items for which data should be generated (**Figure 11.16**). Notice that the range of cells is set to the same range of cells that will be returned by your initial data request, which will eventually contain the top 100 page name values. This instructs ReportBuilder to return the Page Views from your Previous Page to Search report for the same page name values that were in the top 100 pages report. **Figure 11.17** shows the report you'll see when you finish your configuration.

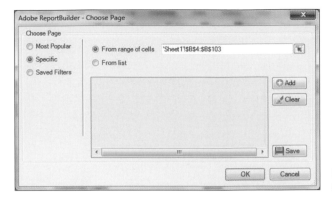

Figure 11.16 Specific filter settings.

	A	B	C	D
1				
2			2012/01/22	2012/07/22
3		Page	Page Views	Page Views
4		Search Results	195552	4674
5		Home	193185	11649
6		Men's Clothing	121032	10566
7		Hiking & Camping Gear	38591	5580
8		Women's Clothing	31227	303
9		Backpacks	24383	1229
10		Climbing	17846	1672
11		Men's Jackets	14064	838
12		Shoes	13398	1960
13		Kids	13323	464
14		Tents	13290	1338
15		On Sale	13273	327

Figure 11.17 Completed dependent data request.

	A	B	C	D	E
1					
2			2012/01/22	2012/07/22	
3		Page	Page Views	Page Views	% PVs to Search
4		Search Results	195552	4674	2%
5		Home	193185	11649	6%
6		Men's Clothing	121032	10566	9%
7		Hiking & Camping Gear	38591	5580	14%
8		Women's Clothing	31227	303	1%
9		Backpacks	24383	1229	5%
10		Climbing	17846	1672	9%
11		Men's Jackets	14064	838	6%
12		Shoes	13398	1960	15%
13		Kids	13323	464	3%
14		Tents	13290	1338	10%
15		On Sale	13273	327	2%

Figure 11.18 Dependent data request with an Excel formula.

You can then use standard Excel functionality to create a calculated metric that divides Search Page Views by general Page Views to see the percentage of Page Views that led to a search (**Figure 11.18**).

Now you can see that the Hiking & Campaign Gear, Shoes, and Tents pages might have some issues because a much higher percentage of people searched from these pages. The next step might be to break down your Previous Page to Search report by onsite search terms to see what people are searching for from those pages (which you could also do using another dependent data request).

Use ReportBuilder for Data Quality

One of the best uses of ReportBuilder is to check the quality of your SiteCatalyst data. Data quality is important to the success of your web analytics program, but if you are using hundreds of variables in SiteCatalyst, it is almost impossible to know when data issues arise. But by using ReportBuilder, you can create data requests for your key success events, conversion variables, and traffic variables that download historical data and compare the latest data to those trends. Then you can apply conditional formatting to be alerted when data might be suspect.

For example, let's say that Greco, Inc. has an insurance subsidiary and the key KPIs it tracks are related to the quote process. Using ReportBuilder, it can create a data quality dashboard that looks at yesterday's data and compares it to a historical average, as shown in **Figure 11.19**.

In this example, it might be worth the company's time to check out the Quote Step 2 and Checkout success events to be sure there are no tagging issues. Although it can take some time to set up a ReportBuilder data quality report, I've found that it can pay great dividends down the road.

Greco, Inc.	QA Dashboard			
Events 1-60				
Event	Yesterday	Same Day Avg	% Change	> 1StDev
QUOTE START	485	493	-1.59%	
QUOTE - STEP 2	231	361	-36.01%	
QUOTE COMPLETE	328	335	-1.94%	
QUOTE CHECKOUT	63	106	-40.38%	

Figure 11.19 Sample ReportBuilder data quality report.

Conclusion

You can use ReportBuilder to insert massive amounts of SiteCatalyst data into Excel. For this reason, many web analysts use ReportBuilder to create professional-looking reports, graphs, and dashboards that they distribute to stakeholders company-wide. Most advanced web analysts use ReportBuilder exclusively because it is more flexible and provides more formatting and graph options than the SiteCatalyst reporting interface. Therefore, I encourage you to take the time to learn how it works so you can spend more time performing analysis and less time creating and sending reports.

Applying Adobe SiteCatalyst

This section focuses on how you can apply the SiteCatalyst concepts covered in prior chapters to your organization. For the most part, instead of introducing new SiteCatalyst concepts, I'll share creative ways that you can apply what you've learned to solve practical business problems. Most of the examples provided in this section are from real companies using SiteCatalyst to solve real business problems.

It would be impossible to cover everything I've helped clients do in SiteCatalyst over the past ten years, so I've chosen some specific topics that are common to many SiteCatalyst implementations. Although some of these applications may focus on one industry vertical or another, each will demonstrate ways you can apply your SiteCatalyst knowledge to generate meaningful website data for analysis purposes. Therefore, even if a particular chapter doesn't seem relevant to your specific industry, I encourage you to read through it so you can increase your SiteCatalyst prowess; you will often identify ways to adapt it to your organization.

As you'll learn over time, there are often several ways to perform tasks in SiteCatalyst. Much of what I'll share are my "best practices" that I've honed over the years based on different client situations. However, I am mindful that there are always other (possibly even better) ways to tackle the business scenarios presented. Keep in mind that the goal of this book and section is to enhance your understanding and education of SiteCatalyst, not to prescribe exactly what you should implement at your organization.

## CHAPTER 12

Tracking Website Content

When organizations initially purchase SiteCatalyst, one of the first details they want to know is how website visitors are using the various pages, types of pages, and sections on their website. There will always be those who ask, "How many hits did our pages get?" Therefore, one of the first action items for a new SiteCatalyst implementation is to develop a good way to organize all of the website content. Unfortunately, many organizations get off on the wrong foot when tracking their content. Normally, the reason is that they are new to SiteCatalyst and don't fully understand it when they need to make important content tracking decisions. Whether you are a brand-new SiteCatalyst client or an existing client, in this chapter I'll share some important considerations to think about when it comes to tracking your website content.

Naming Pages, Sections, and Sites

You can tell a lot about an organization's SiteCatalyst implementation by looking at how it names its website pages and sections. There seems to be a high correlation between good page and section names and a good overall SiteCatalyst implementation. Naming pages, sections, and other page-based attributes is hard work because it often requires tagging rules or integration with content management systems. Similarly, SiteCatalyst implementations take a lot of work and planning via tagging and so on. Therefore, I've often used content naming as a proxy for how an organization approaches implementation. For example, if no page name is set in SiteCatalyst (which results in using URLs as Page Name values), it is normally indicative of an organization that is not willing to devote the time and resources that it should to its SiteCatalyst implementation.

Although there is no one right way to assign names to your website pages and sections, there are definitely some commonsense naming conventions that will help you down the road. The following sections describe some of these practices for you to consider in your SiteCatalyst implementation.

Naming Pages

If you don't apply custom (often referred to as "friendly") page names in the `s.pagename` traffic variable, the URL will be captured by default. This is not ideal for the following reasons:

▶ URLs can be very long and exceed the traffic variable 100 character limit.

▶ URLs are often not descriptive and can be difficult for end users to associate with pages on the website.

▶ URLs can have query string parameters that get cut off, which means that several pages with different query strings can accidentally be treated as a single page name in SiteCatalyst. This makes it impossible to see paths separately by page and query string.

▶ URLs can have "http://" and "https://" versions, which means two versions of each URL. This subdivides one page into many pages, which negatively impacts pathing, page views, unique visitors, and so on.

For these reasons, it is highly recommended that you name your pages the way you want to see them in the Pages report. I generally advise naming pages based on website directory structures or manually through a content management system. Once you determine which approach you'll use to name your pages, you then need to decide the actual structure of your page names. Here are my recommendations:

▶ **Common identifier.** Make sure all pages within each unique website have a common identifier. For example, for three distinct websites that serve different purposes, assign a value in the page name for each website so you can easily filter those pages in a global report suite. For a company like Greco, Inc., which has multiple country websites, you should add a way to identify each page as part of one Greco, Inc. website.

▶ **Section name.** Include the section name in the page name whenever possible. For example, if your website has a section for Products and another for Services, include those in the page name. This allows you to easily filter Page reports to get all of the pages within a section. Some companies also include the subsection in the page name, which is fine as long as you don't exceed the traffic variable character limit.

▶ **Unique name.** In general, all pages should have a unique name. If two pages have the same page name, SiteCatalyst will treat them as a single page and all data for that page will be merged (including paths). The exceptions to this are cases where you might have thousands of pages that serve the same purpose but might be different for each user and cause too many unique values.

▶ **Avoid spaces.** Whenever possible, avoid using spaces in page names because spaces make it more difficult to filter pages using text searches.

Figure 12.1 shows a list of what your pages might look like if you put all of these ideas together. This page naming convention meets all of the criteria in the previous list because it has a company and website identifier, a section, and a name for each page. If Greco, Inc. were part of a larger organization, all of its data could be fed into a higher-level multi-suite tagged report suite that includes other companies as well. For this reason, having a company identifier as part of the website identifier is important. The preceding page name scheme isn't that difficult to implement, and it provides the following advantages when you're using the text search filter (see Chapter 8):

		Pages	Page Views ▼ ⑦	
	1.	grecoinc:us:home:homepage	16,113,652	21.3%
	2.	grecoinc:us:products:products-landing	14,163,351	18.7%
	3.	grecoinc:uk:home:homepage	11,891,155	15.7%
	4.	grecoinc:us:products:product1	7,876,944	10.4%
	5.	grecoinc:uk:products:products-landing	6,267,472	8.3%
	6.	grecoinc:de:home:homepage	4,771,610	6.3%
	7.	grecoinc:us:search:search-results	3,976,342	5.3%
	8.	grecoinc:au:home:homepage	3,484,033	4.6%

Figure 12.1 Sample Pages report.

- ▶ Allows you to filter pages by website (search contains "grecoinc:").

- ▶ Allows you to filter pages by country website (search contains "grecoinc:uk:").

- ▶ Allows you to filter pages by website section (search contains ":products:").

- ▶ Allows you to filter pages by a combination of the preceding items. For example, to see all UK product pages, you can enter "grecoinc:uk:products:" in the text search filter area of the Pages report.

Despite how easy this is, many clients still have incomprehensible page naming, which has a ripple effect through many SiteCatalyst reports. Even if it means losing some historical page data, I always recommend that clients do what it takes to have logical, understandable page names because it makes it easier for your end users to find pages and use Page Pathing reports.

Naming Site Sections

After sorting out page name issues for your organization, you should then move on to site sections. The Site Sections variable (**s.channel**) is useful because it allows you to see a higher-level view of how visitors navigate your website.

The good news is that if you follow the aforementioned advice on designating page names, setting site sections is very easy. The reason is that the Site Section value is already in the page name, and all you have to do is to use the first three parameters of the page name (everything up to the third ":" symbol). Using the example Greco, Inc. page names described in the previous section, the Site Section values would be as shown in **Figure 12.2**. Therefore, if you identify page names well, you might be able to write code to automatically set the site section, which saves time and money.

	Site Sections	Page Views ▾	
1.	grecoinc:us:products:	26,175,690	34.6%
2.	grecoinc:us:home	16,113,652	21.3%
3.	grecoinc:uk:home:	11,891,155	15.7%
4.	grecoinc:uk:products:	10,944,407	14.5%
5.	grecoinc:de:home:	4,771,610	6.3%
6.	grecoinc:us:search:	4,014,212	5.3%
7.	grecoinc:au:home:	3,484,033	4.6%

Figure 12.2 Sample Site Sections report.

Website-agnostic Page Names

Many organizations have different websites with the same general structure and pages. For example, the same website can be translated into different languages or the same website can be used for different brands. If this applies to your organization, it may be beneficial to implement site-agnostic page names. Site-agnostic page names provide a way to see traffic metrics and Pathing reports for all websites that use the same website structure. This allows you to have a higher-level view of how your website is used across multiple countries or brands and complements regular page pathing. For Greco, Inc.'s multiple country websites, this would involve setting an additional traffic variable and passing in the same page names shown in Figure 12.1 but without the country indicator. Pathing can then be enabled on this new traffic variable, and you have a variable that shows pathing of the pages across all country sites into one master page name (in the global report suite only). Another example use for this concept might be comparing the Bounce Rate of an aggregated page to the Bounce Rate for the U.S. version of the page (see the section "Bounce Rate" later in this chapter).

Site Variable

One content-related variable that many clients forget to include is a Site variable. A Site variable can show inter-website pathing in a global report suite if you have multiple websites. Let's look at an example. Imagine that Greco, Inc. wants to see how often website visitors are jumping between its different country websites. Even though all pages are in a global report suite and even with good page names in the Page and Section variables, there are so many different pathing permutations that getting a clear picture of inter-site navigation is next to impossible.

However, you can set a Site traffic variable on each page that has a value corresponding to the site with which the current page is associated. Again, this is easy if you have a good foundational page name because you can just populate this new Site traffic variable with the first two parameters of each page name (e.g., grecoinc:us: or grecoinc:uk). You then enable pathing for the Site traffic variable in the global report suite (which is the only report suite that has data for all Greco, Inc. websites). Now any changes in Site variable values in the global report suite will be shown as a path change, resulting in reports like the one shown in **Figure 12.3**. This is an easy way to see how often visitors view different country sites within the same session. Also, remember that you can see all Pathing reports for these sites in the global report suite, including Full Paths, Fallout, and Pathfinder.

Another reason to capture the site in a traffic variable on each page is for segmentation purposes. Chapter 10 discussed the pros and cons of abandoning multi-suite tagging and relying on Instant Segmentation. Doing so relies on having a Site variable, so it is a good idea to set this as a way to keep your options open or to test the segmentation-only approach.

Figure 12.3 Sample Inter-website Pathing report.

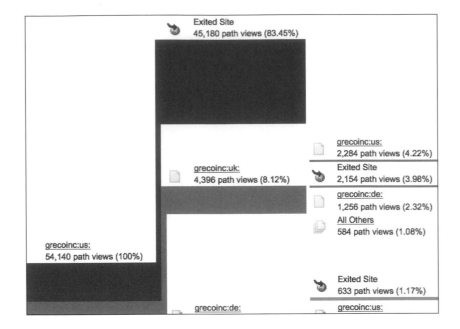

Page Types

Using page types, they key page templates that make up your website, can help you break down your website into its core components so you can better understand how it is being used. Although it is important to effectively capture your pages, sections, and site, there will be times when you'll need to look at your website from a different, more functional perspective.

For example, most websites have a home page, a search page, product pages, campaign landing pages, and more. Behind the scenes of your website, there might be a core set of functions that each type of page serves. For instance, the function of a form page is to get people to complete a form. A checkout page drives an order. Although there may be hundreds of product pages on your site, behind the scenes they are all the same page type—product pages. By identifying a core set of page types that make up your website, you can provide a holistic view of how your website is really used.

Once you can identify your page types, you can use a traffic variable to assign each page to one of a finite number of page types and view Page Views, Unique Visitors, and so on in a way that no other SiteCatalyst report can show (**Figure 12.4**).

		Page Type	Page Views ▼ ⑦	
⊤	1.	Home Page	20,101,354	26.5%
⊤	2.	Product Page	16,314,362	21.5%
⊤	3.	Search Page	13,974,001	18.5%
⊤	4.	Cart Page	7,876,944	10.4%
⊤	5.	Checkout Page	6,267,472	8.3%
⊤	6.	Purchase Thank You Page	3,203,795	4.2%
⊤	7.	Campaign Landing Page	3,014,446	4.0%

Figure 12.4 Sample Page Type report.

Not This Page Type

When I describe page type, I mean the different types of pages contained on your website. However, by sheer coincidence, SiteCatalyst actually has a special variable named (you guessed it) Page Type. Many clients see this variable and incorrectly use it to store the various website page types as described earlier (**Figure 12.5**).

Unfortunately, this won't work. The SiteCatalyst Page Type variable is used for a very special purpose, which is to capture 404 error pages. This variable is meant to be set only on your website's 404 error page, and its only valid value is errorPage. This populates the Pages Not Found report found under the Site Content section in the menu. Don't fall into this trap. Be sure to use a custom traffic variable for your website page types.

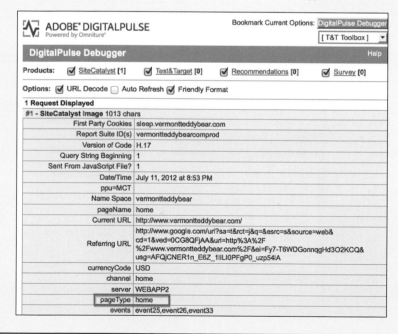

Figure 12.5 Typical misunderstanding of the Page Type variable.

Page Type Pathing

The real magic of page types occurs when you enable pathing on this new Page Type traffic variable. To fully understand why, let's look at an example. Imagine you are a web analyst at a company and your boss asks you, "What is the fallout of visitors starting from the home page, then navigating to product pages, then to product sign-up forms, and finally to the product form thank you page?" Well that sounds easy enough, but is it? You can create Fallout reports from each product, but what if you have hundreds of products? Even Instant Segmentation won't help you if you have a large number of products. After a while, you may be resigned to creating a massive dashboard with Fallout reports for each product or product category. Just then, your boss reiterates that she wants a fallout of all of the steps for *all* of the products in one overall Fallout report (and she wants it every week from now on!). Unfortunately, you don't know how to do this other than manually adding together all of these individual product Fallout reports.

Your boss is actually asking for page type pathing. Many executives don't have time for or care about page or section-level pathing because it contains too much "noise." By lumping pages into a small number of meaningful page types, you can take a step back and see a 50,000-foot view of where people are going on your website. Sometimes, page-level pathing can make it difficult to see that 30 percent of your visitors go from the home page to product pages because all you can see is individual page paths to product #1 or product #2. By implementing page type pathing, you can produce a new Pathing report (**Figure 12.6**).

Figure 12.6 Sample Page Type Pathing report.

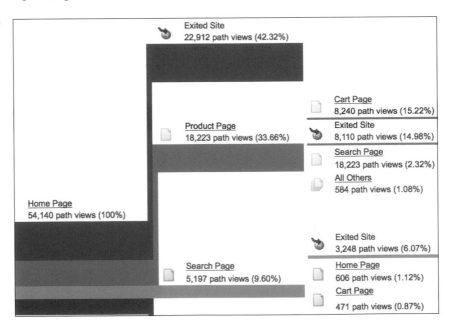

Executives can more easily understand this type of Pathing report because it shows a high-level view of how visitors are navigating the website. And if you find issues in this report, you can always dig into lower-level Pathing reports to see if there are specific sections or products causing these issues. Returning to the example request from your boss, you can use a Page Type Fallout report to show her the exact figures she was looking for (**Figure 12.7**).

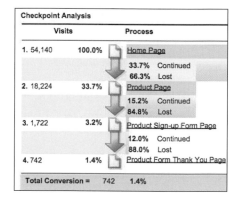

Figure 12.7 Sample Page Type Fallout report.

Implementing Page Types

Implementing a Page Type traffic variable can be a bit tricky because you must map your pages to a finite list of page types. The following outlines some common implementation techniques. Keep in mind that many of these techniques can be used for page names and sections as well.

Content management system

One way to implement page types is to add a field to your website content management system (CMS), which allows you to manually enter a page type and publish it as a readable tag on each page. Because templates drive most CMS tools, there is a good chance that your page types will map to CMS templates so you can simply publish the CMS template type to a tag and have your JavaScript tag insert that tag value into the traffic variable.

DB VISTA

If manual tagging or content management systems aren't options, you can always turn to DB VISTA, a tool that allows you is a tool you can use to set SiteCatalyst variables based on rules and a database lookup (see Chapter 7). In this case, you can create a spreadsheet that associates a page type to each page name and upload these values to a DB VISTA table. When visitors view each page, DB VISTA can use the page name value to do a lookup to its database and populate a Page Type traffic variable with the associated page type. As you add new pages to your site, you'd need to upload new rows to the DB VISTA table.

Adobe Discover

Another alternative is to use Adobe Discover (provided your organization is lucky enough to have it). Implementing page type pathing in Discover can be done in a few hours if you know what you're doing. Recall that it is not possible to see Pathing reports for a classification of a variable in SiteCatalyst. However, it *is* possible to do this in Adobe Discover. Therefore, if you create a Page Type classification of the Page Name traffic variable, you can simply classify the Page Name variable with Page Type values using SAINT. After Discover processes its data, it will pick up that new classification and you'll have page type pathing in Discover.

Bounce Rates

One of the most popular web analytics metrics for website content is Bounce Rate. In web analytics, the Bounce Rate shows how often visitors entering on a page exit the website immediately (bounce). Bounce Rate is most often used in the Pages report but can be applied to other web analytics data points as well. In older versions of SiteCatalyst, Bounce Rate was added to reports by creating a calculated metric (Single Access/ Entries). However, starting with SiteCatalyst v15, Bounce Rate is a standard metric that can be added to almost any report.

Over the years, Bounce Rate has confused many SiteCatalyst clients. Therefore, I'll do a quick review so you know how to access it in SiteCatalyst. The most important detail to remember when you're using Bounce Rate in SiteCatalyst is that it only pertains to variable values when they are entries to the website. For example, page Bounce Rates measure how often those who entered on a specific page exited immediately. **Figure 12.8** shows a sample report. The Page metrics in the figure show many different Bounce Rates. Some clients incorrectly assume that the first row means that of the 101,923 Page

Figure 12.8 Sample Page metrics.

Page Views ▼ ⑦		Entries ⑦		Exits ⑦		Bounces		Bounce Rate
101,923	6.5%	49,186	20.7%	22,470	9.5%	14,114	20.3%	28.7%
51,877	3.3%	857	0.4%	16,846	7.1%	730	1.0%	85.2%
38,814	2.5%	1,650	0.7%	6,863	2.9%	241	0.3%	14.6%
32,584	2.1%	2,127	0.9%	5,008	2.1%	153	0.2%	7.2%
32,581	2.1%	4,285	1.8%	2,517	1.1%	1,133	1.6%	26.4%

Views for this page, 28.7% of those led to a Bounce. That is not the case, because there were 101,923 total Page Views for the page, but of those only 49,186 were Entries. Of those 49,186 Entries, there were 14,114 instances in which the visitor "bounced" off the page. This is reflected in the 28.7% Bounce Rate (14,114/49,186 = 28.7%). Therefore, in the second row, where you see a Bounce Rate of 85.2%, before you start to panic, notice that this particular page had only 857 Entries (or 0.4% of the total website Entries) so it's not as bad as you initially thought. For this reason, you should focus on the pages that have the highest number of Entries when you're looking at Bounce Rates to see which ones can be improved upon.

Another improvement made to SiteCatalyst v15 is that Bounces and Bounce Rates can be used in conversion variable reports. In the past, conversion variable values were often duplicated as traffic variables, solely for the purpose of calculating Bounce Rates, but this is now unnecessary. Because Bounce Rates are now available in conversion reports, you can see a report like the one shown in **Figure 12.9**, which shows Entries and Bounces for a campaign tracking code variable.

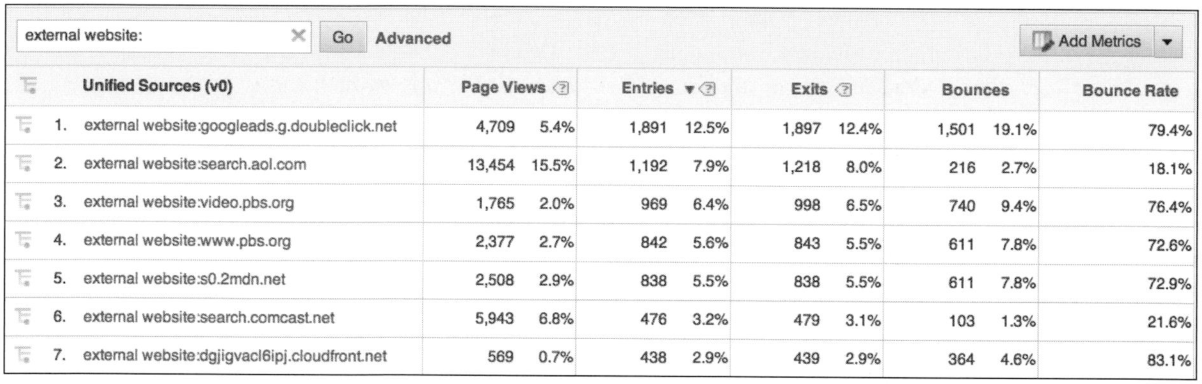

Figure 12.9 Sample Campaign Tracking Code Bounce Rate report.

Here are some other useful ways you can take advantage of Bounce Rates in conversion variables:

▶ View Bounce Rates for search engines and search keyword values.

▶ View Bounce Rates for marketing channels.

▶ View Bounce Rates for A/B tests you are conducting on your website.

Another new addition in SiteCatalyst v15 related to Bounce Rates is the ability to see Bounce Rate metrics in Conversion Variable Subrelation reports. For example, let's say that you want to see the preceding Campaign Tracking Code report broken down by Visit Number. All you have to do is create a normal Conversion Variable Subrelation report with Bounce Rate as one of the metrics to see the report shown in **Figure 12.10**.

Figure 12.10 Sample
Bounce Rate Conversion
Variable Subrelation
report.

Unified Sources (v0) by Visit # Grouping		Page Views		Entries		Bounces		Bounce Rate
1. external website:googleads.g.doubleclick.net		4,709		1,891		1,501		79.4%
1.	First Visit	4,080	86.6%	1,738	91.9%	1,407	93.7%	81.0%
2.	Second Visit	302	6.4%	92	4.9%	58	3.9%	63.0%
3.	Third Visit	211	4.5%	30	1.6%	16	1.1%	53.3%
4.	Fourth Visit	33	0.7%	13	0.7%	7	0.5%	53.8%
5.	Other	83	1.8%	18	1.0%	13	0.9%	0.0%
Show all for external website:googleads.g.doubleclick.net...								
2. external website:search.aol.com		13,454		1,192		216		18.1%
1.	First Visit	8,204	61.0%	802	67.3%	169	78.2%	21.1%
2.	Second Visit	2,566	19.1%	198	16.6%	29	13.4%	14.6%
3.	Third Visit	840	6.2%	75	6.3%	8	3.7%	10.7%
4.	Fourth Visit	639	4.7%	46	3.9%	4	1.9%	8.7%

One caveat to be aware of related to the new Bounce Rate functionality added to Site-Catalyst v15 has to do with non-Page View server calls. There are cases in which a visitor can view a single page on your website, exit, and *not* be counted as a Bounce. This happens if you have items on your page that initiate a non-Page View server call to SiteCatalyst. For example, if a visitor arrives to your home page and after a few seconds a video starts that triggers a server call setting a Video Start success event, that will be enough to tell SiteCatalyst that this visitor did not Bounce. Thus, you should keep this in mind when you're analyzing Bounce Rates for pages on your site.

Page Influence

Another topic related to content tracking is page influence. Page influence represents how often a particular website page leads to a success event taking place. For example, have you ever rummaged through your clothes closet and figured out that you never wear half of the stuff in there? It seems like it is always much easier to buy new clothes than it is to discard old clothes. Well, the same holds true with website content. Most clients have thousands of pages on their website, but in reality, only a fraction of them make an impact on their website success. Having extraneous pages on your website can cost your organization money in many unseen ways. Often, these extra pages on your website make it more difficult for your visitors to do the small number of tasks you want them to do. In this section, I'll share some ideas on how you can use success event participation to "trim the fat" from your website.

So how do you determine which pages matter and which pages don't? The first step is to determine the website success event(s) for which you want to optimize. If you care about multiple success events, this analysis becomes more complex, but the concept is similar. Therefore, let's assume a scenario where one website success event, Website

Registrations, is the primary KPI. You first need to ensure that a SiteCatalyst success event is set for every successful Website Registration. You can then ask your Adobe account manager or ClientCare to enable participation for the Website Registration success event. As covered in Chapter 4, when participation is enabled for a success event, SiteCatalyst will track every page in the flow leading to that success event and give each page "credit" for the success. Over time, the pages that are most often in the flow of Website Registrations will have high participation scores, and those that are not will have low participation scores. **Figure 12.11** shows the report you'll see when participation is enabled. Then you can download this report to Excel and re-sort by Website Registration Participation percent (**Figure 12.12**). With this perspective, you can see that even though this website has 1767 unique pages, Website Registration Participation falls below 3% by the time you reach the top 25 pages. Based on this data, the website could conceivably generate almost the same number of Website Registrations through these 25 pages as it does with the existing 1767 pages. That means that only 1.4 percent of the website pages are contributing to the majority of Website Registrations.

It's important to keep in mind that many of the pages below the twenty-fifth page may have contributed to Website Registrations, but the data suggests that they were less critical than these top 25 pages for this particular success event. Therefore, if the primary purpose of this website is to generate registrations, this type of content analysis might raise questions about the value of maintaining so many pages if they are not contributing to the primary KPI. Another interesting factor to note is that the pages

	Page	Page Views ▾ ⑦	Website Registration Participation
1.	Page 1	104,262	6.5%	37.5% (6,123)
2.	Page 2	52,709	3.3%	25.7% (4,188)
3.	Page 3	40,820	2.5%	3.1% (509)
4.	Page 4	33,450	2.1%	3.9% (632)

Figure 12.11 Sample Page Participation report.

	A	B	C	D
1	1,767	1,603,766	16,324	
2				
3	Page	Page Views	Website Registration Participation	Website Registration Participation %
4	Page 7	29,413	6951	42.6%
5	Page 56	6,754	6585	40.3%
6	Page 1	104,262	6123	37.5%
7	Page 2	52,709	4188	25.7%
8	Page 5	32,893	3199	19.6%
9	Page 91	3,826	3143	19.3%
10	Page 26	12,310	2801	17.2%
11	Page 114	2,889	2583	15.8%
12	Page 172	1,669	1887	11.6%
13	Page 6	31,747	1237	7.6%
14	Page 90	3,965	952	5.8%
15	Page 183	1,566	941	5.8%
16	Page 21	15,684	889	5.4%
17	Page 257	894	861	5.3%
18	Page 24	14,655	723	4.4%
19	Page 316	610	683	4.2%
20	Page 208	1,280	635	3.9%
21	Page 4	33,450	632	3.9%
22	Page 10	25,919	591	3.6%
23	Page 76	4,691	589	3.6%
24	Page 333	556	570	3.5%
25	Page 11	25,134	547	3.4%
26	Page 3	40,820	509	3.1%
27	Page 14	21,108	475	2.9%

Figure 12.12 Website Registrations sorted by Website Registration Participation.

participating in success are not always the most popular pages. In this example, I replaced the actual page names with the page number in terms of page view volume. As you can see, some of the highest contributing pages are those that do not get a lot of page views, relatively speaking.

However, I don't suggest you use this data to immediately start cutting pages from your website, because there may be other purposes served by these pages. Instead, it is reasonable to have an intelligent conversation with your stakeholders about which pages should remain and which should be eliminated. My philosophy is that a website is composed of a set of KPIs, and pages help achieve those KPIs, so if you can show that a page is not "participating" in any of the top KPIs, it may just be taking up space (like that '80s t-shirt that no longer fits). Some clients have used this analysis to shed low-value pages, only to find that conversion either stayed the same or rose as a result.

The other benefits of keeping only the website pages that you absolutely need include:

▶ Cost savings associated with reduced content translation.

▶ Improved website information architecture, including simplified navigation and fewer onsite search results.

▶ Insight into which key pages should be migrated to mobile versions of the website.

▶ Easier web analysis when it comes to Pathing reports because there are fewer pages to view in Pathing reports.

▶ The ability to focus more time improving the pages that matter to success.

File Downloads

One of the out-of-the-box content features available in SiteCatalyst is the ability to track how often files are downloaded from your website. These files could be brochures, pricing sheets, feature lists, and so on. When a website visitor clicks to download a file, SiteCatalyst captures the filename in a special File Downloads report (**Figure 12.13**).

Figure 12.13 Sample File Downloads report.

File Download	Instances	
http://wpc.475d.edgecastcdn.net/00475D/PDF/silverspirits.pdf	3,667	20.1%
http://wpc.475d.edgecastcdn.net/00475D/PDF/your_pretrip_info_2012_2013.pdf	3,149	17.3%
http://wpc.475d.edgecastcdn.net/00475D/PDF/weather-fahrenheit.pdf	1,706	9.4%
http://wpc.475d.edgecastcdn.net/00475D/PDF/bar_menu.pdf	1,687	9.3%
http://wpc.475d.edgecastcdn.net/00475D/PDF/europe_laundry_list.pdf	934	5.1%
http://wpc.475d.edgecastcdn.net/00475D/PDF/electrical_information.pdf	795	4.4%
http://wpc.475d.edgecastcdn.net/00475D/PDF/giftorderform.pdf	767	4.2%
http://wpc.475d.edgecastcdn.net/00475D/PDF/2012gateways.pdf	501	2.8%

File Download Limitations

However, after using SiteCatalyst for nearly a decade, I've found that if you are serious about analyzing file download behavior on your website, the out-of-the-box File Downloads report can be somewhat limiting for the following reasons:

▶ Because the default behavior is to store files using URLs, you can have cases in which the same file is tracked with "http://" and "https://" in the name.

▶ There is no way to use file downloads as a metric in SiteCatalyst, which means it cannot be trended or used in calculated metrics.

▶ You cannot add success event metrics to the File Downloads report, so the only way to see if a file impacts website success is through segmentation.

▶ Often, you'll want to see where a website visitor was when that visitor downloaded a particular file, especially if the same file can be downloaded from different pages on the website. This is not possible out of the box.

▶ There is no way to see file downloads in Pathing reports to see how they are part of page-by-page flows.

These are some pretty substantial limitations. However, because SiteCatalyst is a flexible product, there are ways that you can address each of these limitations if file downloads are important to your organization. The following sections detail ways you can address each of the preceding limitations.

Tracking File Downloads with Custom Variables

To address the first few items on the preceding list, begin tracking file downloads with custom variables. When a visitor downloads a file, set a File Downloads success event and pass the name of the file to a conversion variable. Doing so allows you to produce a regular metric report for file downloads and use file downloads (**Figure 12.14**) in a calculated metric (e.g., File Downloads/Visit).

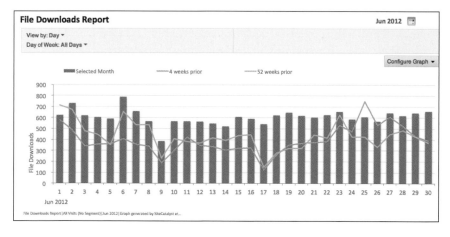

Figure 12.14 File Downloads Metric report.

Having the filename in a conversion variable allows you to duplicate the out-of-the-box File Downloads report and provides an opportunity to set your own filename values instead of relying on URL descriptions (**Figure 12.15**).

As you can see, the same number of file downloads are listed, but the URL portion of the file has been removed, which makes the data more understandable. Another benefit of having files in a conversion variable is that it can be classified (which is not possible for the out-of-box File Downloads report). You can classify files by file type (e.g., PDF vs. PPT) or by purpose (e.g., Brochures, Itineraries, etc.). In addition, because the file download is a conversion variable, you can use it like any other conversion variable to see how values impact other success events. For example, you can see if any of the files had a significant impact on website Form Completion Rate by making the expiration of this File Download conversion variable a "Week" and then adding Form Completion Metrics to the report (**Figure 12.16**).

	File Downloads	File Downloads ▼	
1.	silverspirits.pdf	3,667	20.1%
2.	your_pretrip_info_2012_2013.pdf	3,149	17.3%
3.	weather-fahrenheit.pdf	1,706	9.4%
4.	bar_menu.pdf	1,687	9.3%
5.	europe_laundry_list.pdf	934	5.1%
6.	electrical_information.pdf	795	4.4%
7.	giftorderform.pdf	767	4.2%
8.	2012gateways.pdf	501	2.8%

Figure 12.15 File Downloads Conversion Variable report.

	File Downloads	Form Completion Rate
1.	None	26.9%
2.	your_pretrip_info_2012_2013.pdf	36.5%
3.	weather-fahrenheit.pdf	28.1%
4.	bar_menu.pdf	29.7%
5.	europe_laundry_list.pdf	25.6%
6.	electrical_information.pdf	25.4%
7.	giftorderform.pdf	25.4%
8.	2012gateways.pdf	34.6%

Figure 12.16 File impact on form completions.

File Download Pathing

Seeing where visitors were when they downloaded files and seeing file downloads in page path flows is a bit more complex, so I'll explain why I think this is important through an example. One of my clients had a formal website process. The company wanted visitors to go from the home page or a campaign landing page to a product page and then to the product pricing page. On the product pricing page, visitors could download the pricing sheet and then, if they wanted to, fill out a lead form. In this scenario, the company could see website paths for all pages of this process but were unable to see if the pricing sheet was downloaded in this pathing flow. It was almost as if one of the most important pages in the process was not visible in any Next Page Flow or Fallout report. The reason is that out-of-the-box file downloads are treated more like custom links or exit links than website pages.

To solve this issue, I recommended that the client stop using the File Downloads report and instead modify the SiteCatalyst JavaScript code to treat files as regular pages (using the **s.pagename** variable). This would allow SiteCatalyst users to see file downloads in all Pathing reports. If Greco, Inc. were to do this, here is an example of what it might see in a Pathing report (**Figure 12.17**).

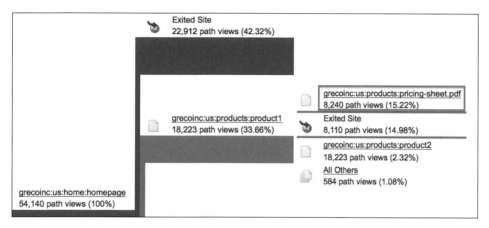

Figure 12.17 Sample File Download Pathing report.

This is not a significant change or JavaScript work effort. However, this simple change provides many other benefits:

▶ You can use any Pathing report, including the ability to see the Previous Page report, which will show you the pages from which visitors are most often downloading a file if it is present on multiple pages.

▶ If visitors can link directly to your website files, you can calculate the Bounce Rate of each file download because it is now part of the Page Name variable, which has Bounce Rate metrics.

▶ You can see Daily, Weekly, and Monthly Unique Visitors for each file download instead of just the instances provided in the out-of-the-box report.

▶ You can enable participation on the File Downloads success event to see which pages on your site lead to file downloads.

▶ Because you probably have participation enabled for your key success events and the Page Name variable, you can see which files "participate" in website success events, just like you can for regular website pages.

▶ If you have any traffic correlations to the Page Name report (which is very common), you now have those correlations to every file on your website. For example, if you correlate Page Name to Visit Number or GeoSegmentation Country, all file downloads will be correlated to these as well and you won't have to pay for any extra correlations or variables.

▶ If you really like this concept, you can also apply it to exit links.

▶**TIP** *If you decide to pass filenames to the Page Name variable, be sure to remove the code that stores files in the out-of-the-box File Downloads report so you don't get charged for two server calls for each file download.*

There are some great advantages if you change your mind-set toward file downloads and try some alternative ways of tracking them. These benefits may only make sense if file downloads are integral to your organization, but the level of effort to make all of these modifications is minimal enough that you can test them and see how they work for your organization.

Conclusion

In this chapter, you explored some ways you can apply what you've learned to improve how you track and analyze website content. Creating logical page, section, and site names can make your pathing analysis much easier. Using page types can give you a big picture view of how your website is used. Bounce Rates and page influence are just two ways you can see how your content is performing and which content is useful to your visitors. In addition, you saw how what you learned about conversion variables and pathing can be applied to file downloads to improve your insight into file usage on your website. Therefore, if you are struggling with answering content-related business questions, consider working with your developers to implement some of the techniques discussed in this chapter.

## CHAPTER 13

Shopping Cart Tracking

The primary objective of many websites is to sell products. In this chapter I discuss some of the ways that you can use SiteCatalyst to monitor how well a website is selling its products. Using SiteCatalyst's predefined attributes and best practices I've created over the years, you'll see how you can track your online shopping cart.

Even if your website doesn't have a traditional shopping cart, you can still take advantage of the shopping cart features in SiteCatalyst. Many of the same principles can be applied to general website conversion funnels that affect healthcare, business to business, automotive, and other types of websites. As you read this chapter, think about how you can apply its lessons to your website.

Product Pages

▶TIP *It is not possible to hide the predefined Product Views (Instances) metric in the Products report; therefore, name your custom Product Views metric clearly so users understand what it represents. Suggested names might be Product Views (Custom) or Product Detail Views.*

Although many SiteCatalyst clients don't treat it as such, the act of viewing a product on your website should be part of your shopping cart funnel. I'm amazed by how few clients use the Product View success event, and I recommend that you take advantage of it in your implementation. SiteCatalyst has a predefined Product View event, but as I alluded to in earlier chapters, it has some inherent limitations because it is simply a renaming of the Instances metric. As a best practice, I recommend that you set a custom Product View success event *and* the predefined Product View success event on every product page of your website (**Figure 13.1**). Having a custom Product View success event allows you to see product views in all reports instead of just the Products report. Custom Product View metrics can also be used in segmentation and calculated metrics. However, you should also set the predefined Product View success event, because failing to do so will make it impossible to filter Conversion Funnel reports by product.

▶TIP *I see too many SiteCatalyst customers storing actual product names in the products variable. Because product names can change over time, consider passing a product ID value instead of a product name to the products variable. Product names can later be added to product IDs using SAINT classifications.*

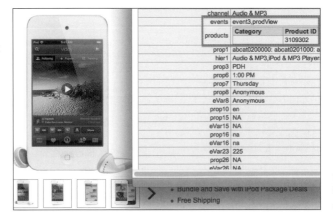

Figure 13.1 Sample tagging of Product View events.

Even if your website doesn't sell products, you should still set the Product View events and the products variable. Let's say that you work for Caterpillar and sell million-dollar machinery. The odds are that you won't sell your product online via a credit card, but that doesn't mean you shouldn't be tracking how often visitors view each product on your site.

Product Pathing

In addition to tracking product views, you should consider *product pathing*, especially if you have many products on your website. Product pathing is the ability to see the order in which visitors view your products. As you learned in Chapter 3, you can use pathing for almost anything in SiteCatalyst. I recommend you pass the product ID to a traffic variable at the same time you set the product ID to the products variable on product pages. You can then enable pathing on the product ID traffic variable and see the order in which visitors view your products (**Figure 13.2**).

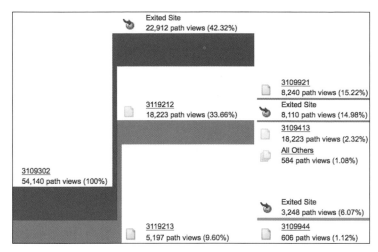

Figure 13.2 Product Pathing report.

The Product Pathing report allows you to see which products are viewed in the same session in case you want to bundle them or cross-sell other products. You also have access to all Pathing reports so you can use Pathfinder and Fallout reports to dig deeper into product browsing patterns.

If you would prefer to have product names in the Pathing report, you can use a DB VISTA rule to translate your product IDs into product names on the fly. As long as you keep the DB VISTA rule updated with your latest product IDs and product names, you would see a report similar to the one in Figure 13.2 but with product names instead of IDs. If you have access to the Discover product, keep in mind that you can also see pathing by product name through your product name SAINT classification.

Product Page Tab Usage

Sometimes clients ask me how they can view visitor clicks on the various tabs featured on their product pages. Often, a series of tabs share additional product information (**Figure 13.3**).

Figure 13.3 Product page tabs.

On this page, the website owner might want to see how often visitors use each of the tabs related to this specific cruise or in general. For example, let's say that a web designer wanted to see data showing whether any of the tabs shown in Figure 13.3 are used for any products. One way to see this would be to pass the name of the tab to a new traffic variable and enable pathing. Doing so would create a "tab" Pathing report that might look like the one in **Figure 13.4**.

If later you want to see this tab behavior for a specific product, you could either concatenate the product name with each tab name (e.g., cruise123|itinerary) or create a segment that has only page views for the product of interest.

Figure 13.4 Product tab pathing.

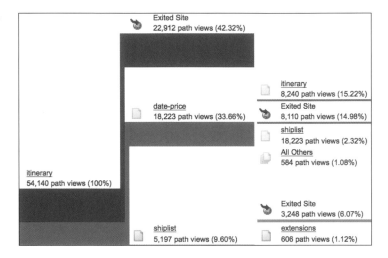

Product List Views

On some websites, visitors are presented with a list of products on one page (sometimes referred to as a "gridwall"). **Figure 13.5** shows an example from L.L. Bean.

On this type of page, you may want to know the following:

▶ What is the click-through rate of each product?

▶ Do products shown at the top get more clicks?

This gets a bit tricky, because viewing these products on this gridwall page does not represent a true product view. Therefore, in this situation, you should set a custom success event to capture Product Gridwall Impressions and Product Gridwall Clicks. At the same time that these new success events are set, you would set the products variable with the product IDs shown on the page or clicked.

Figure 13.5 Sample product list "gridwall."

Let's walk through this example in detail. When the product gridwall shown in Figure 13.5 loads, you might set the following code:

```
s.events="event20";
s.products=";11345;;;;evar30=Row1-Slot1,,11367;;;;evar30=
Row1-Slot2, ;12456;;;;evar30=Row1-Slot3,,11426;;;;evar30=
Row1-Slot4, ;11626;;;;evar30=Row2-Slot1, etc...";
```

This code would create one impression (event20) for each product ID shown on the page. It also uses a Merchandising variable (eVar30) to assign the "row" and "slot number" to each product.

If a visitor clicked on an item in the gridwall, you would set similar code to capture the product ID and location that was clicked, along with a separate Product Gridwall Clicks success event. In this case, if the visitor clicked the top leftmost product, the code would look like this:

```
s.events="event21";
```

```
s.products=";11345;;;;evar30=Row1-Slot1";
```

After this tagging has been in place for a while, you could see a report detailing Product Gridwall Impressions and Product Gridwall Clicks broken down by product (**Figure 13.6**). You can also create a new calculated metric that divides the two to see the conversion rate.

	Products	Product Gridwall Impressions ▾		Product Gridwall Clicks		Product Gridwall CTR %
1.	11345	11,781	13.1%	3,177	14.1%	26.97%
2.	11367	11,556	12.8%	2,567	11.4%	22.22%
3.	12456	10,305	11.5%	2,437	10.8%	23.65%
4.	11426	9,360	10.4%	2,221	9.9%	23.73%
5.	11626	7,448	8.3%	1,650	7.3%	22.16%
6.	15522	5,670	6.3%	1,725	7.7%	30.42%
7.	17881	4,725	5.3%	900	4.0%	19.05%
8.	18651	4,140	4.6%	675	3.0%	16.30%

Figure 13.6 Product Gridwall report broken down by product.

Similarly, you could use the Placement Merchandising variable to see the same report by Gridwall Placement (**Figure 13.7**).

	Gridwall Placement	Product Gridwall Impressions ▾		Product Gridwall Clicks		Product Gridwall CTR %
1.	Row1-Slot1	11,250	12.5%	4,151	18.5%	36.90%
2.	Row1-Slot2	11,250	12.5%	3,296	14.7%	29.30%
3.	Row1-Slot3	11,250	12.5%	2,801	12.5%	24.90%
4.	Row1-Slot4	11,250	12.5%	2,576	11.5%	22.90%
5.	Row2-Slot1	11,250	12.5%	2,768	12.3%	24.60%
6.	Row2-Slot2	9,450	10.5%	2,221	9.9%	23.50%
7.	Row2-Slot3	9,000	10.0%	1,721	7.7%	19.13%
8.	Row2-Slot4	8,550	9.5%	1,271	5.7%	14.87%

Figure 13.7 Product Gridwall report broken down by placement.

If desired, you could also use a Conversion Subrelation report to see both of these elements concurrently (**Figure 13.8**).

The use of the products variable can get complex, but it is extremely flexible due to its ability to store multiple values and pass Merchandising values. This example also illustrates how important it is to understand the core SiteCatalyst concepts introduced in previous chapters. In this case, to solve a specific business question, you needed to know how to use and combine success events, the products variable, Merchandising conversion variables, conversion subrelations, and calculated metrics. Understanding all facets of SiteCatalyst opens the door to web analyses that you may have previously thought impossible.

	Gridwall Placement by Product	Product Gridwall ▾ Impressions		Product Gridwall Clicks	
	1. Row1-Slot1	**11,250**		**4,151**	
	1. 11345	3,888	34.6%	1,646	39.7%
	2. 11367	3,211	28.5%	1,020	24.6%
	3. 12456	1,738	15.5%	604	14.6%
	4. 11426	1,073	9.5%	420	10.1%
	5. Other	1,340	11.9%	461	11.1%
	Show all for Row1-Slot1…				
	2. Row1-Slot2	**11,250**		**3,296**	
	1. 11426	7,261	64.5%	2,023	61.4%
	2. 11626	1,413	12.6%	479	14.5%

Figure 13.8 Product Gridwall Conversion Subrelation report.

Cart Additions and Checkouts

Adding products to the shopping cart and carrying them through to checkout is relatively straightforward. When you're setting the Cart Additions and Checkout success events, you should set the products variable so you can see a proper Products Conversion Funnel or Ranked report (**Figure 13.9**).

However, many SiteCatalyst clients make mistakes or fail to take advantage of functionality in the area of product merchandising. Product merchandising is sometimes set on the product page, but more often is set on Cart Addition. Therefore, while I'm discussing Cart Additions, I'll use it as an excuse to dig a bit deeper into product merchandising.

	Products	Product Views (Custom) ▾		Cart Additions ⑦		Checkouts ⑦	
1.	11345	11,781	13.1%	3,177	14.1%	1,561	12.5%
2.	11367	11,556	12.8%	2,567	11.4%	1,312	10.5%
3.	12456	10,305	11.5%	2,437	10.8%	1,229	9.9%
4.	11426	9,360	10.4%	2,221	9.9%	1,152	9.3%
5.	11626	7,448	8.3%	1,650	7.3%	1,285	10.3%
6.	15522	5,670	6.3%	1,725	7.7%	997	8.0%
7.	17881	4,725	5.3%	900	4.0%	720	5.8%
8.	18651	4,140	4.6%	675	3.0%	266	2.1%

Figure 13.9 Products report with Product Views, Cart Additions, and Checkouts.

Product Merchandising

In Chapter 5, I explained product merchandising and how it worked by using a product category example. That example showed which product category visitors had used to place ceiling fans into the shopping cart so you could attribute orders and revenue to the correct product category for each product. Recall that the benefit of using Merchandising variables is that they allow each product to have its own conversion variable value instead of all products having their conversion values overwritten by the last value of the last product. Therefore, anytime you want each product to have its own conversion variable value, it's best to use product merchandising. With this in mind, let's review some examples of when product merchandising can be useful.

Product attributes

A common use of product merchandising is assigning product-specific attributes like size, color, and so on to products. For example, let's say that you're browsing a retail website and find a shirt that you like. On the product view page for that product, there is most likely a product ID, but there may be different SKU numbers based on which shirt color or size you choose. Most sites will force you to choose your size and color prior to adding the item to the shopping cart (**Figure 13.10**). Therefore, at the point of Cart Addition, you can set the products variable to include the Cart Addition success event, the product ID, and the product Merchandising variables related to the product. In this case, you might populate the Size and Color as two new conversion Merchandising variables like this:

```
s.events="scAdd";
s.products=";11345;;;;evar32=Navy|evar33=XL";
```

Doing so establishes a connection between this product ID and the two Color and Size conversion variable values. No matter what other products you add to the shopping cart, as long as these two conversion variables don't expire, if the visitor purchases this shirt, the order and revenue will be tied to "Navy" and "XL" respectively.

Figure 13.10 Sample product detail page with merchandising options.

Product finding methods

Another common use of product merchandising is called *finding methods*. The idea behind finding methods is to capture the way that visitors found each product on your website. Some examples of ways visitors may find products on your site include:

▶ Clicking on a promo on the home page

▶ Using onsite search

▶ Using top navigation

▶ Using a product selector tool

▶ Watching a product video that has a link to the product

Depending on how your website is structured, there are countless ways to arrive at products. You can use product merchandising to help your organization quantify how many orders or how much revenue should be attributed to each of these finding methods.

To capture product finding methods, you first need to identify which methods you will include on your website. When you're deciding how many and which finding methods to set, keep in mind that until a visitor views or adds a specific product to the shopping cart, these finding methods will continue to replace each other in the conversion variable. Let's review this with an example: A visitor comes to the home page and clicks on a promotion to see product X. When this happens, the visitor is taken to the product X detail page, and if you've done your tagging correctly, you will set the finding methods Merchandising variable to "Home Page Promo." Some SiteCatalyst customers set (or "bind") the finding methods Merchandising variable at this point when the Product View success event takes place; others like to wait until a product is added to the cart before binding the finding method to the product. In the administration console, recall that you can choose when this binding happens and can even bind on the Product View *and* the Cart Addition. In this case, let's assume that your organization only wants to bind on the Cart Addition. The visitor adds the product to the cart, so product X is bound to the finding method of "Home Page Promo."

Now let's assume that from this page the visitor performs an onsite search and clicks to view product Y. At this point, the finding methods conversion variable would be overwritten with the value "Onsite Search" (although it would not change for product X, which has already been "bound"). Next, the visitor sees a cross-sell product Z on the product Y page and clicks it. In this scenario, let's assume that "Cross-Sell" is a valid finding method and is set anytime a visitor clicks on a cross-sell link. Therefore, when the visitor clicked the cross-sell link, the finding methods conversion variable value of "Onsite Search" is replaced with "Cross-Sell." If the visitor then adds product Z to the shopping cart, the value of "Cross-Sell" will be bound to product Z. When all is said and

	Product Finding Methods	Orders ▼ ⑦		Revenue ⑦	
1.	Home Page Promo	1	100.0%	$150	66.7%
2.	Cross-Sell	1	100.0%	$75	33.3%

Figure 13.11 Sample Finding Methods report.

done, **Figure 13.11** shows what the final Finding Methods report would look like if this was the only visitor to the website and both product X and Z were purchased.

This example demonstrates how complex product merchandising can be and why it is important to understand its administration console settings and uses.

Money Left on the Table

Imagine that you are in a retail store and you grab a bunch of items and bring them up to the counter; just as you are about to pay, you decide to push a few of the items off to the side and not include them as part of your purchase. Although this may not happen too often in real life, it happens quite often online. If you manage a retail website, you'll see that these discarded items can add up quickly. In this section, I'll show you how to quantify how much money your organization is leaving on the table for one reason or another on your website. For those not involved in a retail site, I'll try to show how this concept can be applied to non-retail sites as well.

When it comes to seeing money left on the table, not only do you want to see how much money you're losing online when website visitors leave items in their cart, but also, if possible, have the ability to break down the total amount by product. In the preceding retail scenario, this is the equivalent of adding up how much could have been made that day, by product, if no one had left items on the counter when checking out. This might help the store owner determine if there is a pattern in the products that are abandoned, such as a price range or color.

Fortunately, doing this online is much easier than in a physical store because online you already have all of the information you need for these calculations. You just need a bit of creativity and the desire to make it happen. When a website visitor adds one or more products to the shopping cart, you know the product ID and how much the product costs. Currently, you are probably setting the Cart Addition success event and the products variable like this:

```
s.events="scAdd";

s.products=";123456";
```

However, now that you've learned about the other types of success events, you may recognize that you can use a Currency success event to capture the dollar amount associated with the item(s) currently being added to the shopping cart. Here is how the preceding code would change if the item added to the cart cost $50:

```
s.events="scAdd,event25";
s.products=";123456;;;event25=50.00";"
```

Although this isn't a difficult change, passing in the amount associated with the items added to the cart creates a new metric that represents the total dollar amount added to the shopping cart. Let's call this new success event (event25) $$ Added to Cart. Because you are setting the products variable concurrently, you'll also be able to see this new success event in the Products report along with other success events tied to products. This means that you can create a calculated metric comparing the actual revenue with the $$ Added to Cart to see how each product is doing (**Figure 13.12**).

	Products	$$ Added to Cart ▾		Revenue ⑦		$$ in Cart Conversion %
⚎ 1.	123456	$4,099,421	21.3%	$1,037,805	22.7%	25.32%
⚎ 2.	123459	$3,603,251	18.7%	$938,603	20.5%	26.05%
⚎ 3.	123478	$3,025,189	15.7%	$740,199	16.2%	24.47%
⚎ 4.	124321	$2,003,947	10.4%	$480,748	10.5%	23.99%
⚎ 5.	123998	$1,594,487	8.3%	$335,760	7.3%	21.06%

Figure 13.12 Products report with actual Revenue and $$ Added to Cart.

This report allows you to see what percent of $$ Added to Cart is converted for each product. You could also use SAINT classifications to see this by product name, product category, or any other product classifications you have created. In addition, you can use Conversion Subrelation reports to break down the Products variable and $$ Added to Cart by any other conversion variable, such as visit number, campaign, and so on. This can provide valuable data for analysis because it may be easier to convert people already putting items in the cart than to continue trying to find new prospects.

Another great aspect of this new $$ Added to Cart concept relates to the calculated metric you added to the preceding report. Recall that anytime you create a calculated metric, besides seeing it in a Ranked report, you can also see it by itself. This means you have at your disposal an overall $$ in Cart Conversion metric that looks like the one shown in **Figure 13.13**.

In this report, you can see that you're getting about 23% of dollars added to the cart to be purchased. This might be a good KPI to work on because you can calculate the potential revenue lift of raising this conversion rate from 23% to 30%, for example. This also might represent a golden opportunity to use Adobe Test&Target (Adobe's A/B & Multivariate testing product) in the shopping cart process to try different tests to improve this conversion rate.

Figure 13.13 $$ in Cart Conversion % calculated metric.

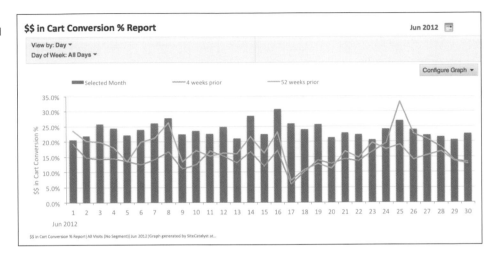

Additionally, you can use the same concept to store the amount of money in the check-out step of the shopping cart. Using similar tagging, when you set the Checkout success event (scCheckout) and the products variable, simply pass the potential revenue amount to a different Currency success event. Doing so allows you to see if you have a bigger issue getting revenue from cart addition to checkout or from checkout to order. In the report in **Figure 13.14**, I created a conversion calculated metric showing what percent of $$ Added to Cart eventually makes it to checkout.

	Products	$$ Added to Cart ▾		$$ Added to Checkout		Cart Add % to Checkout
1.	123456	$4,099,421	21.3%	$1,681,462	19.8%	41.02%
2.	123459	$3,603,251	18.7%	$1,648,409	19.5%	45.75%
3.	123478	$3,025,189	15.7%	$1,495,857	17.7%	49.45%
4.	124321	$2,003,947	10.4%	$1,072,102	12.7%	53.50%
5.	123998	$1,594,487	8.3%	$836,493	9.9%	52.46%

Figure 13.14 Cart Add to Checkout revenue conversion.

Using potential revenue in segmentation

As with many tasks in SiteCatalyst, once you capture additional data, there are often creative ways to use it if you understand SiteCatalyst well enough. A cool side benefit of tracking money left on the table is related to segmentation. Let's walk through an example using the scenario in Chapter 10 in which you wanted to re-market to "cart abandoners." In this scenario, visitors had added items to their cart but had not purchased them, and you created the segment definition shown in **Figure 13.15**.

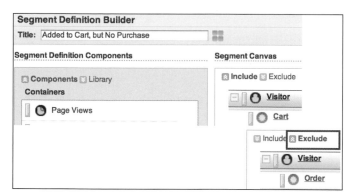

Figure 13.15 Cart Abandoner segment.

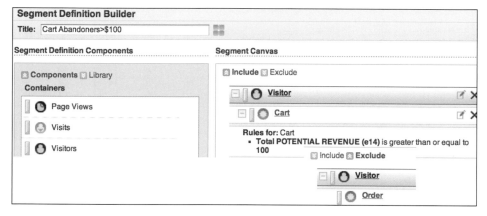

Figure 13.16 Cart Abandoner>$100 segment.

However, what if you wanted to narrow this segment a bit to include only visitors who had added over $100 to the cart? In Chapter 10 that would have been impossible, but now that you're capturing the dollar amount added to cart, you can add this to your segment (**Figure 13.16**).

Beyond retail

For those of you who manage a non-retail website, here are a few ways you could use this "money left on the table" concept:

▶ On a **financial services** site, pass in the total loan amount a person is requesting and compare that to how much that person is eventually loaned.

▶ On a **media** site, pass in the total amount of advertising your site could have earned if ads were clicked.

▶ On an **automotive** site, pass in the total value of cars visitors configure to see your potential vehicle sales.

- On a **lead generation** site, pass in an average lead value for every visitor who starts completing a lead form.

- On a **travel** site, pass in the total value of trips planned online and compare it to the amount actually booked.

You can apply the concept of identifying upper-bound potential and comparing it to actual performance to almost any website to give you another data point for comparison. Using this metric is better than using Visits or Unique Visitors because it is not realistic to think that you'll convert every person who comes to your site. However, once visitors take more deliberate actions, they are self-qualifying themselves; therefore, capturing their potential revenue streams gives you a high, but more realistic, goal to strive for and a KPI that you can use to see how your website converts visitors over time.

Revenue, Orders, and Units

So far, various aspects of the shopping cart have been discussed, including product views, cart additions, and checkout. The final step of the shopping cart is the actual purchase. In SiteCatalyst this takes place via the "purchase" event, which populates the Revenue, Orders, and Units success events with the help of the products variable. Here is what a sample purchase of two iPods at $79 each would look like:

```
s.events="purchase";
s.products=";12321;2;158.00";
s.purchaseID="111222334";
```

As you saw in earlier chapters, you can also set shipping costs and taxes in Currency success events and Merchandising conversion variables if desired. On the final purchase thank you page, you should set a unique Purchase ID to prevent data from being duplicated by refreshes and Back button clicks (if you do not set a Purchase ID, SiteCatalyst will create one for you, but it is recommended that you set your own).

That is really all you need to know about the purchase event. The rest of this section describes some best practices and fun ideas related to orders and revenue for when your organization is ready to do some more advanced implementation.

Validating Orders and Revenue

Over the years, one critical lesson I've learned in the area of web analytics is how important data quality is to an overall web analytics program. Many companies have spent money on people, multiple technologies, and education, but when I crack open their SiteCatalyst implementation, I find poor data quality. As a rule, I believe it is your responsibility to prove that web analytics data is correct so your end users will have faith in it. No one wants to give a presentation advising executives to change the website, only to find out that the data used for the analysis was faulty. As you can imagine, if you sell products on your website, you should be sure that your orders and revenue metrics are within an acceptable range of variance from what your business shows in its back-end accounting systems. Therefore, I'll share some techniques I recommend to give you the peace of mind that these two important metrics are trustworthy. If you don't use orders and revenue in your implementation, you can still apply this concept to compare your key KPIs to your back-end systems.

Order ID conversion variable

As shown in the code at the beginning of this section, you should already be setting the **s.purchaseID** variable with a unique Order ID on the purchase thank you page. This variable is used by SiteCatalyst to ensure order uniqueness. Unfortunately, the downside of this variable is that it is not readily available in the SiteCatalyst interface. Therefore, I recommend that you set an Order ID conversion variable. To do this, pass the same value you pass to the **s.purchaseID** variable to a custom conversion variable. This allows you to see all orders and revenue by Order ID from within SiteCatalyst, just as you would any other conversion variable. You can then open this new Order ID conversion variable with the orders and revenue metrics (**Figure 13.17**).

	Order ID	Orders ▾ ⑦		Revenue ⑦	
1.	111222334	2	0.0%	$150	0.0%
2.	111222346	1	0.0%	$310	0.0%
3.	111222441	1	0.0%	$125	0.0%
4.	111222412	1	0.0%	$75	0.0%
5.	111222398	1	0.0%	$35	0.0%
6.	111222219	1	0.0%	$225	0.0%
7.	111222301	1	0.0%	$245	0.0%
8.	111222976	1	0.0%	$100	0.0%

Figure 13.17 Order ID Conversion Variable report.

If all is going well, you should see only one order for each row. Anytime you have more than one order per Order ID, you know that data has been accidentally duplicated in SiteCatalyst and may require some research (possibly using a tool like Tealeaf). This scenario presents a great opportunity to use the alerts you learned about in Chapter 9. You

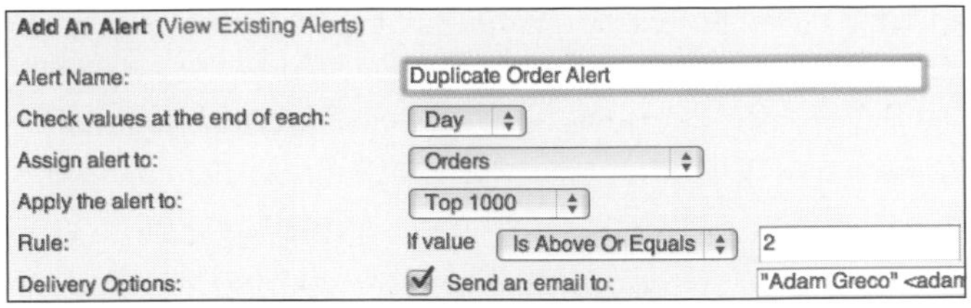

Figure 13.18 Sample Duplicate Order ID Alert.

could create a daily alert to notify you if the orders metric is ever at two or more for a particular order ID (**Figure 13.18**).

Comparing back-end order data

Adding an Order ID conversion variable is helpful to see if you are over-counting orders in SiteCatalyst, but it won't tell you if you are under-counting them or how close your SiteCatalyst revenue data is to your back-end systems. To do this, I recommend you use Data Sources to import revenue and orders from your back-end systems into Site-Catalyst. This provides a way to validate if the data in SiteCatalyst matches your back-end systems.

Now that you have an Order ID conversion variable, you have a "key" that you can use to connect online orders and revenue to back-end orders and revenue. To import this data, you would create two new success events: One would be a Numeric success event called Back-End Orders, and the other would be a Currency success event called Back-End Revenue (**Figure 13.19**). You can then use the Data Sources wizard to create an FTP site and an import template (**Figure 13.20**). In the Data Sources import file,

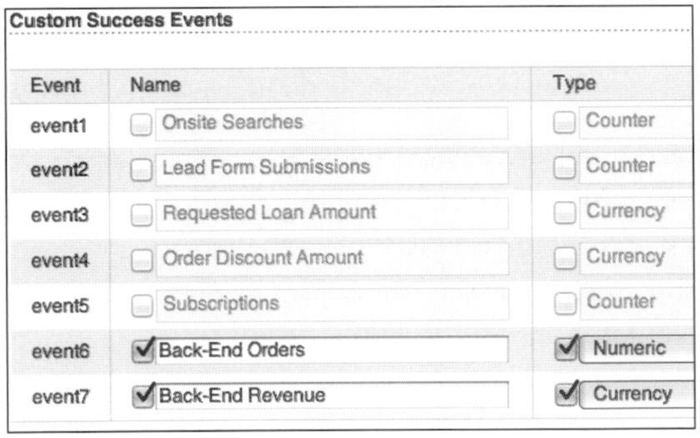

Figure 13.19 Create new events for back-end data.

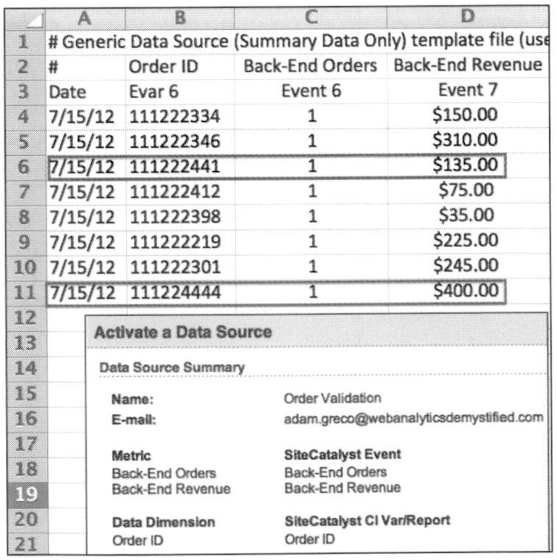

Figure 13.20 Create a Data Sources import file.

Back-End Orders will always be "1" and Back-End Revenue will be the revenue shown in the accounting system. Each row will be updated with the transaction date (not the current date) and the Order ID. Then you just need to automate the process of importing this data into SiteCatalyst.

Once this back-end data is imported, you can look at the Order ID Conversion Variable report (**Figure 13.21**). In this report, you can see that there are a few issues. It looks like one online order (#111222441) has a revenue discrepancy of $10, and it appears that order #111224444 is missing in SiteCatalyst. This example shows two ways this Data Sources import process can help. First, it can point out any cases where orders or revenue do not match so you can be proactive about addressing data issues. Second, it can alert you to cases where your back-end system is seeing transactions that are not being picked up by SiteCatalyst. You can leverage calculated metrics and alerts to be notified of these types of issues.

	Order ID	Orders ▾ ⍰		Back-End Orders		Revenue ⍰		Back-End Revenue	
1.	111222334	2	0.0%	2	0.0%	$150	0.1%	$150	0.1%
2.	111222346	1	0.0%	1	0.0%	$310	0.2%	$310	0.2%
3.	111222441	1	0.0%	1	0.0%	$125	0.1%	$135	0.1%
4.	111222412	1	0.0%	1	0.0%	$75	0.1%	$75	0.1%
5.	111222398	1	0.0%	1	0.0%	$35	0.0%	$35	0.0%
6.	111222219	1	0.0%	1	0.0%	$225	0.2%	$225	0.2%
7.	111222301	1	0.0%	1	0.0%	$245	0.2%	$245	0.2%
8.	111222976	1	0.0%	1	0.0%	$100	0.1%	$100	0.1%
9.	111224444	0	0.0%	1	0.0%	$0	0.0%	$400	0.3%

Figure 13.21 Back-end Order and Revenue validation.

If this process is too cumbersome for your business, the alternative is to push the Order ID Conversion Variable report from SiteCatalyst to Microsoft Excel (using Adobe ReportBuilder) where you can attempt to match back-end data manually. I prefer the SiteCatalyst approach because it is more transparent and allows you to show your users how close the key metrics are directly within the SiteCatalyst interface. This goes a long way to building overall confidence in web analytics data.

As stated earlier, even if you don't sell products online, you can use the principles outlined here for other KPIs. For example, if you have a lead generation website, you can set a unique Lead ID to a conversion variable and import back-end leads via Data Sources to prove that all back-end leads are accounted for in SiteCatalyst. The same could be said of reservations for travel sites, subscription IDs for media sites, and so on.

Product Returns

One formidable challenge that web analysts don't always address is product returns. How often have you bought something online only to ship it back or return it to a brick and mortar store associated with the website? If customers return products in significant enough numbers, all of the great online data you have collected may be inaccurate.

Some companies apply a "rule of thumb" approach in which they discount sales by 10 percent across the board to account for returns. But how does that help you determine if a specific marketing campaign is good or bad, since you cannot tie these returns to specific campaigns? By not tying product returns directly to their corresponding online sales, your web analytic reports will be inherently flawed. Because so few organizations effectively deal with the issue of product returns, I'll show you how to track them in SiteCatalyst and make your product-related reports as accurate as possible. Even if you don't sell items through a shopping cart, I encourage you to read this section because its principles are applicable to any situation in which you have an online success that later is retracted in some manner offline.

Imagine that you are a web analyst for Apple, and a first-time visitor comes to the website from the Google paid search keyword "ipod" and purchases two iPods for $50 each. In SiteCatalyst, when you open the Products report, you would see $100 for the product labeled "ipod," and if you broke it down (subrelated) by visit number, the same $100 would be attributed to visit number one. However, a few days later one of these iPods is returned to a local Apple store. Now the reality has changed. The paid search keyword and first visit combination has now only led to $50, but SiteCatalyst still shows $100. If you create calculated metrics to compare the revenue per marketing spend, suddenly your ROI is cut in half, but this is not reflected in SiteCatalyst. This might cause you to misallocate marketing dollars to campaigns that look good at first, but in reality are not as profitable as others when product returns are taken into account. I don't know about you, but I certainly wouldn't want to be the one telling my boss to invest in marketing campaigns that don't lead to long-term sales.

So how do you fix this? To track product returns, you can use the Transaction ID feature in SiteCatalyst. Recall that Transaction ID allows you to set an ID associated with an online transaction and later import offline metrics that are dynamically associated with any conversion variable (eVar) values that were active at the time the Transaction ID was set. In this case, you need to ensure that you set the Transaction ID value when the original online sale takes place. By doing so, you create a "key" that allows you to import product return data later and back it out of its corresponding online sale. Keep in mind that you'll have to work with your account manager to set up Transaction ID, and you'll want to be sure that the Transaction ID table persists for as long of a time frame that you require to import return data (the default is 90 days but can be extended).

Once you have Transaction ID enabled and have started passing Transaction IDs for online purchases, the next step is to create a new Product Return Amount Currency success event. Then you can use the Transaction ID Data Sources wizard to generate a product returns template that you can use to begin importing product return data. This file would contain the following columns:

▶ **Date.** Make this the date the original purchase took place, not the date of the return, so there is no lag time. Keep in mind that there is a SiteCatalyst restriction that you cannot import a Transaction ID file that has dates spanning more than 90 days. You can import dates that are more than 90 days old, but the date ranges for the entire file import cannot be more than 90 days.

▶ **Transaction ID.** The ID associated with the original online sale.

▶ **Product Name/ID.** This should be the same value you originally passed to the products variable at the time of the original online purchase.

▶ **Product Return Amount.** This is the total dollar amount per product that is being returned.

When you're done, **Figure 13.22** shows what your import file might look like. After you have successfully imported product return data, you can see how all of this looks in SiteCatalyst. Open the Products report and add Revenue and the new Product Return Amount metrics. If you were just looking at the visitor who purchased the iPods described earlier, the report would look like the one in **Figure 13.23**.

# Generic Data Source (Transaction ID) template file (user: 63952 ds_id: 6)				
#	1	Product	Product Return Amount	
Date	transactionID	Product	Event 97	
07/15/2012	1111222	ipod	50.00	

Figure 13.22 Sample Product Returns Transaction ID import file.

	Products	Revenue ▼ ⑦		Product Return Amount		Net Revenue
	1. ipod	$100	100.0%	$50	100.0%	$50

Figure 13.23 Sample Products report with product returns.

In this report, a calculated metric was also created to subtract Product Return Amount from Revenue to create a Net Revenue metric. Because Transaction ID allows you to apply the conversion variable values that were associated with the original transaction to the new "product return" transaction, you can use conversion subrelation breakdowns for the Products report by Visit Number and see revenue, product return amount, and net revenue by any conversion variable (e.g., Visit Number), as shown in **Figure 13.24**.

Figure 13.24 Sample Conversion Subrelations report with product returns.

	Products by Visit Number	Revenue ▾ ⑦	Product Return Amount	Net Revenue
	1. ipod	$100	$50	$50
	1. Visit 1	$100 100.0%	$50 100.0%	$50

As you get more advanced with this concept, you can apply the same principles to back out orders and units, but the preceding steps should be a good starting point if you want to take product returns into account for your web analysis. Additionally, if your website doesn't sell products, you can still use the preceding instructions to deal with any scenario in which you have tracked an item online and later find that you need to back out some or all of this data.

Recurring Revenue

At a web analytics conference, I met someone whose business relied on a subscription model. In a subscription model, you initially sell a product and subsequently have a recurring revenue stream (normally monthly). During the conversation, I explained how I would implement this recurring revenue in SiteCatalyst. Because there are many business models where recurring revenue streams occur, I'll share my implementation here in case it applies to your organization and for educational purposes. The solution for recurring revenue is very similar to what you just learned about product returns.

So why should you care about tracking recurring revenue in SiteCatalyst? Let me explain through an example. Imagine that you sell a CRM product that has an initial sale price and then a monthly subscription. A visitor comes to your website from the Bing keyword "CRM" and ends up purchasing your product for $10,000. You can track this $10,000 sale online and attribute it to the Bing keyword. However, what do you do after that first month? Let's say the customer pays $1000 each month after the initial $10,000. How do you attribute the recurring monthly $1000 to the Bing keyword that originally brought the customer to your website? Many clients stop at the initial sale, but this is problematic. What if some marketing campaigns bring in a lot of initial sales, but those coming from these campaigns quit the subscription after two months? Perhaps other marketing campaigns generate lower initial sale amounts but result in customers who remain subscribed for several years. How do you compare "apples to apples" in this case if you cannot attribute both initial and subscription revenue to the original marketing campaign?

The answer for most clients is to simply pass the original marketing campaign to their back-end system and do all of the reporting outside of a tool like SiteCatalyst. However, this has the following negative consequences:

▶ As a web analyst, you are now out of the loop for a key metric like revenue, which is not good for your analytics program (or career).

▶ SiteCatalyst has related hundreds of online-only data points to the original sale (e.g., visit number, onsite search terms used, internal promos used, etc.). Are you going to pass all of these data points to your company's back-end systems and do analysis there? If you are part of a big company, that may be possible, but what if you are a small or midsize business?

If you're like me, I'd rather have important data in SiteCatalyst so I can use it for web analysis. With this in mind, the following section describes what you need to do if you want to get recurring revenue into your SiteCatalyst implementation and tie it to the same data points as the initial sale. Again, even if your business doesn't have recurring revenue, there may be other ways you can apply this concept.

Viewing recurring revenue in SiteCatalyst

As with product returns, the key to implementing recurring revenue in SiteCatalyst is using Transaction ID. When visitors make their initial subscription purchase, you can set a Transaction ID value on the confirmation page. Doing so allows you to establish a "key" that you can use later to import recurring revenue and tie it to all of the conversion variable values associated with the original sale. Keep in mind that Transaction ID is normally used for only 90 days, but in this case you may want to extend it to at least one year so you can get at least 12 months of recurring revenue data.

Once you have Transaction ID enabled and have started passing Transaction IDs for online purchases, the next step is to create a new Recurring Revenue Currency success event. You would then use the Transaction ID Data Sources wizard to create your import file. In this case, everything will be the same as the product returns file except you'll use a different success event and the date associated with the recurring revenue would be the date that you received the recurring revenue, not the original date of the sale (as it was for product returns). When you're done, **Figure 13.25** shows what your Data Sources import file might look like. When you have successfully imported recurring revenue data, you can see it in SiteCatalyst reports and also create a calculated metric to see total revenue (**Figure 13.26**).

# Generic Data Source (Transaction ID) template file (user: 63952 ds_id: 6)					
#	1	Product	Recurring Revenue		
Date	transactionID	Product	Event98		
07/15/2012	33344433	CRM	1000.00		

Figure 13.25 Sample Recurring Revenue Transaction ID import file.

	Products	Revenue ▼⍰		Recurring Revenue		Total Revenue
	1. CRM	$500,000	38.5%	$1,250,000	16.7%	$1,750,000

Figure 13.26 Sample Recurring Revenue report.

As you learned earlier, because Transaction ID allows you to apply the conversion variable values that were associated with the original transaction to the new recurring revenue data, you can use conversion subrelation breakdowns for the Products report by Campaign and see revenue, recurring revenue, and total revenue (**Figure 13.27**). In this report, you can see an example of the quandary described at the beginning of this section. When you're breaking down the CRM product by campaign, it looks like you should be focusing your marketing spending on Bing-branded keywords. However, when you add recurring revenue to the report, you can see that the majority of the recurring revenue and total revenue is coming from e-mail. This illustrates why tracking recurring revenue can be beneficial and how it can influence your long-term campaign decisions.

Figure 13.27 Sample Conversion Subrelations report with recurring revenue.

	Products by Campaign	Revenue ▼ ⑦		Recurring Revenue		Total Revenue
1.	CRM	$500,000		$1,250,000		$1,750,000
1.	Bing Branded Keywords	$125,000	25.0%	$212,500	17.0%	$337,500
2.	Google Branded Keywords	$75,000	15.0%	$187,500	15.0%	$262,500
3.	SEO	$62,500	12.5%	$125,000	10.0%	$187,500
4.	E-mail	$37,500	7.5%	$350,000	28.0%	$387,500

Revenue and Orders to Date

Website visits don't occur in a vacuum. People who are on your site today may or may not have been there in the past, and if they have been there, some have purchased items and some have not. But how do you know if the current reports you are looking at in SiteCatalyst reflect those who have purchased in the past or not? How do you create SiteCatalyst reports that show *how much* or *how often* they have purchased in the past? Having this context can greatly improve the analysis you are doing. Here I'll describe some techniques that allow you to easily segment your visitors by these metrics.

Before diving into how to do this, let's explore the rationale. Imagine that you are a retailer selling electronics, clothing, and furniture. You might ask, "I wonder how much money all of the people who are on my site today have spent in the past?" Wouldn't it be great to see that 25 percent of the people who bought something today had purchased $500 or more in prior visits? And once you know how much money current visitors have previously spent, there are an endless number of analytics questions you can study. For example, do people who purchased more than $700 in the past convert at higher rates than those who only purchased $300? Do people who bought $400 or more in electronics tend to only buy and look at electronics products?

Surprisingly, there isn't a simple way to do this in SiteCatalyst. One obvious way is to create segments. However, because there are so many segments that could be built, this is not always an easy option. To answer the preceding questions, you'd have to create different segments for each dollar amount and product category (e.g., people who have spent $100, $200, $500, etc.). Of course, this is much easier if you are using SiteCatalyst v15 or later, but it still requires building a lot of segments. A different approach is to use a Counter conversion variable (eVar). As a quick refresher, a Counter conversion variable allows you to retain a number value in a conversion variable and increment it as needed for each website visitor. This counter can be incremented by "1" each time it is set, or as you'll see, it can be incremented by any other number as needed.

With the setup and refresher out of the way, let's dig in. As mentioned earlier, in this scenario, you are a retailer selling three main product categories and want to see how much money each visitor has spent prior to the current visit. In addition to setting the products variable, during the purchase event you would set a Counter conversion variable equal to the amount that is being purchased, like this:

```
s.events="purchase";
s.products=";111;1;300.00,;222;1;400.00,;333;1;200.00";
s.eVar40="+900";
```

Notice that the purchase amount has been added up and passed to a new Counter conversion variable (eVar40). In this example, if the current visitor hadn't previously visited the site, the value in his Counter conversion variable after this purchase would be "900." Because Counter conversion variables don't have a notion of currency, the actual value that will be stored in the report would be "900.00" (I suggest that you round purchase amounts to the nearest dollar because decimals will make applying SAINT classifications difficult.) You should set the Counter eVar to be the Most Recent (Last) allocation and set expiration to a timeframe beyond one visit (e.g., 90 days or 6 months) in the administration console. That is all you have to do from an implementation standpoint.

So now let's look at how you use this. Pretend that the visitor came back to the website the next week and added a few products to the shopping cart. If you pause time for a second and look at the resulting SiteCatalyst report, you would see something like the report shown in **Figure 13.28**.

		Revenue to Date	Cart Additions	
	1.	None	9,800	49.0%
	2.	100.00	400	2.0%
	3.	450.00	350	1.8%
	4.	300.00	325	1.6%
	5.	900.00	275	1.4%

Figure 13.28 Sample Revenue to Date report.

With this report, you can now answer the question of how much money visitors had *spent in the past* at the time they added items to the shopping cart *today*. In this case, it looks like about half (49%) of the people adding items to the cart today had not purchased previously. The visitor mentioned previously would fall into row five in this report as part of the 1.4% of people who had purchased $900 in a previous visit. The same Revenue to Date Counter conversion variable can be used with orders and revenue as the metrics, as shown in **Figure 13.29**.

Revenue to Date		Orders ▼		Revenue	
1.	None	7,800	43.3%	$51,000	46.4%
2.	100.00	250	1.4%	$2,980	2.7%
3.	450.00	225	1.3%	$3,100	2.8%
4.	300.00	200	1.1%	$2,698	2.5%
5.	900.00	175	1.0%	$2,135	1.9%

Figure 13.29 Sample Revenue to Date report with orders and revenue.

When you extrapolate this implementation by thousands of website visitors, you can see some interesting trends that show what percent of website visitors transacting today had purchased in the past and how much they spent. You can also make this report more readable by applying SAINT classifications to the Counter conversion variable to group the dollar amounts spent into buckets (**Figure 13.30**). This report can even be broken down by other conversion variable reports like Campaigns or Products.

Revenue to Date		Orders ▼	
1.	No Purchases	98,800	52.0%
2.	Under $100 Purchased	29,880	15.7%
3.	$101 to $300 Purchased	22,335	11.8%
4.	$301 to $500 Purchased	18,900	9.9%
5.	$501 to $1,000 Purchased	8,990	4.7%

Figure 13.30 Revenue to Date Classification report.

Orders to date

Using the same principle of a Counter conversion variable, you can also track the number of orders that have taken place for each visitor prior to the current visit. In this case, you would just create an additional Counter conversion variable and set it to "+1" each time an order occurs:

```
s.events="purchase";
s.products=";SKU111;1;300.00,;SKU222;1;400.00,;SKU333;1;200.00";
s.eVar41="+1";
```

	Orders to Date	Cart Additions ▼	
1.	None	23,450	21.1%
2.	1.00	8,965	8.1%
3.	3.00	8,225	7.4%
4.	2.00	7,312	6.6%
5.	5.00	7,180	6.5%

Figure 13.31 Orders to Date report.

This enables you to see the report shown in **Figure 13.31**.

In this report, you see that 21.1% of the cart additions that took place today were from visitors who had not ordered on your site in the past. If desired, you could also break down this report by product to see which products they purchased. Keep in mind that this example shows cart additions, but you could just as easily have added orders, revenue, onsite searches, or any other website metric to this report to see how many orders had taken place prior to that success event. You could also use SAINT classifications to group this Orders to Date conversion variable into buckets of say 1–2 Orders, 3–5 Orders, 5–10 Orders, and so on.

The implementation of revenue and orders to date is not complex once you understand how to use Counter conversion variables. This approach is a potential alternative to building multiple segments, but either approach should result in similar data for analytic purposes.

Product Category Revenue and Orders to Date

If your organization has specific product categories that are critical to the business, you can use the revenue and orders to date concept for a specific product category. In addition to setting a Counter conversion variable for the total revenue a visitor has accrued, you can set a second Counter conversion variable with just revenue related to a specific product category. For example, if a visitor purchases $900 in goods and $500 are in the "Electronics" product category, you would pass "900" to one Counter conversion variable and "500" to a second Electronics category Counter conversion variable. This can be repeated for all important product categories. However, keep in mind that this will use many precious conversion variables, so I suggest you apply this only to your top product categories.

Conclusion

In this chapter, you learned the basics of tracking the shopping cart as well as some advanced shopping cart implementation methods that highlighted the SiteCatalyst features discussed in prior chapters. Implementing product views, product pathing, and product merchandising can help you figure out which products and product categories are performing well or poorly. Using advanced techniques, like money left on the table, product returns, and recurring revenue, can help you ensure that your organization knows where its potential improvement opportunities lie. Validating revenue and orders allows you to have faith that your key website KPIs are accurate so web analyses are not done in vain. If you are like the many SiteCatalyst clients only scratching the surface of what can be done with shopping cart tracking, I hope you'll experiment with these techniques and apply them to your organization's business model.

## CHAPTER 14

Campaign Tracking

One of SiteCatalyst's primary uses is to track online marketing campaigns. Most organizations receive website traffic from hundreds of sources. Some are intentional, such as paid search keywords, display advertisements, and affiliate links. Others, like natural search referrals from Google or Bing, are dependent upon website content. Your organization might also send e-mails or embed links within social networking sites like Facebook or Twitter. Regardless of how visitors arrive, SiteCatalyst is a great tool to measure campaign effectiveness.

In addition to these externally driven campaigns, websites often have onsite promotions. These "internal campaigns" steer visitors to content or products of importance.

External Campaign Tracking

When it comes to tracking external campaigns in SiteCatalyst, there are many different approaches. At a high level, the goal of external campaign tracking is to associate as many website referrals as possible to an identifiable code so that any website success events taking place in that visit can be attributed to that campaign tracking code. Once a website session is tied to a campaign tracking code, additional campaign metadata can be added to SiteCatalyst to allow those codes to be grouped by different campaign attributes. Common campaign attributes include campaign name, marketing channel, campaign owner, and so on. Some organizations track only those campaign codes for which they are spending marketing budgets. Others assign every website session to a tracking code, even if that code is "typed/bookmarked" for those who entered the site without a referrer. Some organizations group campaigns by 10 to 20 campaign attributes, whereas others rely solely on campaign tracking codes. A number of organizations care about multi-visit attribution and want to see "first-touch" campaigns versus "last-touch" campaigns.

At the end of the day, it is up to you to understand what your options are and to select the correct level of external campaign tracking based on the time, budget, and resources at your disposal. The following sections detail some of the recommended choices available to you so you can decide which approach is right for your organization.

Unified Sources

▶TIP *A best practice in using Unified Sources is to set the marketing channel as the first part of the tracking code so it is easy to filter and identify tracking codes. For example, if it is determined that a visit was referred by a paid search keyword, the campaign tracking code might be "sem_111515" where "sem" represents paid search and "111515" represents the specific paid search advertisement.*

For those old-timers like me, nothing beats old-fashioned Unified Sources tracking. Unified Sources is the idea that every website visit should have an external campaign tracking code. This means that no matter what marketing channel drove the visit, there is a way to identify the traffic source and tie it to session success events.

To accomplish this, there are two primary implementation methods: The first method is to use a VISTA rule, which transforms referring URLs and codes into campaign tracking codes. This VISTA rule uses a process of elimination to determine which codes should be set for each referrer. For example, a typical rule might first identify if a visit originated from a search engine, and if it did, determine if it contained a paid search query string. These types of rules are used until every visit is assigned to a campaign code. Unfortunately, one downside of the VISTA rule approach is that it costs money anytime you need to modify the rules contained in the VISTA rule.

The second method of implementing Unified Sources is through JavaScript. You can use a JavaScript plug-in called the Channel Manager to assign campaign tracking codes in a similar manner to the aforementioned VISTA rule. The advantage of the JavaScript plug-in over the VISTA rule is that it can be modified as needed without having to pay a change fee that is associated with VISTA rules. However, the disadvantage of the

JavaScript plug-in is that it contains a lot of code and can slow page load times. I prefer to use the JavaScript approach instead of the VISTA rule, because I like the flexibility, and as you'll see, the VISTA rule approach has been effectively replaced by the new Marketing Channels feature I'll cover next. Regardless of which Unified Sources approach you choose, the end result should be similar—a conversion variable report that assigns one value for each visit and persists for the visit or longer. Traditionally, the campaign variable (`s.campaign`) has been used for this purpose, but you can use any conversion variable. Once values are set, you might see a report like the one shown in **Figure 14.1**.

How you structure your external campaign tracking codes is up to you, but it's best to put as much information as possible in tracking codes, because it makes it easier to filter and upload SAINT classifications. In the report in Figure 14.1, if I want to classify all "seo" codes, I can filter by "seo:" and then export to Excel where it is easy to assign the marketing channel to "SEO." Ultimately, the goal is to group all external campaign codes by campaign, marketing channel, and so on, as shown in **Figure 14.2**.

		Tracking Code	Orders ▼ ⑦	
	1.	typed/bookmark	27,240	21.1%
	2.	sem:google:111515	10,414	8.1%
	3.	sem:bing:111527	9,554	7.4%
	4.	seo:google:greco inc	8,494	6.6%
	5.	display:yahoo:777333	8,340	6.5%
	6.	e-mail:1234	6,833	5.3%
	7.	social:facebook:77222	6,575	5.1%
	8.	social:twitter:228881	5,672	4.4%
	9.	seo:bing:greco	5,286	4.1%
	10.	seo:google:greco	4,125	3.2%

Figure 14.1 Sample Unified Sources report.

		Marketing Channel	Orders ▼ ⑦	
	1.	typed/bookmark	27,240	21.1%
	2.	paid search	25,861	20.1%
	3.	seo	25,319	19.6%
	4.	display advertising	22,754	17.7%
	5.	e-mail	15,444	12.0%
	6.	social networks	12,299	9.5%

Figure 14.2 Sample Unified Sources Marketing Channel Classification report.

Marketing Channels

As is often the case, when the SiteCatalyst product team notices that a large number of clients are migrating to the same solution (Unified Sources in this case), it tries to implement product enhancements to meet the need with less work. Normally, these manifest themselves as out-of-the-box features that accomplish the same goal. Hence, SiteCatalyst now offers a Marketing Channels feature that you can use to mimic much of the functionality hacked together by folks like me using Unified Sources. You can use the Marketing Channels feature to configure marketing channel reporting using a set of processing rules that are configured in the administration console (**Figure 14.3**).

These rules are similar to the Unified Sources VISTA rule mentioned previously, but do not have the fees associated with VISTA rules. In addition, within the Marketing Channels, you can configure costs associated with each campaign, apply campaign classifications, and choose when campaigns should expire. All of these options are found in the Marketing Channels menu in the administration console (**Figure 14.4**).

After you configure your processing rules and other settings, you'll see a report like the one shown in **Figure 14.5**.

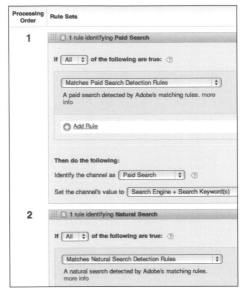

Figure 14.3 Sample Marketing Channels processing rule configuration.

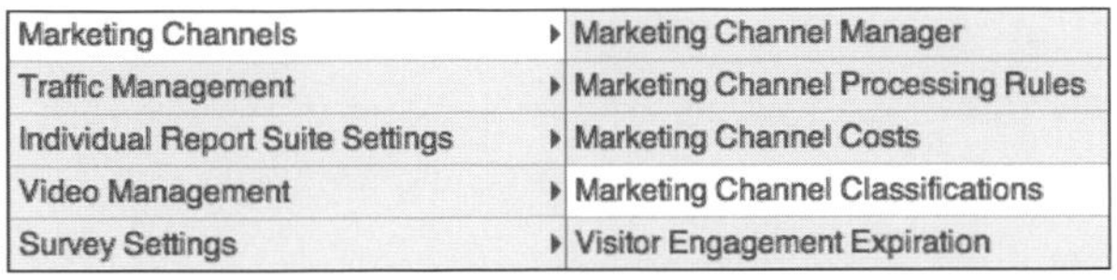

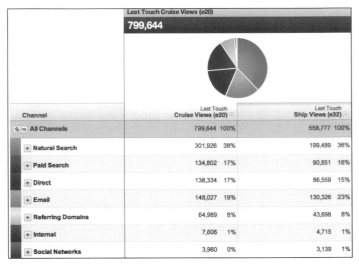

Figure 14.4 Marketing Channels menu in the administration console.

Figure 14.5 Sample Marketing Channels report.

Multiple Campaign Variables

Many organizations use more than one external campaign variable, primarily to have different campaign expiration periods. Because there is no real difference between the campaign variable (`s.campaign`) and a conversion variable, you can pass the same campaign tracking codes into multiple conversion variables concurrently and have each conversion variable expire at a different interval (e.g., week, month, six months). There is no limit on how many campaign variables you can set, but keep in mind that if you have SAINT classifications for your external campaign tracking codes, these will need to be applied to each campaign variable.

Unfortunately, configuring all aspects of Marketing Channels is somewhat detailed, so providing step-by-step instructions is not practical in this handbook. However, you'll find ample information in the SiteCatalyst Knowledge Base should you want to give it a try.

It is important to determine which overall approach is best for your organization. If you are short on development resources, the out-of-the-box Marketing Channels feature is probably best for you. However, if you want complete control of your marketing channel data, you may still decide to use a form of Unified Sources tracking. In some cases, you may decide to use both approaches. Explore both options and determine which one works best for your organization.

Internal Campaigns

Once visitors arrive at your website, you have the opportunity to present them with your own internal campaigns (sometimes called *promotions*). These internal campaigns might be used to highlight current sales, educate about new products, or drive people to a form. Regardless of their intent, you should be tracking your internal campaigns so you can see how each is performing and use them to boost website conversion. In this section, you'll learn how to calculate internal campaign click-through rates and determine how each internal campaign is influencing website KPIs.

Internal Campaign Click-through Rates

As soon as you begin showing internal campaigns (promotions) on your website, it is only a matter of time before someone at your organization will ask how they are performing. This is especially true if the promotion is on a popular page, like the home page. Here is a list of the typical questions asked related to internal campaigns:

▶ What is the click-through rate of each promotion?

▶ How does each promotion perform on different pages?

▶ How does a particular promotional area perform regardless of what promotion is presented?

Unfortunately, answering all of these questions is not trivial in SiteCatalyst, but it can be done. Let's apply the concepts you learned in previous chapters to implement a solution that answers these questions.

The first step is to assign a unique code to each promotion on the page. For example, let's look at the Apple home page (**Figure 14.6**).

Figure 14.6 Sample home page.

For simplicity sake, in this example, let's assume that Apple is treating only the three items highlighted in red as internal campaigns. In this case, you need to assign an internal campaign impression to each of these three promotions whenever the page loads. At the same time, you need to associate those impressions with the internal campaign codes found on the page. Additionally, you need to assign a location to each impression so you can see how each location performs. That is a lot of tracking in a short window of time.

Because the number of impressions is a metric, you know that it will have to be a success event. Therefore, you can create a new Internal Campaign Impressions success event. However, because multiple values need to be tied to that success event, your options in SiteCatalyst are somewhat limited. The conversion variables that are best suited for storing multiple values are the products variable and list conversion variables (only available in v15+). Either of these variable types allows you to track multiple codes. In this case, you'll use a list conversion variable to preserve the products variable for product-related success events. Here is what the coding might look like on this home page:

```
s.events="event55";
s.list1="hero:macbook-pro-retina_12,sub2:ios6_2,
sub4:back2school_4";
```

You may find this tagging a bit strange, so let's review it in detail. For each value of the list conversion variable, you need to identify the location of the promotion (hero, sub2, sub4) and which promotion was shown (macbook-pro-retina, ios6, back2school). By concatenating these two values, you can later use ReportBuilder and Excel pivot tables to split them out by location and promotion. You may also notice that a version number has been added to each promotion (e.g., back2school_4). This version number is optional but can be used to see which version of the "back2school" promotion was shown if there are multiple versions possible.

If a visitor clicks on one of the preceding promotions, you'll follow a similar process but set a new Internal Campaign Clicks success event and pass the code of the clicked promotion to the same list conversion variable. So if a visitor clicks on the main hero spot, you might set code like this:

```
s.events="event56";
s.list1="hero:macbook-pro-retina_12";
```

Now that you have code capturing impressions and clicks, you can see this data in SiteCatalyst. As an example, if the preceding visitor was the only one to view the Apple website, **Figure 14.7** shows what the SiteCatalyst report would look like.

In the report, you can see impressions, clicks, and a calculated metric showing the internal campaign click-through rate for each internal campaign element. Over time, each internal campaign element may be added or removed on various pages, but the preceding reports will be updated accordingly, showing how each promotion and location combination performs. You can break these individual elements into different locations and promotions using a pivot table like the one shown in **Figure 14.8**. This pivot table can then be used to see the click-through rate of a particular promotion anywhere it is shown on the website or can show how a specific location on the website performs over time (**Figure 14.9**).

■ **NOTE** *It is not currently possible to classify a List Variable, but I expect it will be eventually. When it is, you can use classifications to split out these List Variable values by Location, Campaign, etc.*

		Internal Campaign CTR	Internal Campaign Impressions ▼		Internal Campaign Clicks		Internal Campaign CTR %
⊤	1.	hero:macbook-pro-retina_12	1	33.3%	1	100.0%	100%
⊤	2.	sub2:ios6_2	1	33.3%	0	0.0%	0%
⊤	3.	sub4:back2school_4	1	33.3%	0	0.0%	0%

Figure 14.7 Sample Internal Campaign Click-through report.

CTA ID	Internal Campaign Location	Internal Campaign	Internal Campaign Impressions	Internal Campaign Clicks
hero:macbook-pro-retina_12	hero	macbook-pro-retina_12	3459	1400
sub2:ios6_2	sub2	ios6_2	2156	725
sub4:back2school_4	sub4	back2school_4	1987	545
hero:mac-air_10	hero	mac-air_10	988	398
sub4:apple-tv_1	sub4	apple-tv_1	2109	585

Figure 14.8 Sample ReportBuilder Internal Campaign data request.

Figure 14.9 Sample Location Click-through Rate report.

	A	B	C	D
1		Report Filter		
2				
3		Values		
4	Row Labels	Sum of Internal Campaign Impressions	Sum of Internal Campaign Clicks	Internal Campaign CTA %
5	hero	9125	3821	41.87%
6	sub2	7800	2669	34.22%
7	sub4	4625	1301	28.13%
8	Grand Total	21550	7791	36.15%
9		PivotTable Builder		
10				
11		Field name		
12		CTA ID		
13		Internal Campaign Location		

Consider Advanced Internal Campaigns via Test&Target

Once you can see how your internal campaigns are performing, you may want to try using Adobe Test&Target to improve conversion. Test&Target allows you to test different promotions on your website and see which ones perform the best. It also provides a way to target content based on rules or past website behavior. For example, if Apple had a product that was only available in the United States, it could use Test&Target to show different products to visitors from other countries.

Internal Campaign Influence

Although tracking internal campaign click-through rates can show you which internal campaigns are getting clicked, it cannot tell you which ones are leading to success on your website. Ultimately, you want to see if clicks on your internal promotions impact website conversion. However, determining this requires a slightly different configuration of SiteCatalyst. Let's continue with the Apple example to see how you can track internal campaign influence.

If you want to see the long-term impact of an internal campaign, by now you should know that you would set a conversion variable. Because conversion variables persist throughout the visit (or longer), they are ideal for tracking which success events take place after an internal campaign has been clicked. Therefore, in the preceding Apple example, at the same time a visitor clicks on an internal campaign and you pass its value to the list conversion variable, you can pass the internal campaign value to a standard conversion variable like this:

```
s.events="event56";
s.list1="hero:macbook-pro-retina_12";
s.eVar28="hero:macbook-pro-retina_12";
```

	Internal Campaign Influence	Orders ▼ ⑦		Revenue ⑦	
	1. None ⑦	39,255	30.5%	$2,124,184	27.6%
	2. hero:macbook-pro-retina_12	15,625	12.1%	$897,922	11.7%
	3. sub2:ios6_2	12,724	9.9%	$683,654	8.9%
	4. sub4:back2school_4	10,030	7.8%	$504,070	6.5%

Figure 14.10 Sample Internal Campaign Influence report.

	Tracking Code by Internal Campaign Influence	Orders ▼ ⑦	
	1. typed/bookmark	27,240	
	1. None ⑦	9,414	34.6%
	2. hero:macbook-pro-retina_12	7,774	28.5%
	3. sub2:ios6_2	4,209	15.5%
	4. sub4:back2school_4	2,599	9.5%
	5. Other	3,244	11.9%
	Show all for typed/bookmark…		
	2. paid search	25,861	
	1. None ⑦	16,690	64.5%
	2. sub2:ios6_2	3,248	12.6%
	3. hero:macbook-pro-retina_12	2,552	9.9%

Figure 14.11 External campaigns and internal campaigns.

Because visitors can click on multiple internal campaigns within a visit, I suggest that you set this conversion variable to Linear Allocation so each internal campaign receives partial credit if several are clicked. Once this conversion variable is set, it acts like any other conversion variable and allows you to see a report like the one shown in **Figure 14.10**. Additionally, because external campaigns and internal campaigns are tracked using conversion variables, it is possible to see them combined using a Conversion Variable Subrelation report. **Figure 14.11** shows external campaigns broken down by internal campaigns. Also, keep in mind that you can view the preceding subrelation report by marketing channel, internal campaign placement, or any of the classifications associated with either of these two campaign variables.

Conclusion

In this chapter, you learned how to apply concepts covered in past sections to track external and internal campaigns. Tracking both tends to be among the first requirements undertaken in new SiteCatalyst implementations. Various levels of difficulty are associated with internal and external campaigns, but neither is overly complex if you understand the fundamentals of SiteCatalyst. I suggest you review how your organization is currently tracking external and internal campaigns and determine if there is room for improvement.

## CHAPTER 15

Lead Generation

In addition to selling products, lead generation is one of the most common functions websites perform. Accessible to customers and prospects 24 hours a day, 365 days a year, the Internet has become the primary source of lead generation through website forms, which provide the ability to solicit contact information from prospects while they are engaged with your website content.

Business-to-business companies and others have spent years perfecting the art of driving prospects to websites and providing the content needed to get visitors to call or complete a website form. In this chapter, I share some lead generation best practices to provide implementation ideas and continue educating you on the different ways that you can apply SiteCatalyst in real-world business situations.

Lead Generation Forms

Lead generation websites provide content to engage prospects and help them decide if they want to consider the organization's products or services. The primary objective is normally to drive a phone call or complete a form. With SiteCatalyst, you can easily track the completion of a form through a success event. Phone calls are more difficult to track, but I'll provide some ways to do this as well. Let's start with website forms.

Form Views and Form Completions

Most lead generation websites have multiple forms that visitors can complete. The more detail you can collect about these forms, the more actionable your web analysis can be. This includes tracking how often visitors see forms, complete forms, encounter errors, and so on.

The first step is to set success events on any screen where visitors view and complete forms (e.g., Form Views). **Figure 15.1** shows an example of a website form, and the Site-Catalyst code set when this page loads might look like this:

```
s.events="event9";
```

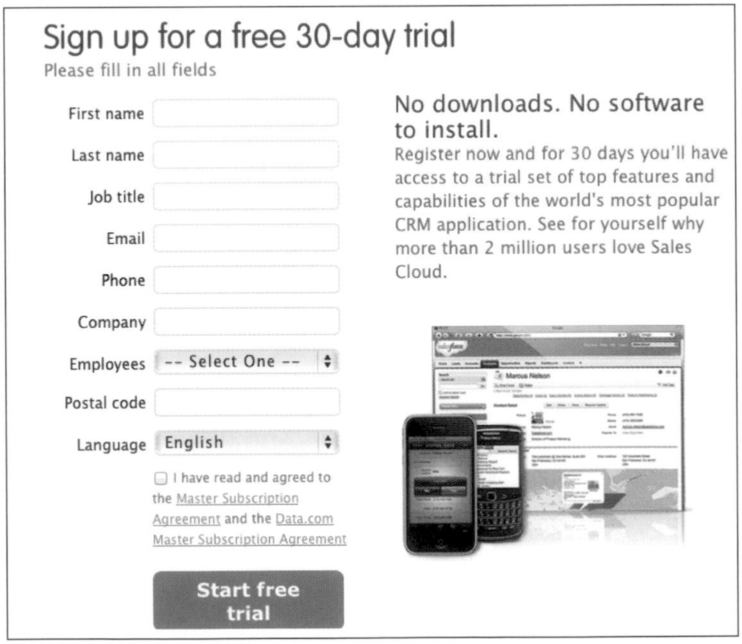

Figure 15.1 Sample lead generation form.

After visitors complete the form, they will often reach a "thank you" page that confirms that their lead information has been successfully processed (**Figure 15.2**). On the form "thank you" page, you should set a second success event (e.g., Form Completions) using the following code:

```
s.events="event10";
```

Setting these two success events enables you to see a metric report for each of these actions. **Figure 15.3** shows an example of a Form Completions metric report.

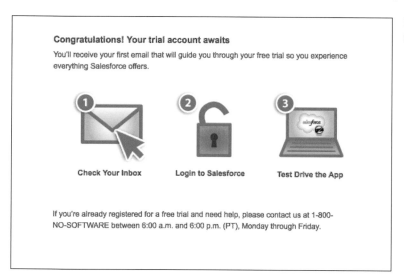

Figure 15.2 Sample lead generation "thank you" page.

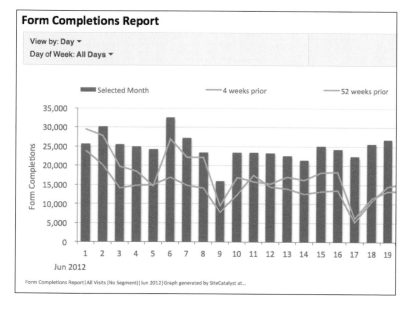

Figure 15.3 Form Completions metric report.

Form Conversion

When the Form Views and Form Completions success events are set, it is possible to create Form Conversion Rates. I tend to focus on two conversion rates: Form Completion Rate and Form Conversion Rate.

Form Completion Rate

The Form Completion Rate is calculated by dividing Form Completions by Form Views. This calculated metric shows you how often visitors who see forms complete them. I often use success event serialization to make sure Form Views and Form Completions are not double-counted and to ensure that this conversion metric is reliable.

When you've created the Form Completion Rate metric, you can open a metric report to see its progress over time (**Figure 15.4**).

Figure 15.4 Form
Completion Rate trend.

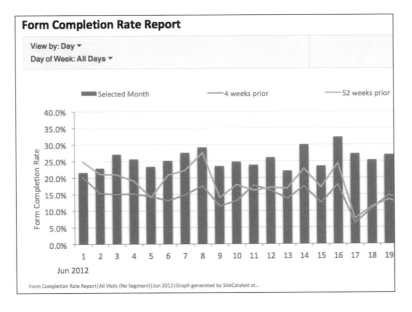

Form Conversion Rate

The Form Conversion Rate is calculated by dividing Form Completions by Visits or Unique Visitors. Which denominator you use is your choice and depends on whether your organization prefers Visits or Unique Visitors. I use Visits because I look at every visit as an opportunity to convert someone. You can even create two form conversion metrics: one using Visits and one using Unique Visitors, as long as you label them appropriately. After your Form Conversion Rate has been created as a calculated metric, you can see its metric trend report (**Figure 15.5**).

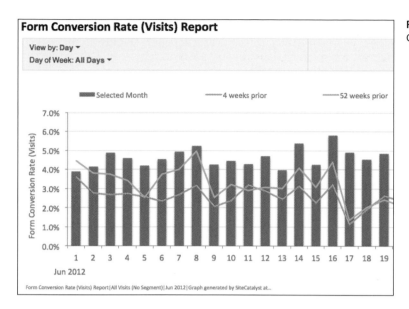

Figure 15.5 Form Conversion Rate trend.

Form IDs

In addition to calculating Form Completion and Conversion Rates, it is often important for lead generation sites to identify which forms are performing well and which forms are underperforming. As with other SiteCatalyst functions, the more ways you can break down metrics, the more web analyses you can conduct. Therefore, it is a best practice to assign a unique Form ID to each form on your website. Having a Form ID allows you to compare forms and see Form Completion and Conversion Rates for each unique website form.

As you learned earlier, the best way to break down success events is through the use of conversion variables. In this case, you should set a conversion variable each time Form Views and Form Completions success events are counted. Also, it is important that you set the same Form ID when both the Form Views and the Form Completions success events are set. Using the form shown previously as an example, you would amend the code provided earlier to set the Form ID conversion variable (eVar25) on the Form Views success event:

```
s.events="event9";
```

```
s.eVar25="freetrial:111";
```

When the Form Completions success event takes place, you would set a second success event, and the Form ID conversion variable (eVar25) would persist and have the same value as the Form Views success event:

```
s.events="event10";
```

This approach enables you to see Form Views, Form Completions, and Form Conversion Rates for the same Form ID value in a conversion variable report (**Figure 15.6**).

Figure 15.6 Form ID report.

	Form ID	Form Views ▼		Form Completions		Form Completion Rate
1.	freetrial:111	670,000	21.3%	170,000	22.7%	25.37%
2.	freetrial:101	621,985	18.7%	153,750	20.5%	24.72%
3.	demo:100	492,500	15.7%	121,250	16.2%	24.62%
4.	demo:210	312,500	10.4%	78,750	10.5%	25.20%
5.	contactus:100	217,750	8.3%	55,000	7.3%	25.26%
6.	freetrial:201	232,450	6.3%	57,500	7.7%	24.74%

Forcing Unique Form IDs

One problem that I've encountered when organizations assign unique Form IDs is that they tend to copy code from one page or site to another. As a result, the same Form ID is sometimes associated with multiple forms. For example, imagine that you have a form on a US landing page and someone from your Australia development team copies the page code to the Australian site. Now the same Form ID is being used on two different pages. This will taint your form conversion data unless the form converts identically on the US and Australian site.

To mitigate this potential issue, one trick I recommend is concatenating the page name to the Form ID conversion variable value (e.g., "grecoinc:us:campaign: landing|freetrial:111") on the Form View page to ensure that each Form ID is unique. This involves adding the page name to the Form ID conversion variable (not changing the actual page name). By adding the page name to the Form ID value, even if the same Form ID value is used in multiple places on the website, the page name portion of the conversion variable will make each unique. This tends to get confusing, so let's look at an example:

The Form View code would be set as:

```
s.events="event9";

s.eVar25="grecoinc:us:campaign:
landing|freetrial:111";
```

The Form Completion code would be set as:

```
s.events="event10";
```

Because the Form ID conversion variable (eVar25) will persist, its value will be identical for both success events and use the page name of the Form View page. This approach, albeit more complex, should guarantee that all forms on all website pages have a unique Form ID. I would then expire the Form ID conversion variable at the Form Completions success event.

Form types

Most organizations have specific types of forms that exist on their website. For example, you might have several different versions of free trial forms, one contact us form, and a few versions of a demo form. If you want to look at the conversion of forms by type, simply apply a SAINT classification to the Form ID conversion variable and look at the same metrics for this classification (**Figure 15.7**).

		Form Type	Form Views ▼		Form Completions		Form Completion Rate
⊤	1.	Free Trial	1,425,890	21.3%	325,875	43.5%	22.85%
⊤	2.	Demo	975,450	18.7%	235,500	31.4%	24.14%
⊤	3.	Contact Us	725,975	15.7%	188,625	25.2%	25.98%

Figure 15.7 Form conversion by Form Type.

Form Submit Clicks

If form tracking is important to your organization, you should consider the concept of Form Submit Clicks, which involves setting a success event when visitors click your form Submit buttons. Let's looks at an example: Imagine that Greco, Inc's website has several ways in which prospects can reach forms unintentionally. For example, there may be a "Learn more about our products" button, and clicking it takes prospects to a form. In this case, the prospect might have wanted to see product descriptions or demos and got stuck with a form. When this happens, prospects see forms that they hadn't intended to see, which might result in lower Form Completion Rates. To mitigate this, you can set a success event when visitors click the button to submit a form. This metric is very similar to Form Completions but excludes cases where visitors encounter form errors. It is a more representative metric for those who are truly interested in filling out your forms, and as such, can be a better proxy for prospect interest than Form Views. I often use this Form Submit Clicks metric as part of a calculated metric with Visits or Unique Visitors to see how effective my website is at getting people to the point at which they are willing to submit their information.

Form Errors

Whenever you have website forms, you have form errors (**Figure 15.8**). Form errors occur when website visitors either knowingly or unknowingly skip required form fields or enter invalid values. As a lead generation marketer, form errors are exasperating because you work so hard and often pay a lot of money to drive people to your website, review your content, and then agree to provide you with their personal information. But all of this work can be wasted if visitors encounter form errors and decide to abandon your website. For this reason, tracking form errors is often "low-hanging fruit" because these are the people who have agreed to provide you with their lead information and all you need to do is get them over the finish line. Resolving issues related to form errors is one of the easiest ways to improve website lead generation. Therefore, the following sections provide you with some of the ways you can use SiteCatalyst to help identify where and why visitors are encountering errors, so you can identify ways to proactively address them.

Figure 15.8 Sample Form Error screen.

Form Error success event

The first step I take to resolve form errors is to identify how often they occur by setting a success event each time a form error takes place (even though an error isn't really success!). Even if a visitor has multiple errors on a form, you only want to set the success event once per form error instance. Therefore, in the case shown in Figure 15.8, only one Form Error success event would be set using code like this:

```
s.events="event12";
```

Setting this success event will produce a Form Error metric report that you can monitor over time (**Figure 15.9**). When you've set the Form Error success event, you can use it with other metrics to create some useful calculated metrics. For example, one metric I like to create is Form Error Rate, which I define as the number of Form Errors per Form Views. In **Figure 15.10**, you can see that Greco, Inc. website visitors are encountering form errors about 32% of the time that they view forms. Alternatively, you can create a similar metric using Form Completions as the denominator. Both metrics will show you whether or not you should be concerned with form errors.

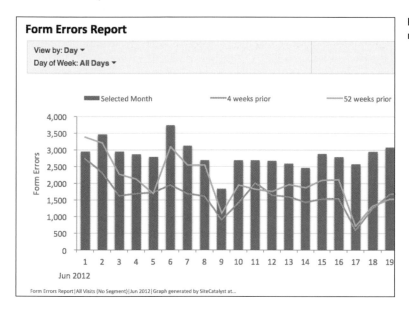

Figure 15.9 Form Errors metric report.

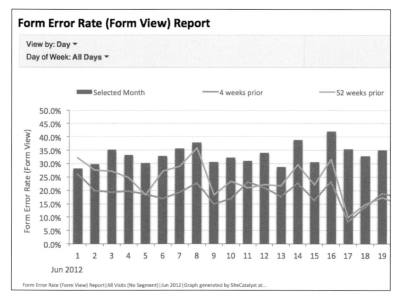

Figure 15.10 Form Error Rate report.

Form Error alerts

Form error tracking is a great use of the alerts functionality you learned about in Chapter 9. Whether you want to be alerted when form errors spike in general or only for a specific Form ID or form type, alerts allow you to be proactive about addressing form errors.

For example, let's pretend that Greco, Inc. wants to be alerted if there is a daily spike in Call Request forms. In this case, Greco, Inc. has classified all of its forms into form types so it can create a classification alert using "Call Request" as the form type and Form Errors as the metric. **Figure 15.11** shows how this alert would be configured.

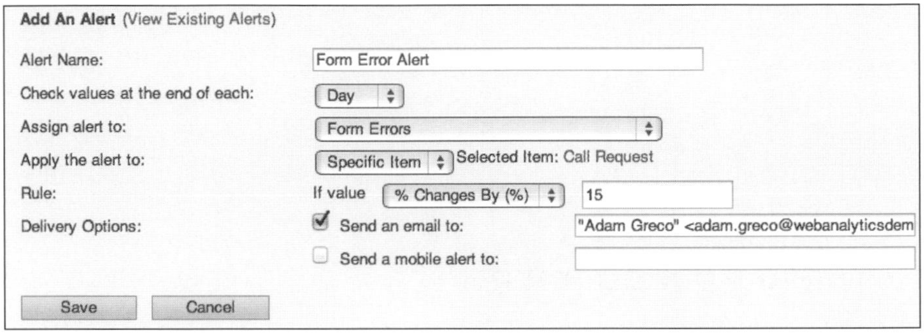

Figure 15.11 Form Type alert.

Fields producing form errors

After quantifying how often form errors take place, turn your attention to identifying which fields on forms are causing the most form errors. Because you already have a success event to quantify form errors, you now need a conversion variable to break down these form errors by the specific form fields that are causing errors. Unfortunately, as you saw in Figure 15.8, often multiple fields can produce errors. This means that you should use a list variable instead of a traditional conversion variable because list variables can store multiple values. For the form shown in Figure 15.8, the code you would use might look like this:

```
s.events="event10";
s.eVar25="freetrial:111";
s.list2="jobtitle,e-mail,phone,company,employees,zipcode,msa";
```

Using a list variable allows you to see how many Form Error success events were associated with each form field (**Figure 15.12**). The report in Figure 15.12 enables you to focus on the form fields that are causing the most errors. In addition, you can use a conversion variable subrelation to combine this report with the Form ID report to see which fields on which forms cause the most form errors (**Figure 15.13**).

	Form Field Errors	Form Errors ▼	
	1.	phone	2,100	42.0%
	2.	e-mail	1,800	36.0%
	3.	msa	1,300	26.0%
	4.	zipcode	800	16.0%

Figure 15.12 Form Field Errors report.

	Form ID by Form Field Errors	Form Errors ▼	
	1. freetrial:111	670,000	
	1. phone	231,552	34.6%
	2. e-mail	191,218	28.5%
	3. msa	103,515	15.5%
	4. zipcode	63,918	9.5%
	5. Other	79,797	11.9%
	Show all for freetrial:111…		
	2. freetrial:101	621,985	
	1. e-mail	401,429	64.5%
	2. phone	78,121	12.6%
	3. zipcode	61,390	9.9%

Figure 15.13 Form ID by Form Field Errors.

Form Field Abandonment

A popular request I get from lead generation clients is to see the order in which visitors complete form fields and to see what the last field was visitors completed if they abandoned the form. The next two sections share the ways you can answer these questions.

Form Analysis plug-in

For years, SiteCatalyst customers have used a Form Analysis JavaScript plug-in to address form field questions. This plug-in sends a server request as visitors navigate from field to field and records the name of the field in a traffic or conversion variable. However, over the years I've grown less and less fond of recommending this plug-in. The reason is that it is difficult to maintain and use, and even the SiteCatalyst Knowledge Base discourages its use. I mention it here only to make you aware of it and suggest you discuss its use with your Adobe account manager or ClientCare.

Form Field pathing

The approach I prefer is Form Field pathing. To implement this, you use custom link tagging to pass the Form ID and form field name (concatenated) to a traffic variable as visitors navigate from field to field. Then you enable pathing on this new traffic variable. Using the sample form shown at the beginning of this chapter (Figure 15.1), a visitor placing his cursor in the First Name field would result in a value of "freetrial:111|firstname" being passed to a traffic variable. As the visitor navigated to the next field (e.g., Last Name), the value passed to the traffic variable would be "freetrial:111|lastname."

■ **NOTE** *If you have Adobe Discover, you can build a Fallout report that shows* all *form fields and see the exact fallout percentages for the entire form.*

As data is collected for all forms, you can take advantage of Pathing reports to learn how visitors are navigating and abandoning your forms (keep in mind that each field will count as a server call, which can end up costing you more money). First, you can open this new traffic report and add the Exits metric to see which fields visitors are exiting on most often. In this case, I have also added an Exit Rate calculated metric (Exits/Page Views) to normalize the data (**Figure 15.14**).

Second, you can also use pathing fallout reports to see the rate of fallout for key website form fields (**Figure 15.15**).

Figure 15.14 Form Field Exits report.

	Form Fields	Exits ▼ ⑦		Page Views		Exit Rate
1.	freetrial:111|e-mail	5,425	21.3%	32,846	12.7%	16.52%
2.	freetrial:111|phone	4,769	18.7%	40,116	15.5%	11.89%
3.	freetrial:111|lastname	4,004	15.7%	56,188	21.6%	7.13%
4.	freetrial:111|firstname	3,223	12.6%	61,537	23.7%	5.24%

Checkpoint Analysis

	Visits		Process
1. 54,140	100.0%		freetrial:111|firstname
		63.1%	Continued
		36.9%	Lost
2. 34,173	63.1%		freetrial:111|e-mail
		61.8%	Continued
		38.2%	Lost
3. 21,104	39.0%		freetrial:111|phone
		88.4%	Continued
		11.6%	Lost
4. 18,655	34.5%		freetrial:111|zipcode

Total Conversion = 18,655 **34.5%**

Figure 15.15 Form Field Fallout report.

Phone Conversion

If your business offers a telephone lead generation option, it is more difficult, but not impossible, to track website success. As a marketer, you will still drive prospects to your website and engage them with content, but when they call you, you can lose that connection to post-website success. This disconnect can prevent you from tying phone conversion to the marketing campaigns and website content that helped drive that success.

The following information describes how you can use what you've learned to address this web analytics challenge.

As you have seen throughout this book, anytime you need to connect online activity to post-website success, the SiteCatalyst feature you want to consider using is Transaction ID. Transaction ID allows you to set a "key" value that will associate online conversion variable values to post-website metrics you import later. In this case, you need to make an association or set the "key" at the point in which a visitor decides to call your organization. You can use two different ways to make this connection: use Click-to-Call or use dynamic phone numbers.

Click-to-Call

One way to connect online behavior to post-website success is to use a website tool called Click-to-Call or "Click to Chat." Several vendors offer this service, which allows you to add a button to your website that prompts visitors for their phone number (or to chat) so your organization can call (immediately). The advantage of using a tool like this is that as soon as a prospect clicks the button (**Figure 15.16**), you can set a unique ID to the **s.transactionID** variable. The Click-to-Call vendor can track the success that happens on the phone and relate it to the same unique ID. Then, metrics related to this post-website success can be imported via Transaction ID, as you saw in Chapter 7.

Figure 15.16 A sample Click-to-Call button on a website.

Dynamic Phone Numbers

Another approach to connecting online visits to phone conversion is to use dynamic phone numbers. Vendors can dynamically populate unique phone numbers (usually using phone extensions) to each website visitor. Then, when a visitor calls this phone number, you can tie the website session with the success that takes place via phone. Using an approach similar to the preceding Click-to-Call example, you can populate the **s.transactionID** variable with the unique phone number during the visit and then later import post-website phone success via Transaction ID.

Conclusion

In this chapter, you learned some ways to track lead generation with SiteCatalyst. This included tracking forms, form conversion, form alerts, and form errors. You also explored some ways to connect online SiteCatalyst data to lead generation success when it happens via phone. If lead generation is important to your organization, consider using these techniques to improve your lead generation conversion rates.

## CHAPTER 16

Onsite Search Tracking

Onsite search refers to the search box most websites contain that allows visitors to find specific content by text string. When SiteCatalyst customers are struggling to understand the nuances of the product, I use onsite search as the most straightforward way to explain key concepts. Even though onsite search isn't at the same level of importance as content, the shopping cart, or campaigns, most SiteCatalyst clients want to track it, and it provides good educational examples of using the features covered in previous chapters.

Therefore, in this chapter, you'll learn some of the ways that your organization can track onsite search. Keep in mind that this is primarily for educational purposes, but you are welcome to try out the techniques presented here if your website has onsite search.

Frequently Asked Tracking Questions

The following are the most common types of questions I'm asked about related to onsite search:

- How often are visitors using onsite search?
- What are the most popular search phrases used?
- Which search phrases lead to success on the website?
- How many results are returned for various search phrases?
- Which search phrases result in clicks on the search result page?
- Which search phrases are used concurrently?
- Do visitors conduct onsite searches from some pages more than others?

Whether you realize it or not, based on what you've learned in this book, you now have the tools to answer all of these business questions. Let's tackle them one by one so you can learn how to apply what you've learned thus far to onsite search tracking.

Onsite Searches and Phrases

▶ **TIP** *Because visitors can use multiple search phrases within a visit, I suggest using Linear Allocation for the onsite search phrase conversion variable. This will allocate success to all search phrases used within the visit.*

To start tracking onsite search, let's begin by looking at a search box on a typical website (**Figure 16.1**). In this example, I've entered the phrase "europe" in the search box, and when I run the search, I would see the results page shown in **Figure 16.2**. From a SiteCatalyst perspective, you would want to know that an onsite search just took place and what phrase was used. To do this, you can set a success event and a conversion variable on the search results page like this:

```
s.events="event7";
s.eVar8="europe";
```

europe
BROCHURES
ABOUT YOUR TRIP
CONTACT US
Find your perfect cruise

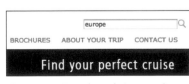

Figure 16.1 Sample website search box.

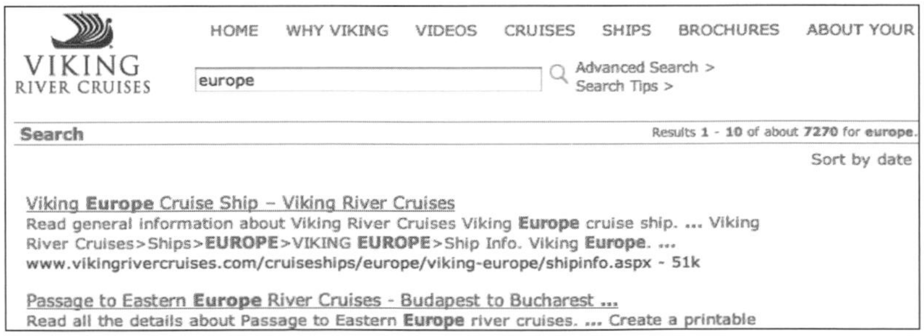
VIKING
RIVER CRUISES
HOME
WHY VIKING
VIDEOS
CRUISES
SHIPS
BROCHURES
ABOUT YOUR
europe
Advanced Search >
Search Tips >
Search
Results 1 - 10 of about 7270 for europe.
Sort by date
Viking Europe Cruise Ship – Viking River Cruises
Read general information about Viking River Cruises Viking Europe cruise ship. ... Viking River Cruises>Ships>EUROPE>VIKING EUROPE>Ship Info. Viking Europe. ...
www.vikingrivercruises.com/cruiseships/europe/viking-europe/shipinfo.aspx - 51k
Passage to Eastern Europe River Cruises - Budapest to Bucharest ...
Read all the details about Passage to Eastern Europe river cruises. ... Create a printable

Figure 16.2 Sample website search results.

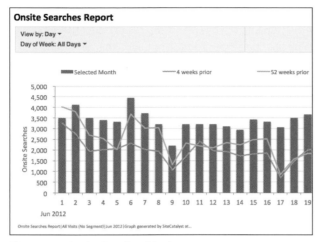

Figure 16.3 Onsite Searches Metric report.

	Onsite Search Phrase	Onsite Searches ▼		Orders ⑦	
1.	europe	10,120	9.9%	2,591	2.0%
2.	itinerary	8,980	8.7%	2,862	2.2%
3.	cabins	7,213	7.0%	2,256	1.8%
4.	destinations	6,206	6.0%	2,462	1.9%
5.	russia	5,178	5.0%	1,122	0.9%
6.	china	4,449	4.3%	1,444	1.1%

Figure 16.4 Onsite Searches Conversion Variable report.

Setting a success event would result in a new Onsite Searches metric report (**Figure 16.3**). Setting the conversion variable enables you to see this new Onsite Searches success event broken down by search phrase. Additionally, if the conversion variable is set to expire at the visit or later, you can also see which other success events took place after the search phrase was used (**Figure 16.4**).

In this example, you can see that the phrase "europe" had 10,120 onsite searches, and that 2591 (or 2%) orders took place afterwards. Using Trended reports, you could also trend the top onsite search phrases over time for either of these metrics. If you have many onsite search phrases, you could use SAINT classifications to group similar types of phrases into buckets. In the preceding example, you might bundle all country phrases into a group and determine what percentage of all onsite searches are devoted to country-specific searches.

Number of Search Results

You might also want to track the number of results for each search phrase. An easy way to do this is to work with your developers to pass the number of results to a conversion variable. In the preceding example, the tagging might look like this:

```
s.events="event7";
s.eVar8="europe";
s.eVar9="7270";
```

As you can imagine, this variable will eventually contain hundreds of values representing all sorts of search result numbers. However, you can use SAINT classifications to

▶**TIP** *One onsite search "best practice" is to set a success event each time the visitor receives no search results. Having a separate success event makes it easy to find onsite search phrases with no results by adding this success event alone to the Onsite Search Phrase Conversion Variable report. This Zero Search Results success event can also be trended like any other metric and used in calculated metrics.*

group them intelligently and ignore the root variable report. Recall from Chapter 6 that it is not possible to classify the value of "0," so if no search results are returned, have your developer pass in a value like "no search results" instead. This can then be classified along with all of the various numbers to see a clean classification report (**Figure 16.5**).

Because you have the number of search results (and its classification) and the search phrase available in two conversion variables, you can use a Conversion Variable Subrelation report to see one broken down by the other. For example, you could use a break-down report to see the most common phrases searched that contain no search results (**Figure 16.6**).

		Number of Search Results	Onsite Searches	▼
	1.	1,000+ Search Results	21,710	21.1%
	2.	1-5 Search Results	17,590	17.1%
	3.	No Search Results	15,052	14.7%
	4.	6-15 Search Results	11,764	11.5%
	5.	16-50 Search Results	9,894	9.6%
	6.	51-200 Search Results	8,230	8.0%

Figure 16.5 Number of Search Results report.

	Number of Search Results by Onsite Search Phrase	Onsite Searches	▼
1. No Search Results		15,052	
1.	flights	674	4.5%
2.	africa	610	4.1%
3.	japan	577	3.8%
4.	kosher	440	2.9%

Figure 16.6 Zero search result terms.

Search Result Click-through Rates

The goal of having onsite search on your website is to get visitors to find the content they need. One way to determine if your onsite search function is adequate is to track how often visitors click on an item in the search results. This will never be an exact science, because visitors can go back and forth between search results, but there are ways that you can quantify your overall search result click-through rates.

On the search results page, if a visitor clicks on a search result link, set a new success event called Onsite Search Result Clicks. Depending on your needs, you might use serialization to count only search result clicks once per search phrase. Once this new success event is set, you can add it to the preceding onsite search phrase report (**Figure 16.7**).

Having this new success event allows you to see onsite search result clicks by search phrase and create a calculated metric for the onsite search click-through rate. This helps determine for which terms your search results are working and for which they are not. Also, as you may recall, once you create a calculated metric, you can see it in a stand-alone metric report. So, you can see a general onsite search result click-through rate for the entire website and take steps to improve it over time (**Figure 16.8**).

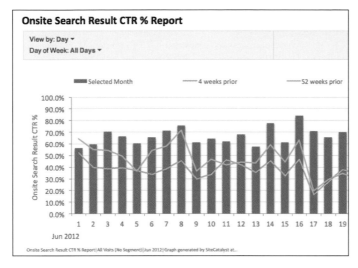

		Onsite Search Phrase	Onsite Searches	▼	Onsite Search Result Clicks		Onsite Search Result CTR %
🔝	1.	europe	10,120	9.9%	5,329	8.0%	52.66%
🔝	2.	itinerary	8,980	8.7%	5,062	7.6%	56.37%
🔝	3.	cabins	7,213	7.0%	4,661	7.0%	64.63%
🔝	4.	destinations	6,206	6.0%	4,314	6.5%	69.52%
🔝	5.	russia	5,178	5.0%	4,087	6.1%	78.93%
🔝	6.	china	4,449	4.3%	3,994	6.0%	89.77%

Figure 16.7 Search click-through rate by search phrase.

Figure 16.8 Onsite Search Click-through Rate report.

Onsite Search Phrase Pathing

At times your organization might want to see which onsite search phrases are used in succession. For example, if you knew that after searching on the phrase "europe" 33 percent of visitors search for the phrase "france," it might change your approach to "europe" search results. If you are a retailer, identifying concurrent search phrases might lead to potential cross-sell opportunities.

Anytime you want to see a sequence of values in SiteCatalyst, you should think about using pathing. In this case, if you pass the onsite search phrase to a traffic variable and enable pathing, you'll be able to see the order in which search phrases are captured in SiteCatalyst within a visit. All you have to do is copy the search phrase found in the conversion variable to a new traffic variable:

```
s.events="event7";
s.eVar8="europe";
s.prop8="europe";
```

You can then see Pathing reports for onsite search phrases (**Figure 16.9**). This report can be viewed with any onsite search phrase as the starting point, and advanced Pathing reports, like Fallout and Pathfinder, can be used as well.

Figure 16.9 Onsite search phrase pathing.

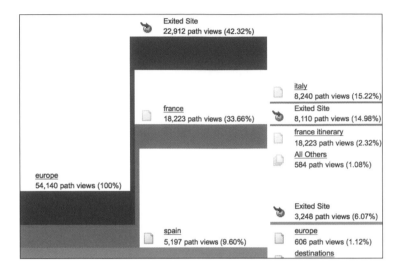

Pages Searched From

If you are using the Previous Value plug-in to pass the previous page name to a conversion variable, it is possible to see what pages visitors are on when conducting onsite searches. Simply add the Onsite Searches metrics to the Previous Page Conversion Variable report. You can also use a Conversion Subrelation report to see from which pages each specific phrase is searched or top search phrases for each page (**Figure 16.10**).

	Previous Page by Onsite Search Phrase	Onsite Searches ▼	
1.	grecoinc:us:home:homepage	3,450	
1.	itinerary	154	4.5%
2.	europe	140	4.1%
3.	ships	132	3.8%
4.	meals	101	2.9%
5.	schedule	87	2.5%

Figure 16.10 Top search phrases by page.

Conclusion

In this chapter, you learned some of the ways that you can track and analyze onsite search. You used many of the various features discussed in prior chapters to answer some of the most common questions related to onsite search. Whether it is conversion variables, subrelations, traffic variables, pathing, classifications, or JavaScript plug-ins, knowing how to apply these various components enables you to create the reports and data you need to answer common business questions.

## CHAPTER 17

Visitor Engagement

Visitor engagement is a broad topic and means different things to different people. In this chapter, I'll review some of the ways you can measure visitor engagement in SiteCatalyst. This includes tracking how visitors engage with your website from a process standpoint (KPI Pathing), quantifying overall engagement, and scoring visitors.

These topics will only scratch the surface of what you can do to track visitor engagement. But keep in mind that the purpose of this chapter is not to provide an in-depth study on visitor engagement, but rather to use it as an example of how you can apply SiteCatalyst to meet day-to-day business questions.

KPI Pathing

The first concept related to visitor engagement is *KPI Pathing* (sometimes referred to as *Success Event Pathing*). KPI Pathing is the process of seeing the order in which visitors complete your primary website KPIs. When you set website KPIs as success events, SiteCatalyst will record how often each takes place, but it does not track the sequence. This is OK most of the time, but in some cases you'll want to see the order in which KPIs take place. Seeing this order allows you to get a holistic view of how visitors engage with your website. This perspective is difficult to see via Page or Section Pathing reports because they are so granular.

Anytime you want to see the sequence or order of data in SiteCatalyst, you must use traffic variables. Therefore, to implement KPI Pathing, you'll pass in a success event description to a traffic variable each time you set a success event that you want to see in the KPI Pathing report (this does not have to be done for all success events). For example, if Greco, Inc. uses success event 1 to track onsite searches, it might use the following code:

```
s.events="event1";

s.prop20="Onsite Search";
```

In this case, the new traffic variable (sProp20) will be used to capture the various success event descriptions, and you'll have pathing enabled by your Adobe account manager or ClientCare. When this is done for all important success events, you'll see a report like the one shown in **Figure 17.1**.

Figure 17.1 Sample KPI Pathing report.

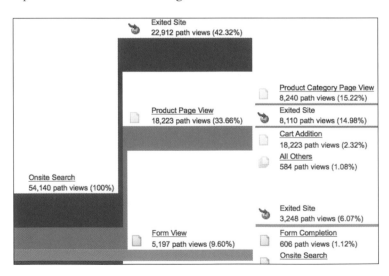

Because only a finite list of success event descriptions is being passed to this traffic variable, the resulting Pathing report is a very succinct view of the website. You can select any success event as your starting point or use the advanced Pathing reports to see all KPI sequences. This high-level view of the website can stimulate numerous discussions about the structure of your website, which can then lead to revenue-generating website redesigns.

Website Engagement Score

Another way to track website engagement is to quantify it by assigning points based on website visitor actions. For example, you might find through web analysis that watching a product video has a high impact on conversion or that the source of traffic is a large factor in website success. Regardless of how you decide to assign points to website actions, having an engagement score can indicate website success or failure.

You can use SiteCatalyst to quantify the specific actions you hope that website visitors take on your website and see if your website visitor engagement is getting higher or lower over time. Because you want to track website engagement as a number, you should recognize that you'll need a success event for this scenario. However, because you'll want to assign different points to different website actions, a simple Counter success event will not meet your needs. Instead, you'll need a Numeric success event, which will allow you to increase the website score by any number of points you'd like at any time.

Once you've configured the new Numeric success event in the administration console, you're ready to start quantifying website engagement. Let's look at this process through an example. Greco, Inc. has found that visitors coming from Google convert much higher than those from any other traffic source. Therefore, it wants to assign a premium to visitors from Google. To do this, it assigns five points to any website visit that comes from Google but no points from visits referred by other channels. The tagging of a Google referral might look like this:

```
s.events="event30";
s.products=";;;;;event30=5";
```

Recall that to set a Numeric success event, you use the products variable, and in this case you are assigning five points to success event30 anytime a visitor comes to the website from Google. But there may be more website actions that you might want to include in your website engagement score. For example, you might want to add points when visitors view website videos, complete lead forms, and complete orders. It is up to you to decide which actions merit website engagement points and how many points

▶ **TIP** *In SiteCatalyst v15 and later, you can build "processing rules" that allow you to set variables using elements and other variables that are passed into SiteCatalyst as part of the image request, such as putting the referrer into an eVar or combining page name and prop1 in prop5. These processing rules don't require tagging and are a great way to avoid having to wait for IT resources to get new data into SiteCatalyst.*

to assign to each. I tend to use statistical analysis to determine these factors and use a numbering scheme like Fibonacci or something similar. For example, you might decide that a product video view is worth ten points and that a lead form completion is worth 25 points if your data suggests that over time a lead form completion is worth 2.5 product video views. Regardless of how you assign the points, the coding would look similar to that of the Google referral. If you assign 25 points to each lead form completion, the code might look like this:

```
s.events="event30";

s.products=";product_111;;;event30=25";
```

Once you've identified and set points for each of your website actions, the new website engagement Numeric success event will accrue points for all website visitors. This will result in an overall Website Engagement report (**Figure 17.2**). This report allows you to trend website engagement over time, but can also be used in any conversion variable report. For example, someone at Greco, Inc. might ask if website engagement is higher for visit number 1 or visit number 2. To see this, open the appropriate conversion variable report (e.g., Visit Number in this case) and add the Website Engagement metric. In this example, I would create a calculated metric to divide website engagement by visits to normalize the data. You'll then see the report in **Figure 17.3**. In this report you can see that most of the website engagement is taking place in the first visit, and it tends to taper off after that. You can run this type of report using any conversion variable, and once you create the new Website Engagement per Visit calculated metric, you can also see the general trend over time, as shown in **Figure 17.4**.

Figure 17.2 Website Engagement report.

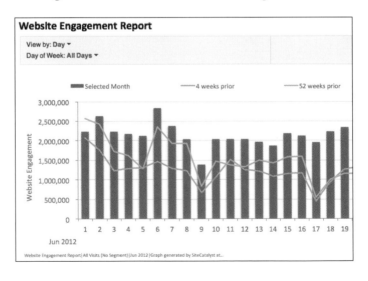

	Visit Number	Website Engagement ▼		Visits ②		Website Engagement/Visit
1.	Visit 1	19,564,850	29.9%	2,843,883	22.7%	6.88
2.	Visit 2	12,248,500	18.7%	2,572,041	20.5%	4.76
3.	Visit 3	8,940,750	13.7%	2,028,357	16.2%	4.41
4.	Visit 4	5,659,200	8.6%	1,317,387	10.5%	4.30
5.	Visit 6	3,700,750	5.7%	920,080	7.3%	4.02
6.	Visit 5	3,261,900	5.0%	961,901	7.7%	3.39

Figure 17.3 Website Engagement by Visit Number.

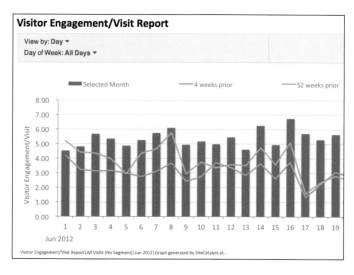

Figure 17.4 Website Engagement per Visit trend.

Visitor Scoring

One area of visitor engagement that can help extend the reach of web analytics in the organization is *visitor scoring*. Visitor scoring is the process of assigning points to each website visitor based on their actions on the website. For example, if one visitor comes to the website home page, views two product pages, and then exits, that visitor might have a low score. Conversely, if another visitor arrives at a product page, watches a product video, adds the product to the cart, and then exits, that visitor might have a high score. Both visitors viewed three pages, but depending on your business model or goals, you might want to assign different points to each in terms of a visitor score.

To accomplish this, you would need to do the following:

1. Determine which actions on your website are worth different point values.

2. Assign these points to each website visitor so that all website visitors have their own unique score generated by their website actions.

The good news is that if you have done the website engagement score steps described in the previous section, you've already completed step one of visitor scoring. You can leverage the points you assigned to each website action and assign those points to each visitor on the site. To do this, you need a variable that can store a point value for each visitor and add points to that value over time as that visitor performs actions that merit additional points. This is a great use of a Counter conversion variable. Through one new Counter conversion variable, you can store a distinct visitor score for each website visitor. To do this, you would use code that looks like this:

```
s.events="event30";
s.products=";;;;event30=5";
s.eVar30="+5";
```

This is the same code from the previous website engagement score example, but you are adding one new Counter conversion variable to set the visitor score. You had originally assigned five points when a visitor was referred by Google. Here you are passing those five points to eVar30 so that the current visitor's website score is increased by five points. This new conversion variable should be set to persist beyond the website visit, possibly until the primary success event takes place (e.g., Purchase). Once this is done, all website visitors will have their own score in their version of eVar30 and any Website success events taking place will be attributed to their current score. In this example, if a website visitor had arrived from Google and earned five points, and then added a product to the cart, it would result in one cart addition success event being tied to a score of five points. If this was the only visitor to the website, the Visitor Score Conversion Variable report would look like the one in **Figure 17.5**.

Because this concept is applied to all of your website visitors, you would begin to see a wide range of visitor scores over time. To mitigate this, I like to apply a SAINT classification to the visitor score Counter conversion variable. This classification groups the various scores into buckets to make the conversion variable report more actionable, as shown in **Figure 17.6**. This report can then be used to determine if there are specific website KPIs that perform better or worse based on the visitor score. Additionally, because this visitor score is a conversion variable, it can be broken down by other

Visitor Score	Cart Additions ▼
1. 5.0	1 100.0%

Figure 17.5 Sample Visitor Score report.

Visitor Score Grouping	Cart Additions ▼	
1. 0-25 (Low Engagement)	120,988	37.5%
2. 26-50 (Medium Engagement)	85,246	26.5%
3. 51-75 (Significant Engagement)	68,841	21.4%
4. 75+ (High Engagement)	47,215	14.7%

Figure 17.6 Sample classified Visitor Score report.

conversion variables using subrelations. For example, the report shown in Figure 17.6 could be broken down by the products variable to see if some products perform better with higher engagement scores.

Other Uses of Visitor Scoring

In addition to using visitor scores to augment your web analysis capabilities, there are some interesting ways you can extend the preceding visitor score concepts. In this section, I'll describe a few of these use cases.

Pass visitor score to CRM

If your organization has a Customer Relationship Management (CRM) system, you might be capturing leads from the website into your CRM tool. Many organizations use their website to capture lead data and then have sales representatives follow up with leads via phone or e-mail. However, there might be times when you don't have enough sales representatives to follow up with every lead. You might also have cases in which sales representatives follow up with unqualified leads and scare them off (e.g., lead says "please don't call me again!"). Visitor scoring can help in these situations. If you are capturing a visitor score, this score can be passed to your CRM system when the lead form is submitted. This allows sales representatives to determine how qualified a lead is and prioritize their follow-up calls. For example, if a sales representative has 30 leads in his queue, and two have scores higher than 90 points, while the rest have scores of less than five points, it might make sense to prioritize the leads with more points.

Passing a website visitor score can also help bridge the gap between marketing and sales. Visitor scoring is a great way for marketing to show that it is passing qualified leads to sales. Sales can also help marketing by explaining which actions on the website, in its experience, lead to good prospect calls. This information can be used to create your visitor scoring model and help build a mutually beneficial relationship between marketing and sales.

Visitor score segmentation

Another benefit of visitor scoring is that you can use scores as part of segmentation. When segmenting website data, it is common to create binary segments that show when visitors did or did not do something. However, sometimes there is value in seeing the scope of what visitors did. For example, a common segment might be to see all visitors who looked at a product but did not purchase it. But what if you wanted to see how engaged visitors were when they looked at a product but did not purchase. Perhaps you only want to consider visitors who have scores greater than 50 points who meet this criteria.

Figure 17.7 Include portion of visitor score segment.

Figure 17.7 Include portion of visitor score segment.

Having a visitor score conversion variable allows you to add this dimension. An example of this type of segment is shown in **Figure 17.7**.

Visitor score targeting

If your organization uses Adobe Test&Target or a similar optimization tool, you can use visitor scores to personalize website content and promotions. For example, if you know that the current website visitor has a high visitor score, you might show different content than if the visitor had a low score.

Time Spent per Visit Report

Another method of measuring website engagement is the Time Spent per Visit report. This report lets you break down success events by time spent on site. It requires no custom implementation and provides a way to see how long it takes your website visitors to complete website KPIs, as shown in **Figure 17.8**.

Keep in mind that this report does not include the time spent on the last page of the visit, and that the times shown only reflect time spent in the current visit versus total time spent across multiple visits. If you need to see the total time spent across multiple visits, you can use the Time to Complete JavaScript plug-in or store the time spent per page (total seconds) in a Counter conversion variable with an expiration longer than a visit.

	Time Spent per Visit	Form Views (e21)		Form Completions ▼ (e22)		Form Completion Rate
1.	1-5 minutes	118,483	25.0%	15,147	42.7%	12.784%
2.	less than 1 minute	236,103	49.7%	8,008	22.6%	3.392%
3.	10-30 minutes	54,998	11.6%	6,048	17.1%	10.997%
4.	5-10 minutes	47,319	10.0%	4,271	12.0%	9.026%
5.	30-60 minutes	14,541	3.1%	1,658	4.7%	11.402%

Figure 17.8 Sample Time Spent per Visit report.

In addition, you can choose to set a different visitor score for specific product categories. For example, let's say that one of Greco, Inc.'s websites sells shirts and shoes. In this case, it may choose to set an overall visitor score Counter conversion variable and also set two additional visitor score variables—one for shirts and one for shoes. In these product category variables, Greco, Inc. would only populate points in the shirts variable when the page being looked at was related to shirts and the shoes variable when the page being viewed was related to shoes. Over time, these variables will provide each visitor with a shirt score and a shoe score. Greco, Inc. can then use these scores to target content and promotions accordingly. If a visitor has a high shirt score and a low shoe score, it might be prudent to show shirt products versus shoe products.

Conclusion

In this chapter, you learned a few of the ways that you can measure website visitor engagement using SiteCatalyst. There are many different uses for this type of data, including engagement trending, analysis of engagement impact on website KPIs, and content targeting. Although only a small subset of the approaches that you can report on in SiteCatalyst were discussed, you can see that the fundamental building blocks presented in earlier chapters come in handy when you're trying to tackle visitor engagement.

In this third and final section, you learned about several common SiteCatalyst topics, such as content tracking, online shopping carts, lead generation, campaign tracking, onsite search, and visitor engagement. Keep in mind that the examples provided in these chapters were meant to illustrate how the concepts explained in previous chapters could be applied. Although you are welcome to implement these techniques, I encourage you to think of them primarily as learning opportunities. Although I could (and might) write an entire second book detailing the various applications of SiteCatalyst I've created or have seen implemented, my hope is that the examples in this section, along with the examples embedded in previous sections, will force you to think outside of the box when you're using SiteCatalyst.

As stated at the beginning of this book, I encourage you to treat SiteCatalyst like a new language and use the features and concepts presented in this book as your dictionary. The better you learn the concepts, the more fluent you will become, and the more successful you'll be at using Adobe SiteCatalyst to help your organization.

SiteCatalyst Cheat Sheet

As you have seen in this handbook, there is a lot to remember about Adobe SiteCatalyst. To help you recall the important product features and nuances, I've created the following "cheat sheet," which you can use as a handy reference when you need a quick refresher. My suggestion is that you photocopy the pages you need and pin them up at your desk for quick access.

Traffic Variables (sProps, Custom Insight)

Variable Purpose: Traffic variables count instances of traffic metrics (Page Views, Visits, Unique Visitors).

Reports and Metrics: All traffic reports focus on Page Views, Visits, Unique Visitors, or participation. You cannot view sProps in conversion reports without Adobe Discover.

1. *Traffic variables are not persistent.* A value must be passed for every instance in which you want a value to be associated with a page. For example, to capture which pages visitors' status is "Logged-in" versus "Not Logged-in," the appropriate value of "Logged-in" or "Not Logged-in" must be passed on *every* page.

2. *Page Name (`s.pagename`), Site Sections (`s.channel`), and Server (`s.server`) are predefined sProps.*

   a. `s.pagename` is special in that if no value is passed, the URL is automatically passed.

   b. Page Name and Site Sections show allocated success event metrics, whereas custom sProps do not.

3. *Traffic variables have a direct relationship to pathing.* To view pathing information, the data must be passed sequentially to a traffic variable. Pathing can be enabled for any traffic variable. For example, to view pathing for Article IDs viewed on site, Article ID must be passed to an sProp on every page that contains an Article.

4. *Traffic variables can be "correlated."* Correlated traffic variables mean that a report is created that shows one traffic variable broken down by another traffic variable. However, both traffic variables must be set in the same image request to be correlated (if not you will see a value labeled "unspecified"). Predefined traffic variables, such as GeoSegmentation, can be correlated to other traffic variables.

   a. For example, to view the most popular "Logged-in" pages, a correlation can be created between the Logged-in Status sProp and Page Name provided that a value was passed to the Logged-in sProp in the same image request that the `s.pagename` was set.

   b. Most correlations are 2-item, but 5-item correlations can be created (allows you to filter by all five attributes in each report).

   c. Correlations created using traffic variables with large numbers of unique values can cause report latency and should be avoided.

5. *Visits and Unique Visitors (Daily, Weekly, Monthly, Quarterly) can be enabled for any sProp (there may be an associated cost in versions 14 and earlier).*

6. *Any custom traffic variable can be "classified" using SAINT.* Classifications allow you to add metadata associated with existing data.

    a. For example, if you capture Product Name in an sProp, you can upload Product Category, Product Type, and so on as classifications, which gives you a separate report for each classification but does not require additional coding or the use of more SiteCatalyst variables.

    b. You cannot classify prepackaged traffic reports (e.g., Browser), but you can do so by moving data to a custom traffic variable.

7. *Hierarchy variables can be used to track data that fits a standard taxonomy.* If there are various levels of your site or filters/choices users can click in sequential order, Hierarchy traffic variables are useful to reduce the number of custom traffic variables. Pathing is not possible on Hierarchy variables.

8. *Participation metrics can be enabled for* `s.pagename` *and other sProps.* Participation is a SiteCatalyst feature in which traffic variables (often Page Name) receive full credit for a success event if they were involved in the path flow of its success.

    a. For example, if participation is enabled for the Revenue metric and a visitor went from the Home page to Page A, then Page B, and then the Purchase Success page and bought $40 of merchandise, all three pages in the flow would receive credit of $40.

    b. Participation can be enabled for any event and tied to any sProp (e.g., Show Order Participation of Internal Search Term sProp).

    c. Alternatively, viewing a Revenue or Orders metric in a Pages report shows Revenue or Orders divided evenly by each page in the flow.

9. *Any sProp can be turned into a list variable, which allows you to pass delimited value strings to an sProp.* Corresponding sProp reports will break out delimited values in reports. However, list traffic variables:

    a. Can only be correlated in v15 or later

    b. Have no unique visitors

    c. Cannot have pathing enabled

Success Events

Variable Purpose: Success events count specific site milestones (or key performance indicators).

Reports and Metrics: Success event metrics can be found in the Conversion area (in both Event and eVar reports) and the Traffic Most Popular Pages or Site Section reports. Success events can only be associated with traffic reports in Adobe Discover.

1. *Success events are normally "counters," meaning that they are incremented (by one) when they are executed (e.g.,* `s.events="event1"`*).*

2. *Success events can be set up as "incrementors," which allows them to contain Numeric or Currency values (increment by more than value of 1).*

    a. Incrementor values are passed to success events from within the Products string (`s.products=";12345;1;20;event2=2.50"`)

    b. Data being imported via Data Sources must use incrementor (Numeric or Currency) success events.

3. *SiteCatalyst provides predefined and custom success events.* Most site key performance indicators (KPIs) use success events.

   a. Predefined success events include Shopping Cart events (Purchase, scOpen, scView, scAdd, scRemove, scCheckout), Product Views (prodView), and Click-throughs. The Purchase event populates Revenue, Order, and Unit metrics.

   b. Any other action on your site can be captured as a custom success event (e.g., Successful Registration, File Download, etc.).

4. *When a success event is executed, SiteCatalyst associates it with related conversion variables (eVar) values and Participation metrics.*

   a. SiteCatalyst automatically associates success events with conversion variables (eVars), such as Tracking Code, Search Engine, Keyword, and so on, provided that they have a value (e.g., If City eVar has a value of "Chicago" when the Registration event executes, Registrations can be broken down by City).

   b. Events can be serialized so they are not double-counted. A unique string (e.g., `s.events="event1:123456789"`) is passed with the success event so that if it is set with the same string, it will be ignored. Success events can also use Once Per Visit serialization.

5. *Success events can be used in calculated metrics.* Success events can be used to create new metrics using the Calculated Metrics tool.

6. *Success events can be used in Conversions and Averages reports.* These reports allow you to create a conversion funnel that shows metrics associated with each event, calculate conversion figures for all metrics added to the funnel, and filter by conversion variable.

7. *Participation can be enabled for any success event and related to any traffic variable (sProp).* Participation is a SiteCatalyst feature in which traffic variables (often Page Name) receive full credit for a success event if they were involved in the path flow of its success.

   a. For example, if participation is enabled for the Revenue metric and linked to the Page Name traffic variable and a visitor went from the Home page to Page A, then Page B, and then the Purchase success page and bought $40 of merchandise, all three pages in the flow would receive credit of $40. This metric is visible when you're looking at the Pages report with the Revenue Participation metric showing.

   b. Participation can be enabled for any success event and tied to any traffic variable (e.g., Show Order Participation of Internal Search Term traffic variable).

   c. Alternatively, viewing a Revenue or Orders metric in a Pages report shows Revenue or Orders divided evenly by each page in the flow.

8. *Some conversion reports have special "report-specific" metrics associated with them.* These metrics often look and act like regular events but are, in fact, different in that they cannot always be used in calculated metrics and in Conversions and Averages reports.

   a. The most common example is the Product View (prodView) event, which only appears in the Products report, so it is recommended that a custom Product View event be set in order to include Product Views in the Conversions and Averages reports.

b. Campaign reports capture Click-throughs, referrals from search engines are reported as Searches, Product reports default to Product Views, and all other reports contain an Instances metric that shows how often the value was passed to the variable.

9. *In SiteCatalyst v15, Visits and Unique Visitors are enabled as metrics in conversion reports.*

Conversion Variables (eVars)

Variable Purpose: Conversion variables (eVars) are used to break down or segment success events.

Reports and Metrics: Each conversion variable (eVar) contains its own report in which the user can choose which metrics they want to view. Conversion variable reports can only be associated with traffic variables in Adobe Discover.

1. *SiteCatalyst provides prepackaged and custom conversion variables.*

   a. Prepackaged conversion variables include Campaigns, Search Engine, Keyword, Visit #, Entry Page, and so on.

   b. Custom conversion variables are unique to each site and are meant for breaking down or segmenting site success events. For example, if, during every Registration event, the City is captured in a custom conversion variable, by opening the city conversion variable report and showing the Registration event, you would see how many Registrations were associated with each city.

2. *Conversion variables are persistent variables, meaning that they can retain their value across more than one page view.*

   a. How long the value passed to each conversion variable is stored is set using the administration console (Visit, Until Success Event occurs, etc.).

   b. Conversion variables must be set at the same time or before a success event takes place to be used with that success event.

   c. Because values can persist, it is necessary to specify which value should be associated with success events. The choices are Most Recent (Last), Original Value (First), or Linear (split evenly among all values passed to a conversion variable—*within one visit only*).

3. *Conversion variables can have Basic Subrelations or Full Subrelations (in SiteCatalyst v15, all eVars have Full Subrelations).*

   Full Subrelations means that a conversion variable can be broken down by any other conversion variable (similar to correlations in traffic). Full Subrelations can be activated for any conversion variable (additional cost in v14 or earlier). SiteCatalyst provides Full Subrelations for tracking code and products variables out of the box.

4. *The products variable is like a conversion variable, but it is not persistent.* The products variable can contain multiple values and can be used to set Incrementor events and Merchandising eVars, which cannot be done in regular conversion variables.

5. *There are two different types of conversion variables: Text String and Counter.* Most conversion variables are Text String and accept text values. Counter eVars increment by one (or more), store this number, and use it to break down success events.

6. *Many conversion variable reports will show a value of "None," which is expected behavior.* When you see a "None" row in a conversion variable report, it means that no value was present in that particular variable at the time the currently chosen event took place. For example, if no City was chosen by a user during the Registration event, that Registration instance would be placed into the "None" row.

7. *Conversion variables can be "classified" to add additional metadata via SAINT.* Classifying eVars allows you to add additional data related to data captured in the image request (e.g., if an eVar captures City, each City value can be classified with a Region to view events by Region).

8. *Conversion variables can be set up to be Merchandising.* Normal eVars associate their value with all subsequent events (until they expire), whereas Merchandising eVars are used to more accurately associate a value (e.g., Category) with a specific product-success event combination. For example, let's say your website contains different sections, such as electronics, clothing, jewelry, and so on, and you want to know your revenue broken down by product category. However, if a user enters the electronics section of the website, adds a stereo to the shopping cart, navigates back to the jewelry section but decides not to buy any jewelry, and instead goes directly to the shopping cart and makes a purchase, the initial value of "Electronics" that had been passed to the eVar has been replaced by "Jewelry." Thus, the resulting revenue is credited to the wrong value. Merchandising eVars alleviate this problem by storing multiple eVar values and associating each with the correct product.

   Another use of Merchandising eVars is to assign a different eVar value to different items contained within one Products string.

Pathing

Purpose: Pathing provides the ability to view the order in which site visitors navigate.

Reports and Metrics: When pathing is enabled for a traffic variable, additional pathing-related reports are enabled.

1. *Enabling pathing for a traffic variable allows you to see new reports and metrics (e.g., Time Spent, Entries, Exits, etc.).*
   a. Once pathing is enabled for a traffic variable, several new metrics (e.g., Visits, Average Time Spent, Average Page Depth, Entries, Exits, etc.) are available for that variable. For example, if pathing is enabled for a traffic variable containing product names, you can use Pathing reports to view the order in which users view products.
   b. Pathing metrics can be used in calculated metrics (e.g., Bounce Rate = Single Access/Exits).

2. *Pathing reports only consider the path to change when a new value is passed to a traffic variable.* For example, if a visitor views Page 1 in the Loans section, then Page 2 in the Loans section, and then Page 3 in the Checking section, Pathing reports will consider this as a flow of Page 1 – Page 2 – Page 3 in the Pages Pathing reports but only a flow of Loans – Checking in the Site Sections Pathing reports.

3. *Fallout reports show how often visitors view specified pages (checkpoints) in the specified order.*

   a. This does not mean that visitors followed the path exactly (they may have gone to other pages along the way), but at some point in the visit they did view the specified items in the specified order.

   b. Fallout reports show only instances where the previous steps have taken place. Therefore, if you want to view how your conversion funnel performs for visitors entering the website on a specific Landing page, simply start the Fallout report from that page, which will filter out all paths not including the Landing page. This concept is often used to view A/B pathing in which a value representing the "A" or "B" test is passed to a pathing-enabled A/B sProp along with the page name (e.g., "Test A:Home Page" vs. "Test B:Home Page") to view navigation differences between page versions.

4. *Pathfinder allows you to dig deeper into flows between a few specific sProp values (limited to four by default).*

   Using Pathfinder, you can add a few items (e.g., Pages, Sections) and see their interaction with others. For example, if you want to see what Site Sections visitors tend to view between the Loans section and the Checking section, you can add those to Pathfinder and include one or more "wildcards" between them to see which other sections visitors of both tend to view.

5. *Pathing is enabled only for the Page Name traffic variable by default, but pathing can be enabled for any sProp.*

   Pathing should be used anytime it is beneficial to see the order in which something took place. For example, if a music site (e.g., iTunes) wants to improve cross-sell by viewing which songs visitors who view XYZ Song also look at, every time a song is viewed, its name can be passed to an sProp and pathing should be enabled. Once this is done, Pathfinder or Previous/Next page reports will provide insight into song affinities.

6. *Using pathing in combination with other products provides additional analysis capabilities.*

   a. Most Pathing reports are available in Adobe Discover.

   b. Adobe Discover allows you to see pathing for classifications of traffic variables.

SiteCatalyst Features

Overview: Often, SiteCatalyst customers fail to take advantage of many powerful SiteCatalyst features that can be used to increase site ROI and analysis capabilities. The following outlines many of these overlooked features.

▶ *Classifications (SAINT).* Any traffic or conversion variable can be "classified" via SAINT. Classifying a variable means adding metadata related to data already existing in SiteCatalyst. For example, if you capture the birth year of a visitor in a variable, you can classify that variable to roll up specific birth years into groups (e.g., baby boomers) for reporting purposes. The only caveat with classifications is that classified data is retroactive, so any changes made to the SAINT file will affect all SAINT data (not originally collected data), including historical data.

If it is important that past data retain its value, it is recommended that it be passed directly to variables. Classifications allow you to:

- ▸ Increase the number of ways you can view/group data
- ▸ Increase the number of reports you can view in SiteCatalyst
- ▸ Reduce the number of variables you have to pass in on each image request

▸ *Correlations.* Correlated traffic variables mean that a report is created that shows one traffic variable broken down by another traffic variable. Although having data in traffic variables may be valuable in and of itself, often viewing one by the other can have a synergistic effect. For example, you may be capturing the internal search term visitors search on in a traffic variable and the number of results they receive in another. By correlating these two variables, you can view a new report that shows what search terms yield zero results.

▸ *Bookmarks.* Once you become a SiteCatalyst user, you will run various reports each day/week. Often, you'll end up referring to the same reports and can save time by saving them as bookmarks. Besides quick access to these reports, bookmarked reports can be shared with other users and can be scheduled for delivery via e-mail in multiple formats.

▸ *Dashboards.* As with bookmarked reports, SiteCatalyst dashboards can be easily saved, shared, and scheduled. However, dashboards are even more powerful in that you can see snapshots of multiple reports at one time, which can be a real time-saver.

▸ *ReportBuilder and Data Extracts.* Adobe ReportBuilder allows you to pull SiteCatalyst data into Excel using predefined data blocks. The power of ReportBuilder is that you can tie key report attributes (e.g., Date Range, Report Suite) to cells in Excel so that changes to those cells result in completely different data without having to alter the report setup in any way. A popular use of this functionality is to build a report that uses variables common to various report suites and to view the data from each report suite by simply changing the cell containing the report suite ID.

▸ *Comparison reports.* Most SiteCatalyst reports come with the ability to conduct a comparison between two date ranges or report suites. Date range comparisons are useful for comparing the same data for different timeframes (e.g., month-over-month), whereas report suite comparison reports allow you to see how data changes for different sites, territories, or segments. For example, if you have one report suite that contains only data for Europe and another for the United States, you can use comparison reports to compare internal search terms between Europe and the United States.

▸ *Alerts.* Alerts allow you to be notified via e-mail or wireless device if specific data criteria are met. A common use of alerts is to be notified if daily revenue is ever less than zero, which could indicate that a coding issue has occurred.

▸ *Participation.* Participation is a SiteCatalyst feature in which variables (often Page Name) receive full credit for a success event if they were involved in the path flow of its success. For example, if participation is enabled for the Revenue metric and linked to the Page Name traffic variable and a visitor went from the Home page to Page A, then Page B, and then the Purchase success page and bought $40 of merchandise, all three pages in the flow would receive credit of $40. This metric is visible when looking at the Pages report with the Revenue

Participation metric showing. Participation can be enabled for any success event and tied to any variable. For example, enabling Order Participation and tying it to the Internal Search Term traffic variable allows you to see which Internal Search Terms "participated" in path flows that led to Orders.

▶ *Targets.* SiteCatalyst provides the ability to forecast values that you expect to take place as targets and view in reports how actual data is performing in relation to targets.

▶ *VISTA.* VISTA allows you to alter data after it is received from the image request but before it is entered into SiteCatalyst data tables (from which reports are generated). VISTA can be used to assign page names, to move data from one variable to another, and in many other useful ways. For example, if a site has a form that asks users for their birth year, zip code, and gender, a VISTA rule can be used to assign each visitor to a grouping (e.g., "Middle-aged Midwestern Men") on the fly and pass that segment label to another variable. To do this, all that is required is a rule definition, which SiteCatalyst can turn into a VISTA rule. Costs are associated with the creation of VISTA rules.

▶ *DB VISTA.* DB VISTA is similar to VISTA except that instead of processing a defined rule, a database lookup is performed to determine what value should be passed to a variable. For example, if a company wants to view true campaign ROI in SiteCatalyst, it may decide to pass in the costs associated with each product purchased. However, this cost information should not be visible in the image request, for obvious reasons. To accomplish this, it can upload a product cost table to DB VISTA, which can then assign the appropriate cost to a Currency success event based on the product purchased.

▶ *Data Sources.* Data Sources is an included SiteCatalyst tool that allows you to import data into SiteCatalyst. Normally, the data being imported is data that cannot be captured online because the event doesn't take place on your site. For example, if a financial services site allows visitors to apply for a loan online, but the approval process takes place offline, it can use Data Sources to upload the number of loans approved and the final approved loan value.

Data Sources imports are tied to a date, and offline data can be integrated with online data by utilizing the Transaction ID option. This feature allows you to associate online conversion variables (e.g., campaign tracking code, visit #, etc.) with offline success provided there is a "key" to tie the actions together (which is passed to the `s.transactionID` variable)

▶ *Plug-ins.* SiteCatalyst customers often require specific functionality that is not provided "out of the box" because it does not apply to every SiteCatalyst customer. To accomplish these requests, SiteCatalyst provides several "plug-ins" that can be added to the standard SiteCatalyst JavaScript file. Some of the most commonly used plug-ins are:

  ▸ **GetQueryParam.** Populates eVars and sProps with values from URL querystrings

  ▸ **GetNewRepeat.** Populates eVars and sProps with "New Visitor" or "Returning Visitor" as appropriate

  ▸ **GetPreviousValue.** Populates eVars and sProps with the previous page (or other value) the visitor was on (useful for correlations)

▶ *XML (Data Insertion) API.* The XML API is an alternative method for sending data to SiteCatalyst servers when image tags are not possible/optimal.

Did You Know?

1. SiteCatalyst has a free JavaScript Debugger that shows you what data is being passed to Site-Catalyst on each page (see the whitepaper in the Knowledge Base for setup instructions).

2. You should minimize how often you pass more than 500,000 unique values per month to traffic and conversion variables.

3. You should not "correlate" traffic variables whose combinations produce a large number of unique combinations.

4. Correlation reports only show Page Views (no Visits, Unique Visitors).

5. Unique Visitors and Visit metrics can be enabled for any traffic variable (done automatically in v15 or later).

6. You cannot do pathing on a classification, only on actual traffic variables, so if you need pathing, pass data directly to an sProp.

7. You cannot view pathing between different websites unless they are in the same report suite or utilize multi-suite tagging.

8. You cannot "classify" some out-of-the-box reports (e.g., Finding Methods, Visit #) but can pass this data to custom variables, which can be classified.

9. Classifications of variables also allow you to view correlations for the classified data.

10. You can upload Campaign Tracking Code costs via SAINT or Data Sources. If done through SAINT, they are treated as Numeric classifications (can be easily modified but have some limitations in usage in calculated metrics). If done through Data Sources, this requires the use of FTP and the setup of new incrementor success events.

11. If you do not pass product names to the products variable using the "prodView" event, you will not be able to filter the Conversions and Averages conversion filter by product (even if a product name is associated with other success events).

12. Conversion calculated metrics cannot be used in the Conversions and Averages reports.

13. The Product Views metric is available only in the Products reports, so it is often recommended that you set a custom Product View success event at the same time.

14. If no success event is set when the `s.products` string is set, the prodView event will be set by default. Therefore, the Product Views metric often acts like other Instances metrics for product-related reports.

15. The products variable is not persistent (like other eVars) and must be set at the same time as related success events.

16. If you set a category for a product using the category portion of the Product string, that product will forever be tied to that category.

17. Total Revenue and Unit values are only accepted via the Products string at the Purchase event (e.g., ignored at scAdd event).

18. When setting incrementor events with products, you must declare the event in the Events area and in the Products string (`s.events= "event6"` *and* `s.products=";;;;event6=.30;` `evar10=Change Mailing Address ";`)

19. Linear allocation is only related to a visit, so any conversion variables specified to Linear should expire at the visit.

20. Although you can change the expiration of Finding Methods eVar variables, the most they will expire at is the visit, so all other settings (e.g., Purchase) have an effect only if they happen prior to the end of the visit.

21. Only files of 1 MB or less can be imported into SAINT without using FTP.

22. When you're importing data into SiteCatalyst via FTP (Data Sources or SAINT), you must upload the file and then an empty ".fin" file.

23. When you're using FTP to upload SAINT files, you can apply them to multiple report suites if the classifications exist for the chosen variable.

24. All variables used for Data Sources imports must be set up as "incrementor" events (non-counter).

25. Data imported via Data Sources is not available for segmentation in Data Warehouse or Discover.

26. Data imported via Data Sources cannot be removed once it is imported.

27. Visit counts in the conversion reports reflect visits in which a conversion variable has been set, not all visits.

28. Using PageViews when you're building a segment (e.g., Data Warehouse) will return data faster than using Visit or Visitor containers.

29. VISTA and processing rules can be created to automate the setting of variables (especially ones based on site URLs).

30. Data feeds are normally available the next day.

31. You can use "objectID" (and associated plug-in) to make ClickMap reporting more accurate (especially for non-Microsoft browsers).

32. You can view any success event in ClickMap if it is enabled.

33. Success events can be "serialized" by using an ID or by a "Once Per Visit" setting.

34. When you're rolling up report suites, Visits and Unique Visitor metrics are summations (not de-duped).

35. When you're rolling up report suites, differing currencies/timezones for child report suites will not be different in the rollup, so these should be the same for each child report suite.

36. Be careful not to allow new line characters, em or or en dashes, or any HTML characters to appear in the page name (and other variables for that matter). Some browsers send new line characters but others don't, which causes the data in SiteCatalyst to be split between two seemingly identical page names. Many word processors and e-mail clients will automatically convert a hyphen into an en or em dash when you're typing. Because en and em dashes are illegal characters in SiteCatalyst variables (ASCII characters with codes above 127), Site-Catalyst will not record the page name containing the illegal character and will show the URL instead.

Index

Symbols and Numbers

$$ in Cart Conversion % reports, 263–264
(–) minus sign, in search filters, 142
(*) asterisk symbol, for wildcard searches, 142
5x5 subrelation reports, 190–191

A

accessibility, of SiteCatalyst reports, 215
accountability matrix, 181
Activated report suite setting, 16, 17
ad hoc analysis, 215
Ad Serving, Genesis integrations and, 126
Add Bookmark option, in Data Extract, 179
Add button, in Segment Builder, 196
Add Metrics button, in traffic variables, 33–34
Add Metrics window
    for calculated metrics, 52, 55, 59
    customize graph metrics and, 190
    double-click to add/remove, 188
Add option, in Request Manager, 221
Add Request option, in Excel right-click context menu, 223–224
Add Segment link, Instant Segmentation and, 205, 206
Admin tab, accessing classification templates, 99
administration console
    accessing calculated metrics via, 55
    accessing Classification Manager screen in, 97
    Classification hierarchy setup in, 106
    conversion variable settings in, 65
    Conversion Variable Syntax Merchandising setting in, 89–90
    enabling Currency success event in, 48
    history of, 4
    managing ASI settings in, 205
    Marketing Channels menu in, 281–282
    Product Syntax Merchandising setting in, 88–89
    reorganizing/hiding menus in, 188
    report suite, 15
    success events in, 42
    traffic variables in, 30
Adobe Discover
    date-based segmentation and, 117–118
    for implementing page types, 244
    option for launching, 177
    segment comparisons in, 187
Adobe ReportBuilder. see ReportBuilder
Adobe Test&Target
    internal campaign tracking and, 286
    in shopping cart tracking, 263
advanced calculations, with ReportBuilder, 214
Advanced Download Options link, 163–164
advanced graphs, with ReportBuilder, 214
Advanced Scheduling Options, 165
Advanced Search tool
    basic search filter and, 140
    complex search filter and, 140–142
Advanced Segment Insight (ASI) slots
    features of, 204–205
    for segment comparisons, 187
Alert Name option, 171
alerts
    classification, 174–175
    Duplicate Order ID, 267–268
    Form Error, 298
    for Metric reports, 171–172
    overview of, 170–171
    for Traffic/Conversion Variable reports, 172–173
All items alert, 172–173
Allocation settings
    for conversion variables, 65–68
    for list variables, 79
allocation, of success events, 57–58
Allow Publishing List Override check box, in ReportBuilder, 218, 226

analytics, web. see web analytics
AND clauses
    basic search filter with, 140
    complex search filter with, 140–141
    in nesting containers, 197–199
    in Segment Builder, 196
Apple home page, 284
Apply Granularity drop-down list, in ReportBuilder, 218–219
Apply the alert to option, in Pages report alert, 172–173
ASI. see Advanced Segment Insight (ASI) slots
Assign alert to option, in Pages report alert, 172
asterisk (*) symbol, for wildcard search, 142
attributes (metadata)
    changing/uploading, 101
    classifications and. see classifications
    limiting number of, 102
attributes, product, 260
automotive websites, 265
Available Metrics column, in traffic variables, 33–34, 35

B

Back-End Orders and Revenue validation, 268–269
Base Currency, in report suite settings, 16, 17
Base URL, 16
basic Ranked report search filter, 139–140
Basic Subrelations conversion variable
    features of, 148
    Status setting, 73–74
Bookmark button, on report toolbar, 166
bookmarking data extract, 178, 179
bookmarking search filter criteria, 142
Bounce Rates, 244–246
breakdown icon, 145–146
breakdown reports
    5x5 subrelations, 190–191
    classifications and, 101
    conversion variable subrelations, 147–149

Instant Segmentation and, 207–208
many-by-many, 215
removing subrelated variables in, 191
search filter for, 141–142
Traffic Correlation, 145–147
unlimited, DataWarehouse and, 204
Breakdowns section, in DataWarehouse canvas, 202
Broken Down By option, in Ranked reports, 138
Browser Export tab, key values and, 99
Browser import, uploading classifications and, 99
Build Report section, in DataWarehouse canvas, 202

C

calculated metrics
  in dependent data requests, 230
  Form Error, 297
  formulating, 52–53
  global, 160
  Instances metrics and, 93
  promotion click-through rates and, 285
  Total metrics for, 56–57
  utilizing, 54–55
Calculated Metrics Manager, 52–53
calculations, ReportBuilder vs. SiteCatalyst, 214
campaign attribution, multi-suite tagging and, 20–21
campaign tracking
  Adobe Test&Target and, 286
  click-through rates and, 283–286
  internal campaign influence and, 286–287
  Marketing Channels and, 281–283
  Unified Sources and, 280–281
campaign variables
  features of, 83–85
  Instances metrics and, 92
  settings for, 85–87
Cart Abandoner segments, 264–265
Cart Additions (scAdd) success events
  Conversion Variable Syntax method and, 89–90
  functions of, 43
  non-retail websites and, 265–266
  product merchandising and, 259–262

segmentation and, 264–265
tracking items left in cart, 262–264
Cart Removals (scRemove) success events, 43
Cart Views (scView) success events, 43
Carts (scOpen) success events
  functions of, 43
  products variable and, 83
Category parameter, of products variable, 81
CEM (Customer Experience Management), 126
Channel Manager plug-in, Unified Sources and, 280–281
check boxes, for graph metrics, 189–190
Checkouts (scCheckout) success events
  functions of, 43
  shopping cart tracking and, 262–264
Checkpoint Canvas, 151
checkpoints, in Fallout reports, 150–151
classification hierarchies, 106–107
Classification Manager screen, 97
classifications
  creating, 97–99
  Date Stamp, 117–118
  None row and, 103–104
  numeric, 104–106
  removing, 104
  retroactive nature of, 103
  setting alerts on, 174–175
  Time Parting plug-in and, 116
  understanding of, 96–97
  uploading, 99, 100
  using/features of, 100–102
classified Visitor Score reports, 314–315
ClickTale CEM tool, 126
click-throughs
  Instances metrics and, 92
  search result rates for, 306–307
Click-to-Call, 301
CMS (content management system), page types and, 243
COGS (Cost of Goods Sold), 121–122
combined Time-Parting variable, 116
comma-separated values (CSV) files, 163–164
common identifiers, page name, 237
company logins, 12–13

Compare Dates selection screen, 185
Compare to Site option, in Ranked reports, 138
comparison reporting
  Date, 184–186
  Instant Segmentation and, 207, 211
  Pathing, 188
  Report Suite, 186–187
  Segment, 187
Comparison Reports-Normalization, 185–186
complex Ranked report search filter, 140–142
Configure Graph button, in Metric reports, 135
Configure Graph option, in Trended reports, 144–145
conservation of variables, classifications and, 101, 102
containers
  defining Segment Builder, 194–197
  nesting in Segment Canvas, 197–199
content management system (CMS), page types and, 243
Converse segments, Exclude tab and, 200
Conversion Funnel reports
  creating, 156, 157
  Fallout reports vs., 156–158
  filtering, 158–160
Conversion Level, in report suite settings, 16
Conversion Variable Ranked report, 159–160
Conversion Variable reports
  Bounce Rates in, 245
  Instances metrics in, 90–91
  setting alerts on, 172–173
conversion variable subrelations
  5x5 subrelation reports, 190–191
  Bounce Rates in, 245–246
  combining internal/external campaigns, 287
  identifying form field errors, 298–299
  in Product Gridwall reports, 258–259
  for product returns, 271–272
  with recurring revenue, 274
  setting targets and, 181
  for top search phrases by page, 308
  types of, 147–149

Conversion Variable Syntax method, 89–90
conversion variables (eVars)
  Allocation settings for, 65–68
  breakdown by traffic variables, 204
  campaign variable, 83–87
  conserving, classifications and, 101, 102
  Counter, 71–73, 275–277, 314
  Cross-Visit Participation plug-ins and, 113–115
  custom. see custom conversion variables
  date comparisons in, 184–186
  expiration settings for, 68–71
  features of, 62–63
  filtering Conversion Funnel reports, 158–160
  Form ID, 293–294
  internal campaign influence and, 286–287
  Merchandising, 87–90
  multiple settings for, 68
  Name settings for, 65
  naming techniques for, 66
  None row in, 74–76
  Onsite Searches, 304–305
  persistence of, 64, 148
  products variable, 79–83
  quality assurance of, 90–91
  Reset setting for, 74
  search click-through rate, 306–307
  settings for, 64–65
  Status settings for, 73–74
  storing multiple values in, 284
  subrelations. see conversion variable subrelations
  success events and, 57–58, 63
  Text String vs. Counter, 71–73
  tracking file downloads, 249–250
Copy Graph option, in More Actions menu, 176
Copy Request option, in Excel right-click context menu, 224
Copy Worksheet w/Requests option, in Excel right-click context menu, 223–224
Correlation report, 146
Cost of Goods Sold (COGS), 121–122
costs
  applying classifications and, 101
  Data Sources calculating, 121–122
  numeric classifications and, 104–106

Counter conversion variables
  Text String conversion variables vs., 71–73
  tracking orders to date, 276–277
  tracking revenue to date, 275–276
  visitor scoring and, 314
Counter success events, 44–45
Create A New Classification screen, 98
Create Custom Report option, 176
Create list now link, 182
Create tab, on ReportBuilder toolbar, 217
criteria elements, Segment Builder and, 195–196
CRM (Customer Relationship Management) tool, 315
Cross-Visit Participation plug-ins, 113–115
cross-website participation, 20
cross-website pathing
  multi-suite tagging and, 19–20
  rollup report suites and, 22
CSV (comma-separated values) files, 163–164
Currency success events
  Back-End Revenue, 268–269
  cart additions and, 262–264
  example of, 46–47
  features of, 45–46
  Product Return Amount, 271–272
  Recurring Revenue, 273–274
  setting/enabling, 48
custom conversion variables
  DB VISTA tables for, 130
  Instances metrics in, 90–91, 93
  tracking file downloads, 249–250
Custom Layout option, in ReportBuilder, 219–220
custom Product Views success events
  features of, 92
  shopping cart tracking and, 254
Custom Reports option, 176
custom traffic variables. see traffic variables (sProps)
Customer Experience Management (CEM), 126
Customer Relationship Management (CRM) tool, 315
customize graph metrics, 190
Cut Request option, in Excel right-click context menu, 224

D
Dashboard button, on report toolbar, 166–167
dashboards
  adding reports to, 166–170
  data requests, ReportBuilder and, 215
  with report target, 181
  for segment comparisons, 187
  updating reports from, 188
Data Extract report, 179
data extracts
  creating, 177–178
  customizing, 178
  saving/sending, 178–179
Data Feeds, 127
Data Filter option, in Ranked reports, 138
data quality, ReportBuilder and, 231
data Request Wizard, 217–220, 225–227
data requests
  creating, 214, 215, 217–220
  dependent requests in, 223
  Excel right-click with, 223–224
  refreshing, 222
data security, Instant Segmentation and, 210
data sets. see report suite(s)
Data Sources
  features of, 120–122
  importing back-end data, 268–269
  importing recurring revenue data, 273–274
data warehouses, marketing and, 7
Database Vista (DB VISTA) rules, 129–130
  for implementing page types, 243–244
  product IDs/product names and, 255
  rules, 129–130
DataWarehouse
  ASI and, 204–205
  facts regarding, 204
  features of, 201–202
  Instant Segmentation and, 206
  report, 203
  scheduling reports with, 197
  understanding of, 201
  utilizing, 202–203

Date Comparison reports
creating, 184
functions of, 184–186
Date Enabled option, classifications and, 98
Date Range selection screen, 135, 136
Date Range settings, 166–167
Date Stamp classification, Time Parting plug-in and, 117–118
Dates area, in ReportBuilder, 218
Day of Week Metric report, 134–135
Days Since Last Visit plug-in, 120
DB VISTA rules. see Database Vista (DB VISTA) rules
de-duplicated success events, 49–51
de-duplicated unique visitors, 20
default metrics, Ranked reports and, 138–139
Default Page, in report suite settings, 16
Define New Metric button, 52–53
Define Visit screen, in Segment Builder, 195, 199
definition selection clauses, 196
Delete option
in ReportBuilder, 219, 220
in Request Manager, 221
Delete Request option, in Excel right-click context menu, 224
Delivery Frequency options, for reports, 165
Delivery Options, for Metric report alerts, 171–172
DemandBase Genesis integration, 127
dependent data requests
in ReportBuilder, 223
utilizing, 228–230
developers, product knowledge and, 8
DigitalPulse Debugger
Get Query Parameter plug-in and, 111, 112
passing data and, 86
Dimensions tab, in ReportBuilder, 219
directional reporting tools, 7
Disabled conversion variable Status setting, 73–74
Discover. see Adobe Discover
Do Not Reset setting for conversion variables, 74
double-click to add/remove metrics, 188
Download button, on report toolbar, 163–164

downloading ReportBuilder, 216–217
Duplicate Order ID Alert, 267–268
duplication, of data requests, 215
dynamic cell references, 217–218
dynamic phone numbers, 301
dynamic templates, 215

E

Edit Request option, in Excel right-click context menu, 224
Edit/Edit Multiple option, in Request Manager, 221
E-mail Marketing integrations, 125
Email Report option, in Data Extract settings, 179
End Delivery Options, sending reports and, 165
eVars. see conversion variables (eVars)
Event ID serialization, 49–51
events, Segment Builder, 194–197
Excel. see Microsoft Excel
ExcelClient, 216
Exclude tab, in Segment Builder, 199–200
Exits reports, Form Field, 300
Expiration settings
for conversion variables, 68–71
for list variables, 79
exporting key values, 99
external campaign tracking
Marketing Channels and, 281–283
Unified Sources and, 280–281
Extract Data option
in More Actions menu, 176
steps for using, 177–179

F

Facebook, Genesis integrations and, 126
Fallout reports
Conversion Funnel reports vs., 156–158
Form Field, 300
functions of, 150–151
Favorites, calculated metric reports and, 54–55
File Downloads reports
custom variables tracking, 249–250
limitations of, 249
pathing and, 250–252
tracking files with, 248
File Transfer Protocol (FTP) sites, 100

filtering
Conversion Funnel reports, 158–159
in ReportBuilder, 219, 220
text search for pages, 237–238
financial services websites, 265
Finding Methods reports, 261–262
First conversion variable Allocation setting, 65–68
fixed start date, reports and, 166
ForeSee tool, 126
Form Analysis plug-in, 299
Form Completion Rate metric reports, 292
Form Completions success events
Form ID variables for, 293–294
functions of, 291
Form Conversion Rate metric reports, 292–293
form error(s)
alerts, 298
fields producing, 298–299
success events, 296–297
tracking, 295–296
form field abandonment
Form Analysis plug-in for, 299
Form Field pathing for, 299–300
Form Field Errors
conversion variables, 91
reports, 298–299
Form Field pathing, 299–300
Form IDs
forcing unique, 294
form field errors and, 298–299
for lead generation forms, 293–294
Form Submission Participation metrics, 58–59
Form Submit Clicks metric, 295
form types, 295
Form Views success events
Form ID variables for, 293–294
functions of, 290–291
Format Options:headers area, in ReportBuilder, 219, 220
Format tab, ReportBuilder toolbar, 217
formatting of reports, ReportBuilder and, 215
From Cell option, in Request Manager, 221
FTP (File Transfer Protocol) sites, 100
Full Subrelations conversion variable
features of, 148, 149
Status setting, 73–74

G

Genesis integrations
    additional, 126–127
    E-mail Marketing, 125
    features of, 124–125
    Voice of Customer/Customer
        Experience Management, 126
Get & Persist plug-ins, 115
Get Query Parameter plug-ins
    for campaign variable, 85–86
    features of, 111–112
Get Val(ue) Once plug-in, 120
global calculated metrics, 160
global report suites
    additional benefits of, 19–21
    example of, 18–19
    Instant Segmentation and, 209–210
    reasons for, 17–18
    Site variables and, 239–240
    standardization in, 21–22
graph metrics
    check boxes for choosing, 189–190
    Form Completion Rate, 292
    Form Conversion Rate, 293
    Form Errors, 297
    ReportBuilder vs. SiteCatalyst, 214
    in Website Engagement reports,
        312–313
gridwalls, product list, 256–259

H

Help tab, ReportBuilder toolbar, 217
hiding option, in ReportBuilder, 219,
    220
hiding report menus, 188
hierarchies, classification, 106–107
hierarchy variables, 37
history
    of products variable, 81
    of SiteCatalyst, 4
HyperText Markup Language (HTML)
    format option, 164

I

If all criteria are met option
    in basic search filter, 140
    in complex search filter, 141
If any criteria are met option, basic
    search filter and, 140
import files
    Product Returns Transaction ID,
        271
    Recurring Revenue Transaction ID,
        273–274

Include tab, Segment Builder, 199–200
Incrementor parameter, of products
    variable, 82
installing ReportBuilder, 216–217
Instances metrics
    calculated metrics and, 93
    in Campaign/Search Engine
        reports, 92
    in conversion variable reports,
        90–91
    in Products report, 91–92
    in traffic variable reports, 34–35
Instant Segmentation
    breakdown reports and, 207–208
    comparing reports and, 207, 211
    data security/complex segments
        in, 210
    features of, 205–206
    multi-suite tagging vs., 209–210
interface layout, SiteCatalyst
    comparison reporting and. see
        comparison reporting
    downloading ReportBuilder from,
        216–217
    general overview of, 162
    Instant Segmentation in, 205–206
    publishing lists and, 182–183
    report toolbar and. see report
        toolbar
    targets and, 180–181
interface time-savers
    5x5 subrelation reports, 190–191
    check boxes for graph metrics,
        189–190
    removing subrelation breakdowns,
        191
    sorting triangle for metrics, 189
    updating dashboard reports/
        reorganizing menus, 188
Internal Campaign Clicks success
    events, 285
Internal Campaign Impressions
    success events, 284–285
Internal Campaign Influence report,
    287
internal campaigns
    Adobe Test&Target and, 286
    click-through rates and, 283–286
    tracking influence of, 286–287
Internet Browser reports, 206–207
inter-website pathing
    global report suites and, 19–20
    rollup report suites and, 22
    Site variables and, 239–240

intranets, company, 13
IP Obfuscation, report suite settings
    and, 16, 17
Item Filter option, in Ranked reports,
    138

J

JavaScript plug-ins
    Channel Manager, 280–281
    Cross-Visit Participation, 113–115
    Form Analysis, 299
    functions of, 110–111
    Get & Persist, 115
    Get Query Parameter, 85–86,
        110–111
    Get Val Once/Visit Number/Days
        Since last Visit, 120
    Previous Value, 112
    Time Parting, 115–118
    Time to Complete, 119

K

key performance indicators (KPIs). see
    also success events
    conversion variables and, 62
    Pathing reports, 310–311
    web analytics and, 40–41
key values, in classification
    exporting with Browser Export
        tab, 99
    Tracking Code report of, 100
Knowledge Base
    JavaScript plug-ins in, 110–111
    suggestions for Time Parting
        plug-in, 116

L

Launch Discover option, 177
Lead Form Submission Counter
    success event report
        None row in, 75–76
        setting, 44–45
lead generation websites
    "money left on the table" concept
        for, 266
    Form Conversion Rates and,
        292–293
    form errors and, 295–299
    form field abandonment and,
        299–300
    Form IDs for, 293–294
    Form Submit Clicks and, 295

Form Views/Completions and, 290–291
phone conversion and, 300–301
left navigation menu, in SiteCatalyst interface, 162
Linear Allocation setting, of conversion variable
functions of, 65–68
internal campaign influence and, 287
for search phrases, 304–305
linear allocation, of success events, 57–58
Link to This Report option, 176
list props
features of, 35–36
limitations of, 36
list variables (List Vars)
functions of, 76–78
identifying form field errors, 298–299
settings for, 78–79
loan application forms, 46, 62–63
Location Click-through Rate report, 286
Lock Report Suite check box, 169
Login tab, ReportBuilder toolbar, 217
logins, company, 12–13

M

Make Public option, in Data Extract, 179
Manage Dashboards screen, 169
Manage tab, ReportBuilder toolbar, 217
many-by-many breakdown reports, 215
marketing
data warehouses for, 7
external campaign tracking, 280–283
improved campaign attribution in, 20–21
internal campaign tracking, 283–287
product knowledge and, 8
SiteCatalyst and, 4–5
Marketing Channels reports
campaign tracking and, 281–282
functions of, 47
None row in, 75–76
Max Values settings, for list variables, 79

media websites, 265
Menu area, ReportBuilder, 218
Menu Customization tool, 188
menu toolbar. *see* report toolbar
merchandising. *see* product merchandising
Merchandising eVars
Conversion Variable Syntax method for, 89–90
Product Syntax method for, 88–89
purpose of, 87
Merchandising parameter, of products variables, 82
metadata. *see* attributes (metadata)
Metric reports, 134–136
Form Completion, 291
setting alerts on, 171–172
Metric Type drop-down box, 52
metrics
applying targets to, 180–181
Bounce Rate, 244–246
calculated, 52–57, 263–264
check boxes for choosing graph, 189–190
double-click to add/remove, 188
e-mail, 125
global calculated, 160
Instances, 34–35, 90–93
selecting Conversion Funnel, 156, 157
showing online/offline, 121–122
sorting triangle for, 189
success event. *see* success events
traffic, 27–28, 33–34
Metrics section, in DataWarehouse canvas, 202
Metrics tab, ReportBuilder, 219
Microsoft Excel
file size limits in, 163–164
ReportBuilder. *see* ReportBuilder
right-click context menu in, 223–224
for segment comparisons, 187
validating back-end data, 269
Microsoft Word, file size limits in, 163–164
minus (–) sign, search filters and, 142
Mobile format option, sending reports and, 164
"money left on the table" concept
non-retail websites and, 265–266
segmentation and, 264–265
tracking, 262–264

More Actions menu
basic actions on, 176–177
Extract Data option in, 177–179
Most Recent (Last) conversion variable
Allocation setting, 65–68
Cross-Visit Participation plug-ins and, 113–115
Expiration settings and, 68–71
Multi-byte Character Support, in report suite settings, 16, 17
multiple values, in products variables, 80
multiple visits
Linear Allocation setting and, 67
Pathing reports and, 156
multiple websites, Site variables and, 239–240
multi-site segmentation, 20
multi-suite tagging
additional benefits of, 19–21
example of, 18–19
Instant Segmentation vs., 209–211
reasons for, 17–18, 209
standardization in, 21–22

N

Name settings
for conversion variables, 65
for list variables, 79
naming pages, 236–238
naming site sections, 238
naming techniques, for conversion variables, 66
nesting challenge, 199
nesting containers, Segment Canvas and, 197–199
Never expiration option, for conversion variables, 70, 71
Next Flow reports, 149–150
next-day availability of data, 22
No Search Results success events, 305, 306
No Subrelations conversion variable
features of, 148
Status setting, 73–74
None items, removing subrelated variables and, 191
None rows
classifying, 103–104
in conversion variables, 74–75
creating classifications and, 98
minimizing, 76

normalization
    of Date Comparison reports,
        185–186
    of Report Suite Comparison
        reports, 186–187
    technique for, 186
Number of Search Results report,
    305–306
numeric classifications, 104–106
Numeric success events
    Back-End Orders, 268–269
    example of, 46–47
    features of, 45–46
    setting/enabling, 48
    for website engagement score,
        311–313

O

offline metrics
    Data Sources showing, 121–122
    Transaction ID connecting,
        123–124
Once Per Visit serialization, 51
online metrics
    Data Sources showing, 121–122
    Transaction ID connecting,
        123–124
onsite search phrases
    plug-ins capturing, 111, 112
    tracking, 304–305
onsite search tracking
    number of search results and,
        305–306
    phrases. *see* onsite search phrases
    questions regarding, 304
    search phrase pathing and,
        307–308
    search result click-through rates
        and, 306–307
    top phrases by page, 308
Onsite Searches reports, 305
Open New Window option, 177
OpinionLab tool, 126
Options tab, ReportBuilder toolbar,
    217
OR clauses
    basic search filter with, 139–140
    complex search filter with, 140–141
    in nesting containers, 197–199
    in Segment Builder, 196
Order ID conversion variables
    for back-end order/revenue
        validation, 268–269
    setting, 267–268

Orders success events, 43
Orders to Date reports, 276–277
orders, validating back-end, 268–269
Orders/Total Orders calculated
    metrics, 56–57
Orders/Visit calculated metric reports,
    54–55
Original Value (First) conversion
    variable Allocation setting, 65–68
out-of-the-box reports, 102
over time reports, 134–136

P

page influence, content tracking and,
    246–248
Page Name variables, 30
page names
    conventions for, 236–238
    previous, capturing, 112
    website-agnostic, 239
Page Participation reports, 247
Page Summary reports, 154
Page Type traffic variables
    implementing, 243–244
    pathing for, 242–243
    tracking website content and,
        240–241
Page Type variable for 404 error pages,
    241
Page Views containers
    nesting rules for, 197–199
    in Segment Canvas, 194
Page Views reports
    list props and, 36
    traffic variables and, 28–29
Pages reports
    basic search filter with, 139–140
    Bounce Rates in, 244–246
    example of, 29
    page name scheme in, 237
    setting alerts on, 172–173, 175
Pageviews per Visit reports, 28
paid search keywords, multi-suite
    tagging and, 20–21
participation
    cross-website, 20
    success event, 58–59
Paste Request option, in Excel right-
    click context menu, 224
Pathfinder canvas, 152–153
Pathfinder reports, 152–153
pathing
    classification values and, 102
    cross-website, 19–20, 22

inter-website, 239–240
    list props and, 36
    Page Type, 242–243
    product tab, 255–256
    traffic variables and, 32–33
    website-agnostic page names and,
        239
Pathing reports
    additional uses of, 154–156
    Comparison reports, 188
    Fallout reports, 150–151
    File Download, 250–252
    Form Field, 299–300
    KPI, 310–311
    Next Flow reports, 149–150
    onsite search phrase, 307–308
    Pathfinder reports, 152–153
    Product, 254–255
    Summary reports, 153–154
    traffic variables and, 32, 102
PDF (Portable Document Format) files,
    163–164
Percent Shown As option, Ranked
    reports and, 138
percentages
    in comparison reporting, 187
    in Conversion Funnel reports, 156,
        157
    in Currency success events,
        263–264
    in Fallout reports, 151
    in Onsite Search Click-through
        Rate reports, 307
    in Pages report alerts, 173
    in Pathfinder reports, 152
persistence
    of conversion variables, 64
    products variable and, 83
    traffic variables and, 31–32
Persistent Cookies filter, 135, 136
phone conversion, connecting online
    visits to, 300–301
Pivot Layout option, ReportBuilder,
    219
Placement Merchandising variables, in
    Product Gridwall reports, 257–258
plug-ins
    Cross-Visit Participation, 113–115
    functions of, 110–111
    Get & Persist, 115
    Get Query Parameter, 111–112
    Get Val Once/Visit Number/Days
        Since last Visit, 120
    Previous Value, 112, 308

Time Parting, 115–118
Time to Complete, 119
Portable Document Format (PDF) files, 163–164
potential revenue, segmentation and, 264–265
Pre-configured segments, 205, 206
predefined Product View success events, 254
Prepend/Postpend Text option, ReportBuilder, 220
Previous Flow reports, 149
Previous Value plug-ins
functions of, 112
tracking pages searched from, 308
Print option, 176
processing rules, 311
product attributes, 260
product categories, 277
product finding methods, 261–262
Product Gridwall reports, 256–259
product knowledge, 7–9, 15
product merchandising
assigning product attributes for, 260
finding methods and, 261–262
non-retail websites and, 265–266
potential revenue and, 264–265
product page tabs, pathing, 255–256
Product parameter, of products variables, 81
Product Pathing reports, 254–255
product returns, tracking of, 270–272
Product Syntax method, Merchandising eVars and, 88–89
Product Views (prodView) success events
Conversion Variable Syntax method and, 89–90
custom, 92, 254
features of, 44
Instances metrics and, 91–92
products variable and, 79–80
for shopping cart tracking, 254
Products reports, classifications for, 104–106
products variable
Carts success events and, 83
classification hierarchies in, 106–107
features of, 79–80
history of, 81
multiple values in, 80

nonpersistence of, 83
special parameters for, 80–83
prodView. *see* Product Views (prodView) success events
promotions. *see* internal campaigns
publishing lists
creating/selecting, 182–183
for sending reports, 164
sending workbooks to, 227
punctuation, classifications and, 103
Purchase success events
Event ID serialization and, 51
success events metrics and, 43

Q

quality assurance of conversion variables, 90–91
quality of data, ReportBuilder and, 231
Quantity parameter, of products variable, 82
query string parameters, 111–112

R

Ranked reports
default metrics in, 138–139
features of, 136–137
of filtered conversion funnels, 159–160
search filters for, 139–142
settings for, 137–138
real-time availability of data, 22
reconfigured data extract settings, 178
Refresh List option, Request Manager, 221
Refresh option, Request Manager, 221
Refresh Request option, in Excel right-click context menu, 224
Refresh tab, ReportBuilder toolbar, 217
refreshing data requests, 222
reorganizing report menus, 188
report area, SiteCatalyst interface, 162
Report Data Columns Canvas column, in traffic variables, 33–34, 35
report formatting, 215
Report Preview section, in DataWarehouse canvas, 202
report spamming, 165
Report Suite Comparison reports, 186–187
Report Suite drop-down list, 217–218
report suite ID, 217
Report Suite Manager, 205

report suite selector, SiteCatalyst interface, 162
Report Suite settings, for dashboards, 169
report suite(s)
comparisons of, 186–187
features of, 13–14
general account settings, 16–17
IDs, 15
multi-suite tagging and, 17–22
rollup, 22
separate logins for, 12–13
Report Time Frame options, 165
report toolbar
alerts on, 170–175
Bookmark button on, 166
Dashboard button on, 166–170
Download button on, 163–164
More Actions menu on, 176–179
Send button on, 164–165
Report Type option, in Ranked reports, 137–138
report types
comparison. *see* comparison reporting
Conversion Funnel, 156–160
conversion variable subrelations, 147–149
Metric, 134–136
Pathing. *see* Pathing reports
Ranked, 136–142
Traffic Correlation, 145–147
Trended, 143–145
ReportBuilder
creating data requests, 214, 217–220
data quality and, 231
dependent requests in, 223, 228–230
installing, 216–217
Internal Campaign data request, 285
refreshing requests/scheduling workbooks in, 222
Request Manager in, 221
right-clicking in Excel and, 223–224
segment comparisons with, 187
SiteCatalyst vs., 214–215
templates, 225–227
toolbar, 217
validating back-end data, 269
Reporting Date section, in DataWarehouse canvas, 201–202

Request Manager, ReportBuilder, 221
Request Name area, in DataWarehouse canvas, 201, 202
Request Wizard, data, 217–220, 225–227
Requested Loan Amount report, 46–47
Reset setting, for conversion variables, 74
retroactive nature of classifications, 103
returns, product, 270–272
revenue
    recurring, 272–274
    validating back-end, 268–269
Revenue reports, with targets, 180–181
Revenue success events, 43
Revenue to Date reports, 274–276
Revenue/Total Revenue calculated metrics, 56–57
right-click context menu, Excel, 223–224
role of SiteCatalyst, 4–5
rolling start date, dashboards and, 166–167
rollup report suites, 22
Rule option, for Metric report alerts, 171–172

S

s.campaign variable
    campaign tracking and, 281
    Get Query Parameter plug-in and, 111, 112
    multiple, 282
s.channel traffic variable, 238
s.events string
    capturing impressions/clicks, 284–285
    Counter success events and, 44
    Currency/Numeric success events and, 48
    product attributes and, 260
s.pagename traffic variable
    applying custom names in, 236
    File Download Pathing reports and, 251
s.products variables, 80
    for Numeric success events, 311–312
    product attributes and, 260
    for purchase event, 266
s.purchaseID variable
    for Event ID serialization, 51
    for purchase event, 266

s.transactionID variable, 123–124, 301
s_account variables
    multi-suite tagging and, 18–19
    report suite IDs and, 15
    report suites and, 13–14
SAINT API, 100
SAINT Bernard tool, 100
SAINT classifications. see SiteCatalyst Attribute Importing and Naming Tool (SAINT) classifications
SAINT classifications link, 99
Salesforce.com Genesis integration, 127
scAdd. see Cart Additions (scAdd) success events
scCheckout. see Checkouts (scCheckout) success events
Schedule Delivery area, in DataWarehouse canvas, 202
Schedule tab, ReportBuilder toolbar, 217
Scheduling options
    advanced, 165
    in ReportBuilder, 227
    for sending reports, 164
Scheduling Wizard for workbooks, 222, 227
scOpen. see Carts (scOpen) success events
scRemove. see Cart Removals (scRemove) success events
scView. see Cart Views (scView) success events
search boxes, website, 304. see also onsite search tracking
Search Engine Dashboards, 168–170
Search Engine Optimization (SEO), 126
Search Engine reports
    Conversion Funnel reports and, 158–159
    date comparisons in, 184–186
    example of, 163
    Instances metrics in, 92
search filters, Ranked report
    additional tips for, 142
    basic, 139–140
    complex, 140–142
Search Keywords reports, 92
search result click-through rates, 306–307
Searches
    Instances as, 92
    onsite. see onsite search tracking

section name, page name including, 237
Segment Canvas
    Exclude area of, 199–200
    nesting containers within, 197–199
Segment Comparison reports, 187
Segment Definition Builder
    cart abandoners and, 264–265
    containers/events in, 194–197
    Exclude tab in, 199–200
    segment nesting and, 197–199
    with visitor scoring, 315–316
Segment drop-down list, ReportBuilder, 218
segment selector area, SiteCatalyst interface, 162
Segment setting, dashboards and, 169
segmentation
    Advanced Segment Insight for, 204–205
    DataWarehouse and, 201–204
    Instant Segmentation and, 205–211
    multi-site, 20
    potential complexity of, 210
    potential revenue and, 264–265
    Segment Builder for, 194–200
    Site variables and, 239–240
    test reports for, 204
    Time Parting plug-in and, 116, 117–118
    visitor score, 315–316
Select All option, in Request Manager, 221
Select Classification Type screen, 97–98
Select insert location area, ReportBuilder, 219, 220
Selected Events link, for Conversion Funnel reports, 156
Selected Items option, in Trended reports, 144
Selected Metrics option, in Ranked reports, 138
Selected Page option, in Metric reports, 135
selecting function, ReportBuilder, 219, 220
Send button, on report toolbar, 164–165
SEO (Search Engine Optimization), 126
serialization IDs, 49–51
serialization, Once Per Visit, 51
Server variable, 30

settings
for campaign variable, 85–87
for conversion variables, 64–65
for list variables, 78–79
Share tab, ReportBuilder toolbar, 217
Shipping Costs, 121–122
shopping cart success events, 43–44
shopping cart tracking
cart additions/checkouts and, 259
implementing Product Views for, 254
non-retail websites and, 265–266
potential revenue, segmentation and, 264–265
product list views and, 256–259
product merchandising and, 260–262
product page tabs and, 255–256
product pathing in, 254–255
product returns and, 270–272
purchase event and, 266
recurring revenue, 272–274
revenue/orders to date and, 274–277
tracking items left in cart, 262–264
validating orders/revenue, 266–269
shortcut links, 176
Show Percentages option, in Trended reports, 144–145
side-by-side graphs, 190, 207
Site Section variable, 30
site sections, naming, 238
Site Titles, 15, 16
Site traffic variables, 239–240
SiteCatalyst
creating reports in. see report types
functions of, 6–7
interface layout, 162
product knowledge of, 7–9, 15
ReportBuilder vs., 214–215
role of, 4–5
v15, instant segmentation and, 205–211
SiteCatalyst Attribute Importing and Naming Tool (SAINT) classifications
applied to visitor scoring, 314–315
creating, 97–99
None row and, 103–104
removing, 104
retroactive nature of, 103
Time Parting plug-in and, 116
understanding of, 96–97
uploading, 99, 100
using/features of, 100–102

Smoothing Applied option, in Metric reports, 135
sorting triangle for metrics, 189
<SPACE>, in search filters, 142
spaces
in page names, 237
search filters and, 142
specific filter settings, 229–230
Specific item alert, 172–173
sProps. see traffic variables (sProps)
standard metrics, 53, 56
standardization, of SiteCatalyst reports, 215
Status settings, conversion variable, 73–74
subrelations. see conversion variable subrelations
success event allocation, 57–58
success event participation, 58–59
Success Event Pathing, visitor engagement and, 310–311
success event serialization, 49–51
success events
calculated metrics and, 52–57
classifications and, 101
comparing back-end order data, 268–269
conversion variables and, 63
Counter, 44–45
Currency and Numeric, 45–48. see also Currency success events; Numeric success events
Expiration settings based on, 69–70
features of, 41–42
Form Error, 296–297
KPIs and, 40–41
Numeric. see Numeric success events
page influence and, 246–248
selecting Conversion Funnel, 157
shopping cart, 43–44
Über, 70
Zero Search Results, 305
Suite Segments area, 205, 206
summary metrics, multi-suite tagging and, 19
Summary reports, 153–154

T

tab Pathing reports, 255–256
tagging, classifications and, 101
targets
functions of, 180–181
visitor scoring and, 316

TeaLeaf tool, 126
team managers, 8
telephone lead generation, 300–301
templates
classification, accessing, 99
content management system, 243
ReportBuilder, 215, 225–227
Test&Target, Adobe
internal campaign tracking and, 286
in shopping cart tracking, 263
Text String conversion variables, 71–73
"thank you" page, lead generation, 291
Ticker Symbol Pathing report, 155
Time frame option, for Metric report alerts, 171
Time Parting plug-ins, 115–118
Time Spent per Visit reports, 316
Time to Complete plug-ins, 119
Time Window report, 117
Time Zone, in report suite settings, 16
time-based expiration for conversion variables, 68–71
top 100 pages data request, 228–229
Top 1000 alert, 172–173
top menu area, SiteCatalyst interface, 162
Total metrics, in calculated metric formulas, 56–57
Total Price parameter, of products variable, 82
tracking
campaign. see campaign tracking
onsite searches. see onsite search tracking
product returns, 270–272
shopping cart. see shopping cart tracking
website content. see website content tracking
tracking codes
campaign tracking and, 280–281, 282
campaign variable and, 85–87
classifications and, 100
e-mail metrics and, 125
None row in, 103–104
Traffic Correlation reports, 145–147
traffic data correlations, 36
traffic metrics
enabling, for traffic variables, 33–34
features of, 27–28

Traffic reports, setting alerts on, 172–173
traffic variables (sProps)
  breakdown by conversion variables, 204
  calculated metrics and, 54
  date comparisons in, 184–186
  enabling correlation of, 145–147
  enabling traffic metrics for, 33–34
  features of, 28–31
  hierarchy variables as, 37
  Instances metric in, 34–35
  list props as, 35–36
  nonpersistence of, 31–32
  Page Type. *see* Page Type traffic variables
  pathing and, 32–33, 102. *see also* Pathing reports
  Previous Value plug-ins and, 112
  Site, 239–240
Transaction ID
  connecting online visits to phone conversations, 300–301
  connecting online/offline data, 123–124
  implementing recurring revenue, 273–274
  tracking product returns, 270–272
travel websites, 266
Trended reports, 143–145
trending, with ReportBuilder, 214
triangle indicating sort metrics, 189
Type settings for conversion variables, 71–73

U

Über success events, 70
Unified Sources, external campaign tracking and, 280–281
uniform resource locators (URLs)
  Base, report suite settings and, 16
  page names and, 236
unique Form IDs, 294
unique page names, 237
unique phone numbers, 301
unique values, unlimited, 204
unique visitors
  calculating Form Conversion Rate, 292
  de-duplication of, 20
  rollup report suites and, 22
  traffic metrics and, 27–28

Unique Visitors report, traffic metrics and, 27
Units success events, 43
unlimited reports, with SiteCatalyst, 215
updating dashboard reports, 188
uploading classifications, 99, 100
URLs. *see* uniform resource locators (URLs)
User Management area, publishing lists and, 182–183

V

validating back-end revenue, 268–269
Value Delimiter settings, 79
values
  attribution of multi-session, 113–115
  capturing previous, 112
  multiple, 284
  storing, 115
  unlimited unique, 204
variables
  conserving, 101, 102
  limited, 22
  Next Flow reports for, 149–150
  number of attributes per, 102
  overview, 26
  quality assurance of, 90–91
  query string parameters and, 111–112
  selecting for classification, 97
  traffic. *see* traffic variables (sProps)
View by setting, in Metric reports, 134
Visit Number plug-in, 120
Visit Number reports
  basic, 143
  Trended, 144
visitor engagement
  KPI Pathing and, 310–311
  Time Spent per Visit reports, 316
  visitor scoring and, 313–315
  website engagement score and, 311–313
Visitor Identification, Segmentation & Transformation Architecture (VISTA) rules
  Database Vista, 129–130
  details about, 129
  features of, 127–129
  implementing Unified Sources, 280–281

visitor scoring
  passing on to CRM, 315
  segmentation of, 315–316
  targeting, 316–317
  visitor engagement and, 313–315
Visitors containers
  nesting rules for, 197–199
  in Segment Canvas, 194, 195
Visits containers
  nesting rules for, 197–199
  in Segment Canvas, 194, 195
Visits reports
  calculating Form Conversion Rate, 292–293
  Metric reports for, 134–136, 143
  traffic metrics and, 27
  in Website Engagement reports, 312–313
VISTA rules. *see* Visitor Identification, Segmentation & Transformation Architecture (VISTA) rules
Voice of Customer integrations, 126

W

web analysts, 8
web analytics
  key performance indicators and, 40–41
  multi-suite tagging and, 18–19
  SiteCatalyst and, 6–7
  team managers, 8
website-agnostic page names, 239
website content tracking
  Bounce Rates and, 244–246
  file downloads and, 248–252
  naming pages and, 236–238
  naming site sections and, 238
  page influence and, 246–248
  page types and. *see* Page Type traffic variables
  Site variables and, 239–240
website engagement. *see* visitor engagement
website engagement scores, 311–313
Website Registrations, 246–248
workbooks, ReportBuilder, 222

Z

zero, classifications and, 103